MONSTERS IN AMERICA

MONSTERS IN AMERICA

OUR HISTORICAL OBSESSION WITH THE HIDEOUS AND THE HAUNTING

Second Edition

W. Scott Poole

BAYLOR UNIVERSITY PRESS

© 2018 second edition by Baylor University Press, Waco, Texas 76798
The second edition ISBN is 978-1-4813-0882-3.

The hardcover first edition was published in 2011.
The paperback first edition was published in 2014.

Cover Design by Natalya Balnova
Cover Image © Jim Zuckerman/Corbis

The Library of Congress has cataloged the hardcover first edition
as follows:

Poole, W. Scott, 1971–
  Monsters in America : our historical obsession with the hideous and the haunting / W. Scott Poole.
  295 p. cm.
  Includes bibliographical references and index.
  ISBN 978-1-60258-314-6 (hardcover : alk. paper)
1. Monsters. 2. Ghosts. 3. Ghouls and ogres. 4. Animals, Mythical. 5. Supernatural. 6. Popular culture--United States--History. I. Title.
  GR825.P626 2011
  398.24'54--dc22
                                    2010053273

Dedicated to Niamh Margaret Carmichael

I don't see any American dream. I see an American nightmare.

—Malcolm X

It's a perfect night for mystery and horror. The air itself is filled with monsters.

—Elsa Lanchester, *The Bride of Frankenstein*

CONTENTS

LIST OF PHOTOGRAPHS

PREFACE TO THE
SECOND EDITION

A beautifully drawn and written graphic novel appeared in 2017 from Emil Ferris entitled *My Favorite Thing Is Monsters*. Ferris offers us a reflection on the relationship of horror and history, takes us from the countercultural Chicago of the late 1960s to classic monster magazines to a Weimar Germany turned lethal with the rise of Hitler and the Nazi party. All of this reflected and intertwined in a love letter to Franken-stein, the Wolfman, the Creature from the Black Lagoon. Even Dracula's daughter makes a very significant appearance in the sumptuously penned monster mash.

Eight years (!) after I first wrote the original version of this text, monsters are still my favorite things. My life as a teacher and a writer revolves around thinking about how horror, culture, and history inter-twine in direct and disturbing ways.

Much of the new material that now appears in *Monsters in Amer-ica* has been fermenting since 2011, born both of the mountain of schol-arly material that has appeared on monsters since 2011 and my own desire to make a book I was generally pleased with into a better one. Some new portions of the book have been added because of import-ant films released, important historical changes that shed light on the past, and social movements that emerged since I wrote the book. Others because I wanted to give the reader a more complete picture of how monsters, and monstrous thinking, have shaped how Americans understand moments in the past, sometimes by practicing complete historical amnesia, sometimes by revising the story, and sometimes by discarding events completely.

I owe my students at the College of Charleston, as well as students in lecture halls and readers in bookstores across the country, a great deal for many of the changes and inclusions. I am particularly grateful to those very precocious and precise readers of the original book who detected both what I hope represents its greatest contribution and paradoxically may have been the first cut's primary limitation.

Many readers intuitively grasped what I meant when I insisted that monsters are real in the sense that they are intertwined with the terrors of history. But not everyone got it, and those that did felt that an important point simply had not been explained well. I hope I am expanding more clearly here on Judith Halberstam's conception of monsters as "meaning machines" while doing what I ask my students to do with topics in popular culture . . . historicize, historicize, historicize!

Much of the practical revision of the book took place in 2016–2017, a time that, as Antonio Gramsci wrote in the years after World War I, had seen the appearance of "certain morbid symptoms." That phrase, sickeningly pungent in its literal form, has sometimes been translated "a time of monsters."

Some new history majors are told that writing about the contemporary moment makes you a journalist, not a historian. Behind this idea lies the notion that, at some point in the past, history stops being history. An academic once said to me, only partially kidding, that everything since the fall of Constantinople in 1451 constituted "current events." One of my students told me of asking a historian when exactly the news becomes history. "Thirty years must pass," he was told, with no justification or explanation for why it takes three decades to bake the human experience into "History."

Historians generally discuss this issue by speaking of the dangers of "presentism," reading the past through the lens of the present. But that's clearly not the same as looking at the present through the lens of the past. If we don't understand past social, political, and cultural realities, we won't even understand the present moment. A quote (often falsely attributed to Arnold J. Toynbee) has it that when we study history we are just studying "one damned thing after another." In point of fact, it is a person without a historical perspective who experiences the news as one damned thing after another, often causing them to do the worst thing . . . throw up their hands in despair, believe they have no agency, or rather accept those structures in our society that want people to believe they have no agency. Apathy results or, perhaps more often, turning to conspiracy theory and demagoguery instead of historical reflection for answers.

I know that some readers will complain, as they did with the first edition, that they just want to mainline their monsters with no reference to America's imperial adventures or the Black Lives Matter movement. There does exist, and I think this theme appears more prominently in this edition than in the first, a significant element of escapism in horror fandom. Some of us want, need, these books, movies, and folktales to, in Žižek's formulation I use in the text, "hide the true horror of the situation."

Monster tales ultimately do not let you hide, something that has always been challenging to me as a lifelong genre fan. You should know that if you fire walk with me that I will not ignore the times in which I write, since this would constitute a failing as a historian, an inability to think through how American history brought us to a perilous moment. In the new conclusion to this volume that keeps its original 2011 title "Worse Things Waiting," I expand on what I hoped to say in that historical moment that feels very distant despite its chronological nearness. Unfortunately, I was right about some of the rather pessimistic points made in that first edition's conclusion.

Morbid symptoms have begun to appear. We live in a time of monsters.

Although much has changed in this book, the central argument remains. Rather than being mirrors of societal anxiety or psychological constructions along the lines of Freud's concept presented in *The Uncanny* (1919), monsters emerge out of the historical context. They are created by but they also help to create the material conditions in which they slither, stalk, and shamble.

There are empathetic monsters, subversive monsters, monsters that we contemplate in order to ponder our own mortality. There are monsters that are out to destroy our self-satisfied sense of modernity and remind us that time, *pace* the Rolling Stones, is not on our side.

There are also monsters born from the systems of exploitation, corruption, and oppression. You will not like all you learn here about American history. But I am telling you that this book reveals, to use the title of one of my favorite television shows that appeared around the time of the first edition's publication, an American horror story, *the* American horror story. Some of our monsters are old friends, some are out to get us. Some come and admonish us with their sorrow, while others are born out of the suffering we have created.

Some are truly morbid symptoms of the times. We too easily become their collaborators and we betray more than we know.

PREFACE TO THE ORIGINAL EDITION

With a Warning to the Unsuspecting Reader

> *Come now,*
> *My Child*
> *If we were planning*
> *To harm you, do you think*
> *We'd be lurking here*
> *Beside the path*
> *In the very darkest*
> *Part of the forest?*

—Kenneth Patchen

Entertaining Comics (usually known simply as "EC") created some of the most subversive images of the 1950s in titles like *Tales from the Crypt* and *Vault of Horror*. These macabre tales of mayhem, taking place in the midst of middle-class American life, used the conceit of a host known as the "Crypt Keeper" to introduce the horror and mix in some black humor. Late-night showings of horror films on local TV used the same convention. In 1954 the world met Vampira, a campy and seductive woman in black, who introduced each film with a bloodcurdling scream.

Here is a favorite introduction to a tale of terror from the Crypt Keeper that seems germane to this book's purpose:

Welcome dear fiends! Come in! Come into the Crypt of Terror! I am your host the crypt-keeper. . . . This one is sure to freeze the blood in your veins. . . . Guaranteed to make little shivers run up and down your crawling spine! This little adventure in terror is about to happen to you! You are the main character.

Right now, I am your crypt keeper and your Vampira. I am going to introduce you to monsters. I aim to give you unpleasant dreams.

Since this is a book about monsters, you probably want to hear how I define the monster. Defining one's terms, I am sure you have been told, is essential to any discussion. Setting out on our nighttime journey with a clear meaning of our terms might help us survive the night. A book about monsters should define its monsters.

But I am not going to do it. At least I am not going to give you a straightforward definition to underline or highlight. I prefer to take you on a wild ride through the darkness of the American past, galloping hard and fast like Ichabod Crane (and not making any ill-considered stops like poor Marion Crane) in hopes we can reach the bridge in time. Maybe if we do, we will have worked out our definition of the monster. Scholars like clear analytical mandates—that is, direct assertions of argument followed by supporting evidence. Since I hope at least some scholars of American history and culture will read this book, let me throw them a bone or two. I will even give them a scholarly citation to munch on like zombies with a nice meaty thighbone. I buy fully into Judith Halberstam's argument that monsters are "meaning machines," exuviating all manner of cultural productions depending on their context and their historical moment. In American history they have been symbols of deviance, objects of sympathy, and even images of erotic desire. They structured the enslavement of African Americans, constructed notions of crime and deviance, and provided mental fodder for the culture wars of the contemporary period.[1]

You see why I did not want to give you a definition? Monsters have been manufacturing complex meanings for four hundred years of American history. They do not mean one thing but a thousand. Only by looking at a multitude of monsters can we come to understand something about them and, in turn, something about American history. This book proposes to examine American history through its monsters.

So do not expect neat definitions when it comes to a messy subject like monsters. A monster is a beast of excess, and monster stories are tales of excess. Part of what makes the horror film so much fun is that it refuses to follow the narrative plot of a simple melodrama. It does not contain conflict and ignore contradictions in order to produce a happy ending. It blows conventions into a million pieces and makes a fetish out of excess. In this the horror film takes on the nature of its subject and its agent: the monster.[2]

The subject of monsters contains too much meaning. It is the *House That Drips Blood* and the thing with 20,000 eyes. It is bigger than it should be, more insatiable than anything in nature; it desires more and frightens you with its yawning monstrous maw. The very messiness of the monster makes it the perfect entry into understanding the messiness of American history. If history were music it would not have the austere balance of a Bach concerto. It would be the opening assault of the Sex Pistols' "Anarchy in the UK," angry, discordant, and yawping at you in combative tones. History issues threats as much as it inspires reflection. Some historians will be less than happy with this book. Many of them will note that I spend more time on sea serpents than the Civil War, or that I dash past the American Revolution in my eagerness to talk about the American Enlightenment's fascination with the homegrown, allegedly carnivorous mastodon. They are right that some events get short shrift and a very different kind of analysis than appears in most historical studies. Obviously a work like this does not aim to deliver the kind of heaping spoonfuls of nuanced historical fact we expect from good textbooks.

As a trained historian, I share these concerns. Even a look at the chapter titles suggests that this author is up to no good. But I also worry that the historian's profession has become deeply problematic because both a younger and older generation have become profoundly disconnected from their putative audience and, in a strange way, from their own topics. Professional historians sometimes see themselves as students and curators of a master narrative. Amateur readers of history, meanwhile, turn to popularly written books on historical subjects because they offer a damn good yarn and literally nothing else.

Neither of these groups sees themselves as enfolded in history, sometimes as its agents and sometimes as its victims. The average reader keeps reading World War II books as if they tell a clear, uncomplicated story. Grad students learn the ropes and take their comprehensive exams and go on to pass the narrative on to their students (or drop the narrative on them like the metaphorical ton of bricks). None of these groups lets history enrage, implicate, and penetrate them.

Master narratives are, by definition, lies and untruths. This is why we need to study monsters. They are the things hiding in history's dark places, the silences that scream if you listen closely enough. Cultural critic Greil Marcus writes, "parts of history, because they don't fit the story a people wants to tell itself, survive only as haunts and fairy tales, accessible only

nd spooks." The secrets and the lies, and perhaps most impor-
:tims of history, are in those stories of monsters, those dark
 ̤̤ waiting to be explored. These places became dark in the first place
because they did not fit the historical story we wanted to tell ourselves.[3]

So, I am wondering if maybe the movie *The Texas Chain Saw Massacre* can explicate issues that a full-scale study of Andrew Jackson's Indian Removal policy cannot. Its lead character, Leatherface, certainly makes an impression, and his house of horrors has a lot to tell us about the American frontier. I am wondering if Frankenstein's monster might offer us a new way to grasp the horrors of scientific racism or if Dracula can teach us something about the early twentieth-century Red Scare.

I do not want to be misunderstood here at the beginning. This is not an effort to use some horrific examples from fantasy literature and film to illustrate important truths about American history. Instead, I am seeking to read the monster as what theorist Slavoj Žižek refers to as "a fantasy scenario that obfuscates the true horror of the situation." The monster reifies very real incidents, true horrors, true monsters. This is why they are always complicated and inherently sophisticated. The monster has its tentacles wrapped around the foundations of American history, draws its life from ideological efforts to marginalize the weak and normalize the powerful, to suppress struggles for class, racial, and sexual liberation, to transform the "American Way of Life" into a weapon of empire.[4]

The reader should also be aware that the author believes in monsters. They are real. Before you shut this book and write it off as Fortean propaganda, know that I do not see myself as a poor man's Mulder from the television show *The X-Files*, here to tell you that the truth is out there. But before we start talking about "monsters as metaphors," let's examine that construction a bit and you will see why I would rather just assert my belief in monsters.[5]

The problem is in the concept of metaphor itself. "My love is like a red, red rose" is metaphorical language expressing a desire to sing the beauty of the beloved (and to get laid by the beloved). But really, who cares? Metaphors can be beautiful, inexact, or just plain silly but, regardless, nobody takes them seriously. The phrase "just a metaphor" sounds suspiciously to me like "just a waste of time."

Lots of books are out there about monsters as metaphors for this or that social or psychological process. I do not think this approach works well when it comes to history. In American history the monsters are real. The metaphors of the American experience are ideas hardwired to historical action rather than interesting word pictures. If you stick with me on the path, I will explain more.

The slipperiness of monsters, whether they are reptilian in nature or not, reminds us that they owe their protean nature to changes in historical context. In this way, they are, above all, ideological constructions. By this I don't mean what the term "ideology" has commonly come to mean: any worldview or set of political beliefs you happen to hold. I'm using the word in Marx's sense of a set of ideas that shapes our social reality while simultaneously blinding us to the forces that produce that social reality.

American historian Barbara Fields has described ideology as "a ready-made interpretation of the world, a sort of hand-me-down vocabulary." Ideological constructions, she insists, are not illusory but as real as the social relations they obscure, even though the vocabulary of ideology may shift over time to suit the needs of those in power. Our monsters are also not simply delusions, whether they slither toward us as folklore, urban legend, or popular entertainment. Nor are they simply mirrors of social fears or expressions of social anxiety, the catharsis interpretation of the horror tale. They are so embedded in the way Americans talk about class, race, gender, and social structure that they offer a way for people to mark, comprehend, and just as frequently, misunderstand their world. Our monstrous vocabularies change, but the monsters of social and economic oppression lurk behind the new horrors.[6]

Once we begin to analyze, as this book tries to do, how even entertainment can shape the way we see our social and historical experiences, we can subvert efforts to blind us. This is what the scholar of culture and history Stuart Hall meant when he famously described the possibility of an "oppositional" reading of the messages the media sends us.[7]

Some of the tellers of monster tales we will meet have done some of the work of challenging ideology for us. Returning to Halberstam's idea of the monster as a "meaning machine," we can see how it's been possible throughout American history for various groups, artists, and authors to seize the means of monstrous production, to burn down the master's haunted house. Horror may be the most dangerous ideological tool in the ruling elite's bag of tricks because it offers a set of symbols with which to, with no metaphor implied, demonize social groups whose agency threatens the social system. But like the archetypal monster of modernity, horror consistently threatens to rebel against its master, to transgress the boundaries set for it, and wreak havoc.

Žižek may go too far when he calls John Carpenter's 1988 *They Live* one of "the forgotten classics of the American left." However, Carpenter's brilliant satire of Reagan's America, taken over by alien invaders already among us, does, as Žižek claims, provide a perfect introduction to the power of ideology and the possibilities of seeing through it.[8]

They Live tells the story of unemployed construction worker John Nada, played with proletarian panache by the late "Rowdy Roddy" Piper, who comes into possession of high-tech glasses that allow him to see the secret codes behind the orgy of 1980s greed on display in advertising, magazines, and all forms of popular culture. A billboard of a beautiful woman in a bikini on a beach actually reads MARRY AND REPRODUCE. Images of luxury carry the subliminal messages CONSUME and STAY ASLEEP. Magazine covers that urge investing and golf playing read NO IMAGINATION and OBEY. The president on television? Only a thinly veiled version of Ronald Reagan that mouths the myths of American exceptionalism and revealed by the glasses as an alien overlord.

They Live offers only one example of how dissenting filmmakers, many of them forged by the 1960s counterculture, began to use horror to transgress social norms and challenge some of America's deeply held beliefs. While many horror films since the 1960s have remained adamantly apolitical, and sometimes even offer viewers conservative cautionary tales, the experimental, countercultural nature of horror has played with some of the most inhumane elements of the historical context that created them, critiquing and challenging an America that began a rapid, transformative, and generally reactionary change in the 1970s.

Clearly, the reader has discovered by now, I take my monsters seriously. I hope they will do the same.

I do not, however, take traditional historical chronologies seriously. Although this book engages in a chronological analysis of a kind, it also ignores some of the basic conventions of historical narrative. We will move back and forth between periods, and listen to voices in the seventeenth century and the twentieth century at the same time, generally mucking up any effort to read the American experience as a linear, and thus progressive, march through time. This is because I hope to trace the ways American monsters form a systemic network, or perhaps a cultural echo chamber, rather than something like a time line.

It is also because I believe that seeing history as a stark glacial formation of dates and facts leads to viewing history as "dead" and definitively "in the past." This, in turn, can make way for the tendency to monumentalize those events, to invest them with the immovable power of marble statues. History as memorizable event becomes at once detached from the present and the embodiment of a profoundly conservative pedagogy, markers of boundaries and parameters that can never be changed. History then becomes dead cultural weight the present must carry on its back rather than living events in conversation and debate. On the other hand, refusing to accept the idea that historical events are dead things on a time line frees us from the incredibly assertive arrogance of the past, its lifeless yet grasping hand. If we do otherwise, we will feel that hand, cold and brutal, holding us tight and not letting us go.[9]

And so we are going to pass a long night together. If you and I make it until morning and find our way out of this dark wood, we will not see American history the same way ever again. Seeing America through its monsters offers a new perspective on old questions. It allows us to look into the shadows, to rifle through those trunks in the attic we have been warned to leave alone. Not all of our myths will make it out of here alive.

I hope one of the first victims, by the way, is that loudmouth "American exceptionalism." This unfortunate philosophy has it that America has always been the innocent abroad, the new nation who teaches the world democracy. This sophomoric notion of world history since 1776 presents the United States as Little Red Riding Hood, setting off on the forest path of democracy and economic liberalism. A hard look at American history raises questions about whether the American nation has been the innocent in the woods or that other, more feral figure in the forest.

So let our midnight ride begin. We will start by figuring out the way monster narratives work and what others have said about them, and hardly catch our breath before we plunge into colonial America's world of witches and wonders. Creatures of scientific nightmare will haunt us in the nineteenth century as we meet Hawthorne and Poe, two old hands at navigating this eldritch wood. The twentieth century seems to open out into a new vista, but we only briefly see some sunlight, and we are back in the dark wood again, hiding from escaped mental patients and seeing strange lights in the sky. We will begin to dream of home and yet also wonder if it is all that safe a place after all before we get chased by creatures of the night eager to chew on us and suck us dry.

I hope you have snuggled back into your favorite reading chair and assured yourself that the world, or at least your little corner of it, is a safe place. Unfortunately for you, I propose to show you that it is not. You are implicated in a violent history, a historical landscape where monsters walk. Like it or not, you are part of the story, and it is not a romantic comedy or a melodrama. You are the main character in this terror-filled little tale.

At about this point, the Crypt Keeper would unloose a demonical laugh, both at the twisted subject matter the audience was about to read and the twisted nature of the audience who wanted to read it. Vampira would give her adolescent audience a bloodcurdling scream to announce that the grisly fun could begin. I cannot pull off that laugh, and in print no one can hear you scream. So, without further ado, let's bring on the night.

ACKNOWLEDGMENTS

W hen I was somewhere around the age of eight, my parents banned me from watching *Shock Theatre* on Saturday afternoons. *Shock Theatre* brought the black-and-white "famous monsters" of the 1930s and 1940s into the lives of the kids of the 1970s. It also gave me a strange combination of hallucinatory nightmares and intense fascination matched only by my near-religious hysteria over the recent 1977 release of *Star Wars.*

Their ban did not last, as evidenced by the endless stream of comic books, TV shows, and movies that soon came into my life. I appreciate my parents' sometimes-harassed patience and hope this book helps them to understand why these things matter not only to me but also to the culture in which we live. I sincerely thank them for their unflagging pride in me, even when my work and interests go places they do not always understand.

I've become a fanboy of Baylor University Press. I would especially like to thank Carey Newman for his unfailing support and indefatigable enthusiasm for the project. Seldom have I had an editor take such a personal interest in a project, including reading and commenting on early drafts. I also very much appreciate the work of Jennifer Hunt, whose helpful, detailed e-mails regarding the original book's production and design answered my concerns and helped prompt new ideas for photographs and images. Thanks to Diane Smith who quickly and helpfully dealt with all my questions and concerns about matters editorial on both editions of the book.

Numerous friends and colleagues take an avid interest in my work and have expressed excitement about this project. I would especially like to thank my many colleagues, in and outside the field of history, who have assigned the book for their courses and whose own work on America's monstrous stories has much improved this version.

I dedicated the first edition of this book to Niamh Margaret Carmichael. I dedicate this revised edition to her as well and to many happy memories at the donut shop, the comic book store, and reading stories before bed. She was three when the book first appeared and already had an intense love of books. I hope one day she will read and enjoy this one.

Christina Butler gave enormous time and attention to indexing the first edition of this book. Many thanks are due to Laura Rashley who prepared the index for the new version. I appreciate her attention to detail and her friendship.

This book would not have happened without my partner Beth Phillips. Her interest in my work never fails to encourage me.

INTRODUCTION
The Bloody Chords of Memory

So ignorant are most landsmen of some of the plainest and most palpable wonders of the world that, without some hints touching the plain facts . . . they might scout at Moby-Dick as a monstrous fable, or still worse and more detestable, a hideous and intolerable allegory.

—Herman Melville, *Moby-Dick*

Joey: The demons, the demons!
Priest: Demons? Demons aren't real, they are only parables, meta-phors. (Church door explodes and Pinhead stands threateningly in the door.) *Joey:* (finger pointing at the monster) *Then what the fuck is that!*

—*Hellraiser III: Hell on Earth*

N ovelist F. Scott Fitzgerald's arrival at the MGM commissary followed fast on a night of humiliation. The author of *The Great Gatsby* had embarrassed himself, in his mind irredeemably, at a party thrown the previous evening by acclaimed producer Irving Thalberg and actress Norma Shearer. Fitzgerald drank too much and launched into a long and embarrassing rendition of "In America we have the dog / and he's a man's best friend," the kind of song, an observer noted, that "might have seemed amusing if one were very drunk and still in one's freshman year at College." Fellow screenwriter Dwight Taylor quickly saw that Fitzgerald's erstwhile audience was not amused. Tolerant smiles turned to a low and ominous hiss of disapproval. In the sober light of dawn, Fitzgerald felt his humiliation compounded by the fear that Thalberg would fire him for his indiscretion, cutting off his income at a time when he was desperate for funds needed to pay for his wife Zelda's care at a sanitarium.[1]

The following day, Fitzgerald planned on a hangover recovery lunch with Taylor. Neither seemed aware that they would share the commissary with the cast of the new Tod Browning production *Freaks*. Browning, coming off his wildly successful production of *Dracula* in 1931, enlisted actual sideshow performers to be the stars of his controversial project. The cast of the film that came to work on the MGM lot included midgets, a small boy with simian features and gait, fully joined Siamese twins, heavily tattooed persons of uncertain gender, and a so-called pinhead, a microcephalic with a tapering cranium and large, heavy jaw.

Almost as soon as Fitzgerald took a seat, Siamese twins known as the Hilton sisters joined him at his table, sitting down on a single stool. Holding a menu in their hands, one of the twin's heads asked the other "What are you thinking of having?" Fitzgerald, already under the weather after his previous night's adventures, became immediately and violently ill. "Scott turned pea green," remembered Taylor, "and rushed for the great outdoors."[2]

Fitzgerald was far from the last person to have a bad experience with *Freaks*. America did not fall in love with the tale's twisted love story that ends in the betrayal of the freaks by a "normal," a betrayal that the freaks answer with a horrible and unforgettable revenge. In fact, the first audiences shrieked, vomited, or simply left the theater.

The preview of the film on December 16, 1931, can only be described as a complete and utter disaster. One observer noted that disgusted audience members not only left the theater, they actually ran to get away from the film. In response to audience reaction, Browning cut *Freaks* by more than half an hour. Despite significant changes, the film still managed to anger and disgust film reviewers as well as religious and civic leaders. Louis B. Mayer, head of MGM, later sold Browning's ode to the sideshow in hopes that he and his company would no longer have any connection to it. *Freaks* went underground for thirty years until it appeared again in 1962 at the Cannes Film Festival and soon became a permanent feature on the art house circuit.[3]

The response to *Freaks* would seem to suggest that Americans have no room for the monster. As the United States faced an economic crisis in the 1930s that appeared to represent the failure and collapse of American

1933 *Freaks* featuring the Hilton sisters

capitalism, the portrayal of such disturbing topics as physical abnormality, torture, and ritual murder hardly seemed the tonic the 1933 moviegoing public needed. The failure of *Freaks* perhaps signaled the public's desire to see more of the kinds of films that Mayer and MGM had become famous for—namely, light romantic fare featuring actors who embodied Mayer's fascination with blonde Anglos of perfect bodily proportions.[4]

Yet this was not the case. The biggest cinematic heroes of the decade before the Second World War, purely in terms of the money they made for their studio, included a foreign aristocrat who drank the blood of his victims in a film with a clear sexual (both homo and hetero) subtext, and a monstrosity knitted together from cadavers and given, by his half-mad creator, the brain of an executed murderer. At the beginning of the next decade, Hollywood's biggest commercial draws included a man transformed into a ravening beast through a satanic curse and a raft of scientists delving into forbidden knowledge. *Freaks* flopped, and yet these other monstrosities shambled, howled, and slithered their way into America's hearts.

The story of American monsters, and how they obsess American culture, allows us a look at the underground history of the United States. While a number of works have examined the horror story as a function of American popular culture, reading them as Rorschach tests for inner pathologies and metaphors for everything from adolescent sexuality to

ɔlence, almost none have made connections with the larger
.ɪcan history. None have looked at the broader story of the
.ɔter in America, analyzing the monster as a historical problem.[5]

Americans have an undeniable taste for the monstrous in all its
forms, a taste in evidence from the time of the earliest colonial settlements.
The narrative of American history can be read as a tale of monsters slain
and monsters beloved. Witches and other night creatures infested the
New England woods, and the devil inspired savage servants to combat
the Puritans. Demonic rites and horrible shapes from beyond the grave
lived in the shadows of the Southern plantation household. Sea serpents
trawled the waters of the oceans where whalers and slave ships knit the
new country into a world of commerce. Wild men and savage beasts
prowled the virgin woodlands where America cut its railroads and canals,
built its settlements, and created a market revolution. After the Civil War,
the American obsessions with race and violence became the bloody chords
of memory that held the Union together, a Union that in the twentieth
century combined an idealistic rhetoric of democracy with the crassest
of imperial endeavors. After World War II, terrifying visitors from other
worlds came to tell this new imperium of its doom, while murderous
maniacs hunted its citizens relentlessly on the highways, in the forests,
and even at summer camp.

Monsters in America are everywhere and come in every genus and
species. American pop culture has had its nauseating monsters, its sexy
monsters, its religious monsters, and even its elegant monsters. They
have menaced us in our fiction and frightened us in our films. Some of
their images, from Frankenstein to Freddy Krueger to Slenderman, are
icons of modern cultural history. This book argues that the origins of all
of America's monster obsessions lie in something more substantial than
media-driven cultural ephemera. American monsters are born out of
American history. They emerge out of the central anxieties and obsessions that have been a part of the United States from colonial times to the
present and from the structures and processes where those obsessions
found historical expression.[6]

While almost all the shambling horrors that walk across our theater
screens and live under our beds have older, transnational roots, the American context shaped them in definitive ways. Vampires and werewolves
came out of the folkloric traditions of early modern Europe. But when
they appear in our local cineplex, in the pages of comic books and prose
fiction, and even in our folklore and urban legends, they are true American
monsters. They are living representations of our darkness, simultaneously

metaphors and progenitors of the American way of fear and violence. They are creatures of American history, their many permutations in folklore and pop culture impossible to explain without that complex history. American history can best be understood through America's monsters.

A Little History of Horror

The Latin word *monstrum* provides us with our English term "monster." *Monstrum* is "that which appears" or reveals itself (the English word "demonstrate" is rooted in *monstrum*). *Monstrum* also has a relationship to the Latin word *monere*, meaning "to warn," and relates to the concept of an omen or a portent. But in world mythology and religious experience, the monster has done more than represent the hideous and abnormal. Monsters have been, from ancient times, invested with meanings divine and demonic, theological or fearfully natural. In every society they appear as multifaceted beings composed of a complicated tangle of symbolic synapses, living messages to those unlucky souls to whom they appear.[7]

Like Dracula leaving his Transylvanian homeland to seek new conquests in the teeming metropolis of London, monsters made their journey to the New World from a European context. Indeed, almost all the monstrous forms that delight and terrify modern America have a longer, intercultural genealogy, sometimes reaching back to the origins of human society.

Humanity emerged from the Stone Age dreaming of monsters. The caves of southern France and northern Spain are covered with figures in red ocher, iconographies of the hunt, of blood and death. Human beings represented themselves not only as hunters but also as prey and victims to the great beasts of the Neolithic world. At least one image, found at Trois Frères in the Pyrenees, presents a human figure, often referred to by historians as a "sorcerer." He is a shapeshifter, imagined by these early artists as being part wolf and part bear. In other words, a monster.[8]

In the Bronze Age, religious epic and theological speculation about the cosmos crafted the concept of the monstrous. Monsters, while certainly transgressive and terrifying, play an ironic role in most religious systems' notions of order. Many Near Eastern and ancient Indian cosmologies imagine the slaying of a monster as central to the construction of the universe. In many of these mythologies, the body and bones of the slain monster are transformed into the architecture of the cosmos.

Monsters even figure into the biblical epic. The Hebrew experience of God drew heavily on its polytheistic antecedents and from the mythic material of its context. Monotheism, and its connection to the idea of the covenant ("One God has chosen one people"), represented a living experience of God's action in history rather than a philosophical sentiment about the nature of reality. Only much later did it become a theological problem for the ancient Hebrews that monsters shared the same conceptual turf as Yahweh.[9]

Monsters, angels, ghosts, witches, and giants all appear in the Hebrew scripture. The meaning of these beings tends to be obscure and, in fact, contradictory. Both the land creature, Behemoth, and the giant sea monster, Leviathan, make an appearance in the book of Job and in the Psalms, beings at once monstrous and miraculous. Religious studies scholar Timothy Beal notes that both beasts appear in Hebrew scripture "in a variety of mutually exclusive ways." The Leviathan of the Hebrew Bible appears as both the enemy of Yahweh and Yahweh's playmate. In both Psalm 74 and in the third chapter of Job, Leviathan acts as the adversary of God, a terrible serpent that must be destroyed so that both creation and the people of God's covenant can be preserved. On the other hand, Leviathan in Psalm 104 and Job 40 appears as God's own creation, a being with a strangely close relationship to the Deity.[10]

Stephen Asma, author of a recent meditation on the nature of the monster, suggests that these competing biblical images reflect a complex conception of God emerging in Hebrew thought. Leviathan represents, in Asma's mind, the effort to reconcile the seemingly contradictory nature of God, a being who elicits both wonder and horror. Timothy Beal, in a close and brilliant reading of the book of Job, argues that God describes Leviathan in detail to his unlucky servant because this creature provides not a "spectacle" of "God's well-ordered world ecology" but instead an image of the "awful chaos that churns just beneath the surface." Both Beal and Asma see religious experience as a kind of horror movie, embodiments of the divine that evoke feelings of terror. The monsters of the Bible are symbols of that horror.[11]

Clashing images of God's monsters reveal both the slow development of ancient concepts of monotheism and the tendency of every human society to hold a deep fascination with the marginalized monstrous, the being that does not exactly fit in the cosmological order and yet is in some sense crucial to it. The horror of the monster goes hand in hand with its attraction. It has always embodied terror, raising questions about its own existence even as it terrifies.

The emergence of Christianity in the first and second centuries of the Common Era played a crucial role in the shaping of the monster in Western Europe. By the second century, the concept of the devil as the enemy of God and the human race coalesced with Hebrew imagery of "the serpent in the garden." This tightly packed symbolic construction gave the Christian church a head full of serpents, a monstrous brood that provided a wealth of demonic symbols. The description, for example, of the great dragon of Revelation chapter 12, identified with the devil, became the paradigm for the West's imagining of everything from sea monsters to the king of the vampires (Dracula means, after all, "son of the Dragon").[12]

The medieval world born out of the ruins of Rome became a world of monsters that shared some of the same contradictory impulses of earlier mythologies. Medievalist Jeffrey J. Cohen describes, in Anglo-Saxon England, legends told of monsters building great houses of stone. In this context of legendary belief, mysterious ruins or rock formations came to be described as "the work of giants." In Anglo-Saxon England, the monster appears as Grendel in the *Beowulf* saga, a loathsome creature that tears through the doors of Hrothgar's mead hall and devours everyone inside. In the medieval mind, the monster appeared as both creator of order and threat to order, a bundle of contradictions that borrowed from Christian images of Satan (both Angel of Light and Prince of Darkness) and from the old Norse cosmogonies in which the original great giant Ymir provided his own body for the foundation of the world, his bones becoming the hills, his flesh becoming dirt, and his skull transformed into the sky. The monster terrified, and yet human beings actually lived within his remains.[13]

Increasingly, the many monsters of the Latin Christian West represented composites of images of Satan, biblical monsters, and the creatures from the folklore of pre-Christian Europe. Folklore about the nature of the devil and his work in the world naturally gave rise to stories of other terrible beings opposed to God and humanity. As historian Jeffrey Burton Russell describes this process in his multivolume history of the devil in the Western world, "the folkloric Devil shades off into other concepts such as the Antichrist, giants, dragons, ghosts, monsters, were animals and 'the little people.'" The process could work the other way as well, with the devil absorbing the myths and legends of pre-Christian monsters. In some parts of Europe, Satan took over the attributes of giants, and unusual geological formations became a house of the devil. Russell points out that this idea persists even into American cultural history with the tendency to name irregular rock formations or mountains "Devils Tower" or "Devil Mountain."[14]

Medieval speculation about the nature of monsters ran the gamut from a simple identification of them as accomplices of Satan to somewhat more sophisticated speculation about their place in relation to humanity and the larger divine design. Medieval scholars' mental maps of the world featured monstrous races of giants, wild apes, and dog-headed men. Christian scholars sometimes speculated that these creatures represented the progeny of Cain, cursed by God for slaying his brother (Grendel, Beowulf's monstrous opponent in the Anglo-Saxon epic, is said to be of the lineage of Cain). Occasionally, glimpses of a more nuanced view of monstrosity can be seen. One minor tradition in the Middle Ages portrayed St. Christopher as a Cynocephalus or "dog-headed man." Scholars in the medieval world debated whether or not monsters had souls, and thus whether, hypothetically, they could receive baptism.[15]

Most of the monsters that rose from the grave in modern America have their distant origins in this context of medieval folklore, legend, and literature. Europeans had portrayed the witch, the vampire, and the werewolf, unlike many of the fantastical creatures located in other climes, as accomplices of Satan. The witch had a clear relationship with the devil, drawing her power from a pact she had made with him. The vampire in Eastern Europe and parts of Germany had some relationship with Satan but also drew on beliefs about revenants and the consequences of a "bad death." Werewolves, and shapeshifters of all kinds, have a more complicated history, at times being portrayed as guiltless figures who labor under a curse (much like Larry Talbot in Universal Pictures' 1941 *The Wolf Man*). Other versions of the werewolf mythos represent them as satanic creatures whose power, like that of the witch, comes from hell. Belief in these creatures assumed that no strict separation of "nature" and "supernature" existed, and that a world of shadows periodically and terrifyingly haunted humanity.[16]

The sixteenth and seventeenth centuries saw the birth of a new worldview. The "scientific revolution" introduced the notion of the universe as a mechanism rather than a playground for divine and demonic spirits. Kepler, Copernicus, and Galileo challenged the domination of Aristotelian cosmology that placed the earth at the center of the known universe. A new mechanical conception of nature began to shape thinking about the world, suggesting that observable, repeatable laws governed everything from the behavior of heavenly bodies to the phenomenon of human bodies. Neither miracles nor monsters would seem to have much of a foothold in this reimagined cosmos.

Ironically, the dawning age of science also became an age obsessed with the work of Satan on earth, specifically his use of witches and other evil accomplices. Witchcraft trials during the early modern period took the lives of perhaps as many as fifty thousand people. Trials of people suspected of being "loup-garou," or werewolves, became common in sixteenth- and seventeenth-century France. Magistrates and church- men described werewolves, seldom imagined anymore as forlorn beings traveling under a curse, as human beings who willfully transformed into a monster with the help of the devil.[17]

The grim realities of the witch hunts suggest that the tenets of the scientific revolution did not filter through all segments of early modern European society. Moreover, this enduring belief in the supernatural during the scientific revolution did not represent a divide between univer- sity culture and peasant village culture. Learned treatises on diabolism, witchcraft, and the etiology of monsters poured forth from the pens of a number of illustrious university scholars. The scientific revolution created new terms for the discussion of the monstrous, but it did not end the discussion. Scholars assumed the existence of powerful nonhuman and inhuman creatures, sometimes giving both scientific and supernatural explanations for their existence in the same breath. The learned sixteenth- century French surgeon Ambroise Pare in his treatise *On Monsters and Marvels* listed thirteen causes for the appearances of abnormality in human beings, some of them natural and some of them purely super- natural, including "the artifice of evil beggars" and the agency of "demons and devils."[18]

The long history of humanity's monstrous fascinations, and the mythologies and theologies that supported them, would seem to have little to do with the early American republic or its citizens. The Amer- ican Revolution grew in part out of the Enlightenment goal of applying rationality to politics. While it is too simplistic to view the creation of the United States as merely the fulfillment of the Enlightenment project, many of America's founders did imagine a new nation reared on the foun- dations of human reason. Patriots forged the United States, it has often been explained to us, out of a wedding of Enlightenment political ideology and a growing sense of national destiny. Adams, Franklin, and Jefferson admired the political philosophy of John Locke, who favored the creation of rational republics where the superstitions of statecraft and "priestcraft" had no purchase. The new republic would live in a sunlit world without shadows, a place where no monster could hide.[19]

The Sleep of Reason

The connection between Enlightenment ideology and the birth of the United States is a complicated one. Many, perhaps most, of the so-called Founders held a combination of Enlightenment belief and what historians of the period call "country ideology"—the idea that the power of small coteries of elites corrupted and destroyed the liberties of the people. Thomas Jefferson and Thomas Paine, two of the most influential thinkers and propagandists in the making of the American Revolution, tied their critique of monarchy to a critique of Old World religion. In their minds, the destruction of political tyranny correlated naturally to the destruction of religious tyranny in both its Protestant and Catholic versions.[20]

These rational revolutionaries did not, however, speak for the broad constituency that helped to make the American Revolution and the American nation. As historian Sean Wilentz shows in his monumental *The Rise of American Democracy*, a significant split always existed between small urban elites in colonial America and, in that era, the much larger population that lived in the rural settlements. Thomas Jefferson expected Americans to become deists by the time of his death. Instead, the so-called Second Great Awakening swept the country, proliferating religious worldviews and sectarian communities. The belief in the supernatural refused to die.[21]

In fact, the Enlightenment itself, most historians now agree, should be considered a complex phenomenon. The eighteenth-century rationalists did not easily relinquish mythical and fantastic beliefs, even as they attempted to wedge them into the new, naturalistic paradigm. French philosophe Voltaire often engaged in speculative reflection about the possibilities of monsters inhabiting the unknown corners of the earth. He suggested, for example, that satyrs might exist and wondered whether or not monsters could be produced in certain tropical regions of the world if human females mated with animals. The latter belief would have calamitous consequences, as we shall see, for the history of racial attitudes in the settler societies of the Atlantic world.[22]

Voltaire, at least, tended to look for natural and scientific explanations for "wonders" in the natural word, for explanations that made these strange creatures parts of a rational framework. Other major thinkers connected with Europe's scientific revolution and Enlightenment exercised less caution. Robert Boyle, the father of modern chemistry, combined the emerging scientific ideology of empirical investigation with a fairly traditional belief in the existence of demons. In the 1670s Boyle interviewed English miners to see if they had made contact with "any subterraneous demons" and "in what shape and manner they appear."[23] Even many early modern thinkers who had become wary of supernatural definitions of the monstrous continued to accept many of the fantastical beings of European folklore. Francis Bacon, whose propaganda text for the scientific revolution *The Advancement of Learning* all but created the notion of "science as progress," believed in the reality of monsters even while arguing, much like Voltaire, that they could be understood in the light of rational empiricism. Swedish scientist Carl Linnaeus asserted that he could explain what he called the "paradoxa" of nature in nature's own terms. Linnaeus showed a special interest in the phenomenon of "wild children," allegedly feral human beings raised beyond the boundaries of civilization. Avoiding the term "monster," he classified these children as a "subgenre" of humanity.[24]

Linnaeus holds a place of honor in the history of science with his detailed and elegant system of classification of the natural world into genus and species. His emphasis on natural history's need for an empirical system of categories marks his work as a clear departure from an earlier willingness to view the natural world as a mysterious place filled with unclassifiable wonders. His taxonomy of nature represented the first effort at creating what cultural historian Stephen Asma has called "a conceptual filing cabinet of the world."[25]

This taxonomy, however, allowed for wonders and marvels. Linnaeus even left open the possibility that a category needed to be created for dragons, and his genera included a spot for troglodytes. Much like Voltaire, Linnaeus had little doubt that further exploration of the globe promised to yield a bounty of fantastic creatures with bizarre anatomies. Linnaeus perhaps represents the Enlightenment attitude toward the monster, the idea that the wondrous remained wonderful even as it became classifiable. Linneaus' conceptual filing cabinet would contain more than a few X-files.[26]

American thinking about the meaning of the miraculous inherited this curious combination of the mysterious and the rational, the desire to understand the physical world while allowing at least a small aperture for the supernatural. Deeply religious notions of the world jostled with skeptical rationalism for supremacy. The Puritans, English religious radicals who represented the bulk of the settlers of New England, viewed the natural world through the lens of their intricate Calvinist theology. Puritan clergy, America's first intellectuals, saw a world full of signs and portents and remained certain of the work of malefic creatures, creatures who swirled around them in an invisible world so close to their own. Thomas Jefferson and Cotton Mather wrestled over the American mind.[27]

One of the earliest American scientific controversies illustrates this conflict. In 1705 a farmer discovered a giant tooth near Albany, New York. Puritan divine Cotton Mather, hunter of witches as well as monsters, wrote a series of letters about the discovery to the secretary of the Royal Society of London, the premier association of scientific thinking in the early eighteenth century. Mather had no difficulty explaining, to his own satisfaction, the origin and meaning of the fossil. The tooth, Mather declared, represented a "wonderful confirmation of Mosaic history," empirical proof of the ancient Near Eastern legend of the Nephilim, found in Genesis chapter 6. This strange tale of angels walking the earth before Noah's flood and mating with human women to produce giants now had, Mather believed, empirical confirmation. The fossil discovery proved that these horny giants had once stamped around western New York.[28]

Even in the early eighteenth century, some American thinkers asserted that the tooth belonged to an animal rather than to an extinct race of giants. As contemporary historian Paul Semonin details so carefully in his book *American Monster,* the controversy over this and other fossils (belonging to what we now know to be the herbivorous mastodon) became one of the major cultural conversations of eighteenth-century America, drawing in Thomas Jefferson and George Washington, numerous theologians, and the museologists. As we will explore more fully in the next chapter, this discussion took place using the terms of debate set by Enlightenment empiricism but also drew on beliefs about fantastical creatures from the Bible and of folklore.[29]

The debate over the meaning of fossils in early America helped shape the development of a huge body of popular belief about other wondrous creatures of the New World, from Big Foot to sea serpents, lake monsters, and lizard men. These strange creatures, like the American mastodon, would terrify and delight the new inhabitants of the American continent, blurring the lines between the natural and the supernatural and incorporating beliefs about topics from religion to nationalism. The horrifying creatures could and would provoke much more than horror, becoming marvels and wonders, secret codes with multiple, complicated meanings.[30]

American monsters are omens, warnings, and portents. Like omens they cause wonder and horror and often refuse to make their meaning clear. Scholars have long understood this combination of fear and delight in the monster to be part of the attraction of everything from folklore about strange beasts to the modern slasher film. A significant genre of scholarly writing, much of it focused on American popular culture, seeks to explain this fascination, to describe the meaning of the monstrous and why it proves such a powerful lure for the human psyche. It is a literature that, while often highly theoretical, can provide much insight into America's appetite for the monster.

Our Monsters, Ourselves

Does the nausea of F. Scott Fitzgerald have much of anything to do with the wonder of Cotton Mather at discovering the tooth of an antediluvian giant? Do we know what the monster is and how human beings respond to it? What is the attraction of these beings that horrify, and why do they manifest to us as horrors?

Although a number of scholars from diverse disciplines have sought to answer these questions, few have examined the monsters produced by a specific national history. Much of the best work on the history of the monstrous has come from scholars of medieval Europe and the early modern period, while the analysis of the monstrous as part of American society has focused almost entirely on pop culture and more specifically on film. This analysis tends to focus on the meaning, often the psychological meaning, of the response of theater audiences both to the monster and to horror narratives more generally.[31]

Efforts to define the nature of the monster are perhaps simpler than they first appear. The critical and popular response to *Freaks* suggests that the monster inspires disgust, anxiety, and even nausea. The marginalized are the monstrous and the monstrous appears as marginalized. The monster, more than our fears, also represents our hatreds. Whatever makes us lose our lunch, whether natural or supernatural, can be defined as a monster. The monster is the sickening Other.[32]

This would work as a definition of the monster if F. Scott Fitzgerald's nausea represented the most common response to the appearance of the despised and damned thing. But this is problematized by the fact that American history provides examples of society reveling in the alien, in the horrifying, and in that which allegedly disgusts. Describing the monster as a trigger for nausea does not explain why Puritans found witches entertaining, why Frankenstein's monster became a major nineteenth-century celebrity, or why contemporary fans flock to horror conventions and subscribe to magazines such as *Rue Morgue* and *Fangoria*.

Image of Elsa Lanchester as the Bride of Frankenstein

The difficulties in defining the monster have led many theorists to instead focus on the feeling of terror the monster elicits. Many interpreters of the terrified cultural response to the other suggest that our hatreds of difference grow out of the fear that our own identities, our very selves, are unstable and could yield to the threat of difference. The monster terrifies because "it" represents the terrifying fate of our own bodies.[33]

All of the creatures of folklore and popular culture raise unanswered questions about the bodies we inhabit. The walking corpse horrifies because our bodies will bear a real resemblance to them someday, sans the perambulation. Medical oddities are disturbing because they remind that the boundaries of the human body are inherently unstable and represent images of alternative bodily experiences. Sea serpents, multiheaded hydra, giant squids, and white whales are too big, have too many eyes or too many heads, revolting us with a gigantism that is awe inspiring but also inhuman. Other members of the monstrous fraternity, even the sultry vampire, threaten to puncture, rend, and ultimately destroy our bodies. We fear the monster perhaps because we fear the death and dissolution of our temporal selves.

Sigmund Freud noted this aspect of human fears in his seminal essay describing the nature of what he called "the Uncanny," that creeping feeling of terror—equal parts nausea and equal parts panic. He credited part of this feeling of horror to the possibility of physical damage, noting the number of children's fairy tales that introduce creatures that wound the eye or steal the head. Freud believed the experience of horror had a close relationship to the fear of physical gore, the horror of the body being disassembled in an especially messy way. He concluded that such fears are tied closely to male sexual panic over the possibility of castration. Sometimes a bloody stump is, in fact, more than just a bloody stump.[34]

Freud saw the severed body part as just the beginning of terrifying possibilities: the ultimate fear, the heart of the uncanny darkness, spilled over from the feeling of nausea evoked by the sense of something that refuses to respect the categories of the known and knowable. In fact, Freud argued, the sudden eruption of what human beings think they have repressed, denied, or defeated constitutes the most terrifying reality of all. In his interpretation, the uncanny "applies to everything that was intended to remain secret, hidden away, and has come into the open."[35]

Numerous scholars of the monstrous have followed Freud in seeing the complexities of the human psyche as determinative of the human response to creatures of horror. Unfortunately, many of these efforts share the two major flaws in Freud's approach. First, like Freud's interpretation, they focus on the individual response to horror, and fail to explore both the societal and historical aspects of horror. Following Freud's path has ended in highly reductive interpretations that consign beliefs about the monstrous to the realm of individual nightmare or even to the exigencies of psychological development and gender differentiation.[36]

Second, Freud's interpretation of the uncanny places too much emphasis on the sense of repulsion that the monstrous provides. Later interpreters of the concept, most notably Julia Kristeva, have insisted that there is something deeply attractive about the horrible, indeed even something erotic about it. The monster may cause us to run and hide but with a frisson that has more Eros than Thanatos. Though it can in no sense be regarded as a pleasant sensation, the terror of the monstrous can, according to Kristeva, "worry, fascinate and beseech desire." Popular fascination with the vampire provides the best example of the strange human tendency to want the thing hiding under our beds to be in bed with us.[37]

American cultural history is replete with examples of the uncanny as a desirable quality; in fact the underground history of America can be seen as a quest for the monstrous that will both terrify and fascinate.

The angry reception to *Freaks* came at the end of a long period, dating from the nineteenth century, when actual "Freak Shows" had been enormously popular in America. Moreover, compare the reception of *Freaks* to Tod Browning's earlier film *Dracula*. Rather than being repelled by the bloodsucking, foreign monster, American audiences welcomed Bela Lugosi's version of the vampire as a new and exciting sex symbol. Today the vampire and its related mythology serve as one of America's primary erotic symbol systems.[38]

Julia Kristeva's discussion of what she calls "the abject" helps to explain this exciting combination of fear and desire, building on and complicating both the work of Freud and Lacan. The abject creates a sense of disgust as something to be cast out while at the same time evokes a desire to know and even possess the object that creates this deep disturbance. While producing this strange combination of what she calls "phobia, obsession and perversion," the abject creates a devoted following.[39]

Popular responses to America's monsters illustrate Kristeva's point. A devoted female following for Bela Lugosi in the 1930s is perhaps explicable by the fact that the audience separated the suave, handsome Hungarian actor from the monster. But monsters on the silver screen are not the only creatures of the night surrounded with an aura of desirability. A real-world case in point is Richard Ramirez, the so-called Night Stalker, who in 1988 went on trial for the murder of thirteen people. His victims had ranged from elderly women to children. The few who survived his attacks described him as dressed in black with long hair, poor teeth, and a bad smell. When finally brought to trial, Ramirez flashed the sign of the pentagram tattooed in his hand at the judge and jury, apparently intimidating both.[40]

Ramirez would seem a highly unlikely candidate as a sex symbol, yet this is exactly what he became. According to one account of the days following his trial, a "line of female admirers formed at the prison" in an attempt to visit him. Ramirez transfixed one female juror, who sent him a valentine during the trial (later voting to convict him anyway). Men also feel this attraction to the serial killer. Author Jason Moss developed an intense obsession with John Wayne Gacy (even reading erotica in an effort to find tantalizing images to include in letters that would pique Gacy's interest). "The victims of the abject," Kristeva writes, "are its fascinated victims." The monster always has its groupies. The power of what Kristeva calls the abject is the power of the monster. It incites, excites, and horrifies all at once.[41]

Interpreters of monsters who have not closely followed Freud have still often relied on psychological theories. A number of scholars, many of them seeking to explain the appeal of the monstrous in pop culture, have seen the monster primarily as part of an inner horror show, the personal nightmares of the ego torn between a reptilian id and the moralistic superego. This interpretation understands the monster as a metaphor of human development, the demons that guard the gates of adulthood and emotional maturity. Monsters, according to this view, are primarily inner monsters. Our desire for them emerges from our desire to embrace our own darkness.

This approach often makes the self, especially the adolescent self, the locus of understanding the horrific. Walter Evans, in a 1984 essay entitled "Horror Films: A Sexual Theory," claims that the appeal of the monster comes from adolescent fear and anxiety over alienation. Monsters, for Evans, embody all the dangers of puberty including threat, bodily changes, and an increased awareness of mortality. Other studies have reached similar dubious conclusions. An article by communications scholars Dolf Zillman and James B. Weaver asserted that horror acts on adolescents to shore up societal gender expectations. Basing their argument on a single experiment in which male and female pairs watched *Friday the 13th, Part 3* and recorded their responses, Zillman and Weaver conclude that horror films teach boys "fearlessness and protective competence," while girls learn "fearfulness and protective need."[42]

Larger, more serious, and more influential studies have come to at least similar conclusions. Cultural historian James Twitchell's massive study of horror over several centuries concludes that the horror tale provides "formulaic rituals coded with precise social information needed by an adolescent audience." Like all myths and fairy tales, Twitchell believes, tales of monsters both "preserve culture and protect the individual." Horror tales, he claims, act specifically on adolescents to excite sexual longings while at the same time explaining the dangers inherent in these longings. In particular, Twitchell insists, tales of monsters contain warnings about the violation of the incest taboo. Even classic tales where such a motif is not readily apparent, such as Bram Stoker's *Dracula*, yield to Twitchell's rather ingenious interpretation. *Dracula*, in his reading, becomes a kind of retelling of the Freudian "primal horde" myth in which "a band of boys" seeks to destroy the "evil patriarch" so they can have sexual access to his "wives."[43]

These examples, when looked at through the broad history of fascination with the monster, fail to cover the full range of possible meanings. Twitchell's description of the "audience" who consumes horror, which he claims is primarily adolescent, neglects to take into account everything from genre to time period. Even more damning of this approach is his concept of audience, which is significantly limited. Twitchell ignores the cultural attraction to monstrosity by restricting the discussion entirely to the productions of popular culture. The history of the American monster has much more complexity than this, and audiences who thrill to the monster are far more diverse and sophisticated than Twitchell allows.[44]

The refusal of much of the literature of horror to consider the larger social context has been challenged, especially by scholars of religion. Douglas E. Cowan's tour de force *Sacred Terror* argues that every cinematic image of terror comes with its own "social history." Cowan describes the American horror film as working in terms of "sociophobics," a symbolic machinery that structures a social order and teaches us to fear through the production of intense cultural images (like horror films themselves). Cowan goes beyond scholars who have sought to locate the sources of pop entertainment terror in the individual self. He suggests that these films register profound fears that are the warp and woof of cultural order, the societal sense of anxiety that Cowan calls the direct collision between "what we hope to be true about the world and what we fear may be the reality."[45]

Cowan is not alone in his insistence that the monster must be understood as embedded in society rather than simply the shadows of the individual psyche. Jonathan Lake Crane, in his powerful criticism of much of the writing about horror, has argued that too many critics have seen images of the monstrous as "archetypes or psychic blackholes" rather than social experiences. Specifically writing about the enjoyment of modern horror films, Crane insists that this is not a solitary experience with one's own psychological terrors but rather "joining millions of others on a roller coaster."[46]

This book will build on the work of Crane, Cowan, and others who have located the monster outside of the human psyche. Monsters of all kinds are far more than malefic explosions of the id, more than a return of the repressed. Monsters occupy a central place in American social and cultural history. They sit like spiders in the center of a web of political identities, economic forces, racial fantasy, and gender dynamics. They are more than the dark side of the human personality or the dark side of popular culture. They are part of the genetic code of American history, ciphers that reveal disturbing truths about everything from colonial settlement to the enslavement of African people, from anti-immigrant movements to the rise of religious fundamentalism in the twentieth century. They are more than fantastical metaphors because they have a history coincident with a national history.[47]

The interpretation of the monstrous as the working out of psychic trauma is deeply flawed in its reductive and overdeterminative implications. Scholars who focus primarily on the psychological symbols that appear in modern monster narratives explain some aspects of pop culture; they tell us something about the unconscious dynamics at work in modern horror films; they help to describe how and why an audience might find a specific horror icon both dreadful and tantalizing. In relation to the event that opens this chapter, they might even be able to explain F. Scott Fitzgerald's nausea—but they do not tell us anything about sea serpents.

The Abyss

In August of 1817 a small group of fishermen sighted a sea monster off the coast of Massachusetts. At that time, wrote the *Boston Daily Advertiser*, the sighting had been assumed to be "a creature of the imagination." But within ten to twelve days, reported the same source, the giant creature entered Gloucester Harbor, one of the most prosperous fishing ports in New England, and had been seen by "hundreds of people."[48]

A broadside distributed in Boston on August 22nd claimed that witnesses who had come within "10 to 15 yards" of the creature had described it as between fifty and seventy feet in length with "the width of barrel." The creature's head, characterized as being the size of a horse or a large dog, periodically raised itself out of the water. The sea serpent slid through the water at terrifying speed and could whip itself round to move in reverse motion "almost instantaneously." *The Salem Register* reported that the sea beast left a wake a mile and a half in length as it moved through the water at prodigious speeds.[49]

The whaling community of Gloucester contained plenty of men who considered themselves experts in seeking out sea monsters. The second day of the sightings, four boats of "adventurous sailors and experienced gunners" went after the creature with guns, harpoons, and all the accoutrements of whaling. The gunners claimed they discharged three musket balls into the head of the sea beast, with no effect other than causing it to dive beneath the waters only to briefly resurface, make for the outer harbor, and disappear. The creature came back a few days later, and this time observers claimed to see a beast even bigger than first reported. Some insisted that the creature, seeming to gambol about just offshore, appeared to be at least 150 feet in length.

Speculation abounded in New England about both the nature and the intent of the sea serpent. One report described how the creature had been the cause of a "variety of conjectures" among both "politicians and philosophers." Some claimed, or rather worried, that the beast that had come into their harbor had been a female of its species and had come to spawn. An 1819 semi-satirical account of the sightings by "Neptune" mockingly noted that the major concern of New Englanders seemed to be over the fate of commerce should their shores become a "serpent fishery." If the beast spawned its young in Gloucester Harbor, then soon, they worried, "the whole ocean within the American coast would be desolated."[50]

The discussions that surrounded the appearance of the sea serpent show the complex messages and omens that American monsters conveyed. Taken together, these accounts give us a much broader sense of the meaning of the monster in American social and cultural history than scholars of the horrific have noted. While the sea serpent became a repository of fear and anxiety, it also elicited fiercer emotions. The monster awakened a desire to destroy, while also eliciting a sense of wonder. On a more pedestrian level, it served the purposes of political discourse, both in printed material and in daily conversation. As with all of America's monsters, part of the monster's monstrousness grew from its many meanings, its profusion of meaning. The Gloucester sea serpent was a highly public experience, impossible to reduce into a psychological symbol.

Numerous New Englanders claimed to have seen it, and everyone tried to invest it with meaning. The Gloucester serpent quickly, in fact almost immediately, made its way into political discussion. The anxious maritime entrepreneurs of Gloucester gave their sea monster the nickname "Embargo," a reference to the controversial Embargo of 1807. This playful moniker reflected the very real uncertainties of the fishing industry, anxieties dating back to New England's opposition to Thomas Jefferson's Embargo Acts, which had threatened their continued commercial expansion. The *Salem Gazette*, in commenting on the popular nickname sailors had given to the serpent, thought a monstrous invasion preferable to a new round of commercial restrictions. "Let our coast then be surrounded," its editor opined, "by multitudes of these sea snakes rather than Jefferson's embargoes."[51]

The fascination with the serpent, fascination that included both a sense of anxiety and wonder, cannot be explained simply in terms of psychological projection and response. As with many of America's monsters, the Gloucester sea serpent represented the monster as social experience, with numerous printed accounts and a very public conversation about its meaning. This was not a monster living inside of individual nightmares. If it was in some sense a "return of the repressed," it had a very public return rather than a secret eruption into individual psyches.

The monster of Gloucester Harbor, like most American monsters, rose out of the boiling abyss of American violence. Richard Slotkin, the cultural historian of American violence and the frontier, argues that while the United States may not display more violence than other "settler societies" in world history, the country remains unique in "the mythic significance we have assigned to the kinds of violence we have actually experienced." Slotkin describes the narrative we tell about ourselves and about our heroes as an act of "regeneration through violence." In this typical American myth, the hero experiences the depths of frontier savagery (through both knowledge of the wild environment and its wild inhabitants) and becomes a mediator "who can teach civilized men how to defeat savagery on its native grounds." American heroes know the wilderness and can tame it, though only and always through violence.[52]

The whalers whose response to the sea monster was to kill it performed this mythic narrative, a narrative that in the previous century had centered on Daniel Boone killing bears and Native Americans and would soon center on Andrew Jackson and his murderous prowess in dealing with "the Indian problem." The same impulse reappeared in the twentieth century when even American foreign policy would be imagined in terms of slaying monsters, first by Theodore Roosevelt and later by the post–World War II architects of the national security state. American heroes are monster slayers, and the monsters are the enemies of America.

The 1817 Boston broadside certainly makes it clear that destroying the monster in Gloucester Harbor was the community's first priority. On the first day of the sighting, "a number of our sharp-shooters" were in pursuit, firing muskets at the serpent. There seems to have been no public discussion of this effort. The town unanimously assumed that killing the monster presented the only possible course. The men of the New England coast killed giant sea creatures for a living, and this particular wonder would receive the same treatment. The monster in American history is not simply that which destroys. It is a being that must be destroyed. As Slotkin's work suggests, there can be no simple border wars in America's conflicts. Every battle is a mythic battle, a struggle against savagery, whether it be a Native American war, the search for a sea monster, or a war on terror.

It would be too simplistic to view monster tales as simply narratives in service of American violence. The monster is a many-headed creature, and narratives about it in American history are highly complex.

Richard Kearney describes the appearance of a monster, in a narrative, in a dream, or folklore, "as a signal of borderline experiences and unobtainable excess." Rather than simply representing personal trauma, he argues, they raise questions about our "neat divisions and borders." The monsters of American history challenge all simple narratives and raise specters of ambiguity. They raise questions about the narratives we trust, even about what we mean by the phrase "American history." Monster tales have at times provided inspiration for massacres and at other times served as haunting reminders of the ghosts of massacres past, the very stuff of American history that is repressed in the American historical consciousness. They are a "return of the repressed" but not simply the return of the repressed personal id. Like the serpent of Gloucester Harbor, they rise out of the abyss to create wonder, consternation, and violence. They are meaning machines that embody the historical structures and trajectory of the American nation.[53]

Metaphors of a Monstrous History:
When Symbols Attack

The American past reads like something of a horror movie, maybe even a low-budget slasher. American history comes at us dripping with gore, victims lying scattered on the ground, eldritch moonlight revealing creeping horrors you never learned from your eighth grade history textbook. The history of the United States offers a chamber of horrors, with clergy transforming the Native American other into demonic beings, mad scientists turning state-funded laboratories into torture chambers, and the photographic revolution of the Victorian era turning toward a morbid fascination with the bodies of the dead and the creation of the category of "gore." History is horror.

In 2009 a debate in Texas over history textbook standards explains why it is important to open up the American chamber of horrors for all to see. During several highly contentious sessions, a committee called by the Texas State Board of Education argued over revisions to the public schools' history standards for the 4.7 million students in the Texas system. In May of 2010 these changes passed and became part of the state's history standards. They remained highly controversial, and, subsequently, some of the more outlandish efforts at hiding significant, if not flattering, parts of American history have been reversed.[54]

Conservative members of the Texas Board, backed by powerful state legislators, proposed some shocking changes to the way central events in American history would be remembered. In the new proposed standards, the legacy of the civil rights movement would include the creation of "unrealistic expectations for equal outcomes." Joseph McCarthy would be described not as the progenitor of a twentieth-century witch hunt but as an American hero. Students would not learn about Pan-Africanist leader Marcus Garvey because, as one Republican board member noted, "he was from Jamaica and was deported."[55]

At the heart of the conservative effort on the Texas Board is the requirement that textbooks, and of course the teachers who use them, teach students the concept of "American exceptionalism." This notion, that the United States has a special place and role in the world, itself has a history. It has often appeared clothed in religious garb, borrowing biblical concepts of the biblical covenant. At other times, it has taken on slightly more secular shading and emphasized America's unique role in world history, the last best hope of earth and an instrument for the betterment of humanity. This vision of America's role in the world, the very concept of exceptionalism itself, trades on the idea of American innocence, that the United States, unlike the rest of the world, has been free from the terrors of history. In this view, the United States is Forrest Gump, wandering innocently through a world of conflict and, more or less by accident, making it a better place.[56]

Such a deeply flawed conceptualization of the American past ignores how fevered dreams of "special destiny" led directly to a genocide of massive proportions against native peoples. It fails to acknowledge how deeply three hundred years of American slavery and the century of Jim Crow that followed compromised the American democratic experience from its inception. This is a vision of an America without monsters. Failing to acknowledge monsters is part of the act of creating them.

The claim that America has always been the Puritans' (and Ronald Reagan's) "city on a hill" echoes Dr. Frankenstein's claim that his creature would "pour a torrent of light into our dark world." Refusing to acknowledge the terrors of American history does not make them go away. Instead they wait, emerging nightmare-like into the images of popular culture and into folktales, in fiction, in films, and in narratives told around campfires. The monster lives at the heart of American identity, giving the lie to notions of American innocence and exceptionalism.[57]

Monstrous narratives not only shape identities, they provide a place to hold conversations about our public anxieties. Our monsters register our national traumas. Eli Roth, the director of the violent film *Hostel*, claims that horror films, especially of an extreme variety, are most popular during times of national turmoil. However, numerous moments in

American social and cultural history suggest that the monster itself, as omen and portent full of cultural meaning, does exist in the middle of a matrix of history and reflection on the meaning of history. The fascination with fossils and the fantastic creatures they may have belonged to peaked during the final years of the American Revolution and the throes of state building that followed. Popular interest and scientific discourses related to the "freak" arose in the midst of discussion about race and its meaning in post-Emancipation society. Slasher films appeared at a moment when American society seemed to be committing suicide in a maelstrom of political violence and social unrest. The so-called torture porn genre, produced by Eli Roth and others, became popular as the United States debated its willingness to use torture against terrorist monsters.[58]

These examples are not meant to suggest that horror narratives exist primarily to offer American society catharsis or that monstrous fascination essentially acts as a kind of national group therapy. This book argues instead that monsters in America are more than reference points for cultural obsessions. Monsters are "real" in the sense that they not only symbolize but also help to configure worldviews and play a role in those worldviews. They live outside of our psyches.

If the history of the American monster could be reduced to the story of psychic wounds opened by national traumas, then this would be strangely comforting. But the monsters walk among us, leaving a trail of gore and ichor in their wake. We wish we could be F. Scott Fitzgerald, having our uncomfortable encounters and then vomiting up our response to them. It is not that simple. There are victims of our monsters. Not victims screaming on the screen or within the pages of paperback horror fiction but historical victims, sacrificed to the nation-state and its some-times bloodthirsty folk culture.

The American past, this book contends, is a haunted house. Ghosts rattle their chains throughout its corridors, under its furniture, and in its small attic places. The historian must resurrect monsters in order to pull history's victims out of what Alice Walker calls "the mud of oblivion." The historian's task is necromancy, and it gives us nightmares. Or at least it should.[59]

The link between the metaphor and the reality of horror, the moments when monstrous fascinations become monstrous acts, appears far too often in American historical experience. Not long before Cotton Mather wrote to the Royal Society describing the appearance of giant fossils, he described the destruction of the Pequot Indians of New England in the 1630s. Mather noted one episode in particular in which settlers attacked a native village on the Mystic River near Long Island Sound, killing, literally, everything that moved and then burning the village to the ground. William Bradford in his *History of Plymouth Plantation* described the aftermath of the same incident as "a fearful sight" with the helpless Pequot "frying in the fyre and the streams of blood quenching the same." Bradford may have thought the sight fearful but also approved of what he saw, describing how "the victory seemed a sweete sacrifice and they gave the praise thereof to God." Mather also expressed pleasure at this brutal massacre, crowing, "no less than 600 Pequot souls were brought down to hell that day."[60]

Something wicked this way comes when we look into the historical narrative. This example suggests that Mather himself embodies something of the monstrous. In figures like Mather and many others whom we will meet as we survey the American historical experience, the monster ceases to be a metaphor and becomes something horribly real, something whose visage flickers in the fire that burned six hundred native men, women, and children alive. Belief and ideology, the social realities produced and reproduced by the images of the monster, turn into historical actions and events. It is not enough to call these beliefs metaphors when they shape actual historical behavior or act as anxious reminders of inhuman historical acts, a cultural memory of slaughter. How limp and pallid to use the term "metaphor" for cultural structures that can burn the innocent to death, lynch them, imprison them, or bomb them. The monster has helped make all these things possible in American history. Mather's justification for the wanton slaughter at the Mystic River echoes throughout the narrative of the American experience. During Mather's own lifetime, the Puritans of New England slaughtered native peoples with abandon. In the savage conflict known to the English as "King Philip's War," numerous raids of villages became wholesale massacres. In May of 1676, for example, a raid by New England militia in the Connecticut River Valley led to the deaths of hundreds of natives. The New Englanders who attacked the village felt that besieging and demanding the village's surrender would take too long. Instead they opted for a surprise attack and took no prisoners, even though the village had not put up any resistance. Increase Mather, Cotton Mather's father, praised the work of Puritan troops in the beheading of an influential female adviser to Metacomet (the Wampanoag leader known as "King Philip" to the English). Mather celebrated the news that Puritan forces had killed so many women, children, and elderly that "nobody could tell how many."[61]

1

MONSTROUS BEGINNINGS

There are terrible creatures, ghosts, in the very air of America.

—D. H. Lawrence

The past is a wilderness of horrors.

—Anthony Hopkins, *The Wolfman* (2010)

Wes Craven's 1991 *The People Under the Stairs* offers a parable of the power relationships of the colonial world. Set in white America's image of "the inner city," the film centers on the story of an African American teenager nicknamed Fool and his struggle with a pair of modern-day colonial overlords, white masters who exude an aura of supernatural evil and control the economic fortune of their Black neighbors.

"Daddy and Mommy," as the white slumlords call themselves, live in a strangely agrarian part of the 'hood, a kind of urban plantation house guarded by a vicious dog and locked behind steel mesh windows. The "people under the stairs," who we expect to be the monstrous villains of the tale, are actually kidnapped white children zombified by the incestuous couple. Fool can defeat Daddy and Mommy only by joining forces with the much-abused white kids living in the nooks, crannies, and secret passages of the old plantation house. The divide of race proves less compelling than the divisions of class, and the master's haunted house, and hegemony, is overthrown.[1]

The monsters in *The People Under the Stairs* are the products of socioeconomic conditions. The sadistic and perverse Mommy and Daddy are described by Fool's Grandpa Booker as twisted in their desire for money: "As they got greedier, they got crazier." The house not only hides its secret of kidnapped children but mountains of ill-gotten gain. "No wonder there's no money in the ghetto," Fool says when he finds the twisted couple's treasure trove. Like white elites since their first coming to the new world, Mommy and Daddy had built their mastery on fear, violence, and economic exploitation.[2]

As in Craven's film, the repressive power structure of colonial America became a forge of monsters. The white European master class exerted power over native peoples and Africans that sometimes seemed supernatural. European settlers, meanwhile, found the monster living in their own settlements and meetinghouses, beings animated by the power of the devil. These beliefs played a crucial role in shaping the American way of violence, the unremitting savagery toward enemies that became characteristic of the American historical experience.

Monsters of the New World

Christopher Columbus came to the "New World" seeking gold, slaves, and monsters. Columbus reported both in his personal diary and correspondence that the native peoples he encountered in the Caribbean in 1492 and 1493 told him of "one-eyed men and other men with dog heads who decapitated their victims and drank their blood." Michael Palencia-Roth notes that the Genoese explorer's private diary of the first voyage shows that finding the monsters of the New World "became an obsession for Columbus."[3]

A long tradition of legend and theological speculation about monstrous creatures informed Columbus' beliefs about what he might find in the new world. Medieval mental maps of a world inhabited by monstrous races prepared Spanish and Portuguese explorers to encounter giants, dog-men, ape-men, and various creatures out of the medieval bestiary. Christian theological speculation about the work of the devil, combined with the ongoing geopolitical conflict with the Islamic powers of the Mediterranean world, encouraged European explorers to see these monstrous races as allied with the evil one, the enemies of God and of the church.[4]

Some scholars argue that the first European conquerors in the New World did not think of the indigenous people themselves as monsters. Contemporary historian Peter Burke, for example, contends that

Europeans always saw the native peoples of Africa and the Americas as part of the human family, even as they categorized them as an uncivilized or even degraded branch of that family. Burke notes that, throughout the era of European expansion, a debate took place among churchly scholars over the ethnic origins of "the savages of America." The very fact that such a debate was held meant that Europeans assumed the humanity, if not the equality, of the native peoples. A monster has no ethnic origin. If Burke is correct, European explorers saw the people of the New World as vastly inferior cousins but not as monsters.[5]

Contrary evidence, however, suggests that such an ambivalent view of the natives had very little traction among most early modern Europeans. The conquerors of the New World saw not simply a savage version of humanity but the monstrous races of their mythology. Even significant Enlightenment thinkers such as the French naturalist Buffon in his *Natural History* connected the creation of monstrosities with the etiology of the "darker races." Monsters represented the progeny of these supposedly savage peoples, a concept that reappeared again and again throughout American history, with a lineage that stretches from Puritan minister Cotton Mather to the twentieth-century horror maestro H. P. Lovecraft.[6]

New kinds of technology in the period of exploration contributed to European monster mania. The print revolution of the fifteenth century, though normally seen as an important moment in the expansion of modernity, provided a way to spread the concept of the monster, locating it in the enemy other. Numerous Reformation tracts portrayed either Martin Luther or the pope as monstrous beings empowered by the devil. In 1727 a popular Portuguese tract, *Emblema Vivente*, described a Turkish monster "fifteen palms high" with an eerie light emanating from its chest every time it breathed. Historians of early modern Europe Laura Lunger Knoppers and Joan B. Landes argue that this tract "blurs the boundaries of science and religion" in its description of the monster both as an oddity of nature and malformed beast. The monster incarnated fears of the religious other whose land it inhabited, the Ottoman Turk.[7]

Emblema Vivente's blurring of conceptual boundaries is representative of the emerging Enlightenment view of the monster. While many eighteenth-century thinkers dismissed theological explanations for the birth of monsters, they did not reject the reality of monsters themselves. The natural scientist Buffon suggested a number of purely natural explanations for the monstrous peoples and creatures that walked the earth. In 1796 the Enlightenment encyclopedist Diderot speculated about the possible natural origins of monsters. The New World, with its strange creatures and peoples, offered new opportunities for sightings of such creatures.[8]

Europeans found the monsters they searched for. Not only did explorers and settlers readily believe wonder tales, they tended to ascribe morally monstrous qualities to the peoples they encountered. This process began with the early explorations of Africa and provided some of the earliest materials for the racist imagination of the modern West. Early European accounts of so-called oranutans (later orangutans) imagined a similarity between various kinds of apes, monstrous ape-men, and the native peoples of West Africa, the region that soon became the primary target for slave traders. Fabulous accounts written by European travelers dwelt on the monstrous appearance of the ape and on the monster's sexual proclivities. According to one account, the apes of India were "so venerous that they will ravish their women," while an African baboon brought before a French monarch allegedly had a sexual organ "greater than might match the quantity of his other parts." These ideas had a calamitous effect on how the white mind encountered native African peoples.[9]

Such imaginings became a familiar part of the racist folklore of the United States concerning African American men and a way to justify the structures of enslavement. An English naturalist, Edward Topsell, wrote in 1607 of African men with "low and flat nostrils" who are "as libidinous as apes that attempt women and having thicke lips the upper hanging over the neather, they are deemed fools." Winthrop Jordan noted that these associations also drew on European folklore about the connection between apes and the devil. Contemporary demonological texts often made this connection explicit, seeing apes as incarnations of Satan or as the familiars of witches. Europeans encountering Africans in the context of the slave trade held in their minds these bizarre associations between monstrous apes, Satan, libidinous sexuality, and enormous sexual organs. They readily applied these folkloric images to the human beings they stuffed into the holds of their ships for a life of enslavement. Such poisonous associations would be reborn again and again in twentieth-century popular culture, most notably in *The Birth of a Nation* (1915) and *King Kong* (1933). They played a role in the folklore that supported lynching, some of the most pathological violence ever to take place on American soil.[10]

Europeans found monsters in the Americas as quickly as in Africa. Some of the earliest Spanish explorers of what would become the southeastern coast of the United States readily accepted Native American tales of monstrous peoples and saw the natives themselves as embodiments of the marvelously monstrous. In the 1520s Spanish explorer Lucas Allyón hungrily devoured the stories of a local Native American Chicora who spoke of all the lands north of Florida as being populated by "a race of men with tails for which they dug holes in the ground when they sat down." Chicora regaled Allyón, and later the Spanish court, with other stories of Native American tribes that stretched their children so that they became enormous giants.[11]

Belief in the monsters of the New World influenced discussions about the moral justification for the enslavement and oppression of native peoples. These debates, with very few exceptions, assumed theological and cultural justifications for the economic exploitation of the New World. European explorers who willingly granted that the natives came from human stock often believed them to be a type of monstrous human, depraved beings whose moral leprosy had its source in the world of the demonic. Even the sixteenth-century friar Bartolomé de Las Casas, a strong proponent of the rights of Native Americans under Spanish law, saw the New World as firmly under Satan's domain. Friar Bartolomé saw the very air of the New World teeming with evil spirits who tempted and destroyed the unbaptized.[12]

Such conceptions of the diabolism of native peoples led some Europeans to imagine the New World as a landscape of horror. Charges of perverse sexuality and inhuman appetites represent some of the most common descriptions of native peoples. Friar Tomas Ortiz described the natives of Terra Firme, colonial Panama, as flesh-eating monsters who had "no sense of love or shame . . . they are bestial and they pride themselves in having abominable vices." Viewing them as "steeped in vices and bestialities," Friar Ortiz saw no reason their personal autonomy should be recognized. Monsters could be enslaved.[13]

The New World itself often seemed a kind of monster to the early modern European imagination. One of the earliest allegorizations of America is Philippe Galle's 1580 "America," in which we see a giantess with spear and bow that has cannibalized a man and triumphantly carries his severed head. Galle's own description of the image refers to America as an "ogress who devours men, who is rich in gold and who is skilled in the use of the spear and the bow." In 1595 Paolo Farinati painted an allegorical representation of the New World as a monstrous cannibal to decorate a villa in Verona, Italy. In Farinati's "America," the artist imagines the New World as a giant roasting a human arm. A crucifix appears to his right, illustrating the hope that conversion to Christianity could tame the beast.[14]

Cannibal Feast

A sixteenth-century Dutch engraving in Hans Staden's *True History* best illustrates this very common representation of the Americas. Staden's work, a captivity narrative that allegedly describes his time among the natives of Brazil, tells a tale of cannibalism that rivals anything a modern master of horror could conjure. One of the more infamous images from that work shows a gory cannibal feast that zombie auteur George Romero might have filmed. A gaggle of cannibals roast human body parts over a fire. A dwarf gnaws on a human hand. Women, sketched according to the traditional European iconography of the witch, chomp on legs, arms, and unidentified bits of human detritus.

Images of a New World filled with monstrous races and the tendency to imagine the New World itself as a kind of cannibalistic beast grew out of the deep roots of European culture. Europeans who settled in the Americas brought with them a head full of monsters and a well-practiced tendency to define the cultural and religious other in terms of monstrosity. A long history of military conflict with the Islamic world converged with early modern religious tensions and age-old legends of the world beyond the borders of Europe to convince most European explorers that they would encounter new lands crawling with monsters. Numerous scholars have examined the European tendency to construct the native peoples of North America as monstrous cannibals and demonic servants. Less attention has been paid to how supernatural beings and occurrences provided a way for white Americans in later historical periods to negotiate the meaning of the colonial period. Simplistic interpretations of folk belief in monsters have seen them as shorthand for death, sexuality, and metaphysical uncertainty. But the monster has, just as frequently, offered a way to ignore historical trauma and historical guilt, to remake the facts into a set of pleasing legends. The grotesquerie of the monster has offered relief from the gruesome facts of history.

Shapeshifter

John Landis, best known as the director of the classic *An American Werewolf in London*, wrote and directed an episode of Showtime's 2005 Masters of Horror series entitled *Deer Woman*. In it a Native American woman becomes an avenging spirit, transforming into a powerful deer whose hooves gore her victims. She vengefully murders white men in a modern world where centuries of oppression have reduced the native experience to tasteless jokes about casinos. Landis' tale drew on a fund of folktales about Native American women and addressed the sexual and misogynistic aspects of the legends, reframing these stories as a dark memory of the American past.

Deer Woman drew on a wealth of legendary material primarily from the tribes of the Plains and the Pacific Northwest. In these stories, a beautiful woman lured men to their deaths, seducing them to join her behind a bush, in a cave, or in some hidden place where she revealed that she was actually a powerful deer and trampled them to death. Landis played with this imagery to great effect, creating a metaphor about the contact between white and Native American culture in which the latter, at long last, strikes back. But such stories could be put to a very different purpose. The tale of a white "Deer Woman," first told in the early twentieth century but portrayed as part of colonial folklore, shows how white elite memory of colonial conquest could be transmuted by a monster tale.[15]

By the late sixteenth century, the decline of Spain as Europe's primary sea power opened the way for English incursions into Spain's Atlantic imperium. In 1584 English adventurer Sir Walter Raleigh pledged to "seek new worlds for gold, for praise, for glory," a promise that led him from the Caribbean to the outer banks of North Carolina and the island of Roanoke. Raleigh found friendly local natives and apparently fruitful soil. This environment seemed to offer the perfect prospect for the first English colony in the New World.

English settlement in both the Caribbean and in North America followed a typical pattern. White colonists founded temporary settlements that became permanent after successful subjugation, through war or diplomacy, of local Native American tribes. These settlements became even more enduring as they developed agricultural and commercial activity that tied them into the larger matrix of the Atlantic economy. The introduction of various forms of unfree labor ensured that they would be profitable ventures.[16]

The experience of the Roanoke colony did not follow this pattern of settlement and conquest. In 1587 a little more than a hundred settlers came to the island off the North Carolina coast under the leadership of governor John White. White spent about a month in the new "planting," helping to build the village of Raleigh. He then returned to England for supplies, a trip that took much longer than expected because of a new war with Spain. When White returned to Roanoke in 1590, all the settlers had disappeared. The only clue he discovered was a word carved across two trees, "Croatoan," the name of a local native group and the nearby island where they lived. The settlers could not be found there either.

Historians have offered a number of plausible explanations for what became known in early American lore as "the lost colony of Roanoke." Settlers may have been killed by natives or perhaps enslaved by them. If the latter, they could have easily blended through intermarriage into local tribal groups. They may also have picked up and moved to an unknown location in Virginia to meet an unknown fate. Whatever became of them, the inhabitants of Roanoke are certainly not the only European colony to face fairly immediate extinction. Further down the coast, near what is today Georgetown, South Carolina, a small group of French settlers abandoned their failed settlement around 1564, building a makeshift boat to return to France. This effort would have resulted in another story of a "lost colony" if the settlers had not been picked up by an English pirate after what one historian describes as "a hell of cannibalism, starvation, and madness."[17]

The lost colony of Roanoke has produced fantasy and romance as well as mystery. Two seasons of the hit television series *American Horror Story* have used the legend, with season 6 actually bearing the title *American Horror Story: Roanoke*. Numerous fictional narratives about the fate of the colony have clustered around Virginia Dare, the granddaughter of Governor White and the first English child born in North America (or as Governor White called her, "the first Christian born in Virginia"). Speculation about her fate has created folk legends, historical romances, science fiction, and even comic book narratives.[18]

One stream of the Dare legend developed into a monster story with Dare suffering a curse that Larry Talbot, Lon Chaney Jr.'s character in *The Wolf Man*, would have recognized. Sallie Southall Cotten's 1901 narrative poem *The White Doe, or The Fate of Virginia Dare* spun a folktale about the young Dare held captive by local natives and becoming a kind of "Indian princess" in her adulthood. Desired by a Native American shaman, Dare's heart instead belongs to a young warrior. The jealous shaman transforms Dare into a white doe who can be killed only by a magic arrow (rather than a silver bullet). After a series of tragic errors, the young warrior, who truly loves Dare, kills her, though Cotten asserts her shapeshifting spirit endured and the people of eastern North Carolina saw visions of her for centuries. In fact, twenty-first-century reports of a white doe along the Eno River near Durham, North Carolina, include the claim that the creature spoke with the voice of a woman.[19]

Although the tradition of Virginia Dare as Deer Woman counts as what is called "fakelore," an invented tradition, Cotten herself insisted otherwise. Writing in a preface to the 1901 edition of the poem that the tale of the White Doe "has survived for three centuries," Cotten added, "From Maine to Florida, lumbermen are everywhere familiar with the old superstition that to see a white doe is an evil omen . . . the rude hunters of the Allegheny Mountains believe that only a silver arrow will kill a white deer." Although Cotten is correct that these ideas have some resonance in American wilderness folklore, and a longer history in Europe, none of these motifs ever had a connection to the last survivor of the lost colony until Cotten made the connection herself in the first years of the twentieth century.[20]

Regional writers quickly built on Cotten's effort to create a mythic history for the earliest efforts to colonize the New World. O. R. Mangum described how Dare "grew into fair maidenhood among the Native Americans but was transformed by a sorcerer into the White Doe." He asserted that the spirit of this creature "haunts continually the place of her birth." Many of these early twentieth-century retellings of Cotten's tale focused heavily on the racial imagery of the white child among the native peoples, transforming both the human Dare and the shapeshifter Dare into a sign of the emerging white dominance over the New World.

A. Denison Heart, for example, described how "the grim old Indians and their dusky squaws looked with wonder and admiration on this little stranger, calling her White Doe."[21]

Imagining the first effort to "plant" an English colony ending in a fairy tale serves a clear cultural purpose. American popular memory has generally ignored the degree of callous brutality that characterized early settlement. Cotten's story of the White Doe soothed anxieties over the nature of the conquest of the New World at a time when the conquest of the American West had recently reached completion. Other early American legends, from the myth of a romance between Pocahontas and John Smith to the legend of "the first Thanksgiving" as a multicultural feast between Pilgrims and Native Americans, hid from generations of school-children the brutal facts of colonial history and by extension the genocidal policies the U.S. government pursued in the American West.[22]

Cotten surely hoped that Dare's tale would serve a similar purpose. An inveterate booster of North Carolina history, Cotten actually took the tale of the White Doe on the road, performing the poem in front of women's clubs, church groups, and in community theaters all across the South while wearing a white-fringed deerskin coat. Cotten created a tragic and romantic monster that hid some of the true monsters of the early American experience.[23]

The development of the tale of Virginia Dare as a Deer Woman reveals many of the anxieties of the colonial experience, including how that experience has been told and retold as part of American memory. Dare's time among the southeastern Native Americans contains some aspects, retold in legendary form, of the colonial captivity narrative. This genre, especially popular among the Puritans of New England, told stories of white English women captured by "savage" Native Americans. The subtext of such tales, that European women endured sexual violation by Native Americans, helped make this some of the earliest sensational literature in America. The captivity narrative offered a strange sort of moral parable, in which the readers received both a sexual frisson and religious edification.[24]

The captivity narrative embodies some of the central conflicts of early American religion. The Puritan woman stands in for the Puritan community, faithful in the midst of savagery and coming out of their "errand into the wilderness" with their faith refined and purified. At the same time, these tests are so extreme that they raise questions about the project itself. Various iterations of the captivity narrative became the basis for all kinds of horrific narratives, appearing again and again in American gothic tales of feminine innocence under threat from dirty old men in dirty old castles. They haunted the American imagination in film as well, from the screams of Fay Wray struggling in the grasp of King Kong in the 1930s to the brutal deaths in *The Last House on the Left* in the 1970s. The captivity narratives not only became one of the first popular American literary forms, they also became foundational for an American brand of horror.[25]

Cotten's decision to weave other motifs into her tale of Dare's transformation borrows a tendency in early American folklore to identify heroic figures with the wilderness of the New World. Like the legendary material that created figures like Paul Bunyan and surrounded actual historical figures like Daniel Boone and Davy Crockett, Virginia Dare became entirely identified with the natural wilderness of the frontier environment. She becomes part of the Native American world and then becomes part of the natural world in the most literal way possible.[26]

Ironically, Dare has become a symbol in the twenty-first century for anti-immigrant hate groups. The website VDARE.com views the lost colony, and Virginia Dare in particular, as a symbol of the white Anglo culture isolated and under assault. Even the tale of the White Doe serves these groups' purposes, suggesting transcendent white purity under threat. Like Dare, white settlers "shapeshifted" into something deeply American, a part of the landscape itself, displacing native peoples in a "natural" process. The tale of a monster became a way for white Americans to hide greater horror.[27]

In the generation following the disappearance of the Roanoke settlement, English settlers established permanent and profitable colonies. Calvinist dissenters came from England in 1620, separatist Calvinists known as the Pilgrims. These first settlers on Plymouth Rock would soon be followed by the Puritans, a much larger sect of dissenting Calvinists, who created the Massachusetts Bay Colony in 1630. Puritan ministers saw the founding of the New England colonies as an opportunity to build "a city on a hill" and create a Calvinist utopia. Cleansed of the mother country's flirtations with sin, the New World would become the kingdom of God. To their great horror, the Puritans found their wide-open wilderness full of monsters.

Sex with the Devil

The Puritan settlements of New England have become representative symbols of early American settlement. Although not the first successful settlements in English North America (Jamestown dates to 1607), they occupy an integral place in the memory of the early American experience. There are many explanations for this importance, ranging from the dominance of New England historians and educational institutions in the writing of early American history, to the way the Puritans' own self-conceptions comport with Americans' tendency to view themselves as bearers of a special destiny.[28]

The special place the Puritans have occupied in American memory made them multivalent signifiers for national identity, appearing as everything from dour-faced party poopers to, ironically, the embodiment of the alleged American appreciation for the search for religious liberty. Their sermons and devotional tracts have provided the grammar of American understanding of sin, redemption, and national destiny, shaping both religious and political consciousness.

No aspect of Puritan experience lives more strongly in American memory than their fear of monsters, specifically their fear of witches that led to the trials of about 344 settlers during the course of the seventeenth century. The Salem witch trials, an outbreak of Puritan witch hunting that ended in the executions of twenty people in 1692–1693, has become central to most Americans' perception of their early history. Salem historians Owen Davies and Jonathan Barry have noted the central role the event came to play in the teaching standards and curriculum of public schools, making knowledge of it integral to understanding the colonial era.[29]

Cotton Mather's *Wonders of the Invisible World*

For many contemporary people, Salem is read as a brief flirtation with an irrational past. At least some of the interest it garners comes from its portrayal as an anomaly, a strange bypath on the way to an unyielding national commitment to freedom and democracy. On the contrary, Salem was far from the first witch hunt in early New England. Nor did the American fascination with the witch disappear after 1693.

Puritans hunted monsters in the generation before Salem. In 1648 Margaret Jones of Charlestown, Massachusetts, became the first English settler accused of witchcraft, and later executed, in New England. The Massachusetts Bay Colony's first governor, John Winthrop, called Jones "a cunning woman," someone with the ability to make use of herbs and spells. Jones was further alleged to have had a "malignant touch" that caused her erstwhile patients to vomit and go deaf. Winthrop, after a bodily search of Jones by the women of Charlestown, claimed that she exhibited "witches teats in her secret parts," which was, by long established superstition, the sign of a witch. The Puritan judiciary executed Jones in the summer of 1648. More trials and more executions followed.[30]

The witch embodied all the assorted anxieties that early New England settlers felt about their new environment, their personal religious turmoil, and their fear of the creatures that lurked in the "howling wilderness." The original Puritan movement in England had grown out of the fear that the English Church retained too many elements of the "satanic" Roman Catholic Church. The Puritan conception of the spiritual life, embodied in John Bunyan's *The Pilgrim's Progress*, imagined the Christian experience as a war with monstrous beings inspired by the devil. This understanding of Christian experience as a struggle with the forces of darkness made its way to the New World. Not surprisingly, this new world became a geography of monsters in the minds of many of the Puritans.

Puritan clergyman Cotton Mather helped to construct a New World mythology that not only included the bones of antediluvian giants but also the claim that native peoples in North America had a special relationship to Satan. In Mather's New World demonology, the Native Americans had been seduced by Satan to come to America as his special servants. This made them, in some literal sense, the "children of the Devil." Other Puritan leaders reinforced this view, seeing indigenous peoples as a special trial designed for them by the devil. Frequently, Puritan leaders turned to Old Testament imagery of the Israelites destroying the people of Canaan for descriptions of their relationship with the New England tribes. The Puritans believed you could not live with or even convert monsters. You must destroy them.[31]

The Puritans embodied the American desire to destroy monsters. At the same time, the Puritan tendency toward witch-hunting reveals the American tendency to desire the monster, indeed to be titillated by it. Contemporary literary scholar Edward Ingebretsen convincingly argues that the search for witches in the towns of New England should be read as popular entertainment as well as evidence of religious conflict and persecution. Ingebretsen shows that Mather makes use of the term "entertain" frequently when explaining his own efforts to create a narrative of the witch hunts. He uses the same term to describe the effect of the testimony of suspected witches on the Puritan courtrooms that heard them. Mather described the dark wonders that make up much of his writings as "the chiefe entertainments which my readers do expect and shall receive."[32]

Mather obviously does not use the word "entertain" in the contemporary sense. And yet his conception of "entertainment" bears some relationship to the more modern usage of the term. Mather believed that his dark entertainments warned and admonished, but a delicious thrill accompanied them as well. Mather himself sounds like a carnival barker when he promises frightening spectacles that his readers "do expect and shall receive." Historian of Salem Marion Starkey, in *The Devil in Massachusetts*, notes that for all of Mather's righteous chest-thumping over the danger the New England colonies faced from the assaults of Satan, it is hard not to see him "unconsciously submerged in the thrill of being present as a spectator." He provided his readers the same thrill.[33]

This thrill had clear erotic undertones, underscoring the close connection between horror and sexuality that became a persistent thread in American cultural history. The genealogy of the witch in Western Europe already included many of the ideas that aroused, in every sense, the Puritan settlements. Folklore taught that any gathering of witches, known as the "witches sabbat," included orgiastic sex, even sex with Satan and his demons. European demonologists frequently connected the tendency to witchcraft with a propensity toward uncontrolled sexual desire.[34]

Such ideas appeared again and again in the New England witch hunts. The trial of indentured servant Mary Johnson not only included accusations that she had used her relationship with Satan to get out of work for her master, but also the assertion that she had flirted, literally, with the devil. Cotton Mather wrote that she had "practiced uncleanness with men and devils." One of the first women accused of witchcraft in Salem village had a reputation for sexual promiscuity, while male testimony against women accused of witchcraft often included descriptions of them as succubi, appearing at night dressed in flaming red bodices. The witch was not only one of the first monsters of English-speaking America. The witch also became America's first sexy monster and one who would be punished for her proclivities.[35]

The end of the witch trials in 1693 came with numerous criticisms of how the cases had been handled. Petitions on behalf of the accused began to appear in the fall of 1692. In October of that year, Boston merchant Thomas Brattle, a well-traveled member of the scientific Royal Society with an interest in mathematics and astronomy, published an open letter criticizing the courts. He especially critiqued the Puritan judiciary for allowing "spectral evidence," evidence based on visions, revelations, and alleged apparitions. Significantly, Brattle did not challenge the idea that supernatural agency had been involved in the trials, only that it had worked by different methods than the Puritan judiciary had supposed. Brattle wrote that the evidence of witches sabbats and apparitions put forward by those who accused (and by those who confessed) represented "the effect of their fancy, deluded and depraved by the Devil." In Brattle's mind, to accept such evidence would be tantamount to accepting the testimony of Satan himself. Like many skeptics during this period, Brattle challenged the courts on how they had used the belief in monsters, without questioning the reality of the existence of monsters.[36]

Salem did not mark the end of the witch trials in America. Fear of dark magic remained a crucial part of early American life. Marginalized women and enslaved Africans remained the most common target of the witch hunt. In 1705–1706 a Virginia couple, Luke and Elizabeth Hill, accused Grace Sherwood of witchcraft. Although the Virginia courts at first found little evidence for the charge, the time-honored search for the witch's teat soon revealed "two things like titts with Severall other Spotts." Sherwood next underwent the infamous "water test" in which the suspected witch was thrown into water to see if she floated or sank. Sherwood floated and faced reexamination by some "anciente women" who, this time, discovered clearly diabolical "titts on her private parts." She was subjected to another trial, although the record breaks off at this point, making her fate unclear.[37]

Enslaved Africans faced accusations of a special kind of witchcraft known as "conjuration" or, more simply, "sorcery." The use of black magic against the white master class became a common charge against the instigators of slave rebellions. In 1779 a trial of slave rebels in the territory that would later become the state of Illinois ended with the execution of several slaves for the crimes of "conjure" and "necromancy."[38]

The Puritans clearly had no monopoly on the belief in witchcraft. Even in parts of colonial America without a strong tradition of witch trials, beliefs that supported such trials remained strong. An Anglican missionary in colonial Carolina, Francis Le Jau, complained in a 1707 journal entry that the colonial court had not severely punished "a notorious malefactor, evidently guilty of witchcraft." While the Puritans pursued their obsession with the most vehemence, the belief in dark powers inhabiting the American landscape remained common throughout the eighteenth century.[39]

Puritans found more monsters in their new world than the witch. Although we tend to picture the dour Puritans in their equally dour meetinghouses, taking in Calvinist theology and morality in great drafts, the actual Puritans lived out at least part of their experience in what David D. Hall has termed "worlds of wonder." The work of Hall, and of colonial historian Richard Godbeer, has uncovered a variety of magical traditions, astrological beliefs, and conceptions of monstrosity among the Puritans that kept alive older European wonder-lore. Puritan conceptions of original sin, for example, contributed to their interest in abnormal births, often termed "monstrous births," that functioned as signs and omens. Spectral, shape-shifting dogs haunted the edges of the Puritan settlements, as did demonic, giant black bears.[40]

Predictably, much of the Puritan ministry saw any portents in nature as signs of the New Englanders' divine mission. The same clergymen, just as predictably, ascribed a diabolical character to any marvel or wonders that did not fit into their theological paradigm. For Puritan clergy, it came as no surprise to find the forests of New England populated with marvelous creatures. Their new world was surrounded by evil spirits of all kinds, as numerous as "the frogs of Egypt" according to Cotton Mather.[41]

Reaction to an alleged sighting of a sea serpent early in the Puritan experiment showcases this attitude. Puritan observers claimed to have encountered sea serpents long before the nineteenth-century sightings in Gloucester Harbor. They also more quickly ascribed dark religious meanings to the appearance of the creature off their shores. In 1638 New England settler John Josselyn reported that recent arrivals to the colonies had seen "a sea serpent or a snake." Nahant native Obadiah Turner described the same creature and worried that "the monster come out of the sea" might be "the old serpent spoken of in holy scripture . . . whose poison hath run down even unto us, so greatly to our discomfort and ruin." The monster could be a portent of divine providence or judgment. The only other possible explanation was that it was a creature of Satan.[42]

Puritans were not alone in finding monsters on the American frontier. Sea serpents swam in many American waters, and strange beasts populated the wilderness that surrounded most new American settlements. But the American response to the monsters they met was not uniform and did not always share the Puritan desire to destroy the monster and cleanse the American landscape. Some even saw the monster as a strange partner in mastering the unruly frontier.

Mastering Frontier Monsters

A practice known variously as "noodling," "bumming," "tickling," or "grabbling" still maintains some limited popularity in the American South and Midwest. Skilled noodlers reach into rivers, their fingers exploring crevices where large, sometimes gigantic, male catfish guard thousands of eggs recently laid by females. The noodlers soon find their hands in the gullet of an enormous and angry fish. Wrenching the creature out of the water in a feat of strength, they both catch their supper and prove their masculinity to the small cadre of fellow noodlers who view this as both sport and initiation ritual. Expert noodlers show off their deeply scarred forearms as proof of their skill.[43]

The roots of this strange pastime are planted firmly in rural traditions of masculinity that are very much a part of America's frontier experience. It draws on a fund of folklore about the monstrous beings that swim America's waters. Through this act noodlers perform an ancient rite that displays masculine strength. Mastery over the monster represented mastery over the American landscape itself.

Persistent tales of catfish that grow to extraordinary lengths and exhibit primal viciousness have a long history in American folklore. Stories of fish in the Ohio River that were able to pull human beings into the watery blackness never to be seen again circulated in the late colonial era. Perhaps the earliest tale of these river monsters comes from French explorers Marquette and Jolliet, who claimed that in 1673 a giant creature slammed into one of their canoes near what is today Peoria, Illinois. The explorers later insisted that the incident had occurred after local Native Americans warned them of a demon that lived beneath local waters that would "drag them into the abyss." In 1780 a Moravian missionary who had come to minister to new settlements along the Ohio River reported a giant catfish that dragged fishermen to their deaths. Into the twentieth century, such stories continued to exert a powerful hold on the imagination. A rural legend from Caseyville, Kentucky, tells of the remains of a human baby found in the gullet of one of the river monsters.[44]

Belief in frontier monsters drew on European folklore and the tendency for frontier communities to produce legendary materials out of the shadowy forests and lakes that surrounded them. But in late colonial America, the question of monsters became a matter of national pride. A debate raged in the eighteenth-century Atlantic world over the theory of "American degeneracy." According to some European natural scientists, including the influential French thinker Buffon, the climatic conditions in the New World produced animals and human beings markedly inferior to their European counterparts. While Buffon did not extend this theory to European settlers themselves (though he came close), he certainly believed native peoples to be a degenerate race.[45]

The theory of the degeneracy of America can be read as cultural propaganda masquerading as scientific theory. Colonial thinkers, including Thomas Jefferson and Benjamin Franklin, responded with cultural propaganda of their own, arguing that, in fact, the American continent had produced gigantic, powerful, and brutal creatures unlike anything anyone had seen on the continent of Europe. The American wilderness, they asserted, had produced monsters. And American monsters had to be bigger than anyone else's.

This discussion had the effect of reopening the debate over the meaning of Cotton Mather's "giant's bones" in Claverack, New York, while also setting off a wave of fossil collection that made the American mastodon a matter for significant public discussion. The collecting of fossils in Kentucky's "Big Bone Lick" and near Niagara Falls, New York, became a passion among amateur paleontologists. During the American Revolution, the bones of the "Incognitum" (the mastodon or woolly mammoth) became what historian of science Paul Semonin has called "an emblem of national honor."[46]

Even George Washington, in one of the most difficult periods of the Revolutionary War, took time out to go fossil hunting. In 1780 Washington established the headquarters of the Continental Army near West Point, New York, as he contemplated an attack on the British stronghold at New York City. A snowfall in December gave him the opportunity to travel to a nearby farm where another "giant tooth" had been discovered. Washington, according to an aide-de-camp who joined him on the outing, claimed that, at Mount Vernon, he had similar specimens collected from the Ohio River Valley.[47]

Thomas Jefferson's 1781 draft of *Notes on the State of Virginia*, a natural history survey of his home state, discussed the fossils of the mastodon in detail. Jefferson sought to refute the claims of European scientists who suggested that the bones belonged to either an elephant or a hippopotamus. "The skeleton of the mammoth," he wrote, "bespeaks an animal of six times the cubic volume of the elephant." The creature was not only the largest that had ever shaken the American continent with its lumbering stride but, Jefferson insisted, "the largest of all terrestrial beings."[48]

Some American thinkers saw the fossil finds as further proof of the biblical account of Noahic giants rather than simply an emblem of national superiority. Ezra Stiles, president of Yale University from 1778 to 1795, at first refused to accept the contention that gigantic teeth unearthed in America belonged to a creature anything like a mastodon. Stiles instead embraced what he called the "Doctrine of Monsters," the belief that anomalies like gigantic fossils proved that the biblical world of wonders existed on the American landscape. Writing about Washington's visit to view fossils in New York, Stiles admitted that most natural scientists "take these bones to belong to Quadrupeds." He insisted, to the contrary, that they belonged to giant humans, "like the bones and teeth at Claverack" that had fascinated Mather. Stiles, a major intellectual celebrity in the early American republic, shows that Mather still had plenty of disciples for this view, bringing together as it did the biblical history and the history of the new nation.[49]

Stiles would eventually reject this idea after a long correspondence with Jefferson. Nevertheless, his doctrine of monsters received new life in a popular account of the Kentucky territory that portrayed the fossil finds at Big Bone Lick as uncovering the remains of a true American horror. John Filson's 1793 *The Discovery, Settlement, and Present State of Kentucky*, popular both in the United States and in France, portrayed the mastodon as "the tyrant of the forest, perhaps the devourer of man."[50]

Filson's strange travelogue used gothic imagery to recreate the frontier landscape as a land of Native American graves, unquiet spirits, and the bones of monstrous creatures. He imagined the herbivorous mastodon as a raging carnivore and suggested that native peoples had to form a large political confederation in order to stamp out the creature that would otherwise have brought about "the extinction of the whole race of animals from the system of nature." Filson had extrapolated from the mastodon fossil finds a secret and terrifying history of the American continent in which Lovecraftian beings had once been a terror to humans.[51]

Filson not only regenerated the doctrine of monsters, he produced the first series of stories about Daniel Boone. Boone was an actual historical character, a brutal Indian fighter and land surveyor who gobbled up vast tracts of land on the Kentucky frontier in the late eighteenth century. Filson, who had accompanied Boone on an expedition through the Cumberland Gap in search of settlement sites, transformed him into America's first frontier hero, a subduer of nature on a wild and brutal frontier.[52]

Filson's mythic language contained a dark truth about early American history. Boone, and men like him, did spill out through the Appalachians in the late eighteenth century, killing and dispersing native peoples. In national mythology, Boone became an archetypal symbol for American masters of the frontier, winning out over a brutal nature that had once been the home of "the tyrant of the forests." Like the noodlers that are their latter-day progeny, early American settlers set out to become masters of the savage beasts of the frontier.

As the nineteenth century approached, many Americans exerted a different kind of mastery. The enslavement of Africans had been part of the American experiment from the very beginning as the Virginia colony introduced the slave system as a replacement for the limited duration of white indentured servanthood. Justifications of slavery on the basis of the inferiority of the African race became increasingly common as the eighteenth century progressed.

Proslavery apologists increasingly turned to the image of the monster to make their case. Even Thomas Jefferson, known for his anxiety over slavery and his condemnation of the international slave trade, still argued in *Notes on the State of Virginia* for the inferiority of Africans (and remained a lifelong slaveholder in spite of his reservations). Jefferson never definitively asserted that this represented a true biological inferiority, leaving open the possibility that African people had been "made distinct by time and circumstances." Whatever the cause of their disadvantage, he fully assented to the belief that African people "are inferior to whites in the endowments of body and mind."[53]

Racism became a new doctrine of monsters in America. Although basing most of his suppositions about African American inferiority on skin color (an aesthetic argument that assumed the superior beauty of white and even of the "tawny" skin of native peoples over the African), Jefferson also borrowed the monster tales of the exploration of Africa. Dismissing Buffon's notions of American degeneracy, he freely accepted the French writer's discussion of giant African apes mating with African women. In one especially startling passage, he suggested that even African people recognized the superiority of the "flowing hair" and "more elegant symmetry of form" of the whites. He then compared this to a strange example of European folklore that claimed that the "Oranootan" showed its preference "for Black women over those of their own species." Paul Semonin comments that Jefferson in this passage "equated the alleged ardor of Black males for white women with aberrant sexual behavior in the animal world." Jefferson the enlightened statesmen told monster stories.[54]

Race and slavery became productive of all kinds of monster tales. Terrifying creatures emerged out of the terrifying realities of the slave trade, with forced immigrations taking place over several centuries. America would be unable to live with the creature it created, and the enslaved found themselves in the maw of a monster.

Ghosts of the Trade

The Atlantic slave trade became the engine that drove the first global economy, the triangular trade that brought enormous wealth to the European powers and fueled colonization and settlement in the New World. The trade in slaves had its beginnings in the late fifteenth century, as early Portuguese explorers, hunting for gold, formed treaties with coastal African merchants to trade metals, guns, and gunpowder for slaves from the African interior. This process disrupted state building in West Africa, setting off round after round of slaving wars between African ethnic groups. As Portuguese and Spanish power waned, Holland, and eventually England, seized control of the trade.[55]

Many of the Africans caught up in the trade came from deep in the interior of West Africa. Slavers marched some of their victims as far as one thousand miles to reach European fortresses built at the mouth of the great West African rivers. The enslaved received a brand, not unlike cattle, that marked them with the national symbol of Dutch or English joint stock companies. Placed in the holds of ships that sometimes had as little as eighteen inches of height between decks, many of the newly enslaved people suffocated, committed suicide, or went insane in the fetid conditions and the terror of their plight. In a number of instances, they rose up against white crews, a deadly gamble that itself often meant a quick death. Slave ships assumed a loss of as much as 30 percent of their cargo as part of operating costs.[56]

The slave ship became a kind of charnel house, haunted with both the reality and the memory of violence. One observer described the deck of an eighteenth-century slave ship as "so covered with blood and mucus that it resembled a slaughterhouse." Historian Marcus Rediker has called the slave ship "a well organized fortress for the control of human beings" in which any attempt at insurrection resulted in brutal retribution. Failed slave rebels found themselves "flogged, pricked, cut, razored, stretched, broken, unlimbed and beheaded." Slave captains often distributed the body parts of the defeated to the rest of their human cargo as a reminder of the punitive cost of an attempted rebellion.[57]

The slave ships represented true houses of horror, machines of torture. Not surprisingly, the forced African diaspora into the New World generated mountains of monster lore that reflected the terrors of the trade. As Olaudah Equiano describes in his reconstruction of the experience of the trade, captives felt they had "fallen into a world of bad spirits." African folklore associated the color white with death, giving an aura of supernatural terror to the creatures that enslaved, beat, and branded them.[58]

The terror of the trade influenced the growth of stories that moved through villages up and down the Gambia River. One such story described the pasty-looking beings who bought Africans from the slave catchers as cannibals, capturing Africans with plans to consume them whole. Equiano described the terror felt by the newly enslaved at seeing the fires burning on the decks of slave ships, fires that slavers believed kept away disease but that the unfortunate victims of the trade interpreted as "cooking fires" in which they would be prepared and eaten "by these ugly men." Some slaves in Louisiana believed that they had found confirmation of their fears when seeing their new masters drink red wine. Unfamiliar with the beverage, they assumed that their masters drank the blood of African victims like vampires.[59]

Historian of the African-Atlantic experience John Thornton has further shown that West Africans entrapped in the slave trade viewed these "cannibal" slavers in the context of witchcraft. West African belief understood the witch as a creature addicted to kidnapping and consumption, so much so that the work of witches could be described as "eating the spirit." Thornton notes a Jesuit priest who described seventeenth-century slaves as believing, almost universally, that their transport across the Atlantic represented "a type of witchcraft" that would end in their bodies being "turned into oil and eaten."[60]

Africans saw the trade as deeply monstrous. Whites, in turn, used the imagery of the monstrous to legitimize the institution the slave trade had created. Slaveholders viewed the slave as a new kind of monster, both useful and dangerous. In nineteenth-century America, such views received the patina of pseudo-scientific legitimacy. Josiah Nott, a respected nineteenth-century physician who became known for his contributions to the treatment of yellow fever, also created a monstrous ethnology in which Africans displayed "immutable characteristics" that distinguished them clearly from other human beings. Nott put forward his ideas in a series of publications between the 1840s and 1870s, constructing a proslavery apologetic based on the alleged genetic savagery of Africans. He saw the African as a monster in the most basic sense, a being outside the limits of the rest of humanity.[61]

Paradoxically, many slaveholders sought to deny the truth of slavery, seeing it as a domestic institution held together by paternal bonds. Planters such as James Henry Hammond of South Carolina used familial metaphors to describe the plantation, viewing himself as the caring patriarch of a large and happy family. Planters hid from themselves and from the world the violent nature of the institution, leaving whippings to overseers and writing proslavery apologetics that insisted that the slave endured no greater hardships than the industrial workers of the North and England.[62]

Many of these same slaveholders feared that they held a monster in chains, one that could break loose at any moment. Slave rebellions, such as the New York Rebellion of 1712 and the South Carolina Stono Rebellion of 1739, greatly increased these fears. Southern newspapers reported, often in lurid detail, revolts in other parts of the slaveholding world, always with the subtext that such horrors could occur on the American landscape. Frequently, these accounts emphasized the supernatural terror of African religious traditions in an attempt to portray the African rebel as a kind of witch and very likely in league with the devil. A Charleston, South Carolina, newspaper account of a revolt in Antigua described its genesis in a ritual involving the drinking of a potion of grave dirt ("goofer dust") and chicken's blood while participants swore an oath to kill every white man, woman, and child on the island.[63]

Slaves became, in the white Southern mind, both monsters and faithful servants. This schizophrenic concept allowed white planters to express their fears while sublimating them. Slaves in revolt represented the perfect monsters, their origins in fearful religious rites. Slaves in the household, meanwhile, were imagined as cheerful domestics, caring for the planter's family or working in his fields out of gratitude for the roof over their heads. The bewildering logic of white supremacy allowed Southern whites to maintain their sanity and, sometimes, to sleep at night.[64]

By the 1830s white fears of the monstrosity of the African increasingly began to draw on the powerful metaphor recently created by English writer Mary Shelley. Shelley's 1818 *Frankenstein*, the story of an inhuman creature that turns on its master, provided slaveholders with a ready metaphor for the possibility of slave rebellion. Elizabeth Young, in her brilliant book *Black Frankenstein*, shows how closely descriptions of the 1831 Nat Turner Revolt in Virginia mirrored Shelley's descriptions of the monster (and theatrical iterations of the story American audiences would have been familiar with beginning in the 1820s). In November of 1831 the *Richmond Enquirer* described Turner as "the monster of iniquity" and "a spectacle from which the mind must shrink in terror." Turner became Frankenstein on a rampage through the countryside. Images from Shelley's nightmare continued to haunt American racial fantasies for two centuries.[65]

The creation of American slavery turned early America into a slaveholder's republic. Slavery constrained the American definition of liberty and democracy, producing some of the fundamental tensions that led to the American Civil War. This war would not destroy the monsters of the American mind, and race would remain central to the American doctrine of monsters into the twenty-first century. The ghosts of the trade continue to rattle their very real chains throughout American history.

The People under the Plantation

Oral tradition in nineteenth-century Florida told of a fearsome, alligator-like creature known as a snoligoster. Despite its comic-sounding name, tales of the snoligoster centered on its size, fearsome appearance, and violence. Folklore frequently associated it with the death of trespassers in the swamps around Lake Okeechobee. One such story has local man Inman F. Eldredge "hunting for an outlaw negro in the swamp" when he comes upon the unlucky man impaled on what Eldredge first believes to be a cypress stump. Eldredge takes a closer look and discovers the stump is actually the razor-edged horn that protrudes out of the back of the snoligoster. He considers shooting the monster but decides, "it was doing a good work and was entitled to live on." Eldredge went on to explain that the "very report of such a creature inhabiting the swamps" would have a good effect on the African American community.[66]

The story of the snoligoster shows how monsters became a part of white supremacy's mythology of power. Runaways in the southeast United States had long taken to the swamps for refuge from the slave patrols. Tales of a monster haunting those swamps inspired fear that reinforced social and political hierarchies. The word "snoligoster," or "snollygoster," became a synonym for "carpetbagger" in the years following the Civil War, suggesting that the creature had a clear connection to racial politics in the American South. Legends of monsters had become assertions of racial power.

Similar stories are common in the antebellum South. One South Carolina planter, concerned that his slaves spent too much time at revival meetings, dressed himself in an elaborate devil costume, complete with a mask that contained a mechanical contrivance that made it appear to move. He used this cartoonish getup to terrify both his slaves and the whites that attended revival meetings with them. Stories such as the snoligoster and this incident raise the possibility that many of the tales of terror of creatures and spirits in Southern woods and swamps may have had their source in the plantation house. Such stories added a supernatural dimension to an atmosphere already fetid with fear and rich with the promise of violence.[67]

This climate of terror proved useful to the emerging American ruling class. In the early years of the nineteenth century, American elites, whether Southern planters or Northern merchants, had a vested interest in maintaining racial and economic hierarchies. Historians of the years following the American Revolution tend to emphasize that the conflict opened up the possibility of social democracy in early American life. At the same time, many of these same historians argue that the years following the revolution witnessed a revanchist move toward the consolidation of power by elites. Confiscation of Loyalist lands in the 1780s led to an increase in independent farmers, though it also helped build the estates of the planter class in the American South. Meanwhile, though some Tory merchant families in New York, Philadelphia, and Boston fled to British imperial protection and left their wealth and holdings behind, these holdings were often claimed by up-and-coming elites. The final years of the eighteenth century represented a changing of the guard rather than a transformation of the basic social structure.[68]

The adoption of the U.S. Constitution in 1787 created the degree of consolidation that the new American elites hoped for, ensuring the protection of commerce. The Constitution also brought an end to the international slave trade following a twenty-year reprieve. The Atlantic traffic in human beings, alluded to in obscure language and never called by its true name in the Constitution, came to an end in 1808.

Slavery in the United States, however, continued and flourished, becoming central to the economic prosperity of the nation, enriching both Southern cotton planters and Northern textile and shoe manufacturers. By the time of the American Civil War, four million African Americans lived under the control of the plantation system in the United States. The institution thrived from enormous profits made from the internal slave trade and the possibility that slavery would move westward.

In Frederick Douglass' speech "Slavery and the Irrepressible Conflict," the great abolitionist and former slave refers to the institution of slavery as "America's pet monster." Douglass chose this frightening metaphor well. He knew from his own experience that slavery played a role in the intimate lives of millions of white Americans and yet was the institution that dared not speak its name in the founding documents. Slavery drove all aspects of American life, from its commercial revolution to its expansion across the opening frontier. America obscured its pet monster in the language of rights and personal liberty, an ideology of democracy for a nation founded, in the most basic economic sense, on slavery. Douglass described how "all our political parties and most of our churches" kneel at the shrine of this thing, a "huge and many-headed abomination."[69]

Monsters in the early republic functioned in a variety of ways. They represented the terrors of the past, the desire by white Americans to obscure the origins of the colonial experience. They could also suddenly leap out from the closet when those same Americans needed a reason to explain why slavery thrived in the land of democracy and why brutality coexisted alongside the high moral ideals of American Christianity. Sometimes they provided the most cynical of masters a way to frighten their chattel, to convince them that the monsters of the plantation house were nothing in comparison to those that lurked beyond the bounds of freedom.

Monsters also invaded the dreams of the oppressed. The belief that supernatural horrors drove the slave trade represented a rational response to the indescribable evil and the terrors of the unknown Atlantic passage. The slave trade, after all, did represent a kind of witchcraft and a kind of cannibalism, a dark blood-magic that transmogrified human beings into a species of property for the consumption of the voracious plantation system, Douglass' "many-headed abomination."

White America also dreamed of monsters, seeing them in slave rebellion and the destruction of the fragile racial hierarchy the world of the plantation had created. Deeply embedded beliefs about African American inferiority, beliefs that included age-old notions of black monstrosity, terrified whites about the fate of the country if the slaves ever gained their freedom. In antebellum America, even many white antislavery reformers believed that the expatriation of Africans, in Haiti or even back in Africa, offered the best solution for the problem of slavery. A multiracial society, in their minds, would be a monstrous society.

Antebellum America was monster-ridden. During the nineteenth century, the shadows only grew longer. The earliest American gothic fictions investigated this underside of the American historical experience as the country itself descended into a truly monstrous conflict.

2

GOTH AMERICANA

One Dark Day in the Middle of the Night
Two Dead Boys Came out to Fight
Back to back they Faced Each Other
Pulled their knives
And each shot the other.

—Traditional rhyme

Believe in Me, Be My Victim.

—*Candyman* (1992)

The stylish 1992 film *Candyman*, based on a Clive Barker short story, succeeds by combining a gothic sensibility with genuine terrors from the American past. A graduate student named Helen (Virginia Madsen), researching urban legends in contemporary Chicago, begins collecting stories of the mythical "Candyman." The story of Candyman contains motifs not dissimilar from other well-known urban legends, including endangered babysitters, unquiet spirits that appear in mirrors when fatally summoned, and maniac killers with a hook for a hand.

Helen's research takes a deadly twist that the ingénue folklorist does not expect. Two African American women at her university, with connections to Chicago's Cabrini Green housing project, connect all the bloody motifs of the urban legend to a recent brutal murder.

Cabrini Green, another scholar tells Helen, is "Candyman country." This monster's folklore comes complete with a historical origin story rooted in America's cruel racial past. Candyman, though the son of a slave, had become a noted artist in the Midwest. A wealthy landowner asked him to paint a portrait of his "virginal young daughter." The two fell in love and the young white woman became pregnant, the ultimate terror in the white supremacist nightmare. This flagrant violation of American racial mores resulted in a brutal lynching. The enraged mob cut off Candyman's hand, covered him with honey so that bees would feast on him, and burned him alive. He haunts the Chicago housing project, and soon he would haunt Helen herself.[1]

The story of Candyman offers the story of a very American monster, born out of the terrors of the past. The film borrowed heavily from nineteenth-century gothic motifs as well as from American anxieties over race, violence, and sexuality. It reflects the ironies and cross-grained tensions of a republic of liberty founded, and then torn apart, over the enslavement of human beings. The influence of the gothic tradition on American literature became a way to deal with the memory of a violent American past and a violent American present.

Nineteenth-century American elites constructed their society out of a number of explosive materials, all ready to detonate. White Americans, though they dominated most of the country's economic and cultural institutions, perceived themselves as under siege. Slaves made up a majority of the population of some American states. Immigrants who shared neither Anglo-Saxon heritage nor Anglo-Saxon values began entering northeastern American port cities in the 1840s and 1850s. Immigrants and slaves provided workers for agrarian and industrial capitalists throughout the century, and yet their presence appeared to native whites as an omen and a threat. The atmosphere was rich with the irony of a nation whose founding documents trumpeted liberty and democracy but whose prosperity rested on slavery and the labor of immigrants hated and feared by the dominant class.[2]

Slavery proved the most combustible element in the young nation. The sectional conflict that led to the Civil War dismembered the nation and transformed the way Americans thought about death. The killing of six hundred thousand men, most between the ages of 18 and 30, caused an enormous shift in social institutions and cultural sensibilities. The collapse of Reconstruction unleashed a violent assault against the African American community in the South. Black men and women faced similar horrors in the urban North by the time of the First World War.[3]

Meanwhile, the postbellum era witnessed a new kind of internecine struggle, an emerging clash over social and ideological values that has remained a part of the American cultural conversation into the present. By the 1870s the struggle for gender equality begun in the antebellum era increasingly turned toward efforts by women to assert their autonomy over their bodies and their sexuality. This struggle inevitably raised questions about the nature of the American family, considered by many a sacrosanct institution protected by religious sanction.

Nineteenth-century stories of the American monster attempted to make sense of unavoidable American social conflicts. American writers, meanwhile, borrowed from the European gothic tradition in an effort to explore the nature of American identity. This identity took on a monstrous shape. Slavery became the greatest monster of all, a horror tale told by both its defenders and its opponents. The American Civil War resulted from this war of monstrous imagery. In the aftermath of the conflict, the United States continued to summon new monsters from the depths as warring cultural visions each had its frightening tale to tell.

Original Goths

During the early 1980s, post-punk music and cultural styles created a new subculture known simply as "goth." Goths embraced the imagery of the macabre in their appearance, sometimes affecting an androgynous style that featured black eyeliner and clothing along with a creative blending of the symbols of medieval Catholicism, punk styles, and a horror film aesthetic. Influenced by the music of Bauhaus and the Damned, goth subculture branched off into numerous alternative subcultures, ranging from steampunk to vampire lifestyles.[4]

The embrace of the goth lifestyle draws on a tradition hundreds of years old. In the eighteenth century the Enlightenment celebration of reason caused a significant cultural backlash. The rise of romanticism exulted in the power of primal feeling over what some regarded as a cold and sterile cerebralism. The "graveyard poets" represent one rivulet of this tradition, as do the canonical works of Romantic poets such as Coleridge.[5]

In 1764 the British writer Horace Walpole published *The Castle of Otranto*, a story of ruined castles, underground passageways, mysterious deaths, and tainted romance. These elements played a significant role in what became known as the gothic literary tradition. In European cultural life, Gothic Revival architecture accompanied this new literary genre, with Walpole himself turning his country estate into a reproduction of a medieval castle.[6]

Gothic fictions elicited a thrill from eager readers with a newfound appreciation for all things old, dreary, ghostly, and built near graveyards. Literary critic Valdine Clemens notes that this aesthetic form appeared at a moment when "enlightenment contempt for the barbarity of the Middle Ages was giving way to a sense of nostalgia." This nostalgia could take a number of forms, including a willingness to revisit the horrors of the medieval period. British gothic novels frequently used the lurid tales of the Inquisition, sexually perverse and possibly supernatural monks, and other anti-Catholic motifs in order to frighten and thrill their audiences.[7]

In the United States the work of John Filson, discussed in the previous chapter, became one of the early conduits of the gothic imagination. His Kentucky travelogue filled the American frontier with unquiet spirits and ancient monsters. Washington Irving built on this tradition with the 1820 "The Legend of Sleepy Hollow." Drawing on the folklore of the Hudson River Valley, Irving describes Sleepy Hollow as a "sequestered glen," paradisiacally rural in its isolation. But the village's agrarian fecundity and preternatural quiet masked horrors. Irving writes of "the drowsy, dreamy influence" that hangs over the land, an atmosphere that local inhabitants attributed to the sorceries practiced by an early German settler or to the influence of local native tribes. Here, Irving drew on Mather, seeing the "devilish" influence of Native American magic over the American landscape as the primary cause for what he describes as "the witching influence of the air."[8]

Irving uses this setting to create an American horror story that attempts, if somewhat whimsically, to give the American continent a gothic past. The chief monster of the tale owes his existence to the Revolutionary War, concluded in 1783. The famous harrowing of Ichabod Crane took place in 1790. Though only thirty years have passed by 1820, Irving refers to these events as occurring during "a remote period of American history."[9]

The publication of "The Legend of Sleepy Hollow" coincided with a period of significant economic shifts and the emergence of the American commercial revolution. In the previous twenty years, seaboard cities had grown in size and in the import and export of commercial tonnage. A significant faction of American congressional leaders began to see the funding of internal improvements (railroads, canals, roads) as crucial for commercial activity and national identity. Most of America remained rural, although most agrarian enterprises interlinked with urban markets and, by extension, to global markets.[10]

Events in 1819 seemed to call into question this commercial expansion and the entrepreneurial spirit that animated it. An economic downturn, known as the "Panic of 1819," grew from a collapse in commodity prices. In 1820s Philadelphia, the city government reported three-quarters of the workforce as unemployed. The panic devastated rural America as well, with millions of farm laborers out of work.[11]

Irving's Ichabod Crane was a representative character of this economic morass. In twentieth-century versions of Irving's tale, Crane has often appeared as the hero, wrongly persecuted by Brom Bones, his rival for the affection of one of the local gentry's daughters. This reading of Irving's characterizations owes far more to the 1958 Disney animated version of "The Legend of Sleepy Hollow" than to the 1820 short story. In the original tale, Crane appears as the very epitome of the money-hungry New England Yankee, indeed as a kind of embodiment of the new entrepreneurial spirit of the commercial revolution. Crane comes to the small, Dutch community and does his best to extract money from this small township and marry one of the prettiest, and wealthiest, of its daughters. Crane is also representative of the American Puritan, eager for stories of monsters and ready to believe in the devilish nature of the American frontier. Irving describes him as the "perfect master" of Cotton Mather's works on witchcraft, with an "appetite for the marvelous" sated only by the old Puritan's "direful tales." In Crane, and in some sense the community he comes to, we have a compendium of all the monster tales that both delighted and terrified colonial America. Irving tells us that one of Crane's favorite pastimes is to sit by the fire with "old Dutch wives" and "listen to their marvelous tales of ghosts and goblins, and haunted fields and haunted brooks." He, in turn, regaled them with tales of witchcraft and of "direful omens and portentous sights and sounds in the air, which prevailed in the earlier times of Connecticut."[12]

Crane's fascination with such legends prepares him to be deceived by Bones, portrayed by Irving as a prototypical frontier hero along the lines of Boone, Crockett, and Leatherstocking. Indeed, his defeat of Crane by subterfuge (we are led to believe that Bones likely disguised himself as the headless horseman in order to terrify away the schoolmaster) constitutes exactly the kind of prank expected of the rough-and-ready men of the frontier often portrayed as skilled tricksters as well as fighters.[13]

Irving shaped a monster story that sought to give America a usable past. The feeling that American nationalism had little strong soil to root itself in, no historic past or ancient traditions, represented a common anxiety in the early nineteenth century. The commercial revolution, which seemed in the process of turning over what thin soil existed for the creation of settled communities with a definable past, only added to this feeling. Irving notes that in America,

> there is no encouragement for ghosts in most of our villages, for they have scarcely had time to finish their first nap and turn themselves in their graves before their surviving friends have traveled away from the neighborhoods; so when they turn out at night to walk their rounds they have no acquaintance left to call upon.[14]

Irving sought to remedy this by creating an American past filled with as many monsters as Europe could boast. Irving believed that this past should be one with monsters, that American identity needed its headless Hessians and haunted places.

While American writers like Irving sought to shape a monstrous past, European romantic writers drew on the folklore of their continent to create new creatures of the night. Many of these would play a central role in America's horrific future. The gothic novel provided the setting for such monsters' graveyards, ruins, and castles haunted with secrets. Major authors in the romantic tradition filled these scenes with shambling night things.

Romanticism gave life to the undead, specifically to the vampire. Vampiric creatures have roots deep in numerous world mythologies but first popped out of their coffins in modern literature through several eighteenth-century German works, including Goethe's 1797 *The Bride of Corinth*. The folklore of Eastern Europe and China viewed the vampire as a bestial creature, barely if at all human. In the shadowy light of German romanticism, the vampire became a dark lover, returning from the grave to reclaim a forbidden bride.[15]

The vampire met the world of English romanticism through the work of Robert Southey. Southey's 1801 *Thalaba the Destroyer* introduced the seductive female vampire. It also included an appendix that translated the work of a French Benedictine who collected and compiled much of the mythology surrounding undead revenants. This translation, much beloved by notables like Coleridge, Shelley, Byron, and Poe, gave the blood-sucking vampire his invitation to make his way fully into the English and the American consciousness.[16]

On a summer holiday in Switzerland in 1816, two bohemian writers created what horror historian David Skal has called the "dark twins" of modern monster mania. The gathering included the poet Lord Byron, seventeen-year-old Mary Godwin (better known as Mary Shelley), the

English poet Percy Shelley, and Byron's personal physician, Dr. John Polidori. One of these early nineteenth-century rock stars (local villagers apparently viewed their holiday as a drug-fueled, sex-frenzied debauch) suggested that they hold an impromptu contest to see who could produce the best ghost story. Polidori's contribution, based on some rough notes of Byron's, would be published several years later as "The Vampyre."[17]

Polidori's tale (for a time attributed to Byron himself) portrayed a very Byronesque character named Lord Ruthven, who becomes a vampire after his death. As in German versions of the vampire legend, Ruthven searches for a forbidden bride (a motif that appears in Bram Stoker's masterwork). Theatrical versions of "The Vampyre" became common, and it eventually worked its influence over Stoker's tale in the 1890s.[18]

Vampires would take some time to make their way to the United States, but the other monstrous creation of that Swiss holiday more quickly shambled ashore. While Polidori dreamed of bloodsucking (and sexy) freaks, young Mary Shelley had nightmares of "the pale student of the unhallowed arts kneeling beside the Thing he had put together." *Frankenstein; or, the Modern Prometheus* would be first published in 1818 and would see quick transatlantic success.[19]

"In less than a decade," writes Susan Tyler Hitchcock, author of an important cultural history of Shelley's creation, "*Frankenstein* had penetrated the public imagination and had become a story told, retold and reinterpreted." Theatrical productions of Shelley's monster story appeared in America as early as 1825. Her dark tale influenced a fascination in American pulp literature with dissection and dismemberment as well as the horrors of resuscitated life. Lurid American novels, such as John Hovey Robinson's *Marietta; or, The Two Students: A Tale of the Dissecting Room and "Body Snatchers"* (1842), drew on the imagery of Frankenstein while also reflecting a debate in the emerging American medical profession over the ethics of dissection.[20]

Although born of the same cultural moment, Frankenstein's monster and the vampire are quite distinct horrors. The Creature is born in a lab, and his creation is an industrial process: an assembling of parts. The vampire has clear supernatural origins in diabolical mystery and black magic. He is not the creation of the Industrial Revolution but a memory of the times before it, a dark nostalgia. Differences aside, the fascination with both monsters grew out of the rapidly changing conditions of contemporary capitalism. The Industrial Revolution suggested that technology had become Dr. Frankenstein, unleashing monsters to walk the earth. A society where technology had seemingly taken the place of the divine raised questions about the nature of the supernatural, questions that the vampire answered in terrifying fashion.[21]

American readers took much more quickly to Frankenstein's monster. The rapid changes brought by the market revolution created significant nervousness in the American public. This theme in Frankenstein, especially when combined with the obvious metaphors of enslavement and rebellion, touched a chord in American audiences. Literary scholar Elizabeth Young shows that the image of Frankenstein as rebellious slave not only appears in relation to white anxiety over the Nat Turner Rebellion but also becomes "the embodiment of racial uprising" in political rhetoric and imagery. The story of a "monster" that rebelled against its master offered a very explicit metaphor for nervous whites.[22]

The vampire would, appropriately, lurk only in the American shadows through most of the nineteenth century. However, he made his influence felt in ways that point to his celebrity status in twentieth-century American pop culture. For example, a number of Poe's tales feature a vampire that lives off the psychic energy, if not the blood, of its victims. At least one unpublished vampire novel of the 1870s drew on the same European influences later so important to Stoker in the 1890s.[23]

The American turn toward the gothic, with its dark castles and shambling creatures, represents only one facet of the nation's monster obsession. America remained a settler society throughout much of the nineteenth century, expanding its frontier and seeking to secure a profit on the seas. Monsters of the deep appeared both in frontier lakes and along its coasts, frightening and appalling but also delighting the new country. Not surprisingly for a seaboard nation tied to the economic engine of the Atlantic world, monsters from the depths haunted the waters.

Melville's Monster

One of America's greatest horror writers frequently described the terrors of the seas. Early twentieth-century pulp writer H. P. Lovecraft's (1890–1937) short story "Dagon" tells the tale of a castaway during the First World War who comes upon a strange megalith on a seemingly deserted island. Under "a fantastically gibbous moon" the sailor sees that the stone is covered in images of horrifying creatures who "were damnably human in general outline despite webbed hands and feet, shockingly wide and flabby lips, glassy bulging eyes and other features less pleasant to recall." Already unsettled by these images, the unnamed sailor is then driven insane when "a stupendous monster of nightmares" slides out of the sea and embraces the monolith.[24]

Lovecraft became a master at creating inhuman horrors connected to the ocean. His famous short story "The Call of Cthluhu" imagines a gigantic, apocalyptic monster sleeping beneath the waves, waiting for the stars to align so that it can rise and destroy all human society. In other tales, creatures from another dimension skitter into our world to wreak havoc and threaten the existence of human life on earth. Terror in Lovecraft's conception came from a philosophical sentiment in which human beings are expendable and unimportant rather than direct victims and prey. The vast heavens and the equally vast deeps contained monsters that will unthinkingly, and uncaringly, destroy us.

The American sea serpent of the early nineteenth century was a much less frightening creature. In no way did it represent a beast that could upset the order of things. The serpent instead became the center of scientific debate, playing a role in discussions about the nature of geological change and evolutionary biology. By extension, "serpent sightings" and their meaning became the basis for an emerging conflict between amateur and professional conceptions of science and a debate over the nature of scientific evidence. The creature also came to occupy a central place in American popular culture in what would become a well-worn path for the monster. In the United States, every frightening apparition and ravening beast has had an afterlife as a media celebrity. Antebellum America remained fascinated with monsters of the deep long after the sightings of the sea serpent off Gloucester Harbor. Between 1800 and 1850, American monster watchers reported over one hundred and sixty-six sightings of alleged sea serpents, both on the high seas and in American lakes. A market in fossils developed as monster hunters claimed to locate the remains of sea serpents in all parts of the new nation.[25]

Sea serpent mania generated a significant amount of scientific interest. Debates over the existence of the creature claimed the attention of important nineteenth-century scientists, including Charles Lyell. Best known for his work on geology that complemented Darwin's theory of evolution, Lyell collected numerous eyewitness accounts of the creature and, at one particularly enthusiastic moment, claimed that these accounts had caused him to "believe in the sea serpent without ever having seen it."[26]

The Boston Linnean Society shared Lyell's interest, and after the 1817 Massachusetts sightings, began a serious effort to compile accounts and work up a zoological profile of the sea serpent. In their zeal to find definitive evidence for the creature, members of the society became convinced that a three-foot snake with strange markings represented one of the sea serpent's young. This alleged find encouraged the speculation that the Gloucester serpent had come close to shore to spawn. Early American newspapers widely reported the society's claims, causing significant embarrassment when further investigations by Harvard zoologist Louis Agassiz revealed the creature as a fairly common land snake with a disease that gave it strangely raised bumps. The debacle helped lead to the dissolution of the Boston society in 1822.[27]

This embarrassment for the New England natural history community did nothing to dampen the broader American enthusiasm for sea monsters that reached fever pitch by midcentury. In 1852 the American whaling ship *Monangahela* allegedly sighted a sea serpent over one hundred feet in length in the South Pacific. The ship's captain, whose reports from sea filtered in to American newspapers throughout the year, described an epic chase in which the giant creature, after being hit with multiple harpoons, pulled the ship for sixteen hours before dying. In his letters to major American magazines, the captain promised to sail into New York harbor with the remains of the sea beast. The excitement over the serpent resulted in multiple stories in the *New York Times* and the *New York Tribune*. Unfortunately, the *Monongahela* was reported lost in the arctic seas in 1853.[28]

Nineteenth-century belief in the sea serpent became a profession of faith in the unknowability of nature combined with, ironically, the willingness to accept unconfirmed personal experience ("eyewitness accounts") as evidence. Belief in the creature lost traction by the second half of the century as scientists fully professionalized their disciplines by placing their work under the umbrella of major universities. Here they would form organizations that would issue credentials based on educational requirements and publish journals that vetted scientific research through the judicial process of peer review. These standards of proof replaced subjective experiences and alleged "eyewitness reports" in determining empirical truths.

The sea serpent fell back into the realm of myth in the wake of emerging scientific consensus about the nature of evidence. Contemporary historian Sherrie Lynne Lyons, in her detailed examination of this debate, describes how the sea serpent came to be seen as an insoluble problem by American science. No specimen of the creature existed. The numerous sightings and affidavits for the creature's existence failed to meet established standards for discerning truth. Given these facts, science refused to say that sea monsters did not exist, but simply pointed out that the lack of fossil evidence or specimens to analyze in controlled settings made it impossible to assert that such a creature did exist.[29]

Popular culture in the United States refused to shed its enthusiasm for the sea serpent as a source of entertainment and wonder, despite the scientific community's refusal to credit its existence. In the second half of the nineteenth century, sea beasts may have been, by far, the most popular American monster. Their alleged existence offered Victorian America a sense of wonder at the marvelous unknown and even seemed to strengthen and support religious belief. Sea serpent entrepreneurs could claim that the serpent was not only a natural animal but a supernatural visitation, perhaps even one of the marvelous, unknown creatures described in scripture as Leviathan. Such ideas proved attractive to religious Americans who felt their beliefs about nature to be under assault after the emergence of Darwinian evolutionary theory.

Promoters quickly claimed fossil finds on an Alabama plantation in 1842 as evidence for a sea monster with sacred meaning. Herman Melville wrote in *Moby-Dick* about these remains, reporting the story that "credulous slaves in the vicinity took it for one of the bones of the fallen angels." In fact, credulity was not limited to Alabama slaves when it came to these fossils. In 1845 a carnival promoter exhibited them in New York and New England, placed in an undulating shape, with head raised. This was the same physical position as most artistic renderings of serpent sightings in Glouces-ter Harbor.[30]

Advertising copy for the Alabama sea monster claimed that carnival-goers would see a creature one hundred and fourteen

Sea Serpent Polka

feet in length. Handbills asserted that the creature did not represent a scientific specimen but rather a sign rich with theological meaning. The advertisement for the beast went back to Ezra Stiles' doctrine of monsters by claiming the creature to be Leviathan from the book of Job. In fact, scientists later concluded that the carnival monster represented an achievement of ingenious taxidermy, a human construction made out of at least five different types of fossil remains.[31]

Exhibitions such as these underscore the celebrity of the sea serpent. Significant sightings became embedded in American popular culture of the period. An original composition known as the "Sea Serpent Polka" became a popular piece of sheet music, its cover replicating the image of the serpent well known from the Gloucester sightings and reenacted by carnival exhibitors. Captains, meanwhile, christened their ships "Sea Serpent," and sightings of similar creatures in America's lakes became common.[32]

Entrepreneurs eagerly sought to cash in on the sea serpent craze. Carnival exhibits promising gigantic fish, sea monsters, and even the

Hydrarchos! Sea Serpent

great kraken of Scandinavian mythology proliferated as the century drew to a close. In November of 1880 a carnival known as "W. C. Coup's New United Monster Shows" promised a "giant devil fish . . . the most perfect specimen of the monster squid ever captured" as being "39 and ½ feet long with tentacles spread." This represented a trimming back of the carnival's claim. The same show had advertised two months earlier that it had the remains of such a creature "fifty feet in length."[33]

By the end of the century, whale shows, the ancestors of today's morally questionable marine spectacles staged at SeaWorld and similar venues, had become popular. Late nineteenth and early twentieth-century whale shows tended to draw much more heavily on monster imagery than today's exhibitions that emphasize the anthropomorphic traits of sea creatures and Disneyify them for their "cuteness." Whale shows of the 1890s, in contrast, emphasized the inhuman characteristics of sea beasts and described the violent struggles in which they had been captured. As late as 1932, a whale show in Georgia described its exhibit as "a monster of the deep captured after 16 hours of death defying combat." Advertisements for the show, like past handbills for sea serpent exhibitions, emphasized the size and power of the creature, insisting that the whale was fifty feet long and sixty-eight tons.[34]

Fascination with sea monsters in nineteenth-century America seems mostly whimsical, even when the power and size of the creatures are emphasized. Unlike Lovecraft's twentieth-century monsters, giant beasts arising from the depths fit into either a biblical or scientific order of things (or both). They were not purely creatures of chaos that would upset the social and cosmic order. But a frightening thing that did threaten the human order swam just beneath these relatively placid cultural waters.

Herman Melville tapped into the dark undertones of America's sea monster obsession with antebellum America's greatest monster tale, *Moby-Dick*. Melville's story of mad Captain Ahab's chase of the gigantic and terrifying beast that maimed him is as daunting in its size and complexity as the great whale itself. Though the vast critical commentary that exists on the novel is not easily navigated, the book offers significant insights into the American obsession with sea beasts. The novel serves as a key to the fascination of nineteenth-century America with monstrous creatures from the sea, a fascination with what Melville called "the unspeakable terrors of the whale."[35]

Cultural critic Andrew Delbanco calls Melville's novel part of "his lifelong meditation on America." It is an America obsessed with violence, fearful of the other, and at times a museum of horrors. The ship on which

Ahab and his unlucky sailors embark on their doomed mission is the *Pequod*, a name directly referencing the Pequot War and the bloody blot that campaign of extermination left on the New England landscape. In his descriptions of the whaling ships, vessels so essential to early New England prosperity, we see floating factories of destruction, covered in the gore of the creatures they hunt relentlessly. Melville presents these charnel houses as metaphors for American expansion, the ugly truths behind America's entrepreneurial fervor.[36]

Melville transforms the emerging American national identity into a haunt of monsters. Throughout the novel, supernatural terror is a brooding presence, preparing the reader for a series of encounters with the great beast of the deep that embodies all terror. When Melville's putative narrator, Ishmael, visits the Spouters Inn, a haunt of New Bedford whalers, he is greeted by a history of horror. On the wall hangs an ominous picture with "such unaccountable masses of shades and shadows" that some artist "in the time of the New England hags" must have painted it to represent "chaos bewitched." This picture, what Melville calls "a boggy, soggy, squitchy picture," evokes all the chaos of the sea and the terrors attendant on the whole project of whaling.[37]

Chaos meets horror on the opposite wall of the entryway. Here "a heathenish array of monstrous clubs and spears" greets Ishmael. These implements allegedly represent weaponry gleaned from the South Sea Islands, a display that causes Ishmael to wonder "what monstrous cannibal and savage could have ever gone a death-harvesting with such a hacking, horrifying implement." But it is not only the weaponry of the cannibal that appears on display. A harpoon belonging to an American whaler shares space with the tools of the monster, a harpoon that is also a "hacking, horrifying" weapon. This juxtaposition destroys any distinction between the whaling industry, a multimillion-dollar engine of prosperity in antebellum America, and the enterprise of cannibalism. Melville makes these links explicit throughout the novel, muddying differences between the American self and the other, and raising questions about the cannibalistic nature of America's search for economic prosperity.[38]

The role of supernatural horror and the constant reminder of the possibility of horrific violence in *Moby-Dick* suggest that Melville's meditation on America caused him to contemplate the darkest undertones of the national experiment. Like Nathaniel Hawthorne, to whom he dedicated *Moby-Dick*, Melville's gothic vision of American life and history help make sense of the antebellum fascination with monsters. Melville's evocation of the Puritan experiment, and its slaughtering of Native Americans and "witches," seems of a piece with his novel of cannibals, barbarous violence, ghostly apparitions, and that great "murderous fish" that becomes the focus of the tale. The wreck of the *Pequod*, the final victory of chaos over order, represents an ill omen for Melville's America, facing its horrific civil war. The ship goes down, "then all collapsed, and the great shroud of the sea rolled on as it rolled five thousand years ago."[39]

Ahab's vengeful search for Moby-Dick, his "tormented chase of the demon phantasm," seems oddly out of place in the midst of sea serpent mania. The American public's fascination with beasts from the sea seems altogether more playful and deadpan literal. Moby-Dick became in Melville's tale a representation of all the unknown terrors of the universe, an uncomfortable imagining of the sea serpent mythology that perhaps explains why the novel proved generally unpopular at the time of its first appearance. Melville presages the terrors of H. P. Lovecraft. Although Hawthorne and particularly Poe are seen as Lovecraft's chief American influences, the terrors of the unknown awakened by Melville, and the "murderous fish" that Ahab chased, prepared the way for Lovecraft's terrible monsters, able to drive human beings insane with their gigantism and uncaring destruction of human life and civilization.[40]

While Melville worked on *Moby-Dick* in late 1850, congressional debates raged over whether or not America would continue to countenance, as it always had, the enslavement of millions of human beings. The "Compromise of 1850" allowed the Kansas territory "popular sovereignty" in deciding whether or not slavery would be allowed when the region became a new state. In one of the many dark ironies of the American democratic experiment, voters would decide in a popular election whether or not they would become a slave society. The compromise did little to tamp down the conflict. Kansas became "Bleeding Kansas," an open wound of partisan warfare on the American landscape.[41]

Slavery had entwined like a snake around the very origins of the republic. The desire on the part of a significant segment of American society to enslave their fellow human beings, and the willingness of a much larger segment to either support or look with apathy on this institutionalized horror, helped to breed even more gothic American tales as the nation edged closer to war.

"Thrill the Land with Horror"

The violence of the institution of slavery produced monsters that filled American popular culture and haunted the African American mind. Contemporary literary critic Theodore Gross once made the point that "the nightmare world of Poe and Hawthorne has become the Monday morning of the negro author," an idea that *Candyman* explores when Madsen's folklorist describes the apparitions in the mirror as a way for a community to express "the horror of their daily lives." Toni Morrison makes this much less abstract when she writes that, for African American people, the existence of horror never surprises. After all, she writes, "we might live right next door to it."[42]

Black and white abolitionists turned to the language of monsters as quickly as did proslavery apologists. Abolitionists especially favored the gothic convention of the "evil double" that suggested that despite the glamorous image presented by the Southern planter, slavery had a true face that sickened and appalled. Boston abolitionist Theodore Weld, for example, wrote that if Americans knew the "true conditions of slaves" the facts would "thrill the land with horror."[43]

Abolitionist tales of slavery's monstrosity made use of the language of conspiracy to describe its power over the United States, suggesting its public face had a dark, hidden visage shrouded in sinister shadow. The phrase "the Slave Power" came into general usage among antislavery and abolitionist forces in the 1840s. Used to describe what was seen as the undue influence of proslavery politicians, the metaphor proved a powerful one in part because it ignored the issue of race. An umbrella term, it was used by everyone from abolitionists who wanted to see immediate emancipation based on a vision of human equality to those who simply thought that slavery, and enslaved Africans, corrupted the American political system.[44]

By the time of the American Civil War, language about the Slave Power morphed into the language of the monster. In 1861 committed abolitionist Charles Sumner, a devoted fan of Mary Shelley, referred to the Confederate States of America as "the soulless monster of Frankenstein, the wretched creation of mortal science without God." Sumner described the new Southern nation as a "monster empire" and the Union war effort as an attempt to exclude "the monster empire from the family of nations."[45]

Monster language came readily from the lips and pens of proslavery writers as well. The Nat Turner Rebellion, as we saw earlier, provided some of the most potent images. Not only did the *Richmond Enquirer* transform Turner into a monster not unlike Mary Shelley's "hideous progeny," other American newspapers tapped into the gothic possibilities of seeing the rebellion as a monster's revolt. A September 1831 account in the *Constitutional Whig* features the reporter retracing Turner's steps and telling a tale of a horrible monster on the loose. Following this route, his "mind is struck with horror." He can see, like phantasms rising out of the earth, "the helpless women and children" killed by Turner and his "banditti." He suggests "in future years, the bloody road will give rise to many a sorrowful legend; and the trampling of hooves, in fancy, visit many an excited imagination."[46]

Literary scholar Teresa Goddu, interpreting this passage from the *Whig*, brilliantly argues that the newspaper created a metaphor that allowed Turner "to haunt the imagination of future travelers much like the Headless Horseman." The slave rebellion became more than a slave rebellion and at the same time a bit less. The transformation of the insurrection against American slavery into a monster tale made it strangely comforting in the way the bloodiest horror film can offer strange comfort through its juxtaposition of extreme violence and unreality. The story symbolizes violence but also contains that violence. If Turner is Frankenstein's monster or the Headless Horseman, he becomes a tale to frighten children rather than a live political option (the film *Candyman* contains some of the same contradictory political messages). He is written off as "a monster" rather than a freedom fighter. Rebellion, the raised fist against the slave system, is reduced to a memory. The slave rebel becomes a character in a fairy tale.[47]

The coming of the American Civil War forced white America to face the monsters it had created. The political struggle between North and South over the fate of slaves in the western territories rode a wave of anxiety over the meaning of millions of enslaved Africans in the midst of white American society. John Brown's raid on Harpers Ferry filled the chamber with powder. Abraham Lincoln's election, the election of a man wrongly perceived by Southern whites as an abolitionist, pulled the trigger. Ironically, South Carolina's secession from the Union in December of 1860 unleashed a nightmare for white America. For enslaved Africans who saw the conflict as an opportunity to destroy the monster empire of slavery forever, the war for the Union became a war for emancipation.

The coming of the war brought out many a monstrous metaphor. Popular illustrator Henry Louis Stephens drew one of the most compelling. Appearing in *Vanity Fair* in May of 1862, it bears the title "The New Frankenstein: A Glimpse of the Horrible Fate in Store for Jeff Davis at the Hands of the Monster Rebellion." The image shows a traditional representation of the Southern planter being lifted violently over the head of a muscular black figure. A crown falls from the Southerner's head (suggestive of the collapse of the Slave Power) as the great creature prepares to hurl him over the ledge and into the abyss.

THE NEW FRANKENSTEIN.
A GLIMPSE OF THE HORRIBLE FATE IN STORE FOR JEFF DAVIS AT THE HANDS OF THE MONSTER "REBELLION."

The New Frankenstein: A Glimpse of the Horrible Fate in Store for Jeff Davis at the Hands of the Monster Rebellion

The image proved prescient. Gradually the American Civil War became a war centered on the issue of slavery. The first efforts to recruit African American troops for the Union Army began in 1862. This also marked the moment when the formerly enslaved began to disassemble the plantation system from within, running away in large numbers to reach the safety of Union lines. Southern proslavery writers had tried to play their rhetorical game both ways, portraying the slave as the docile child and the horrid monster. The image of the new Frankenstein squared the ironic circle, portraying the slaveholding South as destroyed by the institution it had created, a victim of its pet monster.

Gore and Mourning

The violence of the American Civil War far exceeded the expectations of both North and South. At least one Southern political leader claimed that he would be able to soak up all the blood spilled in the conflict with his pocket handkerchief. His fool's prediction became a twisted joke as more than half a million corpses piled up on American battlefields.[48]

Stephen Crane, author of *The Red Badge of Courage*, famously pictured the war as "a machine that produces corpses." These corpses became an object of fascination as well as grief and horror. The war drove an American obsession with the dead body that found an outlet in the nature of the emerging funeral industry, an interest in "death photography" of loved ones, and attachment to new and old practices related to mourning. This cultural meditation on the dead prepared the way for new American monsters, not only in the form of popular ghostly tales but also in the birth of a new kind of horror entertainment. As science continued to detail the origins of the human body, exposing its secrets, a cultural fascination with the literal insides of the human body—gore—began to grow.[49]

The enormous number of Civil War deaths accounts for only part of the macabre atmosphere of postbellum America. Wounded bodies filled American streets in the late nineteenth century; missing arms and legs of disabled veterans testified to the technological brutality of a modern conflict. War wounds had debilitated one-third of elderly veterans that lived in Tennessee and North Carolina "Soldiers' Homes." State governments devoted a considerable portion of their budgets to the care of wounded veterans in the thirty to forty years after the close of the conflict. Traumatized bodies, seared, scored, and amputated, became cultural symbols of the conflict.[50]

The enormous death toll of the Civil War had a strange chronicler in photographer Mathew Brady and his assistant Alexander Gardner (who took many of the most famous images associated with Brady's work). Brady set out to document the war with photography, showing the carnage to the American public in a way that never had been done before. He and his team actually posed the bodies of the fallen for maximum emotional effect. His photographs of the bloody battle of Antietam appeared at a New York exhibition in October of 1862, causing a sensation in the press. Although the popularity of his work faded for a time after the war, his images soon became central to representations of the conflict in both academic and popular works. Congress purchased the images in 1875 to serve as the photographic record of the conflict.[51]

Brady was far from the first photographer of the dead and certainly not the first to pose the dead for photographs. Scholar of American religion and popular culture Gary Laderman has shown the strong impulse in nineteenth-century America to seek comfort from the physical remains of a loved one. Photographic advances in the 1840s made postmortem photographs of loved ones increasingly common, and these were always posed images. Photographers generally hand-colored the image to remove all troubling signs of death while adding to the composition "floral designs, flying angels, and other sentimental iconography."[52]

Brady's Civil War photography ignored such conventions, replacing sentimental comfort with a shocking horror. Bodies lay on the ground, arms and legs in unnatural contortions. Brady and his associates used gothic conventions in their compositions, posing gravediggers with piles of corpses and even skulls. Rather than images of battlefield valor, his photographs showed only the aftermath, fields of corpses instead of heroes. Fascination with these images testifies to a growing interest in viewing the bodies of the dead.[53]

Brady's images, and the cult of death that they served, represent the birth of gore as an American entertainment. Popular culture scholar Annalee Newitz has pointed out a similarity between Brady's photographs and Victorian murder scenes, another subject of growing interest to the American public. Brady gave America nightmare images of death where the murderer had abandoned the images to ruin and rot. These terrifying images could not be dressed up in the language of religious comfort. And yet Americans reveled in such images, both during and after the war, hungry for sensationalist iconography and books that used the destruction of the human body to frighten and entertain.[54]

Brady was not alone in creating sensational images of bodily death from the events of the Civil War. The press in both sections of the divided country reported that the other side had desecrated the remains of the dead. Sometimes this had a basis in fact, while at other times it tested credulity. A *New York Tribune* reporter claimed in the summer of 1862 that gory souvenirs of war were found in a captured rebel camp, including a cup made from the skull of a fallen Union soldier. Even more sensational, *Frank Leslie's Illustrated* showed a woodcut entitled "The Rebel Lady's Boudoir." In a set of images easily imaginable in a Rob Zombie film, a woman sits reading a letter in a room covered with body parts and rib cages. Her child plays with a skull near her feet. The caption purports to contain some lines from her Confederate husband in which he expresses the hope that she has received "all the little relics" he has sent. He promises her that he will soon send "a baby rattle for our little pet, made out of the ribs of a Yankee drummer boy." In a hundred years, slasher film killer-heroes Leatherface, Michael Myers, and Jason Voorhees would emerge from this cultural obsession with bodily mutilation.[55]

In the late nineteenth century, strong countercurrents in American culture sought to prevent the dead body from becoming a gory spectacle. The American funeral industry became the primary proponent of the dead body as the happy soul. The Civil War had introduced embalming techniques that gave rise to the professionalization of the funeral industry. Official associations and trade journals soon followed (journals with names like *The Casket*). The funeral director (a title that trade journals insisted should replace the older, more evocative term "undertaker") made it his job to hide the corpse from the living and surround death with a sentimental language about the passage to "the other side" and the comforts of heaven.[56]

American religious life joined in this effort to ignore the horrors of bodily corruption and focus on death as a safe passage into heavenly delight. Protestant ministers emphasized the idea that the soul successfully escaped the corpse. Death afforded the soul an entry into a world not unlike this one, with all anxieties and discomforts removed. Spiritualism, the belief that the friendly dead could be contacted and convey messages of comfort to the living, reached its apogee of popularity in the 1870s. Even popular evangelical revivalists like Dwight L. Moody deemphasized death in their calls for conversion. When death did make its way into their rhetoric, it appeared as a language about the comfort of heaven.[57]

Nevertheless, the bloodied corpse as entertainment remained a significant part of popular culture, suggesting that the attempts of ministers and funeral directors proved far from successful. The popular writings of former Union officer Ambrose Bierce placed the gored human body at the center of his narratives. Stories such as "An Occurrence at Owl Creek Bridge" imagined death as a fearful end with no possibility of comfort. His popular ghost stories did nothing to take the focus off the bloody corpse. Bierce's ghosts are born of the murdered body, seeking vengeance. They certainly do not convey messages of comfort.[58]

Along with a fascination with ghostly tales, Victorian America showed a growing interest in a new kind of monster, the mass murderer who used techniques not unlike modern surgery to rend and destroy the body instead of to repair it. The rising interest in what a later day would call a "serial killer" tended to focus on the murderer's production of corpses, the form those corpses took, and the manner in which the murders occurred.

News and imagery of the 1888 Whitechapel murders of "Jack the Ripper," for example, became immensely popular in the United States. In fact, interest in the Ripper's crimes seems to have been as strong in the United States as in England. Sensationalist papers like the *National Police Gazette* carried detailed descriptions of the Ripper's crimes and even tried to Americanize the case by suggesting, in 1895, that he might be "at large in New York City." The *Atlanta Constitution* suggested that the unsolved 1884 murders of a number of African American women in Texas had been the work of the Ripper. The American press wanted the great monster of the Victorian era to be an American monster. The recent baseless claims that H. H. Holmes actually was Jack the Ripper should be seen in the light of this apparently continuing obsession.[59]

Dime novels—popular, sensational pulp books and magazines in late nineteenth-century America—often featured Jack the Ripper. These popular and cheaply produced materials frequently sought to Americanize him while emphasizing the savage and gory nature of his crimes. At least one of these narratives, A. F. Pinkerton's *The Whitechapel Murders; or, An American Detective in London*, suggested not only that an American had committed the crimes but that a Native American woman (called an "Indian princess" in the novel) had been responsible. This bizarre theory worked in the late nineteenth century since, as the historian of serial murder David Schmid notes, it drew on the stereotype of the "Indian savage," an image especially powerful in an America seeking to justify its war of conquest on the plains. Schmid also notes that this fantasy both Americanized the tale for popular consumption while it "protected white males" from being represented as homicidal maniacs.[60]

H. H. Holmes provided Americans with horrifying entertainment in the mid-1890s just as he has continued to do in the present. Holmes, a doctor and real estate developer, transformed his enormous and strangely designed Chicago mansion into a factory of corpses, soon to be known as "Murder Castle." Holmes also became the first serial murderer in America to attempt to tap into the potential of the emerging culture of celebrity. He received $10,000 from William Randolph Hearst for an 1896 confession that included such gothic elements as Holmes claiming that a pair of horns was emerging from his skull.[61]

The obsession with the mass murderer is rooted in the battlefields of the Civil War and the efforts of nineteenth-century Americans to deal with the catastrophic number of Civil War corpses and the "living dead" among the wounded. The dead body, especially a dead body outraged by violence, had become a central element in American popular culture.

Fallen Houses and Scarlet Women

Interest in torn bodies seems metaphorical for the dismembered America of the late nineteenth century. America in the 1870s seemed as torn by conflict as it was in the 1850s. A violent white uprising in the southern states destroyed Reconstruction, disenfranchising African Americans and leaving them to the not-so-tender mercies of their former masters. Expanding American settlements on the western frontier encroached on Native American lands, setting off a round of wars of conquest by the American government. Major labor strikes, such as the Railroad Strike of 1877, by workers being ground down by the demands of America's new corporations resulted in violent reprisals from the new industrial giants and their allies in state government.

The ongoing struggle for gender equality became one of the major cultural divides of the late nineteenth century. The national women's suffrage movement splintered in the late 1860s, though this did nothing to abate the struggle for equality. Divisions within the movement allowed more radical voices to gain hearing, voices that raised questions about the nature of the American family and women's reproductive health.

These voices challenged the late nineteenth century's system of gender control. The Victorian ideology known as "the cult of true womanhood" had imagined middle-class women as sequestered in their homes, acting as mothers, wives, and caregivers. This limited set of personal and emotional options coincided with a belief in the asexuality of proper women. Sex was the path to motherhood, not an avenue of self-fulfillment. The "angel of the household" did not go out into the world of commerce or even have any fun in the bedroom. She sat in the parlor, waxen and wan, while servants bustled about her.[62]

Ironically, two male writers from earlier in the century, each with his own gender hang-ups, used gothic fictions to interpret these conflicts over the nature of the family and its relationship to sexuality. Gothic fictions tended to raise questions about the familial household with their motifs of intergenerational violence and incest. Nathaniel Hawthorne and Edgar Allan Poe created monstrous tales of the American family, twisting American expectations of gender and sexuality into lurid shapes to frighten their readers. Late in the century, the conventions they critiqued actually grew stronger, acquiring the force of law as male elites sought to control even the most intimate aspects of women's lives.

Hawthorne's fictions are known for their use of Puritan notions of sin and guilt, taking these concepts and following them to their logical and horrific conclusions. The creepy short tale "The Minister's Black Veil" is one of the most powerful American evocations of the uncanny. Hawthorne's story of the minister that begins to go about with a funeral-pall black mask evokes the frightening unknowability of others and the consequences of Puritan notions of original sin. Meanwhile, Hawthorne's best-known work, *The Scarlet Letter*, uses forbidden sex as the forge to create a story of sin, satanic pride, and revenge.[63]

Hawthorne's most powerful monster tale, "Young Goodman Brown," tells of a young Puritan who is convinced that his community is righteous and his young wife is "an angel." On a night journey, he sees a dark vision of his whole community taking part in a witches' sabbat. Among them is his wife, "Faith," whom, we are encouraged to believe, Brown watches taking part in orgiastic satanic worship. The young Puritan wife, described to us earlier in the story as standing on a threshold with a pink ribbon in her hair, is found cavorting in the woods with devils. The subtext of "Young Goodman Brown" calls into question antebellum America's fascination with female sexual purity and the engines of control built from that obsession. Hawthorne suggests throughout the story that "Goodman Brown" (note the irony of the traditional Puritan title being applied to him) has basically predatory instincts, voyeuristically searching out evil. Brown, who wants to be a monster hunter, is the true monster of the tale. He finds it, he thinks, and becomes a gloomy and forbidding patriarch. He is unable to love his wife because, for the ideology of domesticity, to fail to be an angel is to be a devil.[64]

Hawthorne was not alone in visiting the dark cultural roots of American family life. Edgar Allan Poe rejected the sentimental images beginning to emerge around marriage and family life in antebellum America, seeing behind them predatory control and obsessions leading to insanity. Certainly no proto-feminist, Poe still understood the dynamics of patriarchal families and saw them as producing monstrous visions and monstrous acts.[65]

The work of Poe occupies a bizarre position in the American canon. Vernon Parrington infamously suggested that Poe's place in American literature is a question best taken up by the psychologist rather than the literary critic. He wrote in genres we would classify as comedy, mystery, and satire instead of pure horror. He even wrote a philosophical treatise. His stories of the macabre have won the most attention over the years, seeming so deeply out of step with the America of Ralph Waldo Emerson. Moreover, Poe frequently creates medieval fairylands for his murderers, maniacs, and ghostly apparitions to inhabit.[66]

Poe's ghosts hide behind the fantastic facade. His work delved into the dark undercurrents that ran beneath the surface of nineteenth-century America's anxiety over gender, sexuality, and race. He writes of horrible siblings, marriage as a charnel house where the dead and their desires come back to life, and the possibility of violence that hides at the heart of every human relationship. Poe refused to accept the emerging myths of the American family, and his conception of domesticity as a horror film has had numerous reverberations in how pop culture has dealt with the monster. Tod Browning's *Dracula* and, even more explicitly, Tobe Hooper's *The Texas Chain Saw Massacre* are representations of horrific families who feed on outsiders when they do not feed on each other. In this, they are Poe's progeny.[67]

"The Fall of the House of Usher" in some ways represents Poe's definitive domestic nightmare. It is a tale of two siblings, Roderick and Madeline, who reside in a morbid ancestral mansion. Both of the odd pair suffer from what were popularly known as "nervous illnesses" in antebellum America. Roderick has an "an excessive nervous agitation," while his sister Madeline suffers with "a settled apathy" and "transient afflictions of the cataleptical character."[68]

The narrator, Roderick's boyhood chum who has come to cheer him in his distress, watches in horror Madeline's rapid decline and death and attends Roderick upon Madeline's burial. The nature of her disease, and the fact that she is described as being buried "with a faint blush upon the bosom and upon the face," prepares us to learn that Madeline has been buried alive. The first-time reader is not prepared, however, for the return of Madeline, flinging open antique panel doors and standing enshrouded in burial clothes. Dripping with the blood of her struggle to escape her tomb, she falls on her brother, dying from the trauma of her ordeal and killing her brother with fright. The narrator flees as the House of Usher itself collapses suddenly and violently. Like the *Pequod* sinking beneath the seas that roll endlessly, the House of Usher falls like "the voice of a thousand waters," and the ground closes "sullenly and silently over the fragments."[69]

Shadowy elements of this short story have reappeared again and again in pop culture, its dark progeny including everything from Roman Polanski's *Rosemary's Baby* to Stephen King's *The Shining*. The tale itself presents an utterly deranged version of American family values in which the family unit, in this case the last living members of a family line, become all important to the narrative and to one another. The clear suggestion of incest in the subtext of the story has less significance than the control that Roderick asserts over his sister, literally the power of life and death. Although he knows her to be cataleptic, he rather quickly entombs her. Madeline, who never speaks and who has no control over the fate of her own body, stands in for American women celebrated in the "cult of true womanhood" and entombed in Victorian domestic ideology.

Roderick shrieked with horror when he saw that his allegedly "beloved" sister had broken free of the tomb. The conservative response to the emerging demands of feminism in the late nineteenth century revealed a similar sensibility. Traditionalism constructed women who refused to remain the "angel of the house" as monsters roaming the national landscape, seeking to destroy the family and the scripturally sanctioned rule of male over female in marriage.[70]

The response of conservative forces in American society to feminist leader Victoria Woodhull provides one of the best examples of this mentality. Woodhull became, in the years following the Civil War, an advocate for liberalized divorce laws that would allow women to leave unhappy marriages, retaining both their property and what Woodhull called "the ownership and free use of her sexual organs." Woodhull's demands for gender equality resulted in accusations that she supported "free love."[71]

Woodhull's challenge to American patriarchy made her the target of Anthony Comstock, a lifelong moral crusader who believed that "licentious literature" was poisoning the American spirit. Comstock especially liked the use of monster metaphors to describe his crusade, viewing himself as a Van Helsing seeking to destroy a Dracula-like pornographic evil. In an essay published in the *North American Review* in 1891, Comstock described "spicy stories" of sexuality as "vampire literature." Books that feature human sexuality, especially those that celebrate female sexuality, were in Comstock's view "devil seed-sowing" and "preying upon youth." Comstock saw "indecent" literature as a giant beast, referring to the "hydra-headed monster" of pornography.[72]

Woodhull received Comstock's attention for a number of stories in her newspaper *The Weekly* that exposed the sexual misdeeds of the powerful, including the Reverend Henry Ward Beecher's infamous affair with Elizabeth Tilton. Like "Young Goodman Brown," the gloomy Comstock could not believe that a woman who wrote of such things could be anything but a devil. Woodhull would be imprisoned, along with her sister Tennessee Claflin, for sending "indecent" materials through the mail. Woodhull would be portrayed in the press as a satanic monster tempting wives to leave their marriages for a life of "free love."[73]

The attack on Victoria Woodhull represented part of a larger conservative counterrevolution in the late nineteenth century. Comstock's crusade coincided with the first wave of legislative restrictions on abortion as well as efforts to limit access to improved contraceptive devices. Historian of medicine Andrea Tone notes that obscenity laws during this period increasingly limited access to information about birth control while preventing women (and men) from receiving contraceptive devices in the mails. Between 1866 and 1877 thirty states passed laws restricting abortions. The sensationalist press was filled with tales of the gory deaths of "fallen women" who attempted to procure abortions. The *National Police Gazette* freely traded on the monster metaphor for women who sought and provided abortions. One of the most infamous images the infamous paper ever produced shows a woman with a monstrous creature consuming her womb. A caption reads "The Female Abortionist."[74]

By the beginning of the new century, an obsession with controlling the bodies of women had become firmly embedded in state laws as well as established and defended by the threat of rhetorical and real violence. The world of "conservative society," as Victoria Woodhull described it, labeled monstrous anyone who stepped outside these gendered and racial parameters. A time of cultural fissures that promised to swallow older institutions beneath the ground became a time of reactionary violence. Anthony Comstock embodied a new kind of witch-hunter. In the newly dawning century, angry mobs became monster killers.[75]

"Wading in Blood"

Colonel John M. Chivington promised his soldiers in the summer of 1864 that they would "collect so many scalps" that they would be able to "wade in blood." Chivington targeted a band of Cheyenne and Arapaho Indians, all of whom believed that they lived under the protection of the white soldiers after their leader Black Kettle and six other representatives from the group went to meet with Colorado's Governor John Evans. They could not have been more wrong.

In the early dusk of November 28, 1864, Chivington led seven hundred soldiers along with four highly mobile "twelve pounder" cannons (known as "Napoleons") in a march on the large native encampment near a bend in the Sand Creek River in eastern Colorado. The Cheyenne and Arapaho had not even bothered to set a guard, so certainly did they believe in the government's good faith.

By the end of a terrible night of shooting, torture, and mutilation, most estimates are that one hundred and five Indian women and children and twenty-eight men had been killed. Most of the camp's men had been off hunting. A few successfully dug rifle pits and managed to kill nine of the soldiers and wound thirty-eight, although some of the wounds seem to have come from the poorly trained Colorado troops firing in the dark after drinking whisky on their ride to Sand Creek. Colonel Chivington made an official report in which he claimed he and his men killed four hundred and twenty-eight "warriors." Black Kettle, along with all the other Cheyenne and Arapaho chiefs who had signed a treaty for peace, lay dead among the victims.[76]

Chivington has been seen by many as the reason for the massacre, a sort of "bad apple" that acted largely on his own to initiate one of the bloodiest episodes of native genocide. His words and actions, however, simply embodied the white American view of native peoples as part of a land of monsters. Before the massacre, Chivington had been cheered as he gave speeches to crowds of settlers calling for the complete destruction of Indian peoples, including the murder of infants since "nits became lice."[77]

Dee Brown has described how the Indian in the American mind existed primarily as "the dark menace of the myths." In many respects little had changed since the Puritan wars of extermination against the "children of the devil" or the belief that the frontier hinterlands remained home to monsters that helped legitimize the savagery against native peoples during the colonies' struggle for independence from Britain.

The idea of the monstrous savagery of the American Indian fueled the imperial expansion into the West. Ideas of "monstrous races" that lived on the frontier continued to provide legitimacy for exploitation and conquest. Government policy tended to use paternalistic terms to describe relations to the "sovereign tribes." But on the popular level, the idea that Americans fought monsters that lived in the plains, deserts, and mountains remained a deeply held belief that kept support high for genocidal policies against the indigenous population.

In official pronouncements, such as Andrew Jackson's plan for "Indian removal" from Georgia and the Carolinas (1830), the government created something along the lines of South Africa's "homeland" system of apartheid. The dark reality of American Indian policy proved even more brutal. Jackson himself had come to power based, at least in part, on his reputation as a brutal commander in the Indian Wars he waged for control of Florida and Alabama. These new states, including Mississippi and Louisiana, gave slaveholders a "Cotton Kingdom," an empire for slavery. The annexation of Texas (1845) and the subsequent invasion of Mexico (1846–1848) added a new slaveholding state and allowed the United States to seize vast territories in the west. The expansion of slavery went hand in glove with the young nation's imperial policies toward native peoples.

We would not accurately portray the attitude of Americans toward the diverse ethnic groups of the west by simply saying they regarded these peoples as "inferior." Some, especially among the missionaries, clergy, and the reformist middle class spoke in these paternalistic terms. But the idea of monstrosity remained paramount in the way popular senti-ment regarded the American Indian. The wholesale massacre of native communities, and the ways in which contemporaries legitimized them, underscores how the concept of monstrous races guided and legitimized American expansionism long after the colonial period.[78]

In fact, on those few occasions that white Americans found them-selves tried for violence against Indian peoples, judges excluded the survi-vors of the attack from the proceedings. In Karl Jacoby's masterful account of the 1871 Camp Grant massacre, *Shadows at Dawn*, we learn that the presiding judge over the Arizona trial of the massacre's ringleaders refused to allow the Apache to serve as witnesses. Judge John Titus of Tucson noted in the 1873 trial that "the barbarous codes" of the American Indian made it absurd to give them a place in the white man's judicial system. Meanwhile, newspapers from Arizona to Colorado praised the murder of one hundred and fifty men, women, and children (many of the women raped moments before their death) by suggesting that the event repre-sented the "march of progress" against barbarism. They saw no need to place monster slayers on trial.[79]

They had little to fear. The men who led the massacre soon held elec-toral office in Tucson, welcoming the railroad (with some worries about how it might affect their control of mercantile business in the city) and being lionized in local newspapers in the fashion of boosters for economic growth everywhere. Their leadership led to the founding of the genealog-ical/ancestral group known as the Arizona Pioneers Historical Society that, exactly one hundred years after the massacre, in 1971, had essentially become the official keepers of the state record as the Arizona Historical Society. Local historians ignored or only briefly noted the "Camp Creek Affair" although its memory briefly reemerged, imagined as part of a noble struggle for white mastery, in 1885 when the guerrilla resistance leader known to most whites as Geronimo began what looked at first like an unending campaign against the United States military.

American cultural history has continued to tell lies about the genocide of indigenous peoples. The strangely written box office failure *Cowboys and Aliens* (2011) that combined science fiction, horror, and the Old West proves of interest only because it makes explicit what the hundreds of "cowboys and Indians" tales Hollywood has poured forth since the 1930s has encouraged viewers to believe. The indigenous peoples are, in fact, presented as "alien" in the historical narratives, the "invaders" who tried to break the gears of the engine of American capital's expansion.

They are the shadowy figures that might have prevented the creation of the modern Sunbelt.

The American myth has fully erased the imperial project that began with the slaughter of the Pequot and arguably ended with the 1890 Wounded Knee massacre in South Dakota. American history textbooks write of "American expansion" and, even more, "the opening of the west" with an air of inevitability. Most take the time to speak of genocide as a kind of tragedy without speaking the hard words so necessary to truth telling.

Horror film and fiction has portrayed the house built on "the old Indian burial ground" as a haunted site, a place of spectral power. The symbolic implications are transparent. The United States remains haunted, built on the bones of native women and men murdered to make the nation-state a reality.[80]

"Sweets for the Sweet"

Candyman built on the gothic visions of two hundred years of American history to create its story about white power and paternalism, a story in which the terror of America's racial history comes to life. The Cabrini Green housing project is surely meant to set the frightening tone for white audiences. Surrounded by "gangbangers" who sexually threaten Madsen's white character when she enters one of the buildings, it is covered in graffiti and steel mesh like some funky medieval fortress.

Cabrini Green functions in the film as the same gothic fortress that has been appearing in our nightmares since Horace Walpole. Full of secret passages and the threat of unmentionable acts of violence, it is the public housing project turned haunted house. During the course of the film, the audience learns that the tiny apartment building where Helen lives with her trendy academic husband was once part of the housing project that became Cabrini Green. Rebuilt for white yuppies, it functions as another kind of haunted house, one that has tried and failed to efface its gothic past. The entire American landscape, with its history of slavery, Jim Crow, and lynching, is Candyman country.

"Sweets for the Sweet" is a phrase that appears throughout the film. We learn that it is a phrase intimately connected to the folk homage given to the Candyman. The film never makes the meaning of this phrase explicit, though it clearly emerges out of the entwined symbolism of the romantic gift of chocolates and Candyman's brutal murder at the hands of sexually anxious white men. Slathered in honey and devoured by insects before he burns, he became a true candyman.

This twentieth-century film offers a near-perfect representation of America's historic racial obsessions. Postbellum America had a deep fascination with what was commonly called "miscegenation." A wave of legislation in the 1870s outlawed interracial marriage. White lynch mobs committed acts of inhumane atrocity against Black men, acts of violence that rivaled and surpassed the Candyman tale. Political rhetoric worried the American public incessantly with fears of "amalgamation." The desire to control white women's bodies, even in their most intimate activities, joined with racist folklore about the African American man and his sexual desires. The result could only be, and usually was, horrific violence.[81]

Theories of racial origins proliferated during this era, becoming part of the earliest debates over evolution and the new disciplines of anthropology. Popularized versions of ethnographic theory that claimed supremacy for the white race over other "mongrel races" accompanied discussions of human origins. During the same time period, what became known as the "freak show" attained enormous popularity in America's traveling carnivals, popularity it would retain well into the twentieth century. These shows presented bodily difference as a source of entertaining terror.

Americans became obsessed with the nature of the human body between 1870 and the Second World War. Where the body came from, how Black bodies differed from white bodies, and how women's bodies could be controlled all entered into the political, religious, and pop cultural discourse of the newly dawning century. These bodies under discussion, especially African American bodies, became the targets of violence. This is hardly surprising in a nation that believed in the nobility of its violent origins and that monsters must be purged by violence. Sweets for the sweet indeed.

3

WEIRD SCIENCE

If Poe were alive he wouldn't have to invent horror; horror would invent him.

—Richard Wright, late 1930s

No, I am not a spook like those who haunted Edgar Allan Poe; nor am I one of your Hollywood-movie ectoplasms . . . like the bodiless heads you see sometimes in circus sideshows.

—Ralph Ellison, *Invisible Man*

Lightning jaggedly rips the sky as thunder rumbles in the distance. A steady rain beats on the old stone tower. The air has a faint metallic taste. Chemical vats bubble. Massive Victorian machinery sizzles with electric power that surges through the Thing on the table. The first signs of life are barely noticeable. Hands move. Dead eyes flutter open. It is alive.

James Whale's 1931 *Frankenstein* and 1935 *Bride of Frankenstein* brought Mary Shelley's creature to life in a way that would shock audiences and haunt the American imagination. Whale's use of Shelley's vision confirmed what the young author herself had hoped. After the 1818 publication of *Frankenstein*, Shelley wrote that she "bid her hideous progeny to go forth and prosper." Prosper it did, and not only in Whale's hands. Dr. Frankenstein and his monster became perhaps the central metaphor of

Boris Karloff as
Frankenstein's monster

the last two centuries for anxieties over scientific modernity and the threat
it posed to the human experience. But, in an America built on racial and
class oppression, the monster that rebelled stood in for so much more.[1]

Mary Shelley sutured her creature together out of the ideas of
what has been called "a second scientific revolution," a period in which
Enlightenment-era experimentation explored the nature and origins of
life. In late eighteenth-century England, Erasmus Darwin made a series
of discoveries in chemistry, steam power, optics, and electricity. By the
early nineteenth century, interest in geology and the biological sciences
prepared the ground for Charles Darwin and the publication of *On the
Origin of Species* in 1859. Charles Darwin's paradigm-shifting classic
shows that scientific interest in the late nineteenth century turned to the
nature of the physical self, asking deeply philosophical questions about
the origin of the body and its relationship to the mind. Shelley became
aware of the early discussions of these ideas through her friendship with
the young physiologist William Lawrence.[2]

Lawrence was a devotee of the French anatomical school and especially Étienne Geoffroy Saint-Hilaire. Saint-Hilaire became one of the

founders of what became known as teratology, literally the "study of the monstrous." Interested in why nature at times produced abnormalities when, at other times, there seemed to be little variation, French anatomists like Saint-Hilaire and their English disciples collected malformed human fetuses and experimented with animal embryos in an effort to create "monstrous births" for further study.[3]

Mary Shelley's, and the French anatomical school's, interest in science and its monsters had an unfortunate analogue in the United States. In a deeply racist society, indeed one in which the very structures of power depended on racist folk beliefs to survive, scientific investigation took on a racial cast. In a context of massive violence against African American people in the years following Reconstruction, questions about human origins and human difference informed what became known as "scientific racism," though it is perhaps best understood as pseudo-scientific racism.

The idea that race was a scientifically definable concept had a long history by the time of the American Civil War. Englishman William Lawrence believed that experimentation with human breeding could lead to an evolutionary step forward. Southerner Josiah Nott had used medical theories about the origins of racial difference to argue for the superiority of the Anglo-Saxon peoples. The end of the Civil War came with assurances from some white theorists that African Americans would die out quickly without the paternal care of slave owners. Their view assumed the biological inferiority of the formerly enslaved.[4]

Although some observers thought alleged Black inferiority meant the disappearance of African Americans, the most common view among whites seemed to be that emancipation unleashed the African American male to become a violent, sexually rapacious monster. By the 1870s the idea of racial monsters dominated the white American media and haunted the white imagination. The image of the Black male as the "black beast" became the most common portrayal of African American men in sensationalist literature, political rhetoric, newspaper accounts of crime, and eventually film. This trend continued well into the twentieth century, even informing the earliest debates over evolution in the 1925 Scopes Monkey Trial.[5]

In popular culture, the monstrous found champions in carnival promoters who transformed human oddities into commercial exhibits. The freak show reached the height of its popularity in the early twentieth century, often working in tandem with racist concepts of white biological superiority and racial hierarchies. By the 1930s the monster had become a central part of popular entertainment in films and at the sideshow.

During this same period, true monsters were at work in America's hidden chambers and secret laboratories. The brutally racist assumptions of the years after the Civil War found expression in some of the most horrifying, and least known, events in American history. If the bodies of African American people could be imagined as monsters and brutally murdered like beasts, they could also become lab experiments. America, to paraphrase a comment made by civil rights activist Dick Gregory, became a mad scientist's laboratory.[6]

American historians generally do not see 1870 to the Second World War as a discrete era in national life. However, themes in cultural history explored in this chapter tie together the late nineteenth century, the Roaring Twenties, the Great Depression, and the Second World War. It was the era of Dr. Frankenstein.

"Angry Villagers"

In 1910 Edison Studios produced the first film version of *Frankenstein*. Focusing heavily on the emotional drama of the relationship between monster and creator, it provoked feelings of both terror and sympathy for the misshapen creature. The monster's makeup, wild hair, and patchwork clothing gave him some resemblance to a sideshow performer.[7]

Prior to 1910 the earliest "moving pictures" entertained their audiences with short set pieces called "the cinema of attractions." These short films recorded everything from natural disasters to tourist scenes to sexually suggestive tableaux. Many of these early short films first appeared in the context of carnivals, right beside the sideshow display of human "freaks." By the first years of the twentieth century, theaters became a fixture of urban areas and even small towns. The modern movie audience was born.[8]

Hangings and executions provided this new type of audience with part of its entertainment. In 1898 the American Mutoscope and Biograph Company distributed a film documenting the execution of an African American prisoner in Florida. This was not a singular event. The 1897 inaugural showing of the Edison Company's Vitascope in Dallas featured images billed as "a hanging scene" and a "lynching scene." Reenacted lynchings became common fare, most notably a 1904 production called "Avenging a Crime; or, Burned at the Stake."[9]

Contemporary moralists worry a great deal about the popularity of the "torture porn" genre, a now common description for films in the mode of Eli Roth's *Hostel* or the *Saw* franchise. But motion pictures that employ grisly themes of torture and death as entertainment are not at all new. Public executions filmed for public enjoyment functioned as the first horror films, bundling together pleasure and fright for all age groups. Of course, a crucial distinction existed between these films and the horror-film tradition. The cinema of attractions showed violence against actual human beings, real snuff films enjoyed by kids and adults alike.

In a study of lynching as a type of public spectacle, historian Amy Louise Wood notes that, since theater owners screened these short films in batches to audiences, racist caricature films shared the same bill as images of African Americans being lynched. Groupings of short films seen by early moviegoers included minstrel shows as well as depictions of African American people "stealing chickens, dancing and eating water-melon." Wood notes that these representations made Black men appear "ravenous and voracious" and thus "captured white fears of black sexuality but neutralized them by setting them in a comic setting."[10]

At the turn of the century, a public discourse about the African American man as monster existed at all levels of white society. Ministers, politicians, and other cultural leaders could be counted on for horrific images of the Black male as a horrific beast, utterly uncontrollable, and bent on rape and murder. United States senator Ben Tillman, in a speech defending the practice of lynching, referred to African American males as "a fiend, a wild beast, seeking whom he may devour." George T. Winston, president of the University of North Carolina, editorialized on the neces-sity of lynching to northern audiences using the language of Mary Shelley. "When a knock is heard at the door," he wrote, "the southern woman shudders with nameless horror. The black brute is lurking in the dark, a monstrous beast, crazed with lust. His ferocity is almost demoniacal."[11]

Some white apologists for lynching went beyond using monstrous imagery and created new monstrous mythologies. *The Negro a Beast,* a religious tome written by the Reverend Charles Carroll, offered a new interpretation of the creation accounts of the book of Genesis. In it, he imagined African Americans as literal monsters, allied with Satan from the beginning of human history. Drawing on centuries of racist folklore that gained new life in the age of scientific racism, Carroll described a creature that tempted Eve as an "ape-like being" who promised her a new form of sexuality. Interracial sex became the original sin in this account. By extension, all African American people descended from this original foul tempter.[12]

Racialized images of monsters with uncontrollable sexual desires appear not only in sermons and political speeches but also in major medi-cal journals. It seemed that when scientific thinkers were not measuring craniums, they were measuring sexual organs. In a 1903 issue of the respectable journal *Medicine*, a writer asserted that "the large size of the negro penis" gave African American men a monstrous desire that could not be satisfied by the women of their own race. These uncontrollable desires meant that "sexual madness and excess" were the "African birthright."[13]

By the early twentieth century, every area of authority in American life—medicine, religion and politics, and the press—told monster tales about African American people. The American public eagerly listened. Anxieties over the uncontrollable Black male resulted in one of the most terrifying periods of American history, in which African Americans were regularly assaulted and murdered by angry white mobs. Statistical studies have found that lynch mobs between the 1880s and 1960s murdered more than five thousand African American men, generally in the most grotesque ways imaginable. Frequently accused of rape, innocents became victims of the white image of the racial monster. These were not backwoods affairs perpetrated by "rednecks." The most likely locale was a small town with a degree of urbanization. The violent acts of torture and murder involved the entire community, including all social and economic classes.[14]

Only in the most explicit contemporary underground splatter films can most contemporary Americans see anything approaching the horrifying spectacle of a public lynching. The hanging and burning of African American men generally followed a ritual pattern that included brandings, mutilations, bizarre sexual violence, and the taking of body parts as souvenirs. A description of the Georgia lynching of Black farm laborer Sam Holt in 1899 notes that the crowd of over two thousand people "sent aloft yells of defiance and shouts of joy" as Holt's body burned on a pyre. Before the flames had been lit "the Negro was deprived of his ears, fingers and other portions of his body." After his death "the bones were crushed into small bits and even the tree upon which the wretch met his fate was . . . torn up and disposed of as souvenirs."[15]

The passage of time did little to alter the savagery of these horrors. As late as 1934, a murderous mob killed Claude Neal in Florida, first cutting off his penis and testicles and forcing him to consume them. Burned over and over again with hot pokers, Neale died only after being choked repeatedly by the mob. Locals photographed their victim's broken and mutilated body and sold the images in a downtown store for fifty cents each. A storeowner told an interviewer of a local man who displayed Neal's fingers with pride.[16]

This 1934 lynching occurred only three years after many of the participants would have seen Boris Karloff as Frankenstein's monster chased by an angry torch-bearing mob. The final frames of Whale's *Frankenstein* show the monster burned alive in a windmill, the angry villagers punishing him for the murder of an innocent white child. In 1935 Whale's *The Bride of Frankenstein* made even more prominent use of a lynch mob and the imagery associated with it. Foreign observers could not help but note the similarities between the American lynch mob and the torch-bearing peasants on screen. A British film critic commented that the film's final scene reminded him of nothing so much as a "Georgia Lynching."[17]

James Whale's *Frankenstein* was not the first feature film to employ this imagery. D. W. Griffith's 1915 *Birth of a Nation* presented audiences with a similar, though much more celebratory, representation of mob violence that borrowed directly from the story of Frankenstein. Gus, a former slave portrayed as attempting to rape a white woman, embodied the imagery of Frankenstein's monster, his large and ungainly figure shambling through the woods after a young girl and forcing her to leap to her death. This imagery reappeared in the 1931 *Frankenstein* and again in *Bride of Frankenstein*, the monster threatening little girls and respectable white women. The race-soaked imaginations of the American public brought their history of violence to these films even as Whale sought to engender sympathy for the monster and asked the audience to consider the danger of the mob.[18]

It is not uncommon to hear today that the monsters of the Universal Studios films, and their flagship fiend Frankenstein, are not especially frightening. This is a theme that made it into *Gods and Monsters*, the 1998 biopic of director James Whale, in which contemporary patrons at a bar smirk at a showing of *Bride of Frankenstein*, dismissing it as "not even scary." A number of theorists and film critics have noted the same. Jonathan Lake Crane denies the power of the classic monsters, writing that, today, "these once threatening creatures are for preadolescents who can't get past alert ticket vendors at R-Rated films."[19]

Perhaps the classic monsters do not seem especially frightening because they elicit sympathy rather than fear. We feel for Frankenstein's misunderstood monster and Lon Chaney Jr.'s Wolf Man, both cursed in certain respects. *The Creature from the Black Lagoon* seems less a monster than an intelligent fish literally out of water. But in the early part of the twentieth century, when whole communities believed they burned monsters at the stake, the monster's murder of a small child and his subsequent death at the hands of angry villagers could not have been read the same way. Inhuman creatures, even if they elicited some sympathy, had to be destroyed.

The mob lynched Frankenstein's monster at a time when violent acts against the bodies of men perceived as monsters had become entertainment, producing a bit of horror, a bit of excitement, and a strange kind of pleasure. As heirs to the generation that had marveled at, worried about, and attempted to kill sea serpents, Americans in the 1930s found Frankenstein a worthy successor.

If 1870–1930 saw a massive, violent assault against African American people, it also saw a fascination with human abnormality on display in the "freak" or "monster" show. As Americans passed through a series of social and cultural dislocations, society forced the freak to carry a weighty symbolic burden.

Freak Show

P. T. Barnum, who proudly asserted that "the titles 'humbug' and 'prince of humbug'" were "first attributed to me by myself," can be credited, or blamed, for making freak shows[20] popular in the United States in the antebellum era. In 1842 Barnum had premiered "The Fijee (Feejee) Mermaid," a taxidermy hybrid of a monkey and a large fish, advertised as having the traditional mythic body of a mermaid (including a nude female top half). Barnum admitted that he had tried to sell the public on "a questionable dead mermaid" but claimed that he had also given the American people "wonderful, instructive and amusing realities."[21]

Following the public revelation that his mermaid had been a hoax, an undeterred Barnum wrote to his friend Moses Kimball about the possibility of acquiring some other "monster" with which to entertain the public. Barnum would, in fact, exhibit some of the most famous freaks of the nineteenth century, including Chang and Eng, the conjoined twins from Thailand; Jo-Jo the Dog-Faced Boy from Russia, who had the rare disease hypertricosis or "werewolf syndrome"; and Tom Thumb, the famed midget.[22]

By the late nineteenth century, traveling circuses and carnivals regularly included a freak show. By the early twentieth century, the portrayal of human abnormalities replaced sea serpents as the most bankable public monsters. The Barnum and Bailey Circus, after P. T. Barnum's death, continued to showcase some of the most elaborate of these shows, promising patrons the "smallest people that live" and "the biggest man and woman on earth." A number of traveling carnivals offered customers a menagerie of monsters in which strange animals, human abnormalities, and foreign races with "strange rites and customs" appeared on display.

Frequently, these categories blended together in the minds of the showmen and certainly in the minds of circus-goers. Barnum and Bailey shows at the beginning of the twentieth century promised a "giantess gorilla" along with "fierce dahomy amazons." The same show offered viewers a complete catalog of what white American audiences would have considered exotic and monstrous, including "cannibals, idolaters, fireworshippers, hindoos, mohammedans, pagans, Confucians, heathens, Polynesians and other strange races."[23]

This list that mixed and mingled the categories of racial and religious otherness also included strange animals such as "giant oxes, dwarf cattle and a steer with three eyes, three nostrils and three horns." These "monster shows" thus explicitly racialized the concept of the monster, blending human abnormalities freely with deformed animals and "strange" racial identities.[24]

The exhibition of the racial other as a freak occurred in traveling shows other than Barnum and Bailey. Most circuses in this period featured a so-called ethnological congress, a gathering of races considered exotic (these were almost always African Americans and Hispanics theatrically represented as Eskimos, Polynesians, etc.). Along these lines, W. C. Coup's United Monster Show promised patrons a "Japanese Village Scene" that included "5 Japs." Audiences could see a "Japanese Dwarf" able to make jewelry for customers. In the same breath, Coup promoters promised a "talking dog." Such representations of foreignness as monstrosity became so common that even the highly popular Buffalo Bill's Wild West Show, though focused on the imagery of the American West, exhibited what promotional materials called "an oriental spectacle."[25]

Freak shows reached the height of their popularity in the early twentieth century, offering visions of oddity that encouraged viewers to read the abnormal as the "foreign." Sideshows frequently included "wild people," especially "wild children" presented as coming from a nonwestern context. Promoters advertised the microcephalic twins Elvira and Jenny Snow, who appeared in the film *Freaks*, to circus audiences as "Pip and Flip: Twins from the Yucatan." The twins had actually been born in Georgia. Promoters described nearly every African American freak and some of the "feral children" as having come from "the savage jungles of Africa" or some similar formulation.[26]

Female conjoined twins became especially popular on the sideshow circuit, perhaps because of the questions they raised about sexuality and sexual practice in a time of rapid social change. The "new woman" of the early twentieth century became a figure of great anxiety for conservative

America. Film images of women as "vamps" (often played by Greta Garbo or Theda Bara) emphasized the sexual voracity of the new woman. Many middle-class Americans who accepted Victorian sexual proprieties found in freak shows a free and open space where sexual inquiries could be explored. In this context of fantasy, the attractive conjoined twins known as "the Hilton Sisters" (who had sickened F. Scott Fitzgerald) became famous for their scandalous love affairs. They themselves circulated rumors about their sexually adventurous lives, including their ability to enjoy one another's orgasms.[27]

Married freaks also proved a powerful draw, probably because of the mystery of their sexual relationships. Al Tomaini, an eight-and-a-half-foot tall giant, became remarkably successful in the 1930s and 1940s touring with his wife, Jeanie "the half woman" (she had been born without any legs). Al and Jeanie represented themselves as "the World's strangest married couple" and toured independently with their own show. Perceillia "the monkey girl" and Emmet "the alligator man" launched a similarly successful tour as married freaks, a monster's romance.[28]

Such exhibits allowed customers to react in horror to what conservative, middle-class American culture viewed as the outcome of miscegenation and racial blending. Nativism, the idea of "America for real Americans only," reached pathological heights in the early twentieth century, with even President Theodore Roosevelt warning darkly that white Americans needed to "keep out races that do not assimilate rapidly with our own" and urging white parents to have as many children as possible to prevent "race suicide." By the 1920s a revivified Ku Klux Klan made Jews, Catholics, and other "foreigners" the targets of their terror tactics, as well as African Americans.[29]

Most pop science of the era asserted that monstrous beings, "freaks of nature," resulted from strange mixings, the flouting of natural parameters and boundaries. Freak shows described their goals as "moral and instructive" and they did instruct their patrons in the alleged dangers of racial amalgamation and sexual experimentation. White supremacy became the lesson learned. Even new immigrants, making up the majority of patrons at sideshow venues like Coney Island, could see in the outrageous image of the freak a true outsider. As scholar of the American sideshow Rachel Adams puts it, "the freak's extreme racial and geographic Otherness" provided these unwelcome new immigrants with "confirmation of their status as white Americans."[30]

The popularity of sideshow freakery reached its height during a national discussion about eugenics. A widely held philosophy in turn-of-the-century America, eugenics asserted that "racial hygiene" prevented congenital birth defects as well as the general "weakening" of the race. Eugenics drew on scientific racism as well as worries about racial suicide, finding supporters across the political and ideological spectrum. Criminality, abnormality, and "the degenerate races" came to be seen as the outcome of flawed "racial hygiene," usually imagined as a failure to keep the white race pure.[31]

Eugenics can be understood as an effort to prevent the production of monsters, pseudo-scientific racism's ultimate bid to enforce normalcy via industrial process. Wide support for these ideas led to a number of state laws in America that forced sterilization on women deemed congenitally unfit to bear children. By 1924 Virginia became the first state to create an involuntary sterilization law upheld by the Supreme Court. Over the next forty-four years, law enforcement, aided by welfare officials, sterilized sixty-five thousand Americans without their consent. It is important to note that eugenic practice, used as a powerful weapon of the state against poor whites, African Americans, and Native Americans, continued to be practiced in the United States long after its association with National Socialism in Germany.[32]

This context helps explain the reception of the 1933 film *Freaks*, Tod Browning's love letter to his own days in the carnival circuit that caused F. Scott Fitzgerald to lose his lunch and audiences to react with a mixture of disgust and horror. *Freaks* takes us behind the scenes of a small carnival where the wealthy midget Hans dotes on Cleopatra, a trapeze artist of normal size. Cleo and her lover Hercules (the strong man) seek to con Hans out of his money by having Cleo seduce, marry, and then slowly poison him. Cleo earns the hatred of the carnival community when, at a celebration of her wedding to Hans, she responds to the freak's ritual of welcome with disgust, calling her guests "filthy, slimy freaks!" When Hans falls ill and Cleo and Hercules' plot becomes clear, the freaks take a terrible revenge. The community murders Hercules and horribly mutilates Cleo, transforming her into a half-woman, half-chicken creature and placing her on display.

Audiences certainly did not turn away in disgust from *Freaks* because of its ghastly representations. American moviegoers could have seen more horrifying scenes whenever the carnival came to town. Instead, audience reactions can be explained by the film's dénouement. Popular audiences had become used to freaks as exhibits of the abnormal, warnings and portents about the need to preserve racial and sexual normality. *Freaks*, in contrast, stands up for its subjects. The narrative refuses to recognize "freakishness" as an abnormal state. Rather than assuming the age-old connections folklore made between evil and physical deformation, Browning turned the tables and asserted the moral perversity of "normals" when they deal with the freaks. Although the final act, the killing of Hercules and the torture of Cleo, enacts a moral revenge narrative not unfamiliar to American audiences, Browning showed them social vengeance in precisely the terms American audiences did not want to see. *Freaks* features the lynching of normals, the killing of a traditional masculine leading man, and the mutilation of a statuesque blonde who seemed a copy of every leading lady in every musical and romantic comedy MGM produced in this era. Audiences of the 1930s reacted to this as if one of today's torture porn directors took Sandra Bullock or Jennifer Aniston out of their usual rom-com contexts and subjected them to degradation and death.[33]

MGM tried to recoup its financial loss by selling away the film. *Freaks* survived through the 1940s and 1950s on the underground circuit, often billed along with exploitation and pornographic films of all kinds. Notably, a new coda was added during this underground period that twisted Browning's original vision into something unrecognizable. Calling the freaks "mistakes of nature," it praised modern science for "eliminating such blunders from the world."

If Americans did not want to produce monsters, or even see them when they were not being exhibited for entertainment, they certainly did not want to believe their ancestors had been monsters. In the dawning controversy over human origins, racialized folklore about monsters and monstrosity played a central role. More than just a battle between scientific progress and traditional religious faith, the Scopes trial became a discussion of the nature of race and the nature of monsters.

Scopes "Monster" Trial

The original cut of *Frankenstein* (now generally available in remastered prints of the film) featured a moment right after the creature comes to life in which actor Colin Clive's Dr. Frankenstein shouts in triumph, "now I know what it feels like to be God." In the 1931 theatrical release, sound editors purposefully dubbed over this statement with a peal of thunder. Universal Pictures executives felt that the line might antagonize religious leaders at a time when an impending divorce between science and religion had become irreconcilable and nasty.

The rise of religious fundamentalism in America began in the late nineteenth century with divisions within major Protestant denominations over how best to respond to the changing scientific worldview, a new understanding of the history of religion, and the application of textual criticism to the Christian scriptures. An emergent Protestant liberalism welcomed modernity in all its forms while a recalcitrant fundamentalism saw these innovations as attacks on the old time religion. By the 1920s these divisions led to open splits in many major Christian denominations in America and subsequent wars over the ownership of seminaries and publishing houses.[34]

The average American churchgoer, and certainly those outside the pews, likely found these debates too theologically abstract. Religious fundamentalism found a much more tangible issue in the Scopes Monkey Trial. The war between religion and science, and some of its implicit connotations about the nature of race, became a debate over monsters. For many Americans, Darwinian evolution became a monster story, a tale that broke down the social and cultural barriers they believed so essential to society. Supporters of antievolution laws drew on racial folklore and the heritage of scientific racism to challenge the notion of a common descent of humanity from other life forms.[35]

Weird racial science played a significant role in the intellectual life of nineteenth-century America. Racists who claimed a scientific basis for their ideology influenced the way white Americans thought about their relationship to the natural world throughout the nineteenth century. The so-called American School of anthropology assumed an enormous gulf between the "Saxon" race and inferior races. Louis Agassiz, whose professorship at Harvard and founding of the Harvard Museum of Comparative Zoology gave him enormous influence, never accepted the idea of a common descent of humanity. Until his death in 1873, Agassiz argued for the separate origin of the races and a racial hierarchy of intelligence and ability. Agassiz' taxonomy assumed the superiority of the white race while picturing the darker races as "monstrous races."[36]

Racist science linked brain size, ethnic origin, and criminality. An early scene in the 1931 film version of *Frankenstein* has Dr. Waldman (Dr. Frankenstein's former professor and mentor) giving a lecture about "normal" brains versus "criminal" brains. Pointing to specimens in glass vats on his lecture table, Waldman claims that there are physical differences between the brain of the normal and "inherently criminal." Such ideas (that entered the *Frankenstein* film through the production's scientific adviser) played an important role in scientific racism. The study of the human skull had become a significant part of the theory of racial hierarchies by the late nineteenth century. "Craniometry," or the study of skull size and shape as a method of determining racial characteristics, began to dominate both scholarly and popular writing about racial differences. Works such as William Z. Ripley's *The Races of Europe* contrasted and compared skull sizes of a variety of "racial types" and included photographs of specimens that purportedly allowed white readers to see their superiority for themselves.[37]

Racist science followed its own logic and assumed that differentiation in skull size matched observable differences in the capacity of the brain. In 1909 Edward Anthony Spitzka, a fellow at the New York College of Physicians and Surgeons, compared the brains of the "inferiorly equipped races" to the brains of the "higher races," a comparison he understood as similar to the way "the vacuous, stupid physiogomy of the dull witted individual differs from the bright, animated, forceful and energetic look in the face of the vigorous thinker and talented genius."[38]

American anthropology sought to represent the notions of scientific racism in the most public forums possible. Certainly the strangest and most outrageous example of this is the Bronx Zoo's 1904 display of a human being, a member of the Central African Batwa people named Ota Benga. The young man had been brought to the United States from Central Africa by Presbyterian missionary Samuel Verner for exhibition at the 1904 St. Louis World's Fair. Verner, financially insolvent, later left Benga with the director of the Bronx Zoo. At first allowed to wander about freely, Benga was eventually trapped by zookeepers in the zoo's "Monkey House."[39]

Rachel Adams, in her book *Sideshow America*, shows that zookeepers sought to present Benga as a "racial freak," advertising him as a cannibal and emphasizing his sharply pointed teeth. Seeking to highlight the African as an anthropological missing link, the zoo's director placed an orangutan named Dohong in the cage with Benga. Dohong had been trained to show "human" characteristics and could ride a bicycle and eat at a table. Zookeepers meanwhile urged Benga to charge at patrons and flash his sharp teeth. They scattered bones around the floor of the cage where the man and the ape lived. Adams puts it mildly when she writes that the Bronx Zoo used the exhibit to "suggest an evolutionary proximity between Africans and apes."[40]

The *New York Tribune* commented on the similarity of the freak show and the "anthropological exhibition" in the Bronx. Admitting that there was something "disagreeable" about Ota Benga being placed on display, the *Tribune* also noted that it had been common for "fat women, living skeletons and other eccentric human beings voluntarily to make 'museum freaks' of themselves, exhibited side by side with baby elephants and educated pigs." Of course, the *Tribune* ignored much when it used the word "voluntarily" to describe the similarities. Nevertheless, the author understood that the freak show and the exhibit shared some common characteristics. White middle-class notions of race found their way into both types of spectacles, as did American anxiety over preserving the privileges of class and racial status.[41]

Ota Benga was not the only racialized monster of science put on for public display during the Age of Frankenstein. On exhibit in New York City between 1860 and 1924 was Barnum's "What is it?"—a creature described as "the Most Marvelous Creature Living" that was either "a lower order of man or a higher order of monkey." In fact, "it" was a role played by several human beings from the 1840s into the twentieth century. Although the identity of the first two is unclear, the most famous was an African American man named William Johnson. Born in New Jersey, Johnson was the son of former slaves whose poverty likely induced them to turn him over to the traveling carnival in the 1860s. Johnson also traveled with Ringling Brothers Circus, where he had been known as "Zip the Pinhead."[42]

Barnum's promotional literature portrayed Johnson as an inhuman monster. Promoters dressed Johnson in heavy furs in an effort to create a "savage" appearance and insisted that he had been captured "in the jungles of Africa." New York City patrons who had seen both Ota Benga and Johnson's show had, in their own minds, already tied them into the scientific discourses of the day. Monsters in popular culture blended racist craniology, conceptions of racial brain size, pop Darwinism, and white anxieties about the "black beast."

African American leaders certainly realized that visitors to the Bronx Zoo linked Ota Benga to American racist iconography and responded to his captivity with outrage. Reverend Gordon, an African American minister who headed a New York orphanage, complained in a letter to the zoo, "You people are on top. We have got to rise. Why not let us and not impede us? Why shut up a boy in a cage with chimpanzees to show Negroes akin to apes?" African American leaders, especially the clergy, continued to express this sense of outrage, though the Bronx Zoo and its director William Hornaday remained recalcitrant.[43]

After almost two years of public outcry, Benga was released and taken into the care of some of the clergy who had protested his treatment. Benga committed suicide in 1916 when World War I prevented his planned return to the Congo. Editorials that followed his death tended to warn about the dangers of science when it investigates "backward races" rather than question the racist assumptions that had led to the tragedy. Benga died almost ten years before the Scopes Monkey Trial of 1925 became the first public skirmish in the struggle over the theory of evolution. This very public debate took place soon after a wave of antievolution statutes swept American states in the early 1920s. In Dayton, Tennessee, a small town in the mountainous eastern portion of the state, a biology teacher named John Scopes agreed to teach evolution in his classroom to provide the American Civil Liberties Union an opportunity to challenge antievolutionary laws in court.

The trial that followed, famously represented in the 1960 film *Inherit the Wind* as a struggle between modern rationalism and religious obscurantism, exposed deep divisions in America over a number of cultural and ideological issues. Historians have read the trial, and the spectacle it became, as everything from an emerging religious divide to a struggle for local autonomy.[44]

The concept of racial monstrosity played a significant and generally ignored role in how Americans responded to Scopes and to evolution more generally. The trial firmly cemented the conception of a link between apes and human beings in the American public consciousness. In a country where African American men had frequently been connected to savage apes, it was impossible that audiences would fail to connect the dots to form a crudely racist image. The ghost of Ota Benga haunted the proceedings.

Although religious objections to evolution remained paramount, antievolutionists understood, according to historian of the Scopes trial Jeffrey P. Moran, that believing in humanity's common ancestry promised to destroy the basis of white supremacy. The *Atlanta Constitution*, for example, editorialized that "racial miscegenation" was the only possible outcome of accepting evolutionary theory. Given the white supremacist desire to maintain boundaries between racial types, Darwin's theory threatened to break down those boundaries. The logic of evolution seemingly brought about the dreaded amalgamation so feared by most white Americans in the twenties.[45]

Antievolution forces, however, had no monopoly on the use of monster imagery in the fight. Conceptions of racial monstrosity inspired spokespeople on both sides of the debate. The controversial textbook used by John Scopes contained a taxonomy of "racial types" so beloved by scientific racism. William Hornaday, the influential director of the Bronx Zoo that had imprisoned Ota Benga, wrote during this period, "some sensitive minds shrink from the idea that man has 'descended'" from the apes. I never for a moment shared that feeling. I would rather descend from a clean, capable and bright minded genus of apes than from any unclean, ignorant and repulsive race."[46]

During the same period that the evolution controversy became a permanent part of American cultural life, a fear of "primitive races" and the horrors of racial amalgamation came to represent a significant theme in the work of H. P. Lovecraft. Lovecraft's tales of horror, written between the early 1920s and his death in 1937, became, as Phillip Schreffler puts it, "virtually synonymous with the weird tale." They also reflected deeply racist sentiments born of the paranoia that Anglo-Saxon civilization faced threat from "primitive civilizations."[47]

Lovecraft published some of the most influential stories of horror in American literature, primarily though the pulp magazine *Weird Tales*. Some of these are stand-alone narratives, written quickly to please his audience and receive a royalty check (including his 1922 "Herbert West— Reanimator," the basis for Stuart Gordon's "Re-Animator" films of the 1980s). Many of Lovecraft's later tales are more sophisticated and depend on creating what the author himself called "cosmic horror." Lovecraft imagined a cadre of powerful alien beings, known as "the Old Ones," who had once ruled the earth and now sleep in its dark places or enter our world from dark dimensions.

Lovecraft's horrors often center on human beings in the present who seek to use horrid rituals found in occult grimoire, like *The Necronomicon*, to raise transdimensional monsters from their cosmic sleep. Lovecraft usually pictured these rituals being performed by what he called "the dark peoples of the earth" and taking place either in foreign locations or American seaport cities with a population heavy with the immigrants the author himself personally detested. His heroes, on the other hand, tend to be bookish, bespectacled Anglo-Saxons of Puritan descent, New England Van Helsings who seek to destroy the foreign Draculas.

Lovecraft's "Call of Cthulhu" provides an example of this tendency. A New England scholar begins to fear that the ancient being Cthulhu has been awakened when Black "swamp-cult worshippers" near New Orleans and "degenerate Esquimax" in Greenland are found to be engaged in strange and exotic rituals. Those who take part in the dark occult rites are described as "half-castes and pariah" or "hybrid spawn." Human beings, at least of a "degenerate type," are some of Lovecraft's greatest monsters.[48]

Outside of his writing, Lovecraft frequently made clear his own conceptions of racial difference. During a brief residence in Brooklyn in the early twenties, Lovecraft spewed a torrent of racist venom at his correspondents. A visit to New York's Lower East Side led him to describe the immigrants he found there as "slithering and oozing in and on the filthy streets." He called New York itself "a scrofulous bastard city" and the immigrant communities there a "degenerate gelatinous fermentation."[49]

Given the melodramatic nature of these rants, it is difficult to know how seriously to take Lovecraft's comments on immigrants. Lovecraft had a strangely divided mind over such matters given that he lived in Brooklyn for a time because of his relatively brief marriage to Sonia Haft Greene, a Jewish editor, author, and entrepreneur. However we understand the undeniably great writer's personal prejudices, the idea of racial monstrosity certainly played a key role in his literary output, mirroring the connection between race and monstrosity in the broader American culture. Lovecraft himself claimed that his "The Horror at Red Hook" had been inspired by the "evil looking foreigners" he had seen in Brooklyn. White America largely shared Lovecraft's view of allegedly evil-looking foreigners. This was especially true in the wake of the post–World War I "Red Scare," a national hysteria that painted every Italian laborer or Jewish tailor as a bomb-throwing anarchist. The revivified Ku Klux Klan became an open and respectable organization in the 1920s, using their tactics of intimidation against immigrant communities as frequently as against African Americans. Lovecraft's fiction described horrors that many white Americans believed in firmly, the horror of "degenerate" outsiders.

The Scopes Monkey Trial suggested that two cultures had emerged in America but also that belief in monsters could be found on either side of the divide. Antievolutionists worried that Darwin's theory amalgamated them with monstrous races, while the more scientifically inclined assumed that the racially pure Anglo-Saxon had risen above the world of the monstrous. The terrors of both mind-sets are put in sharp relief in Lovecraft's tales of horrors from the earth, horrors evoked by the "hybrid spawn" of the degenerate. In the first half of the twentieth century, American monster stories became tales of forbidden interminglings, of sex, and of terror. Miscegenated monsters threatened the neat divisions on which middle-class American life depended, and anxiety over racial chaos grew out of interrelated anxieties over sexuality.

White Girls in Danger

The April 2008 issue of *Vogue* magazine featured only the third African American celebrity to appear on its cover since its founding in 1914. It was an appearance not without controversy. The photograph represented basketball star LeBron James unloosing a savage and ferocious cry, while

Top: LeBron James and Gisele. Cover of *Vogue* (April 2008)
Bottom: *King Kong* movie poster with Fay Wray

in his arms he grasps the white model Gisele, who pantomimes screaming terror (though with a smile). Obviously making use of the imagery of
King Kong and Fay Wray, the picture set off a firestorm of controversy
that reminded observers of the secret history of racial imagery in America
and its tendency to transform African American men into monsters with
white female victims.[50]

King Kong (1933) readily made use of white supremacist imagery,
tapping into centuries of white folklore about Africans and apes and the
alleged hypersexuality of Black men. Certain aspects of the narrative
remind us how often America's monstrous metaphors are uncomfortably
close to historical reality and the myths that shape it. The captured Kong
who dies in captivity shows a certain similarity to Ota Benga's story. Its
use of the symbolisms of African American men, sexual desire for white
women, and folklore about monster apes tapped into racist roots going
centuries deep in the American experience.[51]

The 1933 *King Kong* tells the story of a director, Carl Denhem, who
wants to shoot an adventure film on Skull Island off the coast of Africa.
He takes with him Anne Darrow, a willowy white waif played by Fay
Wray. On the island, Denhem and his film crew meet a vicious and possibly cannibalistic tribe that conforms to every colonialist stereotype of
African people. Like Lovecraft's cultists, Skull Islanders worship a giant,
monstrous being, an ape that Denham and his crew capture and take
to New York in chains as an ethnographic spectacle. Kong escapes and
whisks away Darrow, whose screams provide the soundtrack for much
of the rest of the film. The great black beast rampages through New York
until brought down in the unforgettable scene at the Empire State Building. In the final frame, Denham delivers the famous line "'Twas beauty
killed the beast." The uncontrollable, and twisted, desire of the creature
for a white woman became his downfall.[52]

At a time when the American public held the racialized images of the
Scopes Monkey Trial freshly in their minds, the story of King Kong carried
a clear racial subtext. Fay Wray reincarnated D. W. Griffith's unlucky
Flora, an endangered white woman not only chased but this time seized
by the monster. Screen audiences throughout much of the country would
have been used to hearing their politicians and preachers refer to African
American male criminals as "black beasts" and "black fiends" and insulted
as "ape-like" and "monkeyish." At the end of the day, as contemporary film
critic Jim Pinkerton points out, *King Kong* is the story of a "flat-nosed Black
being brought from Africa in chains" who attacks a white girl. Notably,
the 2005 Peter Jackson remake placed Skull Island in an undetermined

Pacific location and not in Africa in a clear attempt to tamp down the story's glaring racial symbolisms.[53]

King Kong was not the only monster film that reflected white America's tragic obsessions. Both of the classic Frankenstein films employ imagery in which the monster endangers white womanhood. In the original film, the monster comes upon a frail young girl throwing lilies into a pond. In his desire to play with her, the monster flings her into the water, killing her. The distraught father carries her in his arms to the town mayor in a scene reminiscent of Flora's father carrying her after her death at the hands of the "black monster" Gus in *Birth of a Nation*.[54]

Frankenstein does not simply rely on carefully coded messages. When the monster enters Elizabeth's bedroom and corners her, all we hear are her screams as the camera cuts away. When rescuers rush into her room, the monster has gone and she lies on the bed, moaning incoherently, her flimsy nightgown looking torn and disheveled. As historian Elizabeth Young notes, this scene is "framed precisely according to the imagery of interracial rape."[55]

In *Bride of Frankenstein*, the monster bends over yet another defenseless young girl to try to save her from drowning, an action perceived as a sexual violation by an angry lynch mob. Elizabeth Young points out that, in the film's famous final scene, even the monster's offer of affection to "the Bride" can be read as an encoded anxiety about sexual threat to a white woman. Young notes that "the Bride" is filmed glaringly white over against the discolored, almost muddy, image of the monster. She is, in fact, wearing the same gauzy robes as Elizabeth in the first film. Her fate (she dies by fire rather than give herself to the monster) again evokes Flora's in *Birth of a Nation*, suggesting that death is preferable to sexual violation by "a beast."[56]

These images reflected anxieties over changing mores in sexuality and gender as well as America's continuing obsession with racial difference. Social changes in American society early in the twentieth century created some of the anxiety over what was labeled "the new woman." Between 1880 and 1900 the number of women employed in the emerging industrial economy doubled. Although much of this new workforce entered traditionally female fields (such as nursing and domestic work), the rise of American business enterprises called forth an army of bookkeepers and stenographers just as the emergence of American retail demanded "shop girls." Conservative voices warned that such changes boded ill for American society, threatening the collapse of the family and encouraging sexual license for women.[57]

By the 1910s urban folklore circulated about "white slavery rings" operating in America's urban areas, kidnapping innocent Anglo-Saxon women fresh off the farm and debauching them in prostitution. Progressive reformers, churches, and even urban police chiefs gave this folklore the legitimacy of their authority and influence. Reformers insisted that by 1910 tens of thousands of women were being whisked away into forced prostitution, almost always by suave foreigners or "brutish" African American men. Books with titles like *Chicago's Black Traffic in White Girls* and *White Slave Hell* combined moral fervor with sensationalism. These lurid tales offered images of country girls gone bad and ignorant immigrant women taken in by vice. In a nod to America's sea monster tradition, *White Slave Hell* featured a drawing of "Vice" as a giant Lovecraftian creature, a "monster" whose "slimy tentacles drag in / the fairest forms to grace the dens of sin."[58]

Almost without fail, promoters of the "white slave trade" scare placed the blame on "the new immigrants." Beginning in the 1880s, an increasing number of immigrants from eastern and southern Europe began coming to American urban centers on the East Coast. After 1890 seventy percent of all new immigrants to the United States came from these regions of Europe, a sharp contrast to earlier waves of immigration from northern European countries. Americans of English and northern German backgrounds looked askance at these new immigrants, who shared few of their customs or religious ideas. A wave of nativistic thinking swept middle-class white Americans, who feared that traditional Anglo-Saxon values had come under assault.[59]

Social reformer Norine Law, in *Shame of a Great Nation*, described the new immigrants as invaders in American cities. "Our immigration has degenerated constantly," Law wrote, "to the poorest breeds of the eastern and southern sections of the [European] continent." Eastern European immigrants came in for special attention from writers who believed the cities had become dens of sin. Samuel Paynter Wilson described the immigrant section of Southside Chicago as a dingy place where "foreign taskmasters" held white American women in thrall whose "groans" (of pleasure or despair?) could be heard over "the discordant rasping sound of the rented pianos."[60]

In 1931 Universal Studios' first successful monster flick starred a foreigner who came from exactly the part of the world so often damned in anti-immigrant rhetoric. Tod Browning's *Dracula* told the story of an undead immigrant, a foreigner on a mission to entice and damn pure Anglo-Saxon womanhood. His offer, which they find more than a little appealing, is an eternal white slavery.

Dracula looked to be a flop rather than a film that would sink its fangs into the zeitgeist. Even casting proved a challenge. Browning originally wanted Lon Chaney Sr., early Hollywood's "Man of a Thousand Faces," to play the vampire. Chaney's early death did not automatically place the relatively unknown Bela Lugosi in the role. When finally given the opportunity to become the immortal count, he was offered a pittance of what some of the supporting actors received.[61]

A shaky beginning seemed an omen of the first responses the studio received to the film. Early critical appraisals damned it as immoral and worried about the effect it might have on the public. "The Author must have had a distorted mind . . . I cannot speak too strongly against the picture for children," opined one early viewer. Others worried about its influence on Americans already overwhelmed by the economic collapse of the 1930s. Reviewers wondered how Universal could bear to show the film's "insane horrible details" to moviegoers "already bowed by human misery." Even the head of the National PTA, Marjorie Ross Davis, entered the fray, insisting that the film would be harmful to children as well as, borrowing the language of eugenics, "the weak-minded."[62]

Warning signs from critics, and the fact that Universal seemed too embarrassed by the film to give it much advance publicity, should have quickly returned Dracula to his ancestral grave. Instead, the opposite happened. Runaway ticket sales made it the most popular film in early Depression America. Americans of all backgrounds lined up to see the foreign monster seduce virginal white womanhood. *Dracula* sold fifty thousand tickets in two days, an enormous haul for 1931. It became Universal's top-grossing feature, making more than a million dollars in a few years' time (at a time when many successful pictures made a quarter of that figure). The film, and the horror cycle that followed, kept the studio solvent throughout the difficult financial decade.[63]

Audience reception and understanding of any film is difficult, if not impossible, to determine. Few viewers would have, in their own minds, made the explicit links between the monster tales of the 1930s and their personal and collective anxieties about sexuality, gender, and the social order. However, as William Patrick Day puts it, stories of vampires are always stories of "sexual sensationalism." They are certainly beings both sexual and monstrous, their penetrating (!) fangs clear references to the animal world of cannibal consumption. Lugosi understood this and tapped into the erotic possibilities of the vampire. Audiences immediately responded to him with fervor. In a world of nervousness over flappers, worries about the disintegrating American family, coeds

Dracula takes a bite out of
Mina Harker

who attended college petting parties, and white slave rings, Dracula drank deeply from America's sexual anxieties.[64]

But the very popularity of narratives of sexual danger, specifically the danger posed to "white womanhood," shows the degree to which movies had become, by the 1930s, a powerful symbolic language that could mix fear with desire. They could, in fact, replicate elements of American society and history in the realm of the fantastic. The audiences in 1931 who watched Frankenstein's monster likely included some who had taken part in lynch mobs themselves. Audiences who saw the strangely accented Lugosi seduce young white girls may have been members of the Ku Klux Klan who feared foreign immigrants doing the same. Middle-class women, who keenly felt the strictures of patriarchal mores, could watch their onscreen counterparts become, in the words of literary scholar Clive Bloom, "corpse brides and demonic sex sirens."[65]

Obviously much of the audience simply sought escape from the Great Depression into fantasy worlds. This has been one of the most common interpretations of the popularity of monster movies in the 1930s. Most of the fare that audiences sought out has been termed escapist, offering Depression-era Americans a way to ignore harsh realities of the 1930s for a couple of hours through an absurdly sentimental musical, a violent gangster picture, or a monster story. Films that dealt in any way with the Depression itself turned out to be, not surprisingly, box office poison.

No matter how fantastic and unreal they may seem at a distance, the horrors of the monster films of the 1930s mirrored the realities of American history. They certainly reflected the psychological anxieties of their audiences, allowing viewers to dream in their waking life their own monstrous fears about race, gender, and sexuality. But the creatures on the screen were more than a metaphor in an America where communities lynched human beings believed to be monsters. The growing popularity of films that dealt with "mad science" reflected scenes from a dark American underworld that grew from centuries of racist fantasies given the patina of scientific legitimacy.

The House of Pain

If American film audiences in the 1930s and 1940s found the vampire creepy and sexually enticing, the mad scientists and the monsters they unleashed on the earth became their primary totemic fear. Andrew Tudor's statistical study of the themes of horror films reveals that only a minority of films during this era dealt with "supernatural, external threats." The overwhelming majority of movies during this classic age of horror imagined a threat created by a "mad scientist" whose moral presumption and lack of respect for human life creates monsters. Dr. Frankenstein represented the true terror.[66]

Frankenstein inaugurated this trend in filmmaking, and numerous films followed that showcased the same theme. In 1931 Paramount released a version of *Dr. Jekyll and Mr. Hyde* starring Fredric March as a scientist whose hubristic exploration of good and evil brings forth a monster. Mr. Hyde is an abomination that seems a living embodiment of the Freudian id. Bestial and barely human, he replicates the "sexual beast" that generations of white Americans had racialized. This time, science had brought him forth.

In 1932 Universal released *Murders in the Rue Morgue* starring Bela Lugosi, a film with content that owes more to nervousness over science and the Scopes trial than to the Poe story of the same name. Lugosi plays a mad scientist who shatters the barrier between the human and animal world. He is an evolutionist so eager to prove a kinship between men and apes that he comingles their blood, transforming the once pacific beast into a murderous creature. A similar theme haunts Paramount's 1933 *Island of Lost Souls*. The island's administrator, Dr. Moreau, experiments on humans and animals, blending them in distorted and disturbing ways. Vivisection takes place in a building the inhabitants call "the House of Pain" and brings about these transformations.

Nervousness over scientific knowledge is perfectly explicable in this era of American and world history. At least some of the supporters of eugenics backed away from the idea by the late 1930s since the thought of "breeding" human beings for perfection looked much like the racial theories emerging from fascism in the same era. World War II would see technology put fully into the service of the destruction of human life. Technology produced horrific weapons, while the Nazi doctors of the death camps became some of the world's best-known "research scientists."[67]

Most Americans at midcentury remained unaware that numerous American medical researchers had engaged in behavior different in degree, but not in quality, to the actions of the Nazi mad scientist Josef Mengele. Moreover, this had not occurred in isolated incidents but formed a significant part of medical research in the United States. Even more damning, given the country's history, racism frequently played a significant role in this story of American mad science as "houses of pain" emerged across the country.

Americans have some awareness of these horrors because of the Tuskegee experiments of the 1930s. Beginning in 1932 the U.S. Public Health Service conducted a series of experiments related to the treatment of syphilis. Drawing their subjects from poor, African American sharecroppers in Macon County, Alabama, researchers promised free medical treatment for the disease. But rather than providing treatment, physicians simply observed the progress of the disease and, after the sharecropper's death, used his body as an autopsy subject.[68]

Few would dispute that the Tuskegee experiments represent a living horror. But few also know of the widespread abuses of African Americans and the poor by the American medical establishment in the early decades of its professionalization. In her award-winning book *Medical Apartheid*, Harriet A. Washington documents a pattern of inhuman research in American medical history that rivals any horror film. Washington and other scholars have shown, for example, that disinterment of bodies from African American burial sites to use in experimentation became a common practice in antebellum America. Even more frightening, persistent legends among both Black people and poor whites of "body snatchers" or "night doctors" found confirmation in an 1886 Maryland case in which it was found that a woman had been murdered and her body sold to the Maryland School of Medicine for fifteen dollars.[69]

Washington's research uncovered numerous cases of the abuse of African Americans by the scientific establishment—much of it occurring between the 1930s and 1950s—that ranged from involuntary sterilization to willfully exposing subjects to disease. These actions are rooted in scientific racism and white racist folklore, two powerful threads in American life that have shaped culture, society, politics, and economics. These are part of the American system, the underside of American history.

So deeply embedded are such ideas that the unethical use of human test subjects did not end with the Second World War, despite the worldwide outrage with Nazi medical experiments in the death camps. In the 1950s and 1960s dermatologist Dr. Albert Kligman performed thousands of experiments on prisoners, the vast majority of them African American, at Philadelphia's Holmesburg Prison. The results of these experiments made the researcher a millionaire for his contributions to cosmetics and pharmaceuticals.[70]

A description of Kligman's research makes for horrific reading. In order to produce skin care products for pimply white teenagers and middle-class women obsessed with clear, blemish-free complexions, Kligman used forceps to remove large chunks of skin and fingernails from prisoners for testing. Washington describes the subject's backs as "so covered by flayed, discolored and scarred skin" that inmates at the prison could be identified by a "distinctive checkerboard" pattern on their flesh. They literally became something out of Clive Barker's terrifying short story "Books of Blood." Kligman revealed his own attitude toward the suffering of his test subjects when he described imagining the prison population as "acres of skin."[71]

By the 1960s Kligman had begun conducting research on his imprisoned subjects for the Central Intelligence Agency (CIA). Harriet Washington notes that the most dangerous experiments conducted by Kligman involved the administration of high-risk drugs to inmates as a part of a long-term CIA plan to produce "the perfect 'truth drug' for interrogating Soviet intelligence operatives."[72]

The work of Washington and other scholars to expose these real-world monstrosities underscores the fact that monstrous metaphors in American historical life have a way of becoming real, that they are intertwined with attitudes and social structures that make the monster possible. The tendency to view American monsters as primarily psychological archetypes ignores how closely they have reflected actual historical events and actual historical victims. A significant segment of America's history of science and medical research is a history of truly mad science. The monster seems more real than metaphorical for the thousands of victims of racist science.

Ignoring the monster when it becomes too real represents one way to deal with them. By the 1940s many Americans seemed to want to see a separation from the horrors on screen and the horrors of the "real world." Films of the 1930s tapped into a variety of anxieties over sexuality and gender, race, and science. By the 1940s monster films disappeared into a fairyland of unreality and juvenile humor. Films like *Frankenstein Meets the Wolf Man, House of Frankenstein,* and *House of Dracula* cashed in on the famous monster's celebrity in narratives with enjoyable, but thoroughly adolescent, plotlines.

Monster stories of the 1940s shared some very real similarities to the way Americans at home dealt with the Second World War more generally. Images of the war, even combat images, often sanitized the conflict. Author and veteran Paul Fussell has pointed out that although the instruments of death used in World War II tore and shattered bodies in horrifying ways, pictures of veterans unfailingly showed them whole and hale. Perhaps the "body horrors" of wolf men and reanimated body parts represented a "return of the repressed," stories about bodies deformed and shattered. More likely the monster stories of the 1940s became simplistic escapism, a denial of the truly monstrous.[73]

Almost no references to the Second World War made it into the horror films themselves. Horror historian David Skal has commented that Chaney's *Wolf Man* appears to be set in England in the 1940s, a place where, strangely, no one seems to know about the war but, in one of the film's famous lines, "everyone knows about werewolves." Only one film, a Lugosi picture made for Columbia long after the King of the Vampires' star had set, makes reference to the war. *Return of the Vampire,* one of the many awful films Lugosi made during this era, had a World War I–era vampire awakened just in time for World War II only to be reinterred by the German "London Blitz" of World War II in the final scene.[74]

By the late 1940s America had seemingly tired of monsters. The end of the war also saw the end of the classic Universal monster cycle after its long period in decline. The 1948 film *Abbott and Costello Meet Frankenstein* is often seen as the definitive end point for the golden age of the monster mash. Farce had replaced fear. But popular culture in the United States, as well as folklore and religion, soon found new kinds of monsters to dread, desire, and seek to destroy.

The United States emerged from the Second World War with a broad sense of optimism. Having suffered the fewest casualties of the major powers, its economy booming with heavy industry, America seemed poised to create an imperium. Veterans, at least those of the race and class favored by American society, came home to prosperity unheard of in their parents' wildest dreams. The atom bomb put enormous power into American hands, a power the U.S. government had shown itself willing to use against a battered Japan in 1945.

Portentous rumblings could be heard beneath the surface of this sunny landscape. President Harry Truman, heir of the enormously popular FDR, faced a challenge in the 1948 election from southern segregationists in his own party. The 1948 "Dixiecrat Revolt" made venomous use of race and represented a style of American politics that shaped the next sixty years of the country's history (and paved the way for the wholesale defection of southern Democrats into Republican ranks in the 1960s). A year later, American intelligence operatives discovered that the Soviet Union had exploded atomic weapons. Fear of communist infiltration helped make paranoia a successful political strategy for the leaders of both major American parties.

Popular culture in the next two decades mirrored real American anxieties over the Cold War, communist subversives at home, the changing nature of American adolescence, and the American family, as well as ongoing concerns about race relations. But in these pop culture mirrors, most Americans saw the world only as they wished to see it. Horror and science fiction became escapist in the worst sense of the word. The monster films of the 1950s in particular told tales that reflected certain aspects of real-world anxieties but that also urged viewers to forget their anxiety and to trust the military, political, and scientific establishment to chase the monsters away.

4

ALIEN INVASIONS

Someday something's coming / From way out beyond the stars / To kill us while we stand here / It will store our brains in mason jars.

—"Lovecraft in Brooklyn," The Mountain Goats

Legendary producer and director Howard Hawks' 1951 *The Thing from Another World* featured a group of American scientists and military men at an arctic station who discover a giant craft frozen in the tundra. An Air Force captain suggests to the team that perhaps the craft belonged to the Soviets since "they are all over the Pole, like flies." Attempting to extract the giant ship ends in its destruction, but the scientists and Air Force personnel manage to save a "Thing" trapped in a block of ice.

The escape of the Thing from its ice prison sets off a debate between Dr. Carrington and the Air Force officers. Carrington believes that the creature can be a "source of wisdom." Unfortunately, the Thing turns out to be a bloodsucking creature, an extraterrestrial Bela Lugosi that the Air Force men have to destroy (though not before it does violence to Dr. Carrington when he tries to communicate with it). After the Americans defeat the alien, a reporter uses the base radio to announce the perilous incident to all humanity: "Here at the top of the world a handful of American soldiers and civilians met the first invasion from another planet," he says. Triumphantly telling his listeners that the Thing has been destroyed,

The Thing from Another World poster

he ends with a warning. "Tell the world. Tell this to everybody, wherever they are. Watch the skies. Everywhere. Keep looking. Keep watching the skies."

America in the 1950s lived in the shadow of the atom bomb. After the Soviet Union developed and tested atomic weapons in 1949, the possibility of a nuclear exchange between the two superpowers seemed both likely and imminent. J. Robert Oppenheimer, the scientist behind the Manhattan Project who publicly lamented his part in creating such a weapon, described the two nuclear powers as "scorpions in a bottle" certain to "kill each other."[1]

Americans in the nuclear age tremulously watched the skies much as the final lines of *The Thing* had insisted. Most watched not for extraterrestrials but for the sudden flash of an atomic weapon, the signal to "duck and cover" if they were not (in the 1960s) one of the few families who built a private bomb shelter. Many convinced themselves, with plenty of help from government and military officials, that a nuclear exchange was survivable, a war in which America would likely even come out on top.[2]

American Cold War culture represented an age of anxiety. The anxiety was so severe that it sought relief in an insistent, assertive optimism.

Much of American popular culture aided this quest for apathetic security. The expanding white middle class sought to escape their worries in the burgeoning consumer culture. Driving on the new highway system in gigantic showboat cars to malls and shopping centers that accepted a new form of payment known as credit cards, white Americans could forget about Jim Crow, communism, and the possibility of Armageddon. At night in their suburban homes, television allowed middle-class families to enjoy light domestic comedies like *The Adventures of Ozzie and Harriet*, *Father Knows Best*, and *Leave It to Beaver*. Somnolently they watched representations of settled family life, stories where lost baseball gloves and dinnertime hijinks represented the only conflicts. In the glow of a new Zenith television, it became easy to believe that the American dream had been fully realized by the sacrifice and hard work of the war generation.[3]

American monsters in pop culture came to the aid of this great American sleep. Although a handful of science fiction films made explicit political messages that unsettled an apathetic America, the vast majority of "creature features" proffered parables of American righteousness and power. These narratives ended not with world apocalypse but with a full restoration of a secure, consumer-oriented status quo. Invaders in flying saucers, radioactive mutations, and giant creatures born of the atomic age wreaked havoc but soon faced their doom from brainy teams of civilian scientists in cooperation with the American military. These films encouraged a certain degree of paranoia but also offered quick and easy relief to this anxiety. Horror film scholar Andrew Tudor, after surveying the vast number of monsters raised and dispatched by science in the 1950s, concluded that such films did not so much teach Americans to "stop worrying and love the bomb" as to "keep worrying and love the state."[4]

America's monsters did not disappear despite the best efforts of conformist 1950s culture. Popular culture produced monster tales that sought to rob monsters of their power, but a growing underground folklore of urban legend warned the nation that the monster might threaten the safe world of midwestern farms or suburban neighborhoods. America's monstrous past even found its way into a post–World War II religious revival as communism and its agents became satanic monsters in the eyes of nervous Americans. And while millions of Americans turned to either to the Reverend Billy Graham or Bishop Fulton Sheen for spiritual succor, others sought out new religious movements that made monsters from beyond the stars into gods and explained the secret history of the world as a story of friendly alien invaders.[5]

Mutant Horrors

Post–World War II America put aside its interest in some of the monsters of yesteryear. The sideshow declined in popularity during the 1950s, as did the freak show that had been its central attraction. The freak shows of Coney Island, for example, closed down in the late 1940s as real estate developers sought to "clean up" area attractions. In 1947 the *New York World* noted that, "freaks still attract curious stragglers on Coney Island midway" but also predicted "hard times ahead" for "the Mule Face Boy" and "the Turtle Girl."[6]

Reformers used the rhetoric of "human dignity" against the sideshow during this era. The increasing medicalization of human abnormality led to the institutionalization of many of the people who would have once performed as freaks. A few found their way into the new monster movies of the 1950s. The 1953 classic *Invaders from Mars* featured eight-foot-six Max Palmer ("the world's tallest man") in an unconvincing green velour mutant costume.[7]

The sharp dip in the popularity of the sideshow freaks grew out of the desire of many Americans to escape the horrors of history in the aftermath of World War II by creating a safe and sanitized public culture. A number of historians have argued that adviser and diplomat George Kennan's notion of "containment" in relation to Soviet communism became a kind of metaphor for postwar culture as a whole. Conservative forces in American government, corporate culture, and religion sought to restrict access to impulses that would shock or produce discontent in American women and adolescents, as well as racial and sexual minorities. The whole culture sought to contain threats ranging from nuclear fallout to deadly microbes to, in popular folklore and popular culture, alien invasions.[8]

This did not mean that monsters disappeared from public life. Fascination with the gothic fears of freakery at the sideshow seems to have been displaced in postwar America by a fascination with the monstrous mutant in the movie theater. Atomic age fears of the dangers of radioactivity and nuclear fallout awakened the possibility of a silent, unbeatable horror—an odorless, tasteless, invisible death that could twist human bodies into horrible shapes.[9]

In February of 1956 the movie industry magazine *Boxoffice* described how "ever since the atomic explosions" the deadly possibilities of "mutations to animal life because of radioactive fallout" had caused a boom for science fiction films. While middle-class America seemingly had little desire to view freaks for entertainment (and certainly not to see them on the streets), science fiction fantasies about mutants, usually created by radiation, became a major box-office draw. In the years after World War II, American moviegoers saw the utter destruction of their major cities by fifty-foot women and giant insects, monstrous beings created by radiation or nuclear testing. American horror in the first years of the Cold War raised creatures from under the earth and sea, gigantic destructive creatures frequently called forth by scientists and government officials but almost always defeated by scientific know-how and the national security state.[10]

Fear of how the public would respond to the realities of radioactivity and fallout led to a massive disinformation campaign by the American government in the years after the Second World War. In the late 1940s, historian Paul Boyer points out, government civil defense plans sought to "downplay the danger of radiation in an atomic attack." Seeking to eliminate public fears about the dangers of fallout from atomic tests, official government educational pamphlets, such as *How to Survive an Atomic Bomb*, advised readers to ignore the "foolish stories" that they had heard of radiation's dangers and to "learn not to be afraid of those words 'radiation' and 'radioactivity.'"[11]

Efforts to dismiss fears of radioactivity quickly found their way into Hollywood films. In 1954 Japanese filmmaker Ishiro Honda's *Gojira* (Godzilla) used the Japanese *Kaiju* ("strange beast") tradition to tell a finely wrought tale of the dangers of the nuclear era. Using imagery borrowed directly from the atomic attacks on Hiroshima and Nagasaki, *Gojira* contained a number of highly politicized digs at the United States and its atomic policy. Atomic testing raises the monster, and it is destroyed not by more scientific/military wizardry but by the willingness of human beings to sacrifice themselves. A 1956 release of the film to American audiences chopped and slashed Honda's moving tale into unrecognizability. Using much of the footage from Honda's original, *Godzilla, King of the Monsters* (as the United States release was called) added an American reporter as a hero and sublimated the atomic theme.[12]

Survivors of America's use of atomic weapons proved a more powerful image than Godzilla. In 1955 the so-called Hiroshima Maidens, twenty-five young Japanese women who as children had been horribly burned and disfigured by the first atomic bomb, came to the United States to receive corrective surgery. A Hiroshima minister, himself a survivor of the attack, joined with *Saturday Review of Literature* editor Norman Cousins in an effort to transform their visit into an act of agitprop against nuclear weapons. Staying in host homes throughout New York City, the women received a significant degree of attention. The American government watched uneasily. Cold War historian Margot Henriksen notes that once-secret communiqués between Washington and American officials in Japan now reveal official concern over whether or not the Hiroshima Maidens represented communist agitation. Washington seemed to believe that anything that raised questions about American foreign policy emanated from Moscow.[13]

Gojira referenced not only Hiroshima and Nagasaki. Honda took the critique further by taking note of America's fondness for its growing nuclear arsenal and willingness to use alleged "testing" of these deadly weapons as part of what increasingly became known as "atomic diplomacy." In *Gojira* we first meet the radioactive monster when it attacks and destroys a Japanese fishing boat.

In 1954 few in Japan could have missed this as a reference to the recent test of a 15-megaton bomb near the Marshall Islands, a weapon estimated at one thousand times the destructive power of the device used against Hiroshima. A radioactive cloud drifted across three of the islands and sickened a generation of its inhabitants. Meanwhile, radioactive white ash fell like a poison blizzard on a Japanese fishing boat named the *Daigo Fukuryu Maru* or *Lucky Dragon*. All twenty-three members of the crew had advanced radiation sickness within days.[14]

The cut-and-paste editing of *Godzilla, King of the Monsters* did not entirely manage to excise all references to the atomic bomb, at least in terms of visual aesthetics. The burning rubble of Tokyo called to mind what Americans had learned about the destructive power of the weapon their government wielded in 1945. In a hospital scene retained from the original film, a doctor inspects one of the casualties with a Geiger counter, while the condition of the patients called to mind the immense suffering of those that survived the initial blast.

Hard as it is to conceive today, many Americans questioned the decision to drop the atom bomb in the months and years following the war, especially after journalist John Hersey's 1946 account of events became widely known. In response, the Truman administration and the larger national security state began what can only be called a campaign of misinformation about the bomb's necessity. For example, many Americans even today are convinced that an invasion of the Japanese home islands would have cost the United States hundreds of thousands of casualties (the numbers have fluctuated; some have claimed "one million"). Left out of this narrative has been the fact that the Soviet entrance into the war, much feared by the Japanese, likely would have prevented an invasion. The Japanese government had *already* offered to surrender as long as they could receive assurances that the emperor could maintain his position. Indeed, they hoped to surrender to the United States, believing they could get better terms from Truman than from Stalin. They may have been wrong. Truman continued to insist on "unconditional surrender." After two atomic weapons were dropped, the Imperial family was allowed to continue to hold its position anyway.[15]

The idea that Truman made the difficult but necessary choice to drop the bomb has, however, become embedded in American historical memory of World War II's conclusion. In fact, when the Smithsonian planned an exhibit for the anniversary of the dropping of the first bomb in 1995, conservative lobby groups became incensed when they learned that the museum would present differing viewpoints on the president's decision. Congressional conservatives took the unprecedented step of forbidding the Smithsonian to present any viewpoints that conflicted with a highly positive reading of the Hiroshima bombing. Given how the United States had criticized the Soviet Union during the Cold War for allowing its citizens to hear only a state-approved set of historical facts, this congressional crackdown on historical debate and discussion seems extraordinary.[16]

Since the first atomic weapons fell on Hiroshima and Nagasaki, the United States has continued its policy of using weapons of mass destruction to forward its foreign policy goals while working toward maintaining a monopoly of those weapons. Nuclear testing continued even after the deadly 1962 Cuban missile crisis; indeed, the United States would perform underground tests in Nevada as late as 1992. In December of 1964, North Vietnam signaled its willingness to open peace negotiations, an offer that Secretary of Defense Robert McNamara responded to with the assertion that the United States might use nuclear weapons in Vietnam and the beginning of chemical warfare and cluster bombs that, for a decade, decimated that country.[17]

Americans have not given up fetishizing weapons of mass destruction, and *Gojira* has continued his rampage across the world. No chemical weapons could be found in Iraq after the Bush administration premised its invasion of that country on their existence in 2004. The only biological agents of war Saddam Hussein ever had in his possession came from the United States in the 1980s when, after a meeting with special envoy Donald Rumsfeld in December of 1983 (he made a second friendly visit in 1984), the Reagan administration allowed the shipment of several strains of anthrax to the country for use in its war with Iran, America's nemesis since that country's 1976 revolution.[18]

After 9/11, new iterations of the Godzilla tale drifted far from the monster's roots in criticism of American foreign policy. Apocalypse became the plot in the years following the attack on the Twin Towers; Godzilla had become just another giant monster, a weaponized image of death that left ruined landscapes in its path with little to no screen time for the millions of deaths such a rampage might effect. The *Kaiju* of these films appears enormous, a bringer of apocalyptic destruction, and devoid of any meaning beyond a reenactment of incomprehensible destruction.

Americans should have had radioactive monsters on their minds. We now know Americans had more to fear from radiation than they ever realized. Secret tests by the U.S. government and major institutions of American medicine, not an all-out nuclear exchange, exposed thousands of American citizens to sickness and death. Between 1948 and 1952 the government released radioactive material on select American communities to "see how it moved." In almost the same period, doctors connected with Harvard Medical School and Massachusetts General Hospital fed small amounts of radioactive food to mentally disabled children in order to study its effects on human digestion and to determine whether they could develop an antidote for radiation sickness.[19]

Exposing developmentally disabled test subjects to dangerous radiation seemed perfectly reasonable to medical researchers in the postwar period. Strong cultural connections between mental and physical abnormality and the idea of the monster remained, even if the freak show had gone into decline. Mental retardation signaled both physical abnormality and social shame, an expendable class of Americans. In an era that fetishized normalcy, birth defects represented a kind of social death.[20]

Ironically, the health of children was very much on the minds of the "baby-boomer" parents who, between 1946 and 1964, brought seventy-nine million children into the world. Given the amount of cultural attention paid to the possibility of radiation creating mutant monsters, it is not surprising that the baby boom created its fair share of monster tales. Unfortunately for many Americans, these horror stories were real and affected tens of thousands of families and their children.

In 1962 a tranquilizer known as thalidomide had been advertised to expectant mothers as a "cure" for morning sickness (and as a general salve for anxiety). Soon afterward, the drug was discovered to act as a reagent for profound birth defects. Extreme craniofacial deformity became a common side effect, along with children born with stunted or missing limbs. A panic ensued. David J. Skal commented that tabloid newspapers "became actual sideshows" with photographs of "freakish" births and headlines like "New Thalidomide Monsters."[21]

Therapeutic abortion represented one humane option for dealing with this living horror, but state laws passed in the late nineteenth century made receiving a safe procedure next to impossible. In this context, Sherri Finkbine became the most public face of the thalidomide tragedy in America. Finkbine, the host of a local Phoenix, Arizona, version of the children's program *Romper Room*, took thalidomide during the first trimester of her pregnancy. Discovering the dangers of the drug and counseled by her doctor, she attempted, unsuccessfully, to obtain an abortion in the United States. Receiving numerous death threats, she and her husband traveled to Sweden to secure medical treatment. The fetus, remarked the attending physician, had no limbs or face and likely would have died at birth.[22]

Mutations seemed to threaten all the cornerstones of American domestic life. If they could live in the womb, they could certainly pay a visit to your neighborhood. The Love Canal tragedy, which unfolded over three decades, further underscored the dangers of scientific mutations. In the early twentieth century, William T. Love imagined a modern, industrial "dream community"—a utopia of middle-class American values and technological innovation in upstate New York. By the 1910s his dream had died, and in the 1920s corporations used the site to dump chemical and industrial waste, buried beneath the earth like the monster of a late-night drive-in feature. In 1958 the Hooker Chemical Company sold the waste site to the city of Love Canal for one dollar. The site became a thriving working-class community, though one with an unusual number of birth defects that became increasingly severe over time. By the late 1970s the Environmental Protection Agency (EPA) concluded that, for a twenty-five year period, eighty-two different kinds of chemical compounds (eleven of them carcinogenic) had leached up through the soil like creatures from the depths.[23]

The outcome of Love Canal seems like a monster tale. An official from the EPA who visited the community in 1979 found a landscape from a postapocalyptic nightmare. "Corroding waste disposal barrels," he wrote, "could be seen breaking up through the grounds of backyards. Trees and gardens were turning black and dying. . . . Puddles of noxious chemicals were pointed out to me in basements, others yet were on school playgrounds. Everywhere the air had a faint, choking smell. Children returned from play with burns on their hands."[24]

Americans had every reason to be afraid of monster mutations in the postwar era. Cultural fears can create strange refractions, a desire to deal with fear by transforming anxiety into desire. This combination of worry and fascination over the menace of mutation appears in the overwhelming popularity of the costumed heroes of Marvel Comics. Marvel's history stretched back to the 1930s when the small company had been known as Timely Comics. Marvel found a large audience during World War II when legendary artist Jack Kirby created Captain America, a super-soldier who fought Axis evil with his allies Sub-Mariner and the Human Torch. In the postwar period, Marvel published popular war comics as well as horror and sci-fi. Many of these titles dealt with the possibility of radiation creating mutated monsters.[25]

Marvel's line took a definitive turn in 1961 when editor Stan Lee and artist Jack Kirby created *The Fantastic Four*, a comic that turned human mutations into heroes. A scientific experiment gone wrong led to the transformation of the four, the soon-to-be heroes exposed to what Stan Lee called in his original synopsis of the story "cosmic rays." These unidentified rays granted all four special powers and changed one of them into a super-powered monster, which Lee called "the Thing" (obviously a riff on the 1951 film). Lee imagined Thing, though a member of the four and a hero, as so monstrous that his fellow superheroes worried that he might eventually lose control of his short temper and destroy humanity.[26]

The popularity of Marvel's new supergroup christened a remarkably creative era. Marvel artists collaborated to produce a lineup of costumed heroes that became icons of popular culture. Almost all of these are mutated human heroes, created from some kind of radioactivity. Peter Parker as Spider-Man premiered in August of 1962, transformed into a human arachnid after being bitten by a radioactive spider. Daredevil receives extraordinary powers after being blinded by radioactive sludge in an industrial accident. The X-Men, young people born with special powers, are actually referred to as mutants. Their strange abilities are seen by the larger society as a kind of birth defect, further proof that Marvel had channeled the nation's collective nightmares.

Given the nation's obsession with monsters, the Incredible Hulk represents the most interesting of Marvel's enduring creations. Lee has said that the possibility of a monster as a superhero triggered his idea for the Hulk (and he had done something very similar already with the Thing). The cover of the first issue featured a stylized subscript that read: "Is he man or monster or . . . is he both?"[27]

Appearing in the summer of 1962, the protagonist was a sympathetic scientist transformed into a monster when exposed to the fallout from a "gamma bomb" he had created. In Bruce Banner, Marvel created yet another scientific expert who raised a monster—and yet who remains a hero. The origin story clearly borrowed both from Frankenstein and Dr. Jekyll and Mr. Hyde, with the twist that the Hulk would be portrayed fighting a myriad of space invaders and evil mutants. Marvel created a monster that battled monsters.[28]

The Hulk corresponded with much of American public opinion's understanding of the terrible weapons developed, tested, and used by their own government and the scientific establishment. Science had created lethal weapons but, the public optimistically thought, such weapons would only be used against America's monstrous enemies. The monster could become an ally of the national security state.

Pod People

Invasion of the Body Snatchers, along with *The Thing*, represents the best of 1950s sci-fi fare, fully making use of very real American terrors. The story follows Dr. Miles Bennell, who finds his hometown of Santa Mira, California, in the midst of a "mass hysteria." His patients claim that their parents are not their parents and their friends are not their friends; they have become emotionless automatons. Dr. Bennell and his love interest Becky discover strange, suppurating vegetable pods all over town, pods that explode to infect, invade, and take over the minds and bodies of their neighbors. These enslaved human beings place more pods around town in an attempt to infect even more people.[29]

What are the origins of these invading body snatchers? Miles speculates, "it may be the result of atomic radiation on plant life or animal life. Some weird alien organism. A mutation of some kind." Later in the film, he goes further and suggests that Americans had opened the door to this invasion of apathy, the death of affect. Miles ruminates that, for a long time, he had been watching his patients allow "their humanity to drain away." Miles' reflection on the stilted, empty nature of American culture perfectly gels with his first diagnosis of the pod epidemic: "mass hysteria" and "delusion" caused by "what's going on in the world probably."

Invasion can also be read as a critique of Cold War–era paranoia about the supposed communist next door. Joseph McCarthy had, for a time, rallied enormous support for his crusade against an internal threat and convinced many Americans that their neighbors were not their neighbors. Beginning in 1950 the Wisconsin Republican made a series of increasingly outrageous claims about communist infiltration at the highest levels of society, an internal alien invasion that transformed even the State Department and the Pentagon into a frightening mass of

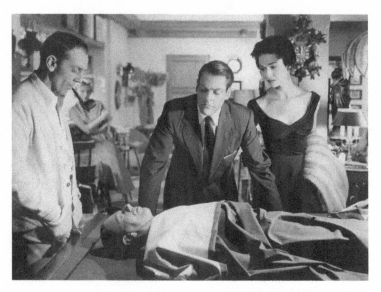

Scene from *Invasion of the Body Snatchers*

pod people. In the same year, Congress passed the McCarran Internal Security Act, which barred immigrants who had belonged to "Communist or Communist-front organizations" from entering the United States.[30]

Late in the 1950s, fear of communist infiltration of American society continued to stir paranoia. Two years after the release of *Invasion*, Federal Bureau of Investigation (FBI) director J. Edgar Hoover published *Masters of Deceit*, a handbook for hunting commie spies in America's own backyard. Sporting a picture of Hoover on the back cover talking on the telephone (as if he were, at that moment, dispatching FBI teams to deal with Russian saboteurs), the book urged its reader to "study your friends. . . . What problems interest them?" Close attention might reveal them as either communist spies or communist dupes. If they are "unemployed workers" or "trade union men" or "a member of a minority group" or even "a mother worried about sending her children to kindergarten," they might be a target, or even a source, of Soviet propaganda. If any of these groups (to which Hoover added "disaffected youth") used language like "restore the Bill of Rights" or "Peace" or "restore academic freedom" it was likely that they had fallen for communist deceit and become carriers of the communist contagion.[31]

Invasion of the Body Snatchers has also been read as less a metaphor for communist paranoia and more a critique of the stultifying conformism of the 1950s. The idea of one's friends, neighbors, and family members becoming emotionless drones seeking to escape into an "untroubled world" fit the fears of many Americans nervous about the degree of conformity created by postwar containment culture. Film critic Sara Hamilton, writing a review of *Invasion* for the *Los Angeles Examiner,* warned her readers that "you too may become a potted plant" and suggested that audiences pay attention to the film's subtext about yearnings for escape into a tranquilized state. Reviewer Jack Moffit, writing for *Hollywood Reporter,* suggested that the film seems "to be saying that modern man [*sic*], tired of facing the mental problems of our intricate age, is prone to welcome the irresponsible life of a human vegetable."[32]

In some respects, *Invasion* worked both as a critique of postwar American apathy and anticommunist paranoia. As American cold warriors worried that communists lurked behind every respectable-looking American face, most of the new middle class sought to become that respectable face, to embody the highly touted values of patriotism, optimism, conformity, and a studied normality. Margot Henriksen notes, in her massive study of Cold War American culture, "there was something unnerving and unnatural about the placidity of America during the 1950s." This placidity seems especially disconcerting given the mixed message of triumphalism and doom coming from official sources. Government-produced educational films described how American families should react in the midst of a nuclear Armageddon, giving precise safety instructions as if an apocalyptic war represented just another natural disaster. John Foster Dulles, Secretary of State to President Eisenhower, gave a number of public interviews in which he insisted that "brinkmanship," pushing the United States to the very edge of war in a high-risk game of international chicken, offered the best promise of peace. Dulles told *Life* magazine in the mid-1950s that "you have to take chances for peace, just as you take chances with war." This policy of inciting conflict in order to promote peace seemed to have provoked little public opposition at the time. Henriksen points out that perhaps "America's trance resulted as much from shock as from contentment."[33]

In the 1950s and much of the 1960s, American pop culture seemed constructed to secure middle-class contentment. Films like *The Thing* and *Invasion* tapped into the middle-class terror and paranoia just below the surface of its unearthly calm. But most of the material put out by Hollywood offered pure escapist fun combined with the message that the authorities had things firmly under control. These monster stories shared the same aesthetic as the government educational films of the same era. Soothing voices becoming suddenly stentorian and alarmed when describing "the Threat" and just as quickly modulated into more soothing tones promising that experts could contain the Threat, even if it could not be eliminated completely.[34]

The experts, in government, in the military, and in the scientific establishment, were in charge. The changing meaning of the mad scientist in the fifties creature features provides the best example of what many audiences hoped to find in their monster fantasies. Before the Second World War, science gone mad had been the prime culprit in the vast majority of monster features. Dr. Frankenstein raising his creature or Bela Lugosi wreaking murder and mayhem with bizarre medical experiments reflected fears of new technology and mirrored, sometimes almost exactly, the real-world horrors being perpetrated on unknowing test subjects. Filmmakers did not represent the madness of their scientists as utter, frothing lunacy but rather as a kind of theological madness, pride, and hubris toward the established cosmic order.

In the vast majority of creature features in the 1950s, the scientist appears as a highly sympathetic figure. While he (and it is always a he) may have unleashed a menace through efforts to better humanity, his scientific know-how, combined with a little help from allies in the military, puts the genie back in the bottle (or the test tube). Horror historian Andrew Tudor makes the point that, while horror films of the 1930s had their occult experts who could destroy the monster and sometimes stop the mad scientist, horror films in the 1950s actually placed the mad scientist in the role of the expert who battles and defeats the threat.[35]

The monsters of these films changed as well. Part of the fascination (and terror) of the 1930s and 1940s monsters came from their human shape. Bodies sutured together from the dead and shapeshifting men still walked like human beings. You would never know the vampire did not share our humanity until she showed her fangs. Even King Kong had strong human characteristics. This tendency to combine the human and the inhuman made the monsters terrifying while evoking more complex emotions of desire and sympathy.

The creatures of the atomic age bore little or no relationship to humanity. Films like *It Came from Beneath the Sea* (1955) and *Earth vs. the Spider* (1958) pitted the scientific-military establishment against giant, slithering creatures. The heavy of *The Beast with a Million Eyes* or *The Fiend Without a Face* evoked no human empathy at all. Creature features stressed the utter helplessness of humanity in the face of these atomic age threats. The scientific-military establishment became the only place to turn. Stephen Whitfield argues that the military and the FBI came to be seen as institutions above reproach in the 1950s, so much so that even Joseph McCarthy's popularity plummeted after he criticized World War II hero General Ralph Zwicker. Creature features reflected this attitude. *Invaders from Mars* intercut its alien invasion with stock footage of American jeeps, tanks, and other armored vehicles riding to the rescue to the strains of martial music, the GIs atop their motorized weaponry giving occasional fist pumps and thumbs up.[36]

An America that trusted Truman when he thanked God for weapons of mass destruction could easily see the American military as an infallible institution and the mad scientist as problem solver. Still, it would create a false picture of the era to suggest that Americans, even white, middle-class Americans, never questioned the words of the experts and relied solely on authoritative voices to tell them when all was well. A sense that perhaps the experts had no idea what they were doing informed at least a small segment of postwar American culture. A rather extraordinary moment occurs in *The Thing* when Dr. Carrington praises science as the best way to understand the world since, after all, science allowed humanity to "split the atom." "Yes," one of the Air Force men sarcastically replies, "and that sure made the world happy didn't it?" Given the degree to which the American public sought to repress the horrors of Hiroshima and the extent to which it responded to government entreaties to trust the bomb and the national security state, this brief jab at the consensus points to a deeper distress. Tales of the fantastic provided a safe forum to vent these minor challenges to the status quo.[37]

Dissent from the American consensus took many forms. While Beat poets expressed their rage or kept their ironic distance from mainstream American culture, others saw the world full of the monsters that the comforts of postwar America had supposedly banished. Some Americans began to worry that the terrible alien creatures threatening Earth at their local theater were something more than Hollywood monsters. Others suspected that not only were such creatures real but that the military had tried to keep their existence from the American public. A few even began to challenge the hegemonic worldview of science, suspecting that more monstrous creatures roamed the world than science had been willing to grant.

Little Green Men

Billy Ray Taylor had been visiting friends on the night of August 21, 1955, when the heat of Kentucky's late summer induced him to go outside and draw water from a hand pump. Taylor saw strange lights in the sky that he immediately identified to his friends, the Sutton family, as "flying saucers." An hour later, strange noises caused Taylor and Elmer "Lucky" Sutton to investigate, shotguns in hand. UFOologist Jerome Clark later described what they saw as a "three and a half foot tall being with an oversized head" with "big floppy pointed ears" dressed in a silvery, metallic garb, with claw-like hands raised in either greeting or threat.[38]

The sighting of what came to be known as the "Hopkinsville Goblins" shaped the formative narrative of the UFO tradition. Although only two witnesses claimed to see the creatures, elements of this story became determinative for much of the folklore about alien sightings, from the appearance of strange lights in the sky to the rural setting (and the stereotype of the local yokel who sees little green men). Alien invaders became the perfect monster for a society seeking containment from outside threats but uncertain if its boundaries could be guarded. But they also expressed wholly legitimate concerns about American institutions in the era of the Cold War and the national security state.

Extraterrestrial goblins in Kentucky were not the first visitors from another world reported by Americans watching the skies. Flying his private plane near Mount Rainier, Washington, in June of 1947, Idaho businessman Kenneth Arnold allegedly saw a bright flash (not unlike the flashes of atomic destruction Americans had been warned to look out for) and a series of circular craft. Arnold described these ships to a journalist as moving across the sky "like a saucer would if you skipped it across water." Referred to in a newspaper story as "flying saucers," the image became iconic in American culture. Notably, Arnold himself suspected the craft might be a secret government weapon and not an alien ship.[39]

The summer of 1947 could be called the summer of the flying saucers. Numerous newspaper stories reported on sightings that followed the general outline of the Arnold narrative. On July 7, UFO watchers in Roswell, New Mexico, added a new element to the developing mythos. They claimed to see a ship crash, and some insisted that the military had found and hidden the wreckage (and perhaps the aliens' corpses). Feeding speculation and folklore, military officials wrote a press release on July 8 that mentioned a "flying disc" as having been recovered. A later release clarified that the "wreckage" had been a weather balloon. Nevertheless, the Roswell sighting became the basis for stories about "Area 51" in Nevada, a military installation that supposedly hid the alien wreckage. The secrecy of Area 51 soon became a metonym for governmental cover-up in general.[40]

The alien visitation/invasion folklore that developed after the Second World War is, of course, perfectly explicable without resorting to extraterrestrial visitations as an explanation. Postwar anxiety about the bomb and its effects, as well as fear of the "masters of deceit" hiding behind the faces of friends and neighbors, fueled paranoid notions about alien visitors and government cover-ups. Popular culture in the late 1940s and 1950s sometimes represented paranoia as a virtue, a sign of knowing what is really going on. This was especially true in sci-fi monster tales where, in films like *Them!* and *The Beast from 20,000 Fathoms*, the first person to identify the threat is considered "paranoid" or "delusional" but is later shown as the only person who really knows what is going on.

Cultural theorist Fredric Jameson once called conspiracy theories "poor people's cognitive mapping." A more accurate description of postwar American conspiracy theory might be cognitive mapping for the confused and frightened. American studies scholar Peter Knight describes conspiracy theory in this period as less about "crackpot delusion" and more about "an everyday struggle to make sense of a rapidly changing world."[41]

Perhaps there was more to America's obsession with little green men than the need to make sense of a confusing world. Although explicable without resorting to literal monsters from the stars, Americans living in the 1940s and 1950s had good reasons to fear conspiracy. The United States government had, after all, made a fetish of disinformation during the Cold War. While there is no reason to believe the American military hid stories about flying saucers and alien autopsies, we know they buried plenty of other secrets from the American people. Beginning in the late '40s, postwar presidents of both political parties began taking unilateral military action without consultation with Congress or any real effort to determine public opinion. The CIA and the National Security Agency (NSA) moved quickly from their original mandate of intelligence gathering to operational activities, conducting secret wars on behalf of American interests around the globe. Later revelations about nuclear testing would reveal a pattern of lying and deception in the name of national security.[42]

The American government's own "culture of secrecy" facilitated rumors of government cover-ups in relation to extraterrestrial life. The Air Force investigated supposed UFO sightings through an official arm known as "Project Blue Book." The real motivation seems to have been to prevent larger questions from being asked by the public about the American military's secret activities. While not bothering to investigate incidents like the Hopkinsville encounter, Project Blue Book head Arthur Ruppelt described the program as having a special interest in any sightings in which the public expressed fear of heightened radiation levels. Cases such as these had to be debunked at a time when official government propaganda urged the American public to stop worrying about radioactivity.[43]

The uncertainties of the age included not only fears of nuclear apocalypse but also anxiety related to gender dynamics and sexuality. By the late 1950s and early 1960s, stories of monsters from the stars increasingly had less to do with national security and more to do with a more intimate kind of security. Private family life had frequently been pictured in postwar advertising as a combination of domestic bliss and consumption, where kindly patriarchs and happy housewives watched over at least two well-adjusted children. Social and cultural changes would threaten this image as the sexual revolution, the struggle for women's rights, and a new kind of American adolescence fomented conservative fears of a new sort of alien invasion.

Getting Probed

In July of 1952 a California maintenance mechanic named Truman Bethurum claimed an alien craft abducted him while he worked on a road project in the desert. Awakened in his tent in the middle of the night by "eight or ten small sized men," he was taken to their mothership and introduced to Aura Rhanes. Rhanes was the beautiful female captain of the alien's ship ("she was tops in shapeliness and beauty," he claimed). Apparently Bethurum spent too much time talking about his meeting with what he called the "Queen of women." Bethurum's soon to be ex-wife mentioned the mythical alien captain in her 1955 divorce petition.[44]

Bethurum represented only one of many flying saucer watchers who claimed to have been contacted, indeed kidnapped, by aliens in the postwar period. Numerous male contactees claimed their abduction included meeting at least one female alien whose beauty overwhelmed them. Increasingly, such fantasies took a pornographic turn. During the mid-1960s UFO researcher (and believer) John Keel eagerly collected stories from college students who, in the midst of the sexual revolution, claimed that alien visitors had raped them. A number of his male interviewees claimed that curious female aliens, both through invasive scientific procedures and in interspecies lovemaking, had extracted their sperm.[45]

Changes in America's sex life fueled many of these tales, changes that pointed to deeper structural shifts in American society. Popular television sitcoms may have pictured husband and wife sleeping like siblings in separate beds, but more happened under the covers than television would or could present. Two postwar books by sex researcher Alfred Kinsey, *Sexual Behavior in the Human Male* (1948) and *Sexual Behavior in the Human*

Female (1953), flew off the shelves. These books, though written in a dry academic style, assaulted traditional assumptions about women's sexual experience and the alleged dangers of extramarital intercourse. Clearly, Harriet wanted more from Ozzie (and sometimes was getting it).[46]

Adolescent experience changed as well with "the teenager" becoming a recognizable demographic pursued by advertisers, magazine publishers, record producers, and even automobile manufacturers. America's new service-oriented economy gave teenagers jobs and pocket money, granting them more independence than this demographic had ever had. This new world of "the teenage years" opened up a frontier of sexual possibilities as courting culture changed dramatically. In her book *From Front Porch to Back Seat*, cultural historian Beth L. Bailey shows that, while American teenagers probably had no more premarital intercourse in the 1950s and early 1960s than at earlier periods, other changes in American society left open the possibility that "the date" could transform into a sexual encounter. The privacy provided by the automobile and the new autonomy of time away from watchful parents inspired many a trip to inspiration point.[47]

Postwar conceptions of family life structured by a male as provider and a female as servicer carried over into postwar notions of sex and romance. The date became an economic exchange in which the purchase of a Coke and fries became fraught with sexual meaning. A male letter writer put this explicitly in a letter to *Seventeen* in which he insisted that "when a boy takes a girl out and spends $1.20 on her (like I did last night) he expects a little 'heavy petting' (which I didn't get)."[48]

Women attempting to navigate the new world of postwar dating often found that the predatory instinct of American misogyny remained firmly in place. Discussions of dating in magazines and guidebooks almost always suggested that women had to protect their sexual purity from men who would likely be unable to control their impulses. These attitudes had real-world consequences in institutional attitudes toward rape and sexual violence. In 1947 a female student at the University of Michigan found herself suspended along with her rapist.[49]

Some cultural arbiters expected and encouraged sexual aggression in young American males, essentially encouraging rape. Albert Ellis, a respected physician who held teaching positions at Rutgers and New York University, encouraged all manner of physical and sexual coercion in *Sex and the Single Man* (1963). Driven by the same "swinging bachelor" fantasies as Hugh Hefner's "Playboy Philosophy," Ellis urged his readers to turn petting sessions into wrestling matches for sexual dominance. "Get as much of her body bare as quickly as you can," he urged. "She frequently will accept the inevitable."[50]

Changes in sexual attitudes and cultural images of male sexual aggression found expression in American monster lore of all kinds. As descriptions of alien encounters became increasingly sexualized, pop culture images reflected this folklore. The 1957 poster for *Invasion of the Saucer Men* featured bug-eyed, cabbage-headed aliens grasping a young woman in their claws, her clothing ripped and disheveled. In the same year, Michael Landon had his first film role as the lead in *I Was a Teenage Werewolf*. Landon played a troubled teen (obviously channeling, or trying to channel, James Dean from *Rebel Without a Cause*) who receives psychiatric treatment for aggression. Hypnosis meant to rein in these impulses instead unleashes the beast. Landon transforms into a wolf in the school gymnasium and kills a young woman. The film barely hid the metaphor of teenage male hormones run wild. Promotional posters and still shots made it explicit with Landon in wolf form threatening scantily clad women who showed a mixture of terror and delight.

By the late 1960s the sexual revolution supposedly reached from college dorm rooms to suburban bedrooms. Most social historians today argue that this profound change in mores and attitudes is a complex phenomenon that did not emerge primarily because of "the pill" but rather from a variety of changes that occurred in postwar America. Indeed, some of the changes in sexual attitudes had roots that went back to the 1920s. Stories of sex with aliens were part of the societal process of coming to terms with these changes. Like other fantasies of sex with monsters, the otherworldly nature of intimate encounters with aliens offered an opportunity to talk, out loud and in public, about otherwise unmentionable topics. This conversation allowed for discussion of very real fears about gendered violence. Stories of rape by aliens registered larger fears about how social change restructured power dynamics between men and women.[51]

The growing influence of religion in postwar America factored into the country's monster obsessions as well as its attitudes toward sex. Religion in twentieth-century America informed how many believers viewed visitors from other worlds. Conventional religion worried that America had enough monsters to deal with in the form of the Soviet Union. Meanwhile, the boom in spirituality of the 1950s and 1960s sometimes transformed monsters into gods.

God Versus the Flying Saucers

Watching the skies in 1950s America often meant hoping and expecting divine intervention rather than fearfully waiting for things from another world. Scholars of American religion point to a dramatic increase in attendance, and membership, of churches and synagogues in postwar America. The year 1959 became the first of the decade in which a religious book did not top the best-seller list. God was in.[52]

Perhaps even more important than evidence of increased personal devotion, the public culture of the United States became more officially religious than ever before. This reflected a new religious interest on the part of the American people, though it received some impetus from the propaganda demands of the Cold War. In 1954 the desire to contrast American religiousness with "godless communism" motivated Congress to officially add "under God" to the Pledge of Allegiance. Senator Homer Ferguson, a Michigan Republican, urged the addition since, he claimed, "It highlights the fundamental difference between the free world and the Communist world." The decision to add "In God We Trust" to American coinage followed a similar logic.[53]

Communism became a special kind of monster in this context. Millions of American Christians believed that the Soviet Union represented not only a rival ideological system, but a diabolical monstrosity engineered by the devil. Billy Graham, increasingly listened to by Americans of diverse faith backgrounds, made the most frequent assertions of this supernatural threat. "My own theory of Communism," he declared in 1957, "is that it is master-minded by Satan . . . I think there is no other explanation for the tremendous gains of Communism." Speaking in the same year that the Soviet Union launched its Sputnik satellite, Graham insisted that such technological progress showed that "they [the Soviet Union] have supernatural power and wisdom and intelligence given to them."[54]

Graham became the foremost spokesman for the notion of communism as a "satanic religion," but other voices fully endorsed this view. It is important to recognize that, for Graham and other anticommunist leaders, this was not a metaphorical language about the nature of evil. Graham's rhetorical construction of communism should be seen in the context of his fundamentalist Christian background in which Satan and demonic forces are literal threats. Graham's assertion of communism as satanic meant that he believed that a powerful, sinister creature had moved against the United States in the form of a monstrous political system.

If a brooding hell beast stood behind communism, God becomes the ultimate monster killer. In fact, the 1952 film *Red Planet Mars* suggests that only by turning to God could human beings be saved from extraterrestrial threat. *Red Planet* exudes the 1950s mix of American nationalism and religious faith. An astronomer receives threatening messages from Mars that promise destruction for the human race. Only a worldwide religious revival that leads to the overthrow of communism in the Soviet Union saves earthlings from extraterrestrial destruction.

Religion also informed a more positive reading of extraterrestrial threats. Alien visitors for some became emissaries of the divine rather than monsters. This had been an element of UFO sightings from the beginning, especially among those who claimed direct contact with these otherworldly forces. What some Americans described as a highly sexualized experience became for others a religious vision with great significance for the world of the atomic age.

UFO religious visionaries during the Cold War era had some background in religious experience outside the American mainstream. One such guru of the space age, George Adamski, had formed a Buddhist religious sect he called the Royal Order of Tibet in the 1930s. By the time of the Second World War, Adamski ran a hamburger stand in Laguna Beach, California, and continued to give lectures on Eastern religious philosophy. In 1952 he became the first UFO contactee to claim the experience as a religious revelation.

Adamski had been sighting flying saucers since 1951 but claimed to have been first contacted by a visitor from another world in late 1952. Adamski quickly placed his experience into print as *Flying Saucers Have Landed*, a book that quickly went through three printings. In it, he claimed that aliens had warned him of an imminent nuclear holocaust and appointed him to share a message of love as the last hope of the human race.[55]

Imitators soon followed. Daniel Fry took a ride in a flying saucer with a creature known as A-lan, who brought a message of peace for warlike earthlings. In 1955 Orfeo Angelucci published *The Secret of the Saucers*, a mystical text of flying saucer religion. Angelucci's account told of "space brothers" who warned of a nuclear apocalypse coming in 1986 if humanity failed to practice the tenets of universal love.[56]

By the mid-1950s networks of contactees had developed through conventions and meetings in major cities. University of California, Berkeley, sociologist H. Taylor Burkner studied one such "flying saucer club" for several years. Made up primarily of the elderly, the membership included veterans of various alternative religious groups. Adherents to various UFO sects borrowed liberally from Christianity and Buddhism and generally viewed visitors from other worlds in messianic terms.[57]

Flying saucer religion remained popular through the 1970s with the best-selling *Chariots of the Gods?* In it, Swiss writer Erich von Daniken claimed that alien visitors came to earth in the early stages of human development. These "ancient astronauts" built the Egyptian pyramids and Stonehenge. Daniken suggested that all major religions emerged from these encounters and that human–alien sex had been responsible for an increase in human intelligence over time. Although never producing an organized religious movement, Daniken's theories gained wide circulation and provided the basis for a History Channel documentary as late as 2009.[58]

Mocked by a variety of critics, from conventional scientists to "young earth" creationists, the durability of Daniken's thesis remains surprising. Religious studies scholar Douglas E. Cowan describes this as "the von Daniken paradox." Lambasted from every side, Daniken's notions have informed popular science fiction narrative from the *Stargate SG-1* series to *Battlestar Galactica*.[59]

Ironically, the source for Daniken's claims of friendly visitors bearing gifts to humanity may lie in the darkest corners of America's monster tradition. Jason Colavito, a writer whose work focuses on debunking alternative archaeology, argues convincingly that a religious reading of flying saucers borrows directly from the stories of H. P. Lovecraft. Daniken's ancient aliens are not unlike the "Great Old Ones" that once ruled the earth and left behind artifacts of their existence. A crucial difference, which Colavito notes, is that the alien beings in Lovecraft's work are indifferent to the human race, indeed terrifying in their indifference. It is unimaginable to think of any of Lovecraft's creatures bringing a message of love and hope or giving humanity an evolutionary leg up.

Lovecraft's influence certainly appears in diluted form among the small religious movements spawned by the age of the alien. However, these groups owe much more to the cultural need to come to grips with the terrifying realities of the nuclear age meeting the often optimistic tenor of postwar American religious life. Benevolent aliens became a *deus ex machina* for Americans anxious about the holocaust their own nation's science and technology could unleash. Like many mainstream religious movements of the Cold War, a belief in alien visitors bearing gifts offered an escape from the myriad dangers and anxieties of postwar America.[60]

Alien visitation as messianic hope underscores once again the multivalence of monsters in America. The otherness of the monster can embody the sum of all fears but also an escape from fear. In the age of the Cold War, the shadow of the bomb represented the most terrible monster imaginable, while rapid social change accelerated the speed of history. Friendly monsters in flying ships offered an escape from history.

Flying saucer cults did more than offer a comforting message, however. They may have offered some adherents a way to experience the frightening power of the sacred at a time when religious faith had become domesticated by America's Christian mainstream. American civic religiousness failed to satisfy the human yearning for transcendence. While most Americans who felt this may have been attracted to the more recognizable horrors of Christian fundamentalism and its tales of monstrous demonic beings (and a somewhat monstrous God), others turned to monsters from outer space, searching for the frisson of divine terror unavailable from the warm and fuzzy world of mainstream American religion.

The postwar religious revival failed to contain American terror of the atomic age. Although America's postwar years look from the outside like an age of consensus, they actually represented a moment of cultural splintering. By the late 1960s loss of faith in American government ignited countercultural protest. A similar distrust in American religious institutions resulted in both the gathering strength of Christian fundamentalism and a growing secular critique of religion's claims. White Americans, in the South and later in the urban North, resisted the African American freedom struggle's claims, often with violence. America seemed, once again, a society cleaved in parts by inherent tensions.

In 1958, on the edge of this cultural precipice, a young logger walked out of the woods and into the offices of the *Humboldt Times* of Eureka, California, carrying a plaster cast of a giant footprint.

Attack of the Cryptids

Jerry Crew worked the logging trails necessary for the building of northern California's Trinity Dam in the hot summer of 1958 when he and his fellow loggers started seeing the unexplained tracks. Minor vandalism of machinery and outsized prints worried some that large bears wandered the vicinity, angry that their habitat had been disturbed. Crew pointed out to his fellow loggers that the lack of claw prints meant that the creature stalking the camp could not have been a bear. Moreover, several of his coworkers claimed that they had seen a hairy creature with long arms run across the road in front of their trucks.

Sightings of mysterious woodland creatures were certainly not a new American phenomenon in the fifties. In the early twentieth century, hunters on the Santa Barbara Channel Islands off the coast of Washington State had sighted, and supposedly captured, a "wild girl" who lived on the island in a cave full of animal bones. During the same period, Canadian Albert Osterman claimed to have been held captive by a family of "ape-like" people near Vancouver Island.[61]

None of these incidents garnered the attention of the 1958 sightings, perhaps because Crew claimed to have empirical evidence in the form of a plaster cast of the creature's footprint. Crew's cast of "Bigfoot's" big foot became the trigger for an explosion of media interest. Not even the fascination with the sea serpent compared to the media storm that made Bigfoot into one of America's most well-known monsters. The sightings in the Pacific Northwest intersected with the worlds of 1950s advertising, entrepreneurism, and the desire for alternative spiritualties. Bigfoot as a popular culture phenomenon was born. The *Humboldt Times* of Eureka, California, happily put a photograph of Crew holding the cast on the front page of their October 5th edition, the strange image and the story of the "mystery in the mountains" providing a distraction for readers from other stories of the day, including the NAACP's struggle to implement *Brown v. Board of Education* and Eisenhower blasting critics of America's foreign policy.[62]

The story proved to have legs as well as giant feet and attracted the attention of a little-known subculture of monster hunters. The story hit Ivan Sanderson, a trained zoologist, like a lightning bolt. Sanderson's career had always displayed a taste for the strange and exotic combined with a penchant for showmanship. Successful nature books in the late 1930s had made him well known, and his interest in "unexplained phenomena" led to his being a frequent guest on both radio and, later, television.

Sanderson's interest in "unexplained animals" went back to his student days. Walking the line between popularizing science and Barnumesque showmanship, Sanderson made it his goal to create a new field of study that involved "the collection and examination of evidence for the existence of any creatures as yet unknown to and unidentified by zoologists."[63]

Sanderson pursued a strange path first cut by the amateur naturalist and failed novelist Charles Fort. In the 1920s Fort mounted a full-throated assault on scientific positivism. His *Book of the Damned* (by damned he meant "facts excluded a priori by science") examined the question of sea serpents, strange climatic conditions, and unexplained wonders in the sky.

Fort mastered a writing style that seemed skeptical and hard-nosed about strange phenomena while also poking at the scientific establishment for its allegedly hidebound notions of truth. His writings are so influential among those interested in unexplained phenomena that "Forteanism" has found expression in quasi-academic associations and popular magazines.[64]

Sanderson saw in Fort's writings a mirror of his own interests and worldview. By the early 1950s Sanderson used the Fortean approach to stake out a claim as a paranormal expert. He had also become a close friend and frequent correspondent with Bernard Heuvelmans, a French zoologist whose 1955 *On the Track of Unknown Animals* became a kind of bible for cryptozoological investigators. Both men served as advisers to Tom Slick, a multimillionaire who made his fortune in the Texas oil boom. Slick had used his fortune in the late 1950s to fund expeditions to the Himalayas in search of "the Yeti," better known as "the Abominable Snowman" (a creature that both Heuvelmans and Sanderson wrote about at length). Slick provided the funds for the first "Bigfoot expedition" in Humboldt County in the fall of 1959.

Slick's expedition caught the imagination of the public. In December, Sanderson published an article in *True*, a popular men's magazine that featured pseudo-journalism and adventure stories, entitled "The Strange Story of America's Abominable Snowman." Bigfoot mania exploded. By 1960 several more expeditions, a Hollywood production company, and even some alternative religious groups made the pilgrimage to Humboldt County. Teams of monster hunters and their yapping dogs filled the Bluff Creek area. The uproar in northern California lasted for close to two years, with funding for Bigfoot research drying up after Slick's death in 1962.[65]

Bigfoot quickly became America's most famous "hidden animal." Interest in his existence tended to blend into fascination with UFOs, sea or lake monsters, and various other cryptids. Sanderson formed "The Society for the Unexplained" in 1965, an organization that focused on unexplained creatures and phenomena of all kinds. In 1967 he wrote a book called *Uninvited Visitors*, which examined UFO sightings. Meanwhile his colleague, Bernard Heuvelmans, published *In the Wake of Sea Serpents*, which called on the scientific community to embark on a new hunt for the creature he insisted had "finished its wandering among the monsters of mythology and returned to the fold of zoology."[66]

These monster hunters represent a profound shift in American cultural attitudes toward science. The late 1950s and early 1960s witnessed a growing cynicism about the scientific worldview and introduced new discourses about the unreliability of science as the final arbiter of significant questions. Belief in cryptids, and in the individuals who publicized them, offered the public an alternative vision of scientific knowledge. At its heart, the cryptid obsession provided a counternarrative to the idea that scientific experts connected to major universities and funded by the government had rationalized the world.

The birth of modern creationism in the post–World War II era represents another strand of this phenomenon. Proponents of so-called scientific creationism rely heavily on the claim that mainstream science exerts excessive control over the basis for knowledge of the world. Creationists make, in essence, the same argument as Charles Fort, that science represents a system of control based on circular assumptions that exclude certain facts a priori. Recent efforts by proponents of creationism (and of its new incarnation as the "Intelligent Design" movement) assert similar claims when they argue that creationism should be taught alongside evolutionary biology so that by "teaching the controversy" the classroom can become a democracy of ideas.[67]

Mainstream science has responded to the claims of monster hunters and creationists much as it did to sea serpent mania. Data never collected and irreproducible can never be analyzed and thus never refuted or proven. Until empirical evidence for Bigfoot or an omnipotent creator deity turns up, such questions are not scientific questions at all. For many Americans then and now, these assertions proved unsatisfying and were perhaps even evidence of the inherent limitations of science. This has had catastrophic effects in the willingness of even political leaders to reject the overwhelming scientific evidence for climate change, one of if not the most serious threat to a human future.

The cryptid hunters themselves became living counter-symbols to the increasingly untrustworthy men in white lab coats. Many of them seemed to embody the explorer and amateur zoologist of an earlier era, setting off on expeditions/safaris that were the stuff of men's adventure magazines. Ivan Sanderson's first claim to fame had been a book about his adventures in Africa. Tom Slick had a photograph of himself taken after his Himalayan Yeti expedition that made him look every inch the gentleman adventurer. Peter Byrne, a cryptid hunter funded by Slick in the late 1950s, was described as looking as if he had "stepped out of a comic strip . . . in safari clothes, replete with ascot and bush hat." A character straight out of central casting, Byrne had been a big-game hunter before he began hunting monsters.[68]

The cryptid hunters seemed more Indiana Jones than Dr. Strangelove. These adventurers searching for the unexplained became a way for many Americans to express faith in science as an investigative system while also doubting the scientific establishment and its authority. Rather than cooking up monstrous creations in test tubes, these were men of science who explored the hidden parts of the earth and brought back tales of wonder. This image suited Americans who had begun to have doubts about the world science had brought them.[69]

The cryptid mania of the 1950s and 1960s reflected changes in the images of science in American pop culture. A number of scholars looking at horror films from this same era have noted that the role of the "expert" begins to change in significant ways during this period. If the 1930s had been the apogee of the mad scientist and the 1950s the age of the heroic professional who makes use of science to defeat scientific threats, the 1960s fully embraced the idea of science out of control. Rather than a rebirth of "the mad scientist," this seems to be the birth of "mad science," chaotic forces outside the control of human agency.[70]

The American tradition of horror began to change in the new decade. By the 1960s alien invaders and mutant monsters departed the film screen and popular consciousness as quickly as they had appeared. Many younger Americans, adolescents, and teens, had already stopped watching the skies during the 1950s. Boomer kids began searching out monsters that came from the tomb (or that lived next door) rather than from Mars, rediscovering the creatures that had frightened their grandparents and finding new horrors in old dark places. America was about to go goth all over again.

Night Falls on the Endless Summer

In 1954 thousands of adolescents in the Los Angeles area cajoled their guardians into letting them stay up after 11:00 p.m. If dubious parents could be convinced, boomer kids could watch, as if hypnotized, a visitor from another world. This was no alien from another planet or multieyed mutant menace, but rather an emissary from the world of gothic past and the future of horror to come. Amid the flying saucers, giant bugs, and false optimism of the 1950s, Vampira struck a sexy, discordant note.

Maila Nurmi became Vampira. Nurmi had worked as an actor and model and had been offered the opportunity to host a block of late-night horror films for Los Angeles station KABC-TV. Dressed in a black rayon cocktail dress, with black nails and arched black eyebrows, Vampira dripped scary and inviting sensuality. Horror historian David Skal remembers her as a being with an "impossible waist-line" and "the cartoon bosom of a sex goddess," who appeared out of the dry-ice mist to the sound of eerie organ music and introduced the children of the atom to a night of 1930s horror.[71]

Nurmi drew on an underground 1950s subculture little known to most Americans. In all likelihood, parents would have locked the television away if they had known that Nurmi took her inspiration not only from the evil queen of Disney's *Snow White* but also from an S&M magazine known as *Bizarre*. Campy and knowing, Vampira represented a cultural pastiche of American dreams and nightmares, Disney and bondage, the vampire and the vamp.

Beloved by adolescents, Vampira struck out with parents who found her simply too shocking. Although she appeared in a four-page photo shoot in *Life*, anxious TV execs cancelled the show after a wild eight-month run. Nevertheless, in that short time, Nurmi had created a cultural icon that reanimated periodically as Morticia Addams, Elvira the horror host, and Vampirella the sexy comic book vampire. America in 1954 was just not ready yet.

Nurmi had drawn Vampira from the dark well of late twentieth-century American culture. At a time when it seemed that flying saucers had brought the monsters destined to take over the world, she heralded the return of a gothic sensibility that never entirely disappeared. Throughout the 1950s, some of the same kids that stayed up late watching Vampira enjoyed the horrific thrills of EC comics and their popular "Tales from the Crypt" series. In the final years of the decade, Vincent Price appeared in

Vampira

enormously successful Poe adaptations produced by Roger Corman that featured apparitions, psychological mayhem, and twisted desires. The schizophrenic fifties, with its sunny optimism and paranoid watching of the skies, would soon worry about the things from the crypt.

Gothic America revived, spinning in every direction through American culture like a spiderweb. Nurmi created her sex-drenched vampire goddess partially as an effort to attract the attention of another 1950s gothicist, Charles Addams. Nurmi hoped that Addams, a cartoonist for the *New Yorker* known for his macabre images and bleak sense of humor, might see Vampira and decide that his drawings had television potential. Addams himself represents the gothic undertow of the postwar era, foreshadowing a host of new American monster obsessions. In 1932 he dropped out of the University of Pennsylvania to take art classes. Soon after, he held his first media position retouching photographs for the popular men's magazine known as *True Detective* (his job was to remove the blood in crime scene photographs). The same year he left college, he sold his first cartoon to the *New Yorker*, and by 1936 he became a regular staff contributor. In half a century with the influential magazine, his macabre sense of humor created an iconography of American gothic, including the characters that became the basis for the television hit *The Addams Family*. Addams himself became an icon of the gothic style, with rumors circulating that he had periodic bouts of insanity (untrue) and that he collected medieval weapons and had been married in a pet cemetery (true on both counts).[72]

Many of Addams' cartoons skewered postwar America's visions of consumer abundance and domestic bliss. These images walked the line between humor and horror, as in an example from his 1950 collection *Monster Rally*, which shows a wife sitting in a chair, munching on a box of chocolates. Her husband is coming up behind her as she says, "Now don't come back asking me to forgive you." What the wife cannot see is that he carries a hatchet in one hand and a bag for her body parts in the other. In another mordant image of postwar married life, a wife looks on as her husband, in an attempt to hang himself, gets his arm caught in the noose. "Can't you do anything right?" she scolds.[73]

American consumerism's relationship to the supposedly ideal family also received a gothic send-up from Addams. In one of his most commented-on images, a happy housewife tells police investigators that she has found her own way of escaping Betty Friedan's "feminine mystique":

I disconnected the booster from the Electro-Snuggie Blanket and put him in the deep freeze. In the morning, I defrosted him and ran him through the Handi Home Slicer and then the Jiffy Burger Grind and after that I fed him down the Dispose-All. Then I washed my clothes in the Bendix, tidied up the kitchen and went to a movie.[74]

Addams' cartoons exuded unease about the central icons of post-war America and challenged any notion of the 1950s as an era of simple consensus. Although powerful corporate, religious, and governmental forces in American life wanted to turn postwar America into a land of consumer bliss and traditional values, dissent appeared everywhere, bubbling to the surface in preparation for the 1960s explosion. Historian Wini Breines captures this mood perfectly when she describes the era as a time of "liberating possibilities masked by restrictive norms."[75]

The aliens had not landed, but more traditional monsters emerged everywhere. Even *Freaks* made a comeback. In 1962, the same year as Tod Browning died, the Venice Film Festival screened *Freaks* in hopes of stirring the growing fascination with "camp" cinema. Browning's masterpiece quickly became a standard attraction on the art house circuit and encouraged numerous writers, theorists, and artists to reconsider the meaning of the freak show. A viewing of the film at the New York Theatre on the Upper West Side inspired the legendary Diane Arbus, whose photographic oeuvre became focused on the marginalized and abnormal. Arbus repeatedly viewed the film and eventually photographed Andrew Ratoucheff, a Russian midget who had starred in Browning's celebration of abnormality.[76]

Vampira's brief and shadowy appearance, the macabre humor of Charles Addams, and the second coming of gothic freakdom signaled sundown for American cultural life, a coming fascination with horror that became a part of American culture for the next half century. Serial killers soon became America's monster du jour, while gothic horrors of all types made a triumphant return from the grave.[77]

By the 1960s postwar social needs had created discourses about mental illness, fears of violence, and the impersonal nature of modern life. You did not have to go creeping about in crypts and dungeons to find something lurking. The monster might live next door, might live in your house, or might even live inside you. Monsters stalked Americans in an age of growing dread. As Norman Bates said in Albert Hitchock's 1960 *Psycho*, "We all go a little mad sometimes."

5

DEVIANT BODIES

*I finally convinced myself that it was good to do it, necessary to do it,
and that the public wanted me to do it. The latter part I believe until
this day. I believe that many were rooting for me.*

—David Berkowitz, "Son of Sam" killer

Welcome to prime time, bitch!

—Freddy Krueger in *Nightmare on Elm Street 3: Dream Warriors*

The story of Marion Crane, a beautiful young woman who wants nothing more than respectable relationship with her beau Sam, seemed at first to follow the plot of most Alfred Hitchcock films. Crane steals money from her boss in hopes of attaining the postwar American dream of domestic bliss and conspicuous consumption. Then she goes on the lam.

Audiences came to see *Psycho* expecting a suspenseful thriller along the lines of *North By Northwest* or simply a big-screen version of the offbeat espionage and crime tales on Hitchcock's popular television series. Packing into theaters all over the country to see *Psycho*, the forty-seventh film by the "Master of Suspense," moviegoers received a shocking, blood-drenched welcome to the 1960s.

Psycho's opening scene titillated viewers with Crane (played by Janet Leigh) in white negligee, talking to her lover in a hotel room about how they needed money to marry properly. Audiences, though they would have likely disapproved of her when she steals from her boss, just as likely identified with her as she sets out for a new life. Viewers experienced a growing unease as Crane gets lost on a dark and stormy night and stops at a hotel with a frightening California gothic house leering behind it. The young proprietor, Norman Bates, though strange, comes across at first as shy and even charming. Moreover, Anthony Perkins played the role of the odd young man, and his previous film work had been in light comedy and romance, suggesting that he might become Crane's ally and maybe even a new romantic interest.

Suddenly, like thrill-seekers on a roller coaster that had slowly bumped its way to the top of the track, audiences felt their stomachs heave as the film took a precipitous and terrifying plunge. As Leigh, alone in her room, begins to take a shower, the curtain suddenly rips open and a shadowy figure with a butcher knife begins plunging the weapon repeatedly into Leigh's naked flesh. Thirty-four segments, edited together at furious speed into a sequence lasting less than a minute, increased the feeling of the attack's suddenness and brutality. Leigh's body crumpled over the edge of the tub with blood swirling down the drain while audiences went from shocked screams to stunned silence.[1]

Esquire called *Psycho* "a reflection of the most unpleasant mind, a mean, sly sadistic little mind." Numerous reviewers exuded distaste and not a little anger at the director himself. The *New York Times* called the film "a blot on an honorable career." Another critic, after calling it "the most vile and disgusting film ever made," added that he found it especially disheartening that a director of Hitchcock's prominence had been responsible for it.[2]

Early critical rejection did not prevent *Psycho* from changing American movies forever. A box-office smash, the film exercised enormous influence over American filmmaking, opening the door for young directors like Arthur Penn and Sam Peckinpah, who made use of explosive violence to create riveting human dramas. *Psycho* also prepared the way for the mainstreaming of violence in widely distributed horror films that gained a much larger audience than older drive-in exploitation fare had ever succeeded in garnering.[3]

Norman Bates also represented a new American monster. The end of the twentieth century belonged to the murdering maniac, a creature not born from the supernatural shadows or cobbled together in a lab, but coming to deadly life in the midst of American family structures. As a debate simmered over cultural change, the horror film accused the American family of producing monsters. *Psycho* wielded its knife in the middle of a broad American conversation about mental health, crime, gender, family life, sex, and the societal changes of the 1960s.

Tales of Love and Death

The very title of *Psycho* shook Americans in 1960, especially given the amount of attention the nation's public culture had given to mental health in the fifteen years since World War II. The enormous growth of the psychiatric profession in those years, as well as the frequent prescription of tranquilizers, responded to a growing number of Americans seeking relief from intense anxiety.

A nervous new citizenry of the atomic age took over one billion tranquilizers annually during the 1950s. By 1956 patients seeking help with mental health issues took up more beds in American hospitals than any other category of complaint. Offhand references to the daily use of powerful drugs, such as phenobarbital, became common in films and television. In *Psycho* Marion Crane's coworker urges her to relieve an afternoon headache by taking powerful tranquilizers she happens to have in her bag.[4]

Even the federal government became concerned about the mental stability of postwar America. In 1955 then–Vice President Richard Nixon used a photo op on the steps of the Capitol to proclaim "mental health week." One civil defense informational film urged its listeners to stock their fallout shelters with tranquilizers "to ease the strain and monotony of life" in a post-apocalyptic world.[5]

American children keenly felt the strain of these years. Todd Gitlin, president of the Students for a Democratic Society in the early 1960s, remembered "duck and cover drills" combined with sudden air raid sirens that made him and his classmates wonder if "the world we had been born into was destined to endure." Adults seemed unaware that adolescent anxiety emerged naturally from the enormously dangerous state of the world. Rather than addressing those seemingly intractable problems, parents, teachers, doctors, and law enforcement sought more easily attainable solutions. Concerns about adolescent mental health found expression in PTA drives for mental health awareness and worry about so-called juvenile delinquency. Leaders in education, law enforcement, and psychiatry became convinced of a growing epidemic of violence and alienation among American teenagers. Concerned adults began to worry that the mischievous hijinks of "the Beave" masked the snarling face of James Dean and Marlon Brando, rebels without causes and wild ones.[6]

Increasingly, parental concerns centered on media and its influence over young minds. Fredric Wertham's popular book *Seduction of
the Innocent* (1954) made the case that comic books exerted a malicious
influence on children, preparing them for a life of crime and delinquency.
Wertham's writing, which frequently made an appearance in magazines
directed at middle-class mothers such as *Family Circle*, led to a full Senate
investigation of comics in the year of its publication.[7]

Wertham and the Senate committee focused their ire primarily on
horror and crime comics, many of them produced by a company known
as Entertaining Comics or simply EC. Entertaining Comics deserves close
examination, as its tales open a dark doorway into postwar American
anxieties. These comics tapped a rich vein of postwar angst about family,
gender, and sex. The bloodletting of the imagination that followed created
material that shocks even contemporary readers with graphic displays of
gore combined with macabre humor and biting social satire (and became
the basis for HBO's successful, long-running horror anthology series *Tales
from the Crypt*).

EC began its existence as a small breakaway comic company from
DC comics, the entertainment behemoth that owned characters such
as Batman, Superman, and Wonder Woman. EC, on the other hand,
produced *Picture Stories from the Bible* and a line of books for very young
readers with names such as *Animal Fables* and *Tiny Tot Comics*. When
William Gaines reluctantly inherited the line from his father in 1947, EC
had fallen deeply in the red.[8]

Gaines attempted to revive the ailing company by bringing in young
artists with a creative vision that would interest adults as well as teenagers in the comic form. The new EC stable of artists turned to crime and
horror stories that, while occasionally employing supernatural themes,
more often portrayed human agency behind horror. In comics like *Crime
SuspenStories*, *Haunt of Fear*, *Vault of Horror*, and *Tales from the Crypt*,
husbands dispatched nagging wives and wives murdered cheating or
abusive husbands in the most grisly and gory of fashions.[9]

Charles Addams cartoons that hinted at murder and mayhem in the
American home found graphic expression at EC. Gaines' merry pranksters
hauled in America's allegedly happy domestic scene for a full interroga-
tion under hot lights. The story "Who's Next?" from *Crime SuspenStories*
featured a barber whose beautiful wife takes a lover. The barber takes
revenge by giving the customer a deadly shave and his wife a "haircut"
that ends with the removal of her head.[10]

Betty Friedan wrote in 1963's *The Feminine Mystique* that middle-class American women, trapped in a round of childbearing and domestic chores, felt a sense of "aching dissatisfaction." EC took grisly note of that dissatisfaction in tales like "The Neat Job," in which a harassed housewife, tired of her jealous and tyrannical husband's insistence that she keep the house clean, kills him with an axe. Police investigators discover that she has done "a neat job" for him by placing his body parts in labeled jars. A similar story had a female axe murderer doing away with her abusive, alcoholic husband and stuffing his body parts into liquor bottles as a symbolic revenge.

Children played a decisive role in EC's tales of domestic mayhem. Stories of adolescents and teenagers taking vengeance on parents and other authority figures became a common trope. In the notorious tale "The Orphan," an abused young girl murders her father and frames her mother, delightedly watching her die in the electric chair while she goes off to live with a loving aunt. In "Stick in the Mud," an unlucky boy watches in horror as his disciplinarian teacher becomes his stepmother. After she murders his father for money, the boy kills her in turn. Blending the supernatural into these tales of intergenerational vengeance, one story features a young orphan who becomes the ward of a family of vampires who plan to feast on him. Luckily for him, he is a werewolf. He transforms and makes dinner out of his foster parents.[11]

The increasing institutionalization of American life in postwar America provided more chilling tales for EC artists. Although significantly reformed by the 1950s, psychiatric hospitals, veterans' homes, and homes for the disabled remained a little-discussed part of American society even as an increasing number of Americans spent time in one of these institutions (as Norman Bates hints to Marion Crane that he had done). Spending time in an institution seemed shameful, an admission of failure, to many in the middle class. At the same time, concerns over deviance in society increasingly caused the public to see the institution as a way to police society, keeping it sane and sanitized for "normal" people.[12]

EC took the side of the incarcerated. In early 1955 *Tales from the Crypt* featured a story entitled "Blind Alleys," in which the inmates of a home for the blind take revenge on a cruel administrator by feeding him to his own dog. The 1951 *Vault* tale "Revenge Is Nuts" featured another cruel administrator whose mistreatment of the inmates leads to more bloody revenge. Tales of equally monstrous medical experts joined these stories of monstrous institutions. In 1950 *Vault* contained a story of an anatomy instructor who begins murdering townspeople to secure cadavers for his class, a story that tapped into the folklore (and the racist reality) of "night doctors" and "resurrection men."[13]

The 1950s proved no more ready for EC's sublime mix of bad taste, subversive humor, and full-on gross-out than it had been for Vampira's blend of sex, death, and laughter. Not only did their horror line challenge every middle-class sensibility, its satirical titles cut American historical memory down to the bone. EC's *Mad* magazine even made fun of beloved comic character "Archie," the all-American high-schooler billed as "America's Typical Teenager" whose character fit perfectly into the safe, domestic dreams of the 1950s. *Mad* responded with "Starchie," the story of an uptight teenager who finds himself lost in an American city and jailed as a juvenile delinquent. More disturbing for some, EC's war comics looked at American history from the standpoint of its victims. EC artist Harvey Kurtzman told the tale of "Custer's Last Stand" as the story of an inept criminal who needlessly murders native peoples. This was a provocative revision of an alleged hero still considered a national icon in post–World War II America. Other EC suspense comics portrayed the lynching of African Americans and made pointed references to the frequency of the practice in America.[14]

EC's ghoulish fun did not last long. Wertham and the 1954 Senate hearings on violence in comics threatened outright censorship. Bill Gaines testified before the Senate and found himself attempting to explain how comic books featuring severed heads in their cover art exhibited "good taste." Gaines gave as good as he got and took a direct shot at Wertham, noting that "it would be just as difficult to explain the harmless thrill of a horror story to a Dr. Wertham as it would be to explain the sublimity of love to a frigid old maid."[15]

Wertham gave equally passionate, if sometimes odd testimony. The psychiatrist asserted, in authoritative tones, that comic books led directly to juvenile delinquency (without describing the link). He also asked one of the strangest rhetorical questions ever entered into the Senate record. At one point in his testimony, Wertham held up a copy of *The Crypt of Terror* that contained a tale of a baseball team who murders its rivals and then plays ball with their body parts. "They play baseball with a dead man's head?" Wertham screeched in his thick German accent, "Why would they do that?"[16]

The threat of censorship led Gaines to call a meeting of the major comic book companies in the United States. If Gaines had hoped to start a resistance movement, he found himself in the midst of a comic book

Vichy. All of the other major companies (many of whom had seen their characters and style mocked by their scrappy, ironic competitor) had decided to adopt their own strict code of censorship before the government could attempt it.

Gaines walked out on the deliberations that created the Comics Code Authority. In the CCA, the industry pledged itself to steer clear of tales of monsters, at least monsters that challenged the consensus view of American history and culture. According to the code, comic books could never portray established authority in a way that would "create disrespect." In fact, comic books had to become purveyors of middle-class American values. Along with banning "walking dead, torture, vampires and vampirism, ghouls, cannibalism and werewolfism," the code insisted that comics inculcate "respect for parents, the moral code and honorable behavior" as well as "emphasize the value of the home and the sanctity of marriage."[17]

The Comics Code Authority ensured a decline in the creativity, and the popularity, of comic books. Comics by the late 1950s became a wasteland of childish stories about one-dimensional superheroes fighting giant robots and creatures from outer space. Superman appeared as "America's Secret Weapon," with covers showing him fighting alongside American paratroopers (presumably in Korea). Not until the 1960s, when Marvel began producing its more adult tales of angst-ridden mutant heroes, would comics revive as a popular form (and would still not find a largely adult audience until the 1980s).[18]

As the 1950s drew to a close, America found itself hungry for monsters. America discovered the creature it had been waiting for outside the pages of comic books. The macabre tales of EC and the sense of mental and emotional instability in American life found their living incarnation in the serial murderer.

Dead-Eyed Monster

In 1957 police searching for a missing woman in the tiny town of Plainfield, Wisconsin, followed a hard lead to the home of Ed Gein. Inside, they found a veritable chamber of horrors that sent these adult men screaming and vomiting into the cold northwestern night.[19]

Most of Gein's nineteenth-century farmhouse had been walled off and left just as his mother had kept it at the time of her death in 1945. Contemporary newspaper accounts described these forbidden rooms as decorated in "the style of forty years ago." Gein himself lived in two small rooms that included the kitchen. In these rooms, a shambles of garbage and detritus, police found evidence of Gein's crimes and the gruesome trophies he had taken from them. Gein had a refrigerator full of human organs. Human skulls had been turned into bowls and decoration for his bedposts. Vulvas were discovered in a shoebox, one of them grotesquely painted silver. A chair and lamp had been made of human skin and bones. Gein had sewn masks and an outfit made of skin. The missing woman herself was found hanging on a hook, her body hollowed out in the manner a Wisconsin hunter would dress a deer.

If Gein's story sounds hideously familiar to readers, it is because it served as the ghastly inspiration for films ranging from *Psycho* to *Texas Chain Saw Massacre* to *The Silence of the Lambs*. A serial killer before law enforcement coined the term, Gein, and his brutal crimes, ushered in the age of the maniac murderer in American popular culture. The serial killer became central to American discussions of public order, criminality, celebrity, and the nature of sexuality in the final third of the twentieth century.

"Stranger killings," the term used before the serial killer panic, had obviously occurred in America before with H. H. Holmes and, in the 1920s, Albert Fish. Gein's bloody crimes came to light just before the United States began an ongoing pageant of national trauma. The assassination of President Kennedy in 1963 serves as only a symbolic beginning to a period of disillusion among many Americans, the sense that the democratic experiment had come apart at the seams. The assassinations of Malcolm X in 1965 and then of both Robert Kennedy and Martin Luther King in 1968 further underscored this sense of chaos. By the late 1960s, on any given night, the newscast could contain a story about escalating casualties in Vietnam, an exposé of the drug-fueled sex romp many middle-class Americans imagined American youth to be engaged in, or the tale of a civil rights protest being violently squelched in the American South. The white, middle-class America that Nixon would dub "the silent majority" watched it all with mounting anxiety.[20]

The 1960s also, of course, represented a revolutionary period during which the struggle for minority and women's rights registered significant gains. In 1965 the Voting Rights Act ensured African Americans the franchise, while acts of civil disobedience had crippled, if not destroyed, Jim Crow's hold over public life in much of the nation. In 1966 the National Organization for Women (NOW) became instrumental in defining the political program of second-wave feminism that found expression in struggles for reproductive freedom, economic justice, and attempts to change both laws and attitudes about rape and domestic violence. By 1965 the small but growing gay and lesbian rights movement held public political demonstrations for the first time.

The escalation of the Vietnam War in 1968 galvanized college students into mass protest of every aspect of American institutional life. The American Indian Movement (AIM) used the tactics learned from the Black freedom struggle combined with demands that the federal government adhere to its numerous broken treaties. Public protest sought to call attention to the denial of jobs and education for native youth, continued governmental seizure of Indian lands for environmentally dubious schemes (including the mining of uranium), and numerous examples of police brutality and the mass incarceration of native men.[21]

By the early 1970s even those who had participated in the revolutionary struggles of the 1960s felt a growing sense of unease over the direction of American society. Incremental change had come with great effort and yet many elements of American life remained essentially the same. The desegregation of public schools proceeded slowly with many parts of the American South only moving to unitary school districts in the early 1970s. Controversy and violence erupted over busing and housing in the urban North. Federal law enforcement targeted groups such as the Black Panthers that called for revolutionary change in the economic structure of American society. By the mid-1970s, the United States government had incarcerated, murdered, or driven into exile the Panthers' leadership. The pace of change seemed glacial to a generation that had been asked if it wanted a revolution.[22]

In the midst of slow change and violent responses by the military and the police, the feminist movement won two major victories. The first came in 1965 when the Supreme Court struck down state laws limiting the distribution of birth control in *Griswold v. Connecticut*. The high court declared a "right to privacy" inherent in the Constitution. Another major achievement came in the 1973 *Roe v. Wade* decision that similarly eliminated state laws that restricted access to abortion.[23]

Change came slowly and victories elicited a massive reactionary response. Although many Americans today look with horror on the shooting of antiwar protestors at Kent State on May 4, 1970, many at the time approved of the action of the National Guard. Major media outlets ignored the shooting of antiwar and civil rights protestors at South Carolina State in Orangeburg (1968), Jackson State in Mississippi (1970), and in East Los Angeles (1970).[24]

Reactionary forces outside politics, law, and government organized primarily into what we now call the "Religious Right." The newly enthused

Right created the Reagan Counterrevolution of 1980, a movement that fused a libertarian ideology of limited government that pleased big business with an assertion of "traditional values" that appealed to Nixon's silent, and often very religious, majority.[25]

Shadows quickly fell on the landscape despite Reagan's now famous campaign commercial declaring "morning in America." Although serial murder has played a significant role in the history of American crime since the founding of the nation, a noticeable uptick in its frequency occurred during the 1970s. Many analysts have argued that this represents a return to the normal number of seemingly random homicides after a brief post–World War II decline. Others have noted that the growth of media—print, televised, and electronic—simply made it easier to gather statistics. Moreover, even with what looks like a surge in serial murder cases, they represented between only 1 and 2 percent of the total number of homicides in the United States each year during the 1980s. Given that the United States has the highest murder rate of any industrialized nation, this still accounted for a significant number of deaths.[26]

Although statistically tiny, serial homicide and its perpetrators became, during the Reagan years and beyond, the subject of a mountain of books and films. Sociologists and criminologists examined the phenomenon from every angle. Probably the majority of material on serial murder came from so-called true crime authors, such as Ann Rule, and from FBI agents who sought to publicize Bureau efforts at hunting down psychotic killers. These accounts often portrayed the serial killer as a monster who threatened not only the lives but also the values of middle-class Americans. Their books, sometimes purposefully, provided ammunition for conservative proponents of a return to traditionalism.[27]

By the Reagan years, FBI profilers became the most prolific source of popular information on the serial killer. In 1988 FBI agent John Douglas, a significant figure in the Bureau's efforts to profile serial homicide, appeared in a television special called "The Secret Identity of Jack the Ripper." Douglas claimed that he had profiled the Whitechapel killer "as an asocial white male, perceived by others as a quiet shy loner and probably with a heavy-drinking promiscuous mother." Douglas' description represented the FBI's basic template of a serial murder, one that defined it exclusively as a male activity with its origins in oedipal drama. Profilers held on to this paradigm with ferocity as the Bureau increasingly defined itself as the American institution best able to deal with this new American monster. Douglas inculcated future FBI agents with his views through a coauthored training manual called *Sexual Homicide*. He also became a best-selling author with books like *Mind Hunter, Journey into Darkness,* and *The Cases That Haunt Us.*[28]

FBI agent Robert Ressler did more than any other public figure to invest the serial murderer with traits the uneasy public would fear the most. Ressler organized a decade-long study of serial murder in the 1970s, and in October of 1983 he helped put together an FBI-hosted press conference that announced his findings. At this conference, Bureau officials declared a firm link between serial murder and sexual sadism. For reasons not at all obvious, alternative sexuality had to be a part of the serial killer's profile. The definition of a serial killer, Ressler argued, could not include any murders or series of murders that took place because of "greed, a fight, jealousy or family disputes."

The Justice Department's highly restrictive definition excluded all but a very tiny percentage of homicides in the United States. The 1983 news conference, however, had the effect of generating a panic over an alleged epidemic of serial murder. Roger Depue, head of the FBI's Behavioral Science Unit, promised that the FBI would give closer attention to open and unsolved cases. He noted that 28 percent of the nation's 20,000 murder cases went unsolved each year, and that the percentage was rising. Depue at least implicitly suggested that these unsolved cases were the work of serial killers. Media sources immediately began to suggest that shadowy serial killers committed as many as 4,000 murders every year.[29]

In the wake of skewered reporting, wildly inflated statistics began to appear everywhere. *Newsweek* and *Life* magazines speculated about "hundreds" of serial killers at large. At least one novelistic account of an FBI training session had a Bureau official make the absurd claim that the typical middle-class American has "about a 37 percent chance" of crossing paths with a serial killer. In truth, the small number of Americans who did become the victims of serial killers came from groups marginalized by American society, including sex workers, drug users, and the homeless.[30]

Panic over serial murders created an appetite for stories about their adventures, making "true crime" authors like Ann Rule immensely popular. Rule had written on mass murderers since working for *True Detective Magazine* in the late 1960s. During most of the 1970s she wrote pieces on brutal murder for a number of unlikely venues, including *Cosmopolitan, Ladies' Home Journal,* and even *Good Housekeeping.* Her 1980 book *The Stranger Beside Me* detailed the crimes of Ted Bundy, a prolific serial murderer who beat and strangled at least thirty-five women between 1974 and 1978. Rule continued to write accounts of serial murder as public interest crested in the late 1980s and literally hundreds of imitators put out their own chilling accounts.[31]

These narratives gave America a new creature to fear. Images of the serial killer in true crime, television police procedurals, films, and even official police accounts invariably used the term "monster" to describe the killer's activities. In her book *Lust Killer*, Rule notes, "convoluted medicalese" might seek to explain the psychological underpinnings of serial murder but that to "the man on the street," they are "always a monster." Robert Ressler has portrayed himself again and again as a "monster hunter," writing books with titles like *Whoever Fights Monsters* and *I Have Lived in the Monster.*[32]

While asserting the inherent monstrosity of the mass murderer, almost all popular images simultaneously used the language of sickness and psychosis, tracing the emergence of the murderous impulse to childhood trauma or oedipal confusion. Ann Rule, so insistent that we see the serial murderer as "always a monster," finds in Ted Bundy's unstable childhood the seed of his crimes. Two books on Ted Bundy, one by Stephen G. Michaud and the other by Hugh Aynesworth, share a similar contradictory stance. On the one hand, they assert that Bundy had an inner madness that he hid with "a mask of sanity." On the other hand, they take issue with a Florida attorney who had argued that American culture too frequently thinks of the criminal as a "hunchback, crosseyed little monster slithering through the dark" rather than a human being. Michaud and Aynesworth disagreed, writing that "the slithering hunchback" did live inside of Bundy, uncontrollable and irredeemable.[33]

Serial killers in popular culture appear as both evil monsters and insane maniacs who have suffered childhood trauma. This obviously represents two warring discourses united in the same terrifying figure. Insanity suggests a severe mental disability, one that could perhaps receive and respond to various therapies. A monster is, however, beyond the ken of human experience. Monsters cannot be treated and rehabilitated, only destroyed.

On close examination, the term "monster" seems remarkably imprecise if we want a word to describe people like Gein, Bundy, Henry Lee Lucas, Jeffrey Dahmer, and other well-known criminals. After all, the monsters Americans have encountered include sea serpents bubbling out of the ocean, Bela Lugosi in eveningwear, Lon Chaney Jr. in yak hair makeup as the wolf man, and goblin-like extraterrestrials in flying saucers. The term has been elastic enough to include all sorts of phenomena beyond the normal range of expectations and experiences. The friendly sea serpent would seem to have little to do with Ed Gein happily sewing his skin suit by firelight on a wintry Wisconsin night.[34]

The serial murderer, sick psycho and malevolent beast, behaves in the popular mind very much like these earlier monsters in one very significant way. Mass murderers as "monsters" takes us back to Judith Halberstam's argument that the monster acts as a meaning machine. The creatures of our imagination absorb meaning out of their historical context and, in turn, invest that context with meaning. In the case of the serial murderer, we fashioned a new horror that owes its existence to the struggle to define the cultural direction of America in the wake of revolutionary social change.

The definition of the serial killer as "sexual deviant" offered a new cultural image on monstrosity, a powerful tool for emerging forces in politics and society that sought to counter the sexual revolution, second-wave feminism, and the emerging struggle for gay and lesbian rights. Combining a discourse of madness and monstrous evil made the serial killer into a powerful symbolic construction of all that had gone wrong since Woodstock. A "sick" and "degraded" society produced monsters.[35]

Sex and the Single Serial Killer

In the 1984 presidential race, Ronald Reagan made an assertion of allegedly traditional moral values central to his campaign. Reagan declared that "promiscuity" had become "stylish" and transformed a "sacred expression of love" into something "casual and cheap." This claim went hand in hand with Reagan's rhetorical war on poor single women (he coined the term "welfare queen") and his opposition to abortion. His supporters in the Christian Right, represented by Tim LaHaye and Jerry Falwell, asserted that America had gone into social and political decline because of the gains of the social protest movements of the 1960s.[36]

Descriptions of the serial killer phenomenon reflect this deeply conservative representation of America's supposed plight. Ann Rule, for example, suggested that the seed of Bundy's sexual murders had been planted in the unstable environment created by his unwed mother, who moved frequently and pretended to be his older sister (allegedly to become more attractive to sexual partners). This alleged connection between a "sexually promiscuous society" and the serial killer persisted. By the 1990s even dating guides hinted at a connection between being sexually active and random homicide. The enormously popular 1995 dating and relationship guide for women entitled *The Rules* not only argued for a neotraditional relationship in which "the man must take charge" but told young women to "never get into a car with a man you meet at a party; you might end up in his trunk."[37]

The FBI profile of the serial killer as sexual sadist invited conservative commentators to connect the dots between the dangers of sexual revolution and the brutalities of wanton murder. A 1984 opinion piece in the *New York Times* reported that "many officials" believed that an increase in serial murders had some link with "sweeping changes in attitudes regarding sexuality that have occurred over the past twenty years." An article that appeared the same year in *Omni* described the possible profile of a serial killer as "homosexuals who kill their anonymous partners after sex."[38]

Conservative commentator Joel Achenbach in the *Washington Post* went even further. Achenbach saw the serial murderer as a kind of divine judgment, "the price we pay for slavish devotion to individualism, mobility, the right to buy smut, the right to ignore one's neighbors even when they seem weird." Achenbach's latter comment reveals a great deal. While suggesting that Americans needed a more communitarian spirit, he implies that the primary reason one might want to pay attention to the neighbors is to keep tabs on their weirdness. Increasingly, conservative cultural texts encouraged Americans to understand "weirdness" in sexualized terms.[39]

Two events in the 1990s seemingly sealed the connection in the popular mind between alternative sexualities and the murdering maniac. Jonathan Demme's brilliant 1991 film *The Silence of the Lambs* and the real-world horrors of Jeffrey Dahmer both appeared to underscore the conservative claim that deviant sexuality threatened family values and American lives. In representations of Dahmer, and in both the novel and the film versions of *The Silence of the Lambs*, alternative sexualities are presented as a kind of gateway drug to serial murder.[40]

The discovery of the carnage wreaked by Jeffrey Dahmer in the summer of 1991 riveted the nation. Dahmer's neighbors frequently heard the sounds of buzzsaws, loud thumps, and occasional screams coming from his apartment. The police had, by accident, come close to discovering Dahmer's crimes earlier than they eventually did. In May of 1991 two women found a drugged, dazed fourteen-year-old boy wandering the street who had escaped from Dahmer's apartment of horrors. Dahmer managed to convince police that the boy was his nineteen-year-old boyfriend. The officers on the scene allowed him to take the boy back to his apartment.[41]

In July another of Dahmer's intended victims escaped and this time brought police back to the apartment. Police arrested Dahmer after finding a human head in the refrigerator, chemical vats with human organs, and the beginnings of an altar made out of human skulls in his bedroom. Gein, who had died in prison in 1984, seemed back from the grave.

Dahmer's atrocities became fodder for the culture wars. Law enforcement officials in Milwaukee assumed a link between Dahmer's homosexuality and his monstrous murders. Jeffrey Jentzen, the medical examiner for Milwaukee County, termed the murders "homosexual overkill." The two police officers that came close to arresting Dahmer in the late spring of 1991 made a series of homophobic comments when reporting the incident, joking with the dispatcher that they had reunited the "lovers." Both officers were fired for the incident soon after Dahmer's arrest. In what has become almost the paradigm for dealing with police misconduct in the years since the incident, the officers successfully appealed their termination and even received back pay. One of the officers, John Balcerzak, later became president of the Milwaukee Police Association.[42]

The perception of a link between homosexuality as a "deviant" lifestyle and violence commonly appears in the literature on serial murder. The image of the "gay serial killer" emerged in both tabloid journalism and true crime literature. In 1951 a popular exploitation paperback entitled *Terror in the Streets* described the "homosexual prowler" as "the sex deviated version of what we call the 'wolf.'" More contemporary accounts of serial murder indulge in the same kind of monster making. Dennis McDougal's book on California serial killer Randy Kraft claimed that heterosexual murderers have little interest in "torture or dismemberment," whereas the homosexual killers can barely discern the difference between gay sex and violence. The discovery of young male corpses, McDougal asserted, "could generally be traced back to a lover whose anger or ecstasy—or both—got out of hand." Even gay victims of serial killers, or victims portrayed as gay in media sources, are demonized and dismissed. Anne Schwartz, the wife of a Milwaukee police officer, wrote in her book about Dahmer that the murderer's "victims facilitated him in some way." She further insisted, "their life-styles and unnecessary risk-taking contributed to their deaths."[43]

In retrospect, 1991 seems the year of the cannibal. The day before Valentine's Day, Jonathan Demme's *The Silence of the Lambs* introduced audiences to Hannibal Lecter, a sophisticated psychiatrist with a taste for art, classical music, and human flesh. Lecter becomes a strange kind of Van Helsing figure, instructing FBI ingénue Clarice Starling (Jodi Foster) in the method and lore of serial killers. Starling uses this secret knowledge to track and kill "Buffalo Bill," a deviant serial killer who murders young women in an effort to sew together, like Ed Gein, a "skin suit."

The Silence of the Lambs, despite its garish subject matter, showed strong conservative instincts. The film portrays Buffalo Bill as seeking a new, transgender identity, and his crimes are motivated by a sexual deviancy that can find release only through violent means. He clearly has no sexual interest in the women he kidnaps and kills, but rather wants to leave behind his male identity by taking their skin and creating his gruesome skin suit. One scene, designed to create unease about abnormal sexuality, has Bill camping it up in drag queen fashion. Buffalo Bill represented more "homosexual overkill."[44]

The film and literature of the serial killer clearly exhibited conservative anxieties over the increasing plasticity of sexual identity in America. While authors and film producers infrequently had overt political intent, their efforts to pitch their products to the broad mainstream resulted in a demonizing of alternative sexual identities. In the "gay murderer" and the "sexual maniac," themes of evil and mental sickness came together in a single figure.

By the early 1990s conservatives had come to use the languages of mental sickness and of moral depravity as a single language, suggesting that frightening deviant forces posed both an internal and external threat. In a book entitled *Body Count*, Reagan adviser and "virtue czar" William Bennett described America's Black neighborhoods as suffering primarily from "moral poverty." Meanwhile, conservative scholar James Q. Wilson combined savage monster imagery with the language of mental sickness. African American men in urban environments, he wrote, had become "feral, presocial human beings." These ideas had a public policy component in the restoration of the death penalty in a number of states and a prison population that grew by 130 percent between 1980 and 1990.[45]

The Silence of the Lambs, like most sophisticated works of art, contained more than a simple political message. The film's dénouement does not give us the straightforward destruction of the monster. Instead, we learn in the conclusion that Hannibal Lecter has managed to outwit his captors and make good his escape. This raises questions about whether or not Starling and the FBI's quest for one monster had only served to unleash a more vicious one to walk the earth.

The Silence of the Lambs offered mainstream audiences a stylized version of the popular, youth-oriented slasher genre. The maniac killers of the earlier slashers had provided a way for a generation of screenwriters and directors to comment on America's family values, both as an ideology and a reality. The slasher had, at first, been one of the most subversive American film genres. Previous horror films had used the monstrous to picture the marginalized. Increasingly, horror imagined normalcy as the truly monstrous.[46]

The *Silence of the Lambs* itself has a number of sometimes conflicting ideological currents flowing though it. But a more complete examination of the history of the slasher film reveals the changed nature of the monster in America and its role as a creature that unleashed anarchic impulses on the American landscape. In many respects utterly apolitical, the slasher film's celebration of excess, dark humor, and complex portrayals of gender made it a subversive art form in an increasingly conservative America.

. . . Meanwhile, on Amity Island

The box office–shattering success of Steven Spielberg's *Jaws* (1975) strangely presaged the slasher phenomenon, even as it seemed to forecast brighter skies for a film industry that, during the same period, had taken on the grittier aspects of the American 1960s and 1970s with *Easy Rider, Chinatown, One Flew Over the Cuckoo's Nest,* and *Taxi Driver.* The reader may balk at the idea that a film about a man-eating monster from the depths eating beach-goers proved lighter fare (no pun). However, for post-Vietnam America, *Jaws* meant an escape from recent history to the degree it meant anything at all.

Spielberg had no particular ideological axe to grind at a moment in cultural history when many in his generation hoped to make the socially relevant film, the film as art and politics, the film that, as the phrase went, "had something to say." Spielberg took a wholly different route, building his career from movies that blended adventure with childhood fantasy. In decades to come, he employed melodrama even when dealing with events of incredible sensitivity such as the Holocaust (*Schindler's List*) or with moments central to American historical memory such as D-Day (*Saving Private Ryan*).[47]

The carnage of *Jaws* offered a peculiar start to such a career. Ostensibly a horror film with the haunted American tale of Moby Dick as a major influence, the bloody, corpse-ridden *Jaws* played out on the sun and sand of the American summer. Spielberg introduces Roy Schneider as "Sheriff Brody," a literal "new sheriff in town" but one who has come to a suburban beach frontier. Amity Island usually has no bigger problems than kids "karate chopping the fences." Cindy, the teenage boy's dream of a 1960s Gidget-girl, may have washed ashore in pieces, having run afoul of a Great White. But no one wants to think about a shark just before the big tourist-opening weekend on the Fourth of July. Don't let the shark win. Can't we all just get back to being Americans and making money?

The answer turns out to be yes, and more deaths follow until the film's third act, which takes us away from the island of friendship and back to the wild, aquatic frontier. We, all of America, go along on a shark hunt undertaken by Quint, a salty old captain who sings his sea shanties and tells his gruesome stories like an ancient mariner from the nineteenth century. His crew includes Hooper (Richard Dreyfuss), a marine biologist who represents technical and rational prowess of a younger generation, and Brody, the calm, levelheaded American hero who sets the world right. Or, in the case of Amity Island, even more right than it had already been.

Quint, our Captain Ahab for the 1970s, dies in one of the most carnage-ridden moments ever featured in a "PG"-rated film. But Hooper and Brody literally shrug off his death at the end of the film as they paddle back to the inviting shores of Amity, a Huck Finn and Tom Sawyer playfully splashing about in the water as they float along toward the setting sun, the monster and the American past (bound up in Quint's identity and his horrific tales) behind them.

Jaws premiered on June 20, 1975. The Fall of Saigon had just occurred on April 30th, marking the complete collapse of America's puppet government in South Vietnam. Nixon had resigned in disgrace less than a year earlier. The facts of his criminal regime continued their slow leak into the American consciousness, though it is an open question whether the country ever fully faced these facts. The economy had come apart at the seams, the OPEC embargo of 1973 precipitating an energy crisis that forced Americans into waiting in long lines for gasoline. Real wages and manufacturing jobs began a forty-year decline and a revolutionary transformation of the economy began as American capitalism migrated from its base in building, manufacturing, and raw material extraction toward a service, retail, and information economy.[48]

Spielberg ignored these issues and made it all about the shark. By the late summer of 1975 the image of the gargantuan monster rising out of the sea toward an all-American bikini-clad young girl appeared on a million t-shirts and posters. Peter Benchly's best-selling 1974 novel *Jaws* had contained references to adultery, drug use, and Vietnam, all of which Spielberg stripped out of the script.

Studio execs wanted a horror film ending, with a thousand shark fins shown heading to Amity's beaches. Spielberg said no, and the film closed with the idyllic ending described above. It capped a tale of mythic American adventure where the monster has been killed along with that decidedly weird two-second shrug for Quint, the death of Ahab. This moment is so strange in part given how Spielberg and Tom Hanks have spent the last twenty years sometimes mawkishly praising the greatest generation, a generation that, embodied in the World War II navy man Quint, dies mauled and screaming in *Jaws.*

The America of the late seventies represented anything but an island separated from the world. As unemployment rose to its highest levels since the Great Depression and corporations deindustrialized the American city, capitalism appeared to enter the crisis phase long predicted by some Marxist intellectuals. Meanwhile, tensions with the Soviet Union reached dangerous levels not seen since the early days of the Kennedy presidency when Jimmy Carter adopted a tough stance on the Russian invasion of Afghanistan and began a military buildup in 1978 that would grow to gigantic proportions in the Reagan years, soon consuming fully one fourth of the American budget.[49]

The formula for the slasher film may have been established with *Black Christmas* (1974), featuring a psychosexual killer slaughtering sorority sisters, or *The Texas Chain Saw Massacre* in the same year. *Jaws* does, however, deserve a counterintuitive spot in this pantheon. We are to understand the shark in terms different from nineteenth-century conceptions of the sea serpent. He (the shark seems consistently gendered and Spielberg himself called it "he") has dead eyes, exists only to kill, and even does some of the moralistic slasher films one better by slaughtering the nude young woman pre-coitus, obliterating the sexual revolution on Amity Island before it can even begin. The murderous shark, although appearing in a film awash in sea-blues and the sun's glare, builds his abattoir in a fashion not so different from Michael, Jason, and Freddy going about their wet work amid shadow and fog. The fact that the first summer blockbuster represented a kind of "feel good slasher" tells us much about why audiences understood the politics of such films so differently and why the films stated their politics in often confusingly contradictory terms.

Slasher Dreams

Jaws took America on a trip to the beach, but the country had far darker dreams. The story of *Psycho* borrowed from the Ed Gein narrative the theme of oedipal fixation and the archetypal terror of cadavers being kept and preserved rather than properly buried or destroyed. The story left unprepared audiences in 1960 deeply shaken with its psychosexual meanings. Hitchcock, however, left out the most gruesome aspects of the Gein story.

Director Tobe Hooper's 1974 *The Texas Chain Saw Massacre* went to those dark places with a howling, power-tool-wielding vengeance. Jim

Van Bebber, a director heavily influenced by *Chain Saw*, remembered that, prior to 1974, horror had tried to frighten audiences by "jumping out from behind the door." *The Texas Chain Saw Massacre* was different. "This thing was coming out in fucking clown paint, blood-spattered, with homicide on its brain."[50]

The Texas Chain Saw Massacre followed five countercultural teenagers making their way across Texas. A brother and sister, Nancy and Franklin Hardesty, have family roots in the region of rural Texas where the group is traveling and convince the others to leave the main road in search of their grandfather's old homestead. What they find is a psychotic, all-male family of murderers and cannibals who had once been workers in a local slaughterhouse. Leatherface, the youngest son, lives in a preverbal, infantile state, his face covered in a mask of human skin, his chainsaw the screaming embodiment of the family's madness and violence.[51]

Hooper describes the origins of *Chain Saw* as both an outgrowth of the verbal transmission of American horror tales and a reflection of the times. Hooper recalled in an interview that Wisconsin relatives had terrified him as a child with tales of Ed Gein as well as other stories of psychotic maniacs. *The Texas Chain Saw Massacre* attempted to tap into the weirdness of American families, exacerbated by the generational split of the 1960s, the emerging culture wars, and the consequent struggles over the nature of the family.[52]

Hitchock's *Psycho* and Hooper's *Chain Saw* provide symbolic bookends for the turmoil of the 1960s and early 1970s. In the thirteen years since 1960, political assassination, a violent response to the civil rights struggle, the massive escalation of the Vietnam War, and the rise of countercultural protest and meteoric changes in the household rocked American culture. A significant number of POWs who returned from Vietnam in 1973 felt like, and sometimes compared themselves to, Rip Van Winkle. The sister of Lieutenant Everett Alvarez, shot down over North Vietnam and captured in 1964, described how her brother had left an America where "there was complete faith in the government, the government knew best." His sister told him on his return: "All of that had changed considerably." Other POWs complained that all their friends seemed divorced, while the meek housewives they had left behind had become financially independent, and often sexually adventuresome, women. Others simply complained about X-rated movies, the men in "women's clothes," and Andy Warhol.[53]

Certainly any vets who went to see *The Texas Chain Saw Massacre* the year of their homecoming received a very different image of American history than their 1950s history textbooks had offered. The setting of Hooper's film on the Texas frontier evoked the violence of the American past and situated it in the troubled present. The name of the family (introduced in Hooper's sequel) conjures both cutting (the saw) while playing with the notion of American innocence on the frontier (Tom Sawyer). When asked what *Chain Saw* was really about, Tobe Hooper, whose only previous feature had been an antiwar drama, laughingly responded in a 2000 interview, "It's about America, man."[54]

It is about America. The Sawyer family represents all that the Puritans feared about the howling wilderness, the alleged savagery of the Native Americans who lived in the dark woods beyond the settlement. And yet, the Sawyers are not the American other, the enemy of the nation. They are deeply American, intricately tied to national myths of the frontier hunter-hero. This is the implicit message when the Sawyer homestead appears as a kind of frontier cabin full of hunting trophies, both human and animal. Leatherface himself obviously references James Fenimore Cooper's Leatherstocking, the hunter who becomes part of the natural landscape.[55]

The 1986 sequel to *Chain Saw* underscores similar themes. The patriarch of the family (known simply as "the Cook") is now presented as a 1980s entrepreneur who rides the wave of Reagan's free-market cowboy capitalism by becoming Dallas' favorite barbeque purveyor. At the beginning of the film, he appears in front of an adoring crowd dressed like a car salesman, proudly taking his award for winning a chili cook-off with his special recipe. "I love this town," he cries. "This town loves meat." The Sawyer clan's less public face has relocated from their homestead to a bizarre, blood-drenched chamber of horrors beneath a Frontierland-style theme park. Giant, creepy statues of Davy Crockett are joined by images of forts and wagons. Meanwhile, Dennis Hopper played a former Texas Ranger ("the Lone Ranger") on the trail of the Sawyers. Hopper used his signature style to portray this typical American hero as utterly deranged, not so different from Leatherface himself. Hopper appears in the film as a maniacal lawman the same year he channeled utter, terrifying madness in "Frank," the unforgettable villain of David Lynch's *Blue Velvet*.[56]

Chain Saw sliced and diced the American dream of the past. Increasingly, the slasher genre mocked the American dream of the present. Wes Craven's 1972 *The Last House on the Left* prepared the way for a new kind of horror film that combined extraordinary violence with a countercultural critique of American institutions and their violent origins and trajectory. Craven's film showed the brutal rape, degradation, and murder of two teenage girls by a "family" of murderers that mirror the dark family of Charles Manson. The killers' car breaks down and they find themselves the houseguests of the parents of one of the brutalized young women. The middle-class parents discover the crime and that they are playing host to the perpetrators. Rather than calling the authorities or running for their lives, the bourgeois couple take vengeance themselves, slaughtering the murderers in ways that actually cause some shift in audience sympathies and raise questions about primal violence beneath the veneer of middle-class America.[57]

Craven has described the film as growing out of his desire to take the American public's thirst for violence to its logical conclusions. Craven believed this would expose the foundations of violence at the heart of Nixon's silent majority. He purposefully sought to give *Last House* a photo-graphic intensity resembling the raw footage coming from Vietnam by using high-speed, documentary-style film. The original script called for the murderers to be Vietnam veterans, while one of the slaughtered girls would die giving the "V" sign, with all its metonymic evocations of the peace movement.[58]

John Carpenter's *Halloween* (1978) soon joined Hooper and Craven's challenges to the dreams of America's past and the hopes for its future. Carpenter took urban legends about endangered babysitters and turned them into a critique of the American suburb. The film portrays the Hallow-een night return of Michael Myers, a mental patient who fifteen years earlier brutally slashed and killed his older sister, to the small, quiet town of

Jamie Lee Curtis—On the set of *Halloween*

Haddonfield, Illinois. Pursued by psychiatrist Sam Loomis, Michael invades the quiet streets and four-bedroom ranch homes of Haddonfield, impassively slaughtering teenagers the same age as his sister. He meets his match in Laurie Strode (Jamie Lee Curtis, the daughter of *Psycho*'s Janet Leigh) who manages to best Michael by turning everything from coat hangers to knitting needles into weapons, even taking Myers' signature butcher knife away from him and using it against him. Curtis' portrayal made Strode into what horror scholar Carol Clover has described as the archetypal "final girl" of slasher convention, a heroic figure who slays, or at least holds at bay, the monster.[59]

Michael Myers came home to a world that was supposed to be safe. Suburban life since the 1950s had increasingly become the image of middle-class success. In the master narrative of domestic life, hard work and frugality allowed an American family to purchase a suburban home that offered refuge from the world of commerce. At the same time, the home became a place to display the rewards of financial success, a showcase for the latest model of refrigerator, self-cleaning oven, and color television set.[60]

The civil rights struggle had given another meaning to the suburban refuge. The phenomenon of "white flight" from urban centers created the perception of the suburb as an escape from social change. New school districts blossomed around the nation as the educational system integrated in the early 1970s, and new schools often became the epicenter for developing communities. The desire to flee the consequences of the Black freedom struggle generated the enormous and violent anger over busing, as white families watched their children's court-ordered rides back to what they increasingly called "the ghetto" rather than the neighborhood.[61]

The masked killer's assault on Haddonfield tapped into white middle-class anxieties that the secure world they had created could easily become a literal shambles. Carpenter pictures Haddonfield as in every way idyllic, except that one of its perfect families in one of its perfect homes produced an unstoppable killer. In 1984 Wes Craven would build on this theme with his *A Nightmare on Elm Street*. As the title suggests, a safe suburban street could easily become a slaughterhouse where, to paraphrase Malcolm X, the fulfillment of the American dream actually represents the nightmare.

The legacy of the 1960s lived on in other aspects of the new American monster film. The critique of the alleged safety of the suburb is joined in the slasher film by a strong antiauthoritarian strain. The role played by teens has led many commentators to see such films as parables of adolescent hormones run wild. In fact, the motif of teenagers in danger has been less an opportunity to explore adolescent sexuality than a chance to satire various kinds of established, institutionalized authority. Young people are generally left to themselves in these films, forced to cope with the monster alone. Parents, police, camp counselors, and ministers are frequently held up for ridicule as either ineffectual or participants in the mayhem.

Chain Saw created the paradigm of this approach, portraying countercultural teens as victimized by a family in a domestic setting—the American home turned slaughterhouse. In *Friday the 13th*, the killer turns out to be a middle-aged mom who despises the young for their treatment of her son Jason. In *Halloween*, Laurie Strode's father (whom we see only briefly, in one scene) puts her in harm's way by sending her to "the old Myers place" on an errand. In *A Nightmare on Elm Street*, the parents of an entire town endanger their children by keeping secret a horrible act of violence, the lynching of an alleged serial killer. The older generation's acts of violence, and the secrecy that surrounds it, unleashes Freddy Krueger into the nightmares of their children.[62]

Craven's 1984 *Nightmare* represents the crest of the slasher film's creativity as a form. Independent auteurs such as Hooper, Carpenter, and Craven increasingly moved on to big-budget studio projects and left the indie slashers to lesser talents eager to cash in on the maniac-with-a-knife craze.

By the late 1980s, Reagan-era conservatism seemed to influence many of the films being made in the genre. Sequel after sequel drew less and less from their seminal sources of bloody inspiration and degenerated into simplistic morality tales of besieged communities seeking to destroy a monster, a reimagining of the themes of 1930s horror with less creativity and lots more blood and skin.[63]

Indeed, only an extremely naïve view of popular culture's political possibilities can claim that the flood of slasher films that stalked behind the classics challenged the American status quo. Many of them simply propagated the era's ideological message of individualism and consumerism. The 1980s allowed America to reimagine its own adolescence. Too many of the cheaply made, but almost always financially successful, slasher films represented exactly the kind of sleazy commodities the decade became famous for advertising, desiring, and acquiring.

One offbeat example, though now a cult classic that represents the genre's political pliability, appears in the 1986 *Chopping Mall*. The absurd film, marketed as a traditional slasher, offers one especially cynical take on maniacal murder. Made seven years after George Romero's *Dawn of the Dead* satired the emergence this new kind of American shopping culture, the mall became less a haunted space than an endangered space. Consumerism is not the enemy; it, along with human survival, has become a value worthy of defense.

The film celebrated American gun culture in much the same way as Romero had parodied it. The young men of *Chopping Mall* load out a supply of weaponry from a store called "Peckinpah's Sporting Goods," a clear reference to Sam Peckinpah's *Wild Bunch*. This is no revisionist western, however, but something closer to Reagan's desire to reclaim manifest destiny and the constructed image of the Old West, complete with inhuman forces to slaughter and evil to destroy. The characters use Rambo as a heroic point of reference and, along with misogynistic tendencies all slashers have been alleged to display, the film feels like the right-wing fantasy *Red Dawn* fought to keep the mall safe.

By the late 1980s the Reagan Revolution came to fruition in yuppie dreams, a vision of youthful experience in which brutally ambitious MBAs fought their way to the top of corporate America. From Michael J. Fox's Alex in television's *Family Ties* to Michael Douglas' Gordon Gekko in *Wall Street*, the yuppie worldview saw American life as a wild frontier and men in Brooks Brothers suits as the new Davy Crocketts.[64]

The serial killer remained the icon of this era though revisions of his image left behind some of the themes found in the slasher films. Increasingly, the monster wore the mask of success, American style.

Mainstreaming Murder

Bret Easton Ellis' 1991 *American Psycho* transformed Norman Bates into a 1980s American yuppie turned (maybe) into a serial killer. Ellis' novel tells the story of Patrick Bateman, a corporate-ladder-climbing monster whose obsession with the accumulation of status commodities and utter hatred of women leads him to commit a series of bizarre and brutal murders. While Ellis leaves unresolved the question of whether or not these murders actually occurred or only took place in Bateman's mind, his graphic descriptions seem more than real to the reader.[65]

Ellis' title makes clear that Bateman represents a peculiarly "American" psycho. Bateman works for "Pierce and Pierce Mergers and Acquisitions," a typical 1980s financial firm practicing slash-and-burn capitalism. His antifeminist obsessions and love of status symbols (a brilliant and unforgettable scene in the book and the film has Bateman wax poetic over the paper quality of his business cards) perfectly tied together the obsessions of the New Right, its freebooting entrepreneurialism, and reactionary response to the women's movement.[66]

A cult classic today, *American Psycho* had a bumpy ride to press. Simon & Schuster originally picked up *American Psycho* for publication. The rumors of the novel's alleged misogyny set off intense and heated prepublication criticism from NOW and other women's organizations. Simon & Schuster dropped the book one month before its planned publication date, though it was quickly picked up by Vintage Books and became a controversial best seller.[67]

Ironically, during the period when Ellis' book received a rough handling by the censorious at both ends of the political spectrum, images of serial murderers saturated American culture. Bateman's deeply American psychosis mirrored a fascination with the serial killer that intertwined with the country's culture of celebrity. This had been a facet of the serial killer's appeal since Ted Bundy, whose crimes brought him enormous media attention while he waited for execution on Florida's death row. Bundy became one of the first serial killers to create a romantic following. Women sent him flowers in prison and wrote him love letters. One admirer, Carol Anne Boone, moved from Washington State to Florida in order to be near him. They later married and had a child.[68]

The growth of serial killer fandom led to the phenomenon of murderabilia, the auctioning of personal items and artwork belonging to "celebrity murderers." The Internet helped to fuel this phenomenon. A murderabilia site called murderauction.com offered a John Wayne Gacy collection with a starting bid of ten thousand dollars, as well as less expensive single items such as a Henry Lee Lucas drawing of a vampire with a starting bid of seven hundred dollars.[69]

Public obsession with serial murderers by the 1990s fed off new cultural realities. Historic changes in technology since the appearance of *Psycho* in 1960 facilitated the rise of a cult of celebrity. In the late 1960s satellite technology made possible the broadcast of multiple channels and the emergence of cable television. Entrepreneurs like Rupert Murdoch proved especially adept at transforming cable TV into one strand of a larger web of media outlets (including magazines and radio stations) that literally covered the globe. By the 1980s this media monster had become voracious for material to fill hundreds of channels playing twenty-four hours a day. The explosive growth of the Internet by the mid-1990s created an even greater need for fresh content. Serial murderers and their stories provided a simple narrative that did not ask audiences to confront larger social and political realities.

The cult of celebrity that centered on murderers invited satire. Oliver Stone's 1994 *Natural Born Killers* used the serial killer as a symbol of media madness, posing questions about the nature of the monster in a world that simultaneously hates, fears, and glamorizes it. Stone's psychedelic imagery perfectly captured the frenetic pace of the twenty-four-hour news cycle. The film used the device of a TV sitcom to tell the story of one of the killers' dysfunctional family background, mixing the inanity of a laugh track with the severe sexual and psychological abuse that allegedly created the murdering maniac.[70]

The mid-1990s perhaps represent the apogee of the American fascination with serial murder. Talk shows, twenty-four-hour news outlets, true crime novels, a raft of movies, and innumerable television police procedurals dealt time and again with the knife-, axe-, and chainsaw-wielding maniac. This dark obsession in American culture did not disappear in the twenty-first century, although history would alter and complicate it.

Al-Qaeda's attack on the Twin Towers in 2001 gave America a new set of monsters. Anger and a desire for revenge led politicians and the public to load the terrorists down with monstrous imagery. As if ideologically inspired terrorists with no respect for human life were not fearful enough, political leaders and commentators referred to the terrorist network as a "cult of evil" and made use of satanic imagery to describe the threat. The idea of the terrorist as the monster became a common media trope.[71]

Shadowy terrorists did not completely replace the maniac with a knife. The 2006 Showtime hit *Dexter* recreated the serial killer for a post–9/11 world. The gruesome drama of the Emmy Award–winning series featured Dexter Morgan (played by Michael C. Hall) as a serial murderer that works by day for the Miami Police Department as a blood spatter expert. By night, he splatters quite a bit of blood on his own in the vigilante killings of "the guilty" who have slipped through the criminal justice system. *Dexter* represents both the best fiction ever produced about the serial murderer and a revisionist reading of America's serial killer craze. *Dexter*, successfully running for eight seasons, asks the audience to identify with the serial murderer in a way that no other imaginative reconstruction of the genre has ever done before.[72]

Dexter's creators provide a significant number of cues that audiences can recognize from the national mythology of the mass murderer. We learn, for example, that Dexter endured a significant childhood trauma. Moreover, he believes, and we are urged to believe, that Dexter is a monster on a basic level. He makes numerous references to his "Dark Passenger," a need to kill born out of a traumatic event. We also learn that Harry, his homicide investigator stepfather, recognized the signs of this inner monster in Dexter's early childhood. Knowing that the beast could be controlled but not destroyed, he taught Dexter "the Code," a complex mix of injunctions against killing the innocent, combined with precautionary measures to keep from getting caught.

A desire to see vigilante justice in the messy post–9/11 world explains only part of Dexter's appeal for audiences. Like Patrick Bateman, he is a very American psycho and a much more appealing one. When we first meet Dexter, he is successful in his work and lives in a small but stylish apartment that offered the perfect domestic nest for the metrosexual male, outfitted with the latest technology and IKEA minimalism. The show's creators also make it clear that he is no sex maniac. The first episode of season 1 forcefully underscores Dexter's heterosexuality by introducing his beautiful girlfriend (Julie Benz), a sweet single mom with perfect children who lives in a comfortable suburban home.[73]

Dexter is the un–Norman Bates in numerous ways. He does not choose his victims in a psychosexual frenzy but rather on the basis of the Code. His issues are primarily paternal rather than maternal, an effort to come to terms with the demands, strictures, and, ultimately, the limitation of patriarchal authority. His fondness for his girlfriend and her children doesn't humanize him so much as it Americanizes him, giving him, for a short time in the series, a traditional family unit that makes his other, secret life seem both comprehensible and compartmentalized.

Dexter taps more into America's dreams than its nightmares. Like numerous characters in successful franchises since the late 1990s, Dexter attempts to live a prosperous, fulfilled, materially rich family life grounded in dark, nighttime activities that, in some sense, make that life possible. Not unlike HBO's *The Sopranos*, AMC's *Breaking Bad*, or Showtime's other hit *Weeds*, *Dexter* critiques white, middle-class dreams while affirming them. Dexter's appeal is that he departs in one significant way from the prosperous, successful mainstream and yet he still desires to be a part of it, to live a life where his boat, his family, and, during season 4, his suburban home form a web of personal fulfillment. He is the perfect suburban warrior, meting out justice from the minivan he acquires in season 3.

While signaling audiences with a recognizable mythology of the serial murderer, Dexter's writers also revise and question that mythology. Did Harry recognize something inherent or, more likely, did he create something through investing Dexter with his bloody and unforgiving Code? Dexter may be a monster, but is he a Frankenstein's monster, cobbled together out of his stepfather/creator's own darkness? Perhaps monsters are made in our society more purposefully than we realize. In fact, perhaps our own beliefs about monsters and their intractable nature help to produce the monsters we fear the most.[74]

By the end of the fourth season of the show, which aired in the fall of 2009, the cracks began to appear in Dexter's persona and in the audience's sympathy for him. The show's writers radically called into question Dexter's suburban lifestyle in an especially dramatic fashion, simultaneously suggesting that the murderer as celebrity is so deeply problematic that a miniature apocalypse is the result of our cultural romance with the murdering maniac. However, his Code does not disappear, and the loss of the suburban fantasy arguably makes him into an even more lethal practitioner of social vengeance.

Dexter forces its audience to have the experience of realizing that they are fully and completely sympathizing with the sum of all fears: a being who kills with no remorse and whose all-consuming self-regard allows him to decide who is innocent and who deserves execution. Dexter implicates us in the crimes of a murderer. At a time when the president of the United States could refer to himself as "the decider" in matters of war and peace, Dexter used his code to decide who gets to live and who gets to die. The audience's total identification with Dexter asks how much we are all humming along to the executioner's song.[75]

The fascination with the serial killer sat at a very complex nexus of cultural nerve endings in late twentieth-century America. This newest American monster truly became a meaning machine that glossed attitudes toward sexuality, crime, mental illness, and celebrity culture. The excitement of the narrative grew from the clear lines it drew between good and evil and the lurid shock value of the most gruesome of the serial murderer's escapades. Moreover, these monsters might be part of your everyday experience. Media interviews with neighbors and acquaintances of accused killers invariably told the same tale. He was "quiet and shy." He was perhaps a loner but "seemed normal." The monster was within, the stranger was beside us, and the call was coming from inside the house.

Maniac murderers as a growth industry in popular culture blurred the line between fiction and reality, changing with the transformation of American society over a forty-year period. A clear line of development can be seen between Leatherface and Dexter, one that mirrors social and economic changes in American society. The meaning of the maniac killer changed dramatically from the proletarian murders in Texas, at Crystal Lake, and on Elm Street, to the sophisticated killers of Wall Street and South Beach. The American monster had come to the suburbs not as an invader like Michael Myers but as a permanent fixture. Along the way he became a fully Americanized psycho, willing to go a bit further to get the penthouse or the McMansion, but sharing the same values as the white middle class and those who imitated it.

The origin of the monster did not change over this long period of development. Norman Bates, Leatherface, Jason Voorhees, and Dexter all share a common tale of family dysfunction. In this way, the serial killer as monster spoke to the social upheavals of the 1960s and 1970s. These narratives found their greatest resonance at a time when the nature of the American family changed forever, when family values became a battle cry, and gender and sexuality occupied the center of political rhetoric. If Americans in the 1960s and early 1970s worried about the last house on the left, they soon worried that monsters might be living in the bedroom at the top of the stairs.

6

HAUNTED HOUSES

She doesn't need a psychiatrist, she needs a priest ... Jesus Christ won't somebody help me!

—*The Exorcist*

Mark glued the Frankenstein monster's left arm into the shoulder socket. It was a specially treated Aurora model that glowed in the dark, just like the plastic Jesus he had gotten for memorizing all of the 119th Psalm in Sunday School class.

—Stephen King, *Salem's Lot*

In late December 1973 film patrons lined up around the block in every American city to watch some of the most terrifying images ever put on film. Using a documentarian style that created both a sense of *cinema verite* and of claustrophobia, director William Friedkin's *The Exorcist* dragged America, literally kicking and screaming, into the bedroom of a teenage girl and forced them to face the devil.

The Exorcist invites us into a comfortable, toney Georgetown townhouse, the home of movie star Chris McNeil (Ellen Burstyn) and her daughter Regan (Linda Blair). Chris is starring in a film being made at Georgetown University about campus protest and the Vietnam War (that she laughingly describes as "the Walt Disney version of the Ho Chi Minh story"). The household rattles busily with the demands of McNeil's career and social life, while Regan, her adolescent daughter, seems well adjusted in school, has an artistic bent, and wants a pony. All in all, this does not seem the setting of an American monster tale.

But strange things begin to happen to Regan. A Ouija board planch-ette moves on its own. Regan's bed shakes violently, and she uses foul language at the most inappropriate moments possible. At one point, she interrupts one of her mother's fashionable dinner parties standing in her nightgown and voiding her bladder on the carpet. She then pronounces doom on one of the guests, an astronaut who is about to begin an orbital mission. "You're going to die up there," she snarls.

McNeil goes first to the medical establishment, certain they will find some somatic explanation for her daughter's behavior and the odd events that surround her. Neurosurgeons put the young girl through a battery of torturous examinations. Regan worsens and her upstairs bedroom becomes a chamber of horrors. She displays enormous strength, hurling a doctor across the room. Her skin turns a garish green, covered with gashes and scar tissue, while her eyes have become feral and inhuman. In one harrowing scene, she masturbates with a crucifix.[1] Unable to find a medical solution, Regan's physicians suggest to Chris that she find a priest to perform an exorcism, noting that "the power of suggestion" might help the young woman. McNeil revolts at the idea of finding a "witch doctor" but finally turns in desperation to Father Damien Karras, a young Jesuit with training in psychiatry. Karras receives permission from church authorities to conduct an exorcism with the help of an older priest, Father Merrin, who has experience with the ritual.

The ensuing struggle with the demon that possesses Regan adminis-tered a series of visceral shocks to audiences. The high production values of the film, unusual for a horror film in the early 1970s, made the makeup and special effects especially convincing. Perfectly paced, Friedkin's film created massive unease, followed it up with shock, and moved to a climax of fear and, for some, the feeling that the ending had left the devil in charge.[2]

The Exorcist released right after Christmas 1973. Horror author Stephen King remembered that a terrified America could not get enough and began "a two-month exorcism jag." At one New York theater in early January, patrons waited four hours to purchase tickets. Showings of the film became spectacles that reflected the action on the screen. First-time viewers fainted, ran out of the theater, and vomited. Others reported weeks of sleepless nights. Catholic priests, and soon Protestant pastors, received requests for exorcisms from frightened moviegoers, convinced that they

The Exorcist movie poster

WILLIAM PETER BLATTY'S

THE EXORCIST

Directed by WILLIAM FRIEDKIN

Something almost beyond comprehension is happening to a girl on this street, in this house ... and a man has been sent for as a last resort. This man is The Exorcist.

ELLEN BURSTYN · MAX VON SYDOW · LEE J. COBB
KITTY WINN · JACK MacGOWRAN   JASON MILLER as Father Karras
LINDA BLAIR as Regan · Produced by WILLIAM PETER BLATTY
Executive Producer NOEL MARSHALL · Screenplay by WILLIAM PETER BLATTY Based on his novel
From Warner Bros. A Warner Communications Company

had become possessed. One ticket-buyer for an early showing of the film told an interviewer that he or she "just wanted to see what all the throwing up was about."[3]

Friedkin's brilliant direction and the film's revolutionary manipulation of cinematography and special effects accounted for some of the extreme audience reaction. Perhaps even more significant than these factors, *The Exorcist* touched on both the transformation of the American family and the place of religion in American society. Linking family breakdown to supernatural terror proved a powerful concoction in 1973–1974 at a time when both family and religious faith became an arena of profound cultural contest.

Families and kinship networks have, for more than five millennia, served as a central organizing principle in human societies. Powerful patriarchal forces in traditional civilizations, including government, religion, medicine, and education, have viewed the family as the first line of defense for male privilege. The combination of intimacy and authority that exists within the household provides the opportunity to inculcate societal conceptions of gender, sexuality, and morality as well as to examine and police behaviors deemed abnormal or dangerous.[4]

Struggles for the liberation of women and sexual minorities in the 1960s raised numerous questions about the nature of family life in America. Second-wave feminism called for a radical redefinition of family life. A powerful and energized conservative response emerged by the late 1970s. Spearheaded primarily by religious leaders, the conservative movement fought back against what it perceived as an "attack on the family." Unwilling to accept the transformative changes that rocked American society, conservatives mounted a highly successful sexual counterrevolution in the 1980s.[5]

Underlying this titanic cultural struggle, anxieties over the body and its processes presented America with a new set of monsters. As the most intimate aspects of Americans' biological experience became battlegrounds of the culture war, monstrous images came crawling out of the womb. Fear that the patriarchal family had risen from its grave to wreak terror, or the anxiety that rapid changes to the family would twist and corrupt America, became the basis of both horror films and popular urban legends. The human body itself, especially the female body, came to be seen as a monster or at least a monster-birthing machine.[6]

Monstrous Moms and Scary Babies

Women's bodies became the literal source of horror during the beginning of the culture wars. *The Exorcist* used the emerging sexuality of a teenage girl as a metaphor for diabolical evil. Brian De Palma's film version of the Stephen King novel *Carrie* did something very similar. At the onset of menarche and with a growing interest in boys, Carrie becomes a conduit for powerful forces that lead to a blood-drenched dénouement. Women's sexuality and reproductive abilities became the focus of numerous horror films throughout the 1970s, exposing America's nervousness over contraception, abortion, the sexual revolution, and the changing nature of the family.[7]

Sexually powerful women proved especially frightening to family values advocates as the sexual revolution came to full fruition in the 1970s. Freedom to experiment with sex and to imagine a life with more than one sexual partner became, especially for women, an extension of the politics of liberation born in the 1960s. Ready availability of effective forms of birth control as well as wide dissemination of knowledge about sex dimmed the possibility that sexual pleasure could lead to terrible consequences.[8]

Given the intimate nature of the subject, statistical formulations of just how sexualized American life became during the 1970s are impossible to offer. Interviews done by sex researchers with a disparate sampling of American women do suggest that sexual experimentation, and improved sexual experience, became more common than ever before. One housewife in her mid-thirties described to interviewers how "a bunch of us girls on the same block started reading books and passing them around—everything from how-to-do-it sex books to real porno paperbacks." She noted that while some of the men complained about the "garbage" their wives read, her own husband "was always ready to try out everything." Even the willingness to talk about sex to interviewers proved that once seemingly invincible cultural barriers had collapsed. Containment, at least the domestic version, had ended.[9]

The willingness, even eagerness, of women to talk about their own sexuality registered the gains of the women's liberation movement in life's most intimate arena. Sexual guides like *The Hite Report* and *My Secret Garden* celebrated a woman's sexual pleasure and the uniqueness of her sexual experience. Many women in the 1970s began to describe both giving and receiving orgasms as a celebration of personal agency and autonomy. One woman described how oral sex gave her "sort of the Amazon mentality—all powerful woman." Another said that giving her partner fellatio meant that she was "exerting power" and that "the giving of pleasure is a powerful position."[10]

New technological innovations contributed to the new relationship American women had to their sexuality and their sexual partners. The introduction of Enovid-10 in 1960, better known as "the pill," provided a safe and highly effective means of preventing conception. Mary Calderone, a feminist on the frontlines of the growing sex education movement, saw the pill effecting a decisive separation between sexual pleasure and pregnancy. By the 1970s, for the first time not only in American history but also in human history, a combination of scientific progress and dramatic social change made it possible to decouple sex and reproduction entirely.[11]

The emerging New Right coalition wanted to end what they saw as party time in America. Conservative rhetoric in the 1970s and 1980s focused on the dangers of the sexually empowered woman who acted on her own agency. Conservatives feared that the family home had become a haunted mansion of female desire run amok, of monstrous reproduction free of patriarchal constraints. The untethering of reproduction from sexual experience transformed the American mother into an American monster.

Conservative critics of feminism explicitly portrayed sexually liberated women as unnatural monsters. Notably, they often conjoined sexual power and the ability to reproduce as an especially fearful mixture. Toni Grant, in a mix of pop psychology and conservative politics entitled *Being a Woman* (1988), warned that men had become only "a means of procreation" that would be used by breeding women and then "discarded in black widow spider fashion." Grant luridly described the independent woman as a "devouring, consuming monster" and suggested that the growing divorce rate meant that men were fleeing for their lives from these omnivorous *vagina dentatas*.[12]

Monstrous women threatened, according to conservatives, to destroy the American economy as well as the American home. Conservative commenter Allan Carlson described the dangers of the "displacement of the patriarchal family by the matriarchal state." Author and Republican activist George Gilder's 1986 attack on feminism, entitled *Men and Marriage* (originally entitled *Sexual Suicide*), argued that women had become "masculine" even as men had become emasculated. This monstrous description of gender-bending had consequences in the marketplace as well as the bedroom. Men, faced with the devouring female, would "lose their procreative energy and faith in themselves and their prospects." Markets, Gilder asserted, would go into decline as America's economic energy became focused on "welfare programs and police efforts required by a culture in chaos."[13]

The Reagan years saw both a rapidly growing inequality of wealth and the slashing of social programs that provided a safety net for the poor. The "welfare queen" became a common trope used by conservatives who wanted to move from a critique of feminism to a warning about the dangers of the maternal state. While James Wilson warned of the "feral, presocial" state of "the ghetto," other conservative critics suggested that monstrous African American women, breeding huge numbers of fatherless, violent creatures, represented an apocalyptic danger. Gilder warned, "the worst parts of the ghetto" featured "a rather typical pattern of female dominance." As scholar, fiction writer, and filmmaker Joshua Bellin points out, conservative writers imagined the typical African American woman as "a spectacularly fertile teenage incubator," a monstrous womb that poured forth crime, poverty, and addiction as well as an army of angry African American men.[14]

A number of horror films in the 1970s and 1980s mirrored, usually unwittingly, conservative critiques of women's liberation and transformed rhetorical monsters into literal ones. David Cronenberg, the Canadian auteur of a number of disturbing body horror films, created a powerful nightmare of anxiety over female reproductive power in his 1979 *The Brood*. Nola Carveth's husband has her committed to an institution that employs a new method of psychiatry in which patients give literal form to their anger through cellular changes in the body. Carveth's feminine rage becomes a dark energy fueling an asexual conception and producing dwarf mutant children who begin killing and maiming all they come in contact with. In one especially unsightly scene, Nola, the monstrous mother, animalistically licks blood and effluvium off of one of her recently gestated egg sacs.

Nola's husband appears in the film as a sympathetic figure in contrast to his monstrous wife. Even before Nola begins breeding little monsters, the film constructs her as callous, foulmouthed, and generally unpleasant. Her psychological problems are rendered as both severe and unsympathetic. Cronenberg suggests that she is suffering from the ennui of the liberated woman who has it all and yet still cannot find a way to be happy and mentally stable. Her search for personal growth shows her to be such an angry feminist that she produces monsters that destroy her family.[15]

Notably, Cronenberg has described the film in highly personal terms, explaining that it emerged out of *his* anger over a recent divorce and the subsequent child custody battle. He has also described the scene of Samantha licking the membrane as no more disturbing than "a bitch licking her pups." Horror historian David Skal has suggested that Cronenberg considered his subject "to be a bitch on any number of levels" and quotes a contemporary *London Observer* review that concluded the film "has something pretty terrible to tell us . . . about the fears of North American males."[16]

In the same year that Samantha's brood wreaked havoc, another monstrous mother attempted to reproduce herself, and slaughter anyone who got in her way, aboard the spaceship *Nostromo*. Ridley Scott's *Alien* combined science fiction with the sensibilities of gothic horror to give the 1970s its most iconic monstrous mother.

Alien offered a complex message about women, the body, and reproduction. The monster, an insect-like, transgender birthing mechanism, uses the *Nostromo* as a nest to breed its young, transforming human victims into incubator. In the film's most notorious scene, a fetal alien explodes out of a male crewmember's chest. The power of the Alien to reproduce on its own also involves outraging the male body, literally tearing it to pieces. In the sequels, the films tend to render the Creature as more specifically female ("the Bitch is back" became the promo line for *Alien 3*).

The Alien's savaging of the *Nostromo*'s crew could easily be read as a reactionary message that toyed with male anxieties over women's increasing control over their bodies and reproduction. This reading must be set alongside the portrayal of Lieutenant Ripley, Sigourney Weaver's character who fused the typical action hero with the slasher genre's "final girl," the

Alien 3 by David Fincher

one who uses courage and ingenuity to survive the night. Moreover, as the classic *Alien* sequels show, Ripley becomes a kind of mother who, in the film's final install-ment, asserts her own ability to control her biological destiny by destroying the alien spawn growing within her. In this final sequel, Ripley has shaved her head and become a "bitch" in the politically conscious sense of the term, refusing to allow biology to be her destiny. Notably *Alien 3* appeared in 1992 after a series of Supreme Court rulings that allowed states to place barriers between women and abortion, including parental consent for minors and strictures against family planning clinics counseling abortion as an option.[17]

Numerous films in the 1970s joined *Alien* in playing with the fright-ening potentialities of female biology and the politics of reproduction. *It's Alive* (1974), with its tale of a clawed, mutant horror that comes out of its mother's womb as a killing machine, appeared one year after the *Roe v. Wade* decision.

It's Alive directly addressed the politics of sexuality and reproduc-tion. We learn that the couple, the Davies, considered an abortion early in Ms. Davies' pregnancy since, the husband tells a police detective, "every-one inquires about it these days . . . but we decided to have the baby." "Everybody makes mistakes," the detective responds, aware that the couple has created a monster.

The increased role that technology played in human reproduction haunts *It's Alive*. The title is, of course, a reference to Dr. Frankenstein's infamous cry of triumph in the 1931 Universal film. Mad science run amok seems to be behind the horror. But the origin of the mutation is never explained, though we learn that Lenore Davies had been taking birth control pills for thirty-one months prior to her pregnancy. A doctor working for a major corporation recommends "absolute destruction" of the monster child to prevent any discovery of malfeasance on the part of the pharmaceutical industry or laxness on the part of the FDA. At one point, Frank Davies calls the child a "Frankenstein" and ruminates on how he always thought that Frankenstein was the name of the monster when he was a kid but, when he read the novel in high school, he learned that it was the name of the monster's creator. "Somehow," he says, "the identities got all mixed up." "Best not to take escapist literature too seriously," responds a scientist who wants to use the monster's body for research.

It's Alive, and all of the 1970s films of fetal terror, owe something to the 1968 Roman Polanski film *Rosemary's Baby*. Polanski had already explored how the sexual counterrevolution could become a horror film; his movie *Repulsion* tells of a repressed young girl's descent into psychosis and murder. *Rosemary's Baby* gave the director, infamous for his own sexual violence against women, the opportunity to examine the emerging clash between second-wave feminism and religious conservatism.

Rosemary's Baby tells the story of Guy and Rosemary, a young couple given the chance to move into a Gilded Age apartment building known as the Bramford (actually filmed at New York's famous Dakota building). The film opens like a Doris Day–lite picture with the attractive young couple beginning their life together in a well-appointed apartment and getting to know their wacky, elderly neighbors. Soon enough, the monster begins to appear. Rosemary has disturbing dreams of being raped by a demon. Guy, a struggling actor, gets a part in a play but only after his rival suffers a sudden and mysterious onset of blindness.

When Rosemary discovers that she is pregnant, she finds herself the center of attention at the Bramford. The film enjoins the audience to share her mounting sense of paranoia as everyone from her doctor to her neighbor attempts to sequester and control her, feeding her a disgusting mixture that's supposed to be herbal and constantly monitoring her body and behavior. The film becomes increasingly surreal as Rosemary discovers that her quirky neighbors are, in reality, a satanic coven, and her husband has made a very literal Faustian pact, giving her body and her womb to Satan in return for a career boost. She gives birth, against her will, to a child that has "his father's eyes," the eyes of the devil.

Rosemary had her baby in the same year that Pope Paul VI promulgated the encyclical *Humanae Vitae* ("On Human Life"). Given the progressive changes brought to Catholicism by Vatican II, many Catholics, especially in America, expected a liberalization of the church's traditional strictures against contraception. Ironically, a devoutly Catholic doctor who believed it represented a "natural" method of birth control that cooperated with female biology had developed the pill to prevent conception. Pope Paul's advisory committee, made up of laypeople as well as bishops and theologians, had recommended that the church alter its stance.[18]

Paul VI's encyclical, instead of a new vision of human sexuality, represented a battle cry of the most conservative forces in the Vatican, a declaration of war against the sexual revolution. American Catholics responded by leaving the church in droves. Over the next several decades, an increasingly hard-line stance, taken by the American Catholic hierarchy on matters of gender and sexuality, created an unlikely alliance between traditionalist Catholics and the evangelical Christian Right.[19]

Rosemary's Baby makes good use of the growing religious crisis. Rosemary is herself a lapsed Catholic, and her pregnancy coincides with the Pope's visit to New York City. In her doctor's office, the infamous 1965 *Time* magazine cover with the stark question, "Is God Dead?" sits on the waiting room table. The child has a demonic nativity, complete with visiting foreign satanists who appear as diabolical wise men. Like the birth of Christ in Christian theology, the satanists hail the birth of the "Promised One" as the beginning of a new satanic millennium.

Religious groups reacted with fury to *Rosemary's Baby*. The Catholic Office of Motion Pictures (formerly the Legion of Decency) attacked the film's "perverted use . . . of fundamental Christian beliefs." If Polanski had not perverted, he had at least inverted Christian symbols in order to create a powerfully political aesthetic document. *Rosemary's Baby* wrapped American sexual and religious anxieties into a single disturbing package.[20]

In Polanski's vision, the satanists are urging typical bourgeois American values, indeed "family values," on Rosemary. They force her to make the child the center of her experience and to allow her once-beloved apartment to become a literal and psychological prison. In a prescient satirical move, Polanski created a satanic send-up of religious conservatism's efforts to control women's bodies, particularly to control their role in reproduction.[21]

Most of the cinematic body horror watched by Americans during the culture wars did not have the rapier thrust of Polanski's satire. As the culture attempted to navigate the transformation of the American family and attendant issues of sexuality and gender, a popular form of folklore became a way to talk intensely about intimate anxieties. This folklore, known generally as "urban legend," increasingly found its way into America's horror films, and even its politics. These legends would have real-world consequences, creating monsters that ruined lives and reputations.

A Hook for a Hand

Alone in the house, the teenaged babysitter does her homework and watches TV as the children sleep peacefully upstairs. The phone rings and she picks up the receiver. "Hello?" Silence. A few minutes later, the phone rings a second time and she answers. Again, silence.

She returns to her homework, a feeling of unease beginning to grow. Soon, the phone is ringing ominously every few minutes, and a male voice finally says in a threatening tone, "Have you checked the children?" Terrified, the babysitter calls the police, who arrange to trace the call. The phone rings again, and the threatening male voice urges the sitter again to "check the children." The police call, warning her to "Get out of there! The call is coming from inside the house."

This nasty little chiller is undoubtedly familiar to every reader. Folklorists refer to it as the motif of the "Babysitter in Danger" or "The Babysitter and the Man Upstairs," an American urban legend that became popular in the 1970s and the basis for the 1979 hit film *When a Stranger Calls*. It became part of a large fund of rapidly circulating modern folklore that told monster stories of sexual danger and deviance. Frequently, these tales are punishment narratives triggered by behavior that mainstream culture considered immoral, inappropriate, or at least anxiety producing.[22]

Although oral folklore that combines elements of rumor, legend, and narrative are as old as human society, the "urban legend" is a distinctly modern phenomenon. These materials are not "urban" because they always take place in cities but because they travel at light speed along communication media typical of modern, industrial society. The telecommunications boom of the 1960s and 1970s and the growth of pop culture industries in the same period ensured that urban legends traveled from coast to coast and became national phenomena. The babysitter in danger became such a common trope in the 1970s that it provided fodder for both John Carpenter's *Halloween* (1978) and *When a Stranger Calls* (1979). The latter represents a milestone in the growth of American folklore, the first time that an urban legend had been used as the narrative basis of a major feature film.[23]

Babysitting had become an American institution by the late 1950s. The emerging teenage demographic supplemented the parental allowance (a new phenomenon of the middle class) in the prosperous post–World War II years with all manner of part-time jobs. Baby-boom parents seeking a night away from the kids paid teenage girls to stay in their home, eat all they wanted from the refrigerator, and not have any friends over. By the 1970s, as women entered the workforce and rising divorce rates significantly increased the number of single-parent families, hiring childcare went from being a luxury for middle-class parents to an economic necessity for most parents.[24]

Anxious parents frequently worried that leaving a teenager in charge of their home and child may not have been the best idea. Parents' practical concerns fed off larger anxieties about gender, parenting, and intergenerational conflict. Meanwhile, babysitters themselves, especially in the 1950s and 1960s, often saw their part-time jobs as preparation for motherhood, an initiation into domesticity.[25]

The babysitter-in-danger motif reflects the fear that teenagers, especially in the intergenerational conflict of the 1970s, had failed to prove themselves ready for the responsibility of babysitting. The story, in which the parents are a missing element, exploits the teenage girl's fears of being unable to protect either herself or her charge from a masculine attacker. Sometimes these stories drew specifically on parental fears. The same genre of urban legends includes the story of "the Cooked Baby" or, an especially telling title, "the Hippy Babysitter." In this cautionary tale, a countercultural babysitter, often described as being high on pot, alcohol, or both, mistakes a baby for a roast or a turkey and cooks it in the oven (later variants of the story made it a microwave).[26]

These stories, circulating through oral transmission and later on the Internet, encoded a profoundly conservative message. Urban legends became tales of matriarchal failure, a conservative critique of women's unwillingness to fully domesticate themselves. Variants of the cooked baby tale had an unhappy mother roasting the baby or a mother "taking pills" to deal with depression (usually rendered unsympathetically in these stories as a "woman's illness" or "nerves"). Monsters, either as home invader, babysitter, or bad mother, suggested that women's liberation threatened the very lives of America's children.

Monsters came in handy for other deeply conservative purposes in the post-1960s era. Urban legend provided a way to police the sexuality of teenagers and to suggest that immediate, bloody, moral retribution awaited the sexually adventurous. Notably, teenagers themselves often became important transmitters of a genre of stories, generally described by folklorists as the motif of "the Hook" or "Hook Man." In this story, a teenage couple parks at a local inspiration point, making out and listening to the radio. The music and the mood are interrupted by a radio announcement that a "lunatic" has escaped from a local asylum. The announcer helpfully observes that the public can recognize the escapee by a hook used to replace his amputated hand. This terrifies the girl, but the boy wants to stay and have some more fun. Finally, she convinces him to leave and he angrily pulls away, tires squealing. When they arrive at the girl's house, the boy opens the door for her and passes out when he sees the bloody stump of a hook hanging from the passenger door.[27]

The monster of the story of the Hook served the need of post-1960s American society to rein in the kids and their hormones. In this most common version of the tale, the girl resists the boy's advances, "holding out" while he seeks to make her "give it up." His hormones almost bring about their deaths, leading folklorist Bill Ellis to suggest that "Hook Man" plays the role of "moral custodian" in a time of shifting mores. Some versions of the story make this point even more strongly when the amorous boyfriend meets his death while the "good girl" gets away. "Only the strictist sexual standards can save you" is the message to teenage girls. Lie back and think of the Hook.[28]

Monster tales became part of a larger project in post-1960s America to produce a solid and respectable citizenry. Churches, schools, and civic groups sought to socialize teenagers in ways that limited the effects of the sexual revolution and the political repercussions of the counterculture. Nervousness over sex, drugs, and rock and roll called forth a powerful cultural movement to direct young Americans down more traditional paths. This effort took the form of an increased and intensive concern about "the youth" in churches where programs directed specifically at them blossomed. Parents and teachers sought to attract adolescents to the Boy Scouts of America even as the organization's membership declined ("He's such a boy scout" became a common, derogatory phrase). Summer camps advertised themselves as centers for moral education that taught middle-class values. The wilderness became a training ground for life in the suburbs.[29]

The growth in popularity of summer camps for children and teens promised a deeply American experience, a replication of the frontier experience that would inculcate "good values." Activities tended to reinforce gender conventions, while counselors insisted that campers maintain high standards of cleanliness and hygiene even in allegedly natural settings.

After 1960 camps featured areas designated for specific recreational pursuits, often with the idea that such predetermined arenas of fun and learning (waterfront, archery range, craft cabins) created safe environments that facilitated supervision and discipline. Above all, summer camps insisted on full participation of all campers. "Teamwork" represented a primary social value.[30]

The campfire tales of mindless, unstoppable killers who haunt the woods around the campers' cabins present an odd counterpoint to the wholesome fun. Most major American summer camps have such a story told and retold every year by camp counselors. Camp Robert Meecher in northern Kentucky has "Headless Haddy," a dark-clad woman who rides a horse and beheads male campers. Camp Clifton in Ohio has "The One-Armed Hermit" who rips and tears at campers' screen doors trying to get in. Camp Ranger, just outside of New York City, has a maniac who had once been a counselor but was burned up in a fire trying to save a camper. Despite his altruism in life, the unquiet spirit of the counselor has become murderous.[31]

In various ways, the murderers who haunt the edges of the campfire are figures that violate the norms that summer camp seeks to inculcate, or they dispatch those that do. Many of the stories fit a general motif that folklorists refer to as "The Disfigured Hermit," a physically repulsive monster that chooses social isolation over the values of teamwork and community spirit that almost every summer camp seeks to impart. Folkloric monsters may also punish campers who fail to live up to camp standards of health and hygiene. Camp Ranger in New York State promises "fellowship" and "athletic competition." Apparently, not accepting these values can have dire consequences. Its counselors warn that the camp's resident murdering maniacal ghost will "pick the fattest kid out of the bunch" and will tear "all his limbs off."[32]

Monsters by the 1970s had become instruments of social discipline. Urban legends and campfire tales shed light on the role of the horror film in relation to America's late twentieth-century struggles over gender and sexuality. A number of feminist critics of American horror films in the 1970s and 1980s argued that slasher films celebrated violence against women and punished sexual behavior. *Halloween* seemed to critics to represent the first and one of the worst offenders until slasher films became one long post-coital massacre in the 1980s. John Carpenter himself took note of the raft of cultural criticism his film and its imitators had received when he jokingly apologized for bringing an end to the sexual revolution.[33]

These critics fail to note that some slasher films, though certainly not all, turn upside down powerful narratives that contained profoundly conservative messages not only about sexuality but also about the role of women in the household. The classic slasher films citique these stories, expressing, if not a clear political message, at least discontent at the vision of society propounded by traditional authorities.

Halloween provides a good example. On one level, the film borrowed all the imagery of babysitters in danger from urban folklore. But it also transformed one of those babysitters into a hero, the final girl whose courage and cleverness allow her to outwit and even outfight the monster. *Friday the 13th* drew directly on tales of unstoppable maniacs haunting the summer camp with its story of Jason Voorhees stalking and killing teens at Camp Crystal Lake. Notably, however, Jason had once been a child at this camp, and his mistreatment by the counselors had turned him into a monster. He reserves his hatchets, knives, and, at one point, even a spear gun for the counselors themselves, the ones who tell scary stories to keep the kids in line.[34]

Filmmakers seeking to transform social nightmares into successful film franchises are not the equivalent of social prophets. Their entertaining intervention in the culture wars did little to prevent deep anxieties over social change from spilling out into the real world. The moral panic, often with horrifying consequences, became a staple of American culture in the Age of Reagan. Urban legends transformed into public morality plays that found their way into the court system and into the ideological rhetoric of the New Religious Right.

Halloween poster

The Monster and the Moral Panic

Generations of New Yorkers who spent time at summer camp know the legend of Cropsey. In its canonical version, told by generations of camp counselors, Cropsey and his son lived near the site where the nervous kids are spending the summer. Campers accidentally caused the death of Cropsey's child. Driven insane by grief, Cropsey disappears into a shack in the most isolated part of the woods. One year later, on the anniversary of his son's death, he returns to kill one of the campers with an axe, a meat cleaver, or a hook. The power of such tales comes from performance. Counselors would regularly end the story by saying: "Cropsey is still out in these woods. Tonight is the anniversary of his son's death and he may pay a visit to your bunk at midnight. Good luck."[35]

The Cropsey narrative functions similarly to other gruesome campfire tales, encouraging group solidarity against an outside menace. Unfortunately, Cropsey found its way into the darkest paths of America's forest of urban legend. In an America fighting the culture wars, monstrous metaphors frequently became actual monsters.

In 1987 the kidnapping and search for twelve-year-old Jennifer Schweiger united the story of Cropsey with both an actual crime and rumors of new kinds of monsters. Staten Island residents became convinced that the stories they had heard of a hook-handed or axe-wielding maniac were not only true but had a larger, more conspiratorial dimension. Rumors of Satan worshippers hunting children for use in bizarre rituals joined with the legend of the disfigured hermit to create a terrifying (if not altogether coherent) new narrative of horror. The arrest of Andre Rand, a local homeless person, for Schweiger's kidnapping abated, but did not end, the belief that the worship of Satan played a part in the disappearance of Schweiger and other unsolved cases in the region.[36]

The Staten Island panic is connected to a national moral panic that struck American culture in the 1980s. During that decade, American church leaders, social workers, heads of civic organizations, and even law enforcement officials came to believe that a widespread conspiracy of satanists provided the explanation for social problems as diverse as child abuse, teenage vandalism, missing children, teen suicide, and serial murder. Borrowing heavily from pop culture images of satanic covens, the satanic panic morphed from urban legend into a full-scale moral panic as day care workers, parents, and alienated teenagers found themselves accused in the court system of the most horrific crimes imaginable based on rumor, theological beliefs, and occasionally even something like the "spectral evidence" that had been used by witch-hunting justices in seventeenth-century Salem.[37]

Sociologists and anthropologists generally ascribe the cause of moral panics to anxiety produced by social dislocations. Sociologist Jeffrey S. Victor, in his brilliant and important book *Satanic Panic: The Creation of a Contemporary Legend*, notes that factors that influenced these lurid stories in the 1980s and 1990s include the high American divorce rate, the anxiety produced by stepparents and stepchildren, and the sense, across the political spectrum, of corruption in the American experience. On the latter point, Victor points out that the 1970s and 1980s gave America Watergate, Oliver North and the Iran-Contra affair, D.C. mayor Marion Barry's lies about drug use, Pete Rose's gambling and tax evasion, televangelist Jim Bakker's and Jimmy Swaggart's embarrassing fall from grace, and numerous Wall Street moral debacles, including the savings and loan crisis that called into question the basic integrity of America's allegedly free-market system.[38]

A sense among conservatives that something had gone profoundly wrong with American society certainly contributed to the satanic panic, especially in its ability to find resonance with people across the political and religious spectrum. But the monsters created by the panic also had a profoundly political dimension shaped by the culture wars and the rise of the Christian Right. Conservative evangelicals began to organize themselves politically in the early 1970s, specifically in response to the 1973 *Roe v. Wade* decision. By the late 1970s, national conservative evangelical leaders such as Jerry Falwell and Tim LaHaye assembled a network of organizations such as the Religious Roundtable and the Moral Majority to lobby representatives and mobilize voters.[39]

Narratives of supernatural terror and danger have always been part of American Christianity, dating back to Jonathan Edwards' "Sinners in the Hands of an Angry God" and the Puritans' tales of devils and God's wrath. The Christian Right created a powerful symbolic language out of that traditional message of hell and damnation combined with cultural unease over controversial social issues. Stories of a massive satanic conspiracy perfectly suited this worldview. Portraying themselves as the defenders of the American home proved especially powerful when the enemies of the traditional family could be constructed as satanists brainwashing, torturing, and murdering children. The powerful metaphor of satanic conspiracy allowed for extreme attacks on books, music, comics, and films viewed as baleful influences, attacks that saw these media as instruments of a sadistic, supernatural monster. Political debate and discussion became impossible when conservative evangelical rhetoric linked pro-choice advocates, feminists, heavy metal musicians, liberal Democratic congressmen, and child-killing devil worshippers into a single web of diabolical conspiracy.[40]

These beliefs did not exist simply as sermons or fragmentary folk belief. In 1983 accusations of child abuse against workers at the McMartin Preschool just outside Los Angeles included charges of cannibalism and forbidden rites dedicated to the devil. Several years of investigations and a twenty-eight-month trial followed, at the time the longest trial in American history. Although no physical evidence of actual abuse ever surfaced, one of the accused spent five years in prison until he found a way to post a $1.5 million bail. Heavy media coverage of the McMartin case helped set off day care panics across the nation.[41]

Moral panics over satanic monsters became a basic feature of life in 1980s America. In 1985 a sheriff near Toledo, Ohio, claimed that satanic cults had sacrificed fifty to eighty children and buried them in a wooded area near Holland, Ohio. What became known as the "Toledo dig" attracted significant media attention but no physical evidence. In 1988 absurd national rumors of a satanic cult that planned the kidnappings and sacrifices of blue-eyed virgins on May 13 (Friday the 13th) led to deeply irrational and dangerous behavior. Jeffrey Victor's research on the small town of Jamestown, New York, during this rumor panic revealed that what the era called "alternative" teens had been bullied and beaten up, parents kept their children home from school, and more than a hundred cars appeared at a wooded location rumored to fuction as a satanic meeting site, many of the cars containing parents and teens who came armed with guns, knives, and blunt weapons. Other incidents, usually centered on schools, blossomed all over the country.[42]

Conservative evangelical churches and law enforcement often allied with one another in seeking out satanic cults and fomenting base-less rumors. The involvement of churches is easily explicable. Satanic panics did not have to be founded on concrete empirical evidence since beliefs about the devil depended on inviolate positions of faith. The willingness of law enforcement officials to believe and act on these rumors proves more difficult to explain. A full study of so-called occult cops has shown that police officers that made themselves "experts" on satanic cults usually held conservative Christian beliefs and that many of them spent the 1960s involved in the surveillance of antiwar and civil rights groups.[43]

The media's need for monster tales to fill a twenty-four-hour news cycle further abetted these moral panics. In May of 1985, the television news magazine *20/20* ran a lurid special entitled "The Devil Worshippers" that provided a national platform for conservative evangelical ministers and occult cops to speak as experts on the topic of Satanism. Authorities accepted gothic claims of cannibalism and child sacrifice uncritically. The Toledo dig provides another example of the role of the media in the panics. Alleged occult expert Dale Griffis found doll's clothing and a few curved knives at the site and insisted that this provided evidence of satanic cult activity. Television news widely reported these claims with no alternative explanation offered.[44]

The satanic panic of the 1980s drew on the worst aspects of the American monster tradition, the power of horror narratives to construct cultural and political opponents as the ultimate other. Religion has always needed its monsters, but the ideological struggles of the late twentieth century increased the temptation to draw on monstrous imagery to describe political opponents. Americans already nervous over changes in family life and gender roles, especially those prone to think of these changes as "attacks on the American family," proved easy targets for rumor panics that had the blessing of church and community leaders.

Moral panic and the American monster tradition also appeared in the phenomenon of Christian-themed haunted houses that became popular in the 1970s, a cultural form that combined the most gothic aspects of Christian theology with imagery from the battlefields of the culture war. Jerry Falwell's Thomas Road Baptist Church featured an event in 1972 known as "Scaremare," a strange mixture of traditional haunted house frights (at least of the tamest sort) and a crucifixion scene, followed by the distribution of gospel literature. By the early 1980s other evangelical churches in Florida and New Mexico began including social and political imagery in their alternative Halloween productions.

So-called Hell Houses and Judgment Houses owe a great deal to American monster culture, often referencing the gory effects of bargain basement slasher films and the demonic terrors of post–*Rosemary's Baby* horror. Social problems that evangelicals perceive as part of America's "moral degeneration" in particular are portrayed with a horror film aesthetic. Hell Houses almost always include an "abortion scene" in which buckets of fake blood and a cold, dismissive medical staff turn the patient into their victim. In 1991 one controversial Hell House in New England used animal intestines in a jar to represent an aborted fetus. Blood and other effluvia fly in scenes that replicate a school shooting, a teen suicide, and a drunk driving accident.[45]

Hell Houses not only borrow images directly from horror films, they tell tales of cultural and theological monsters. Images from hell frequently employ an S&M sensibility with masked and leather-clad male demons whipping and torturing attractive teenage girls. These images owe something to Clive Barker's *Hellraiser* series of the late 1980s and early 1990s in which demonic spirits in bondage-wear rip the flesh of unlucky souls with a pain that becomes pleasure.[46]

Author and religion scholar Jason Bivins reports from his site visits that exorcism and possession scenes are common fare in Hell Houses. These scenes often borrow directly from both *Alien* and *The Exorcist*, with demons exploding out of chests and heads doing a Linda Blair–inspired 360-degree turn. Bivins goes on to describe how the aesthetic of the Hell House makes liberal use of "blood and meat. . . . The sets of Hell House are littered with broken bodies, blood, weapons and debris, with demons and malevolent spirits flitting between worlds to torment the waking who suffer through graphic portrayals of late-term abortion, murders, risen corpses and sexual trauma." Showing no sense of irony, one Hell House in Texas featured a scene in which a young woman, described as a lost soul who "directs horror films in Hollywood," falls screaming into hell for poisoning the minds of the young.[47]

The Hell House phenomenon shows the usefulness of monster narratives in the American culture wars. The willingness to make use of the aesthetics of modern horror, a genre often deplored in official evangelical rhetoric as an example of society's moral depravity, suggests that America's monsters are an inescapable part of the rhetoric of moral crisis. This does not represent a cynical use of monster imagery since most evangelicals believe in a literal supernatural monster with monster allies—Satan and his demons. The moral panics are a conservative counterassault on the 1960s, informed by the literal belief that real monsters are stalking American kids.

The Christian Right appeared at a moment of manifest changes in social and cultural history. Some children during these years turned to monsters and found them comforting companions rather than terrifying apparitions. They certainly were not scarier than what was happening in their own homes or in the world's Cold War geopolitics.

Little Monsters

Children and adolescents in the 1960s and 1970s rediscovered the pleasures of the classic Universal Studios horror films and helped to create what has been called "monster culture" or the "monster kid" phenomenon. The impetus behind this was really twofold. In 1958 Universal Studios sold fifty-two of its classic horror films as a package to local television stations across the nation, a package they called *Shock Theatre*. Featuring all of the significant Universal releases (and followed up with a second package called *Son of Shock*), late-night showings of these films made Dracula, Frankenstein, and all their pals suddenly cool again.[48]

By the 1960s hosts for the late-night programs borrowed some of Vampira's old tricks, mixing horror and laughter, without quite attaining her level of camp and dark sensuality. John Zacherle, better known as "Zacherley the Cool Ghoul," set the standard for the new horror hosts. The Philadelphia TV personality created a character equal parts mad scientist and vampire. In this persona he used wacky humor to introduce Universal's classic monsters, intercutting himself into movie scenes and spoofing them. He soon had imitators like "the Gorgon" in Fort Worth, Texas; "Morgus the Magnificent" in New Orleans; Baltimore's "Dr. Lucifer"; and Cleveland's "Ghoulardi."[49]

The renewed popularity of the classic Universal films led to the creation of a magazine that gave style and structure to the monster kid phenomenon, Forrest J. Ackerman's *Famous Monsters of Filmland*. "Uncle Forry," as Ackerman became known to his enormous fan base, filled his black-and-white publication with photographs of the classic monster films and simple fan tributes to every horror and science fiction movie of the 1930s and 1940s. Key to *Famous Monsters'* success was its ability to create an imaginary community of fellow monster lovers, kids who cared more about Bela Lugosi than baseball and who in *Famous Monsters* had their own "private" club. Joe Dante, the horror director best known for *The Howling* and *Gremlins*, remembered his utter delight at finding a copy of *Famous Monsters* at a Safeway supermarket in New Jersey. "Here all of a sudden," Dante told David Skal in a 1991 interview, "was this magazine that was a validation that there were other people out there like us." Dante recalled buying as many of the magazines as he could and having them regularly confiscated by parents, teachers, and camp counselors concerned about his reading habits.[50]

Changes in American toy production and design in the 1960s proved a boon for the monster kids. Prior to the 1960s, toy manufacturers assumed that their products should offer miniature models of adult reality that prepared children for future tasks and solidified gender identities. Boys would play with dump trucks while girls would play with dolls. Moreover, American toy makers created products that children would play with in cooperation with their parents. Since the early twentieth century, Kodak marketed a toy camera for children that they could use to snap pictures, with parental supervision. Chemistry sets, such as Hasbro's Chemcraft, promised to introduce boys to "industrial chemistry," though they needed their dads supervising the experiments. Model airplane kits, also popular in the 1950s, were assumed to be father–son weekend projects. Parents would also be in on the fun of scale model trains and Erector sets.[51]

Intergenerational conflict in the 1960s led toy makers to a different set of assumptions. Increasingly, toy manufacturers began to work off the theory that children desired toys that took them to the realms of the fantastic rather than to the world of workaday adulthood. Moreover, an adversarial relationship between parents and children over the nature of play came to be assumed by advertisers. Toys, and the worlds they conjured, offered an escape from parental oversight and even a subversion of parental values.[52]

These assumptions found their clearest expression in Aurora Plastics' "monster models," which first appeared in 1962. Advertised in comic books and in *Famous Monsters*, these scale models of figures and scenes from the Universal horror cycle were marketed directly to kids, often with the suggestion that these toys would cause at least a minor domestic disturbance. "Decorate your room! Surprise your mother! Create your very own chamber of horror!" suggested one Aurora advertisement. *Look* magazine did a cover story on the phenomenon, writing, "Toyland '64 looks like a charnel house . . . there's a monster for every child, and toy dealers figure this ghoul game will pay a clammy $20 million this year."[53]

By the early 1970s the Universal monsters had become an incredibly marketable commodity. Toy companies sought to capitalize on adolescent fascination with the horrifying fantastic. In 1964 Aurora attempted to market a toy guillotine that caused such a parental backlash that the company pulled the model after only a few months. In the early 1970s Aurora tried to push boundaries once again by marketing a "Pain Parlor" torture chamber model complete with a scantily clad female victim. This time they found themselves criticized by second-wave feminists rather than by parents. Aurora's troubles did not prevent Mattel from selling the "Thingmaker," which allowed kids to mold various insect-like monstrosities, or Hasbro from marketing a "Queasy Bake Oven," a satire of its own "Easy Bake Oven," in which kids could bake a "Bugs and Worms" mix or a "Mud and Crud Cake."[54]

I had the opportunity to be part of the monster kid phenomenon as it took its last gasps in the late 1970s and early 1980s. My own interest in the classic Universal monsters grew from a local television station that owned the *Shock Theatre* package and screened it on Saturday afternoons (without, unfortunately, a horror host). This led in turn to a fascination with the monster kids commodities that included a plastic model of Lugosi as Dracula beside a gnarled tree (plastic bats flapping in the background), a cardboard haunted mansion with adhesive plastic images of the classic monsters and their accoutrements, and a "Mad scientist's laboratory," where plaster molds of the Wolf Man, Franken-stein, Dracula, and the Mummy could be crafted and painted.

Behind the fun for all of us who participated waited the serious business of social transformation. Monster kids, especially my fellow Gen Xers, are the kids who watched a complete restructuring of Amer-ican family demographics. The divorce rate in the 1960s began to rise sharply. Economic slowdown in the 1970s created increased tensions in households already struggling with the changing nature of gender roles. During that decade, a little over half of all the marriages in the United States ended in divorce. By the 1980s, about 40 percent of all children in the United States had, by the age of eighteen, experienced the divorce of their biological parents. A significant number of these children saw subsequent remarriages and divorces and dealt with various stepparents and stepsiblings along the way.[55]

Many of these changes in American family life are likely more posi-tive than negative. The high divorce rate can be attributed in part to liberalized divorce laws in many American states that made it possible for women to leave unhappy or abusive partnerships. Nevertheless, there is no question that many adolescents experienced this period of instabil-ity and change in American social history as a kind of "crisis." Monster culture gave them not only a fantastic world to escape into but also a subculture to be a part of, a community to belong to. The community of monster fandom offered an exciting alternative to the much-discussed "breakdown of the family" as well as the more general malaise in Amer-ican institutions during the 1960s and 1970s. The monster kids are the first wave of a gigantic subculture still present in American life that is made up of comic book fandom, sci-fi and fantasy "geekdom," and parts of the goth and steampunk communities. San Diego's annual ComicCon, attracting one hundred and twenty thousand fanboys and fangirls, had its origins in the alternative community of the monster kids. A network of similar conventions, websites, and comic bookstores have inherited Uncle Forry's dream.[56]

Not every monster kid enjoyed his or her ghoulish fun in a single-parent household (I'm an example of this), so fears about the transformation of America's family do not account entirely for the sudden return of the famous monsters of filmland. Like their parents in the 1950s, children of the 1960s and 1970s continued to live in the shadow of the bomb. The global political tensions of the 1970s made American children more certain of the possibility of nuclear apocalypse. As these kids became teenagers in the 1980s, Ronald Reagan's blunt rhetoric reheated the Cold War to a temperature it had not reached since the early 1960s and the Cuban missile crisis.

Universal monsters perfectly suited kids who lived in a world of vast nuclear stockpiles. The classic monsters had told stories of death and decay combined with the promise of eternal life, at least of a ghastly sort. In an America where political leaders toyed with the possibility of global apocalypse, the black-and-white horrors of an earlier era offered minor frissons and an escape from a real world of horrors.

The end of the monster kids phenomenon in the 1980s (the original *Famous Monsters* ceased publication in 1983, although it has returned from the dead many times since) did not signal the end of a gothic fandom. The monster magazine received a gory makeover in *Fangoria*, a magazine dedicated to the gruesome narratives and effects of the new American monsters, the murdering maniacs discussed in the previous chapter as well as all manner of supernatural terrors that would emerge in the 1990s. Horror comics have grown in popularity, and newer magazines like *Rue Morgue* offer their readers a gothic lifestyle of clothing, music, art, and social opportunities that defines modern American experience through the eyes of the monster. Moreover, the Universal monsters did not disappear entirely. Almost all of the classic characters have reappeared in periodic remakes and reimaginings, such as Francis Ford Coppola's stylish 1992 *Dracula*. These creatures of the classic American film tradition have continued to horrify audiences right alongside Jason, Freddy, and demonic creatures from womb and tomb.[57]

Americans feared a diverse set of monsters at the close of the twentieth century. Despite their differences, they shared a common origin in the national historical process. Devil babies competed with "the Hook" to elaborate social anxieties over abortion, religious conflict, the sexual revolution, birth control, single-parent families, intergenerational conflict, and women's liberation. The revival of the Universal monsters showed the continuing power of the gothic in American historical experience. Horror showed an increasing tendency to subvert conservative values, causing commentators such as art scholar Henry Jenkins to draw attention to the horror film's relationship to progressive politics and avant-garde art.[58]

Monsters as markers of social change, perhaps its harbingers, continued to shape American entertainments in the 1970s and into the 1980s. Economic transformation, much of it dangerous for American workers, also marked this era. The deindustrialization of America really began in the 1970s, as did a boom and bust cycle in economic life more pronounced than at any time in American capitalism since the Gilded Age.

Working-Class Monsters

Alien certainly deals with body politics in the age of the sexual revolution. However, the monstrosity that stalks the crew of the *Nostromo* had a more complicated genealogy than second-wave feminism, even if it is impossible to imagine a character like Ripley in the science fiction horror films of the 1950s and 1960s when Jane Fonda's *Barbarella* appeared to represent the limits of feminist possibility.

Alien appears, as Harvey Greenberg describes it, as "a Linnaean nightmare . . . crustacean, reptilian and humanoid." Its hulking mass rises over the crewmembers with its absurdly phallic head, but it also moves like a lethal insect. Lumbering about like Frankenstein's monster, it skitters across bulkheads like a Lovecraftian nightmare. It's the monster defying all possible categories and that looks as if it has twenty different ways to rip our bodies to shreds.[59]

The film opens and closes in the void of space, a vast expanse of emptiness. This further explains the enduring strength of this film that almost became a Roger Corman production (Dan O'Bannon had entitled the script "Star Beast," and it seemed destined for B-movie cultdom instead of becoming a horror classic). The inhuman exoskeleton of Alien embodied a universe that has little place for humanity.

Swiss artist H. R. Giger drew much of the early concept art for Alien and later joined a team of set designers to give the creature, the one otherworldly environment we see, and the *Nostromo* its look that blends ancient Near Eastern archaism with biomechanical futurism. Ridley Scott discovered Giger's work through his 1977 collection entitled *The Necronomicon*, a reference to a powerful occult grimoire imagined by H. P. Lovecraft and recycled again and again by his imitators.

Giger's designs not only invested the film with a topos of bleak Lovecraftian message of cosmic indifference to humanity, a very different vision of life beyond the stars that audiences received in the flood of space operas that attempted to cash in on the *Star Wars* phenomenon.

The *Alien* series, even as it descended into the drive-in comedy depths of the *Alien vs. Predator* film, never departed fully from this vision. Scott's return to the series in *Prometheus* (2012) essentially retold Lovecraft's *At the Mountains of Madness*, placing the story of humanity's origins among uncaring Great Old Ones in space rather than Antarctica.

Lovecraft's cosmicism sat alongside a set of much more human, contemporary concerns of the late 1970s. The Alien prowls a floating factory that feels very much as if it belongs to the class politics and economic ravages of 1979. The ship where the extraterrestrial massacre takes place is no Amity Island. When Hooper announces to Quint that "he's tired of all this working-class hero crap," we know he'd never find a berth aboard the *Nostromo*.

There is another villainous character aboard ship; indeed, the environment itself has been created by it and it guides the tragic events of the film. "The Company," as the crew calls it (we come to know it as Weyland-Yutani in the sequels) runs the floating factory and processing plant in space, controlling every aspect of the crew's lives. "Mother," as the ship's onboard computer is known, has an incarnation in the character of Ash, an artificial intelligence hated by the crew (especially Parker and Brett, the mechanics / outer space machinists that keep the whole flying manufacturing plant running below decks). Ash reminds them of the nature of their contracts and obligations to the Company, an apparently necessary technocratic voice of authority as both Brett and Parker begin the film grumbling about an unexplained "bonus situation."

Scott released *Alien* just as the 1980 election season began, an election that ended disastrously for the labor movement just as the new kind of highly mobile, international capital that emerged in the era began to fundamentally reshape the economy of America and the world. In 1977, 160,000 miners went on strike under the aegis of the United Mine Workers. They received a favorable settlement but had to concede much, particularly after the intervention of the Carter administration on behalf of the coal companies. In 1981 Ronald Reagan handed the American labor movement perhaps its biggest defeat in history with the firing of 11,000 striking air traffic controllers. "The Company" could not be trusted.[60]

Ironically, before he became shop steward on the *Nostromo*, African actor Yaphet Kotto's previous role featured him as a labor leader killed on an assembly line that has replaced people with robots in Paul Schraeder's 1978 *Blue Collar*. Corporations had been part of life since the nineteenth century and controlled huge portions of the economic landscape after World War II. But by the 1970s, Americans had become nervous about the new ways they worked, where they worked, and if they could work at all. They would increasingly wonder about the monstrous possibilities of such entities even as the pro-business climate of Reagan's America urged them to think of the corporate world as "Mother."[61]

The end of the Cold War in 1989–1991 did nothing to slow down America's monster mash. George H. W. Bush's pronouncement that a "new world order" had come, a world no longer defined by conflict between the United States and the now-defunct Soviet Union, combined with the economic bubble, that at the time appeared to be a boom, of the Clinton years seemingly created a sunny optimism that had no place for lurking creatures of the night. A sense of cultural optimism did inspire social philosophers such as Francis Fukuyama to proclaim "the end of history." Liberal Western democracy wedded to barrier-breaking entrepreneur-ialism had, according to Fukuyama, ended the long struggle of warring social and economic systems. The American ideal represented the most complete and the most successful form of government, triumphing over all its rivals.[62]

The 1990s did not represent the escape from history that Fukuyama predicted. The bombing of the World Trade Center in 1992 and of the Alfred P. Murrah Federal Building in Oklahoma City in 1995 offered ominous signs of a new kind of danger in the post–Cold War era. America's domestic culture became increasingly volatile as a host of cultural clashes centered on controversial moments in entertainment and poli-tics. A twenty-four-hour media cycle brought narratives to America both gothic and incendiary, such as the O. J. Simpson trial, the Rodney King beating and the Los Angeles uprising, the confirmation hearings for Supreme Court justice Clarence Thomas, and the sex scandal that impeached a president.[63]

Americans made their way through this labyrinth of sex, race, and power while being pursued by well-beloved monsters whose unnatural appetites did nothing to prevent their entry into celebrity culture. The 1990s saw the dawn of the hungry dead.

7

UNDEAD AMERICANS

Ain't no grave / Gonna hold this body down

—Traditional Gospel hymn

Wish me monsters.

—Buffy in *Buffy the Vampire Slayer*

"They're coming to get you Barbara."
George Romero's 1968 *Night of the Living Dead* opens in a cemetery in western Pennsylvania, well marked with flags honoring the recently buried Vietnam dead. A brother and sister, Johnny and Barbara, are visiting their father's grave. Both siblings are uneasy. Johnny did not want to come, and Barbara clearly still grieves their father's passing. She kneels beside the grave to pray while Johnny, clearly uncomfortable, jokes about a man, perhaps an indigent, lurching toward them. "They're coming to get you Barbara," he says, doing his best Boris Karloff impression.

They did come to get Barbara, and everyone else. The shambling figure turns out to be a zombie who kills Johnny as Barbara escapes to a nearby farmhouse and becomes catatonic with terror. A young African American man named Ben also occupies the farmhouse as does, we learn soon, a family that has been hiding in the cellar. The group, fighting among themselves, also must defend against a horde of hungry zombies who

Dracula from Hammer

surround the small house. Ben learns from a radio he has discovered that "those things" are a global phenomenon, a zombie apocalypse. Humanity has been besieged by hordes of cannibalistic, animated corpses.

Shot for a little over one hundred thousand dollars in rural Pennsylvania, Romero's film was filled with local actors and friends from his native Pittsburgh. Filmed in black and white (for financial as well as aesthetic reasons), *Night of the Living Dead* became a staple of drive-in theaters around the country, and created five sequels and numerous remakes, tributes, and reimaginings.[1]

Night of the Living Dead shaped the modern zombie genre, a new monster for the dark American pantheon. Zombies had played some role in African American folklore in the coastal American South and appeared in Universal's tellingly titled *White Zombie* and RKO's *I Walked with a Zombie*. Both films borrowed the zombie figure from the religious traditions of the African Atlantic and its folklore about an evil *papaloa* (shaman able to channel spirits) that had the power to transform corpses into undead servants. Romero's hordes of zombies broke with this tradition. He and his imitators imagined undead humans in various states of decay, driven by their hunger rather than by a necromancer's will. The rising dead, in this new version, could create more zombies, passing on their infection through a bite. The whole human race could be transformed into monsters.[2]

Zombies retained their popularity in American culture through the 1970s and 1980s in Romero's follow-up films *Dawn of the Dead* and *Day of the Dead*. Their popularity spiked in the early part of the new century. During the same period, American pop culture witnessed the ascendancy of a monster that, in some respects, never fully went out of style. A new version of the American vampire rose from its coffin in the 1970s and followed a similar trajectory of celebrity as the zombie, his more proletarian monster cousin.[3]

Like the zombie, the vampire had appeared in slightly different incarnations earlier in the twentieth century. Lugosi's *Dracula*, featuring a monster sophisticated enough to stalk his victims at the opera, had enormous popularity on his first appearance but soon found himself eclipsed by Boris Karloff's *Frankenstein* and the barrage of mad scientist movies that followed. In 1958 American audiences thrilled to Christopher Lee's new interpretation of the vampire in the British Hammer Studios' *Horror of Dracula*. Lee's version of the Count kept the sexual allure of Lugosi's vampire king while adding an animalistic cruelty and hungry, bloodshot eyes that transformed Dracula into a savage and sensual Miltonic Satan.[4]

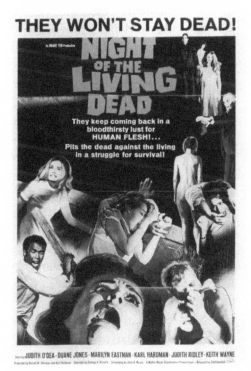

Night of the Living Dead poster

Alluring and yet monstrous, the Lugosi–Lee vampire tradition would be replaced by Anne Rice's Louis and Lestat in *Interview with the Vampire*. Rice's 1976 novel framed its story around a young reporter listening to Louis relate his more than a century as one of the undead, a story that introduced the reader to a larger community of vampires and a secret vampiric history of the world. Rice told this tale of hunger and eternal life as one rich with pathos, passion, and exquisite suffering (so much so that at the end of the novel the reporter, who clearly stands in for the reader, begs to become one of the undead). Rice followed up the best-selling *Interview* with a cycle of vampire tales centered on Lestat who, like Louis, is a tortured, glamorous, undead soul. The sexy, sadistic monster had become the sexy, sympathetic monster.[5]

The mythologies and cultural meanings of these two creatures, zombies and vampires, are very distinct. At the same time, they have certain similarities that led to their coregency as the undead monarchs of American popular culture. Both the zombie and the vampire draw on themes embedded in the history and theology of American Christianity and its struggles in the late twentieth century. Both are, in fact, heavily redacted versions of the American Christian millennialism's hopes for immortality. They each articulate meanings theologically important to Americans since the Puritan era and are the walking, flying, roaming, and shambling embodiments of the "resurrection of the dead and the life of the world to come."[6]

The vampire and the zombie are monstrous keys to American experience over the last five decades. These creatures, flesh eating or blood drinking, decomposing or forever young, appeared as pop culture phenomena at a historical moment when the body had become of central concern in American culture as the vehicle of pleasure, of theological meaning, or of personal happiness (or all three at once). Anxiety over threats to the body became a paramount concern as evidenced by the popularity of dieting and exercise regimens, public health campaigns, and the growing acceptance of plastic surgery as an aesthetic renovation of the aging or unsightly physical self.[7]

Vampires and zombies are further linked with one another in their origins and popular mythologies. Unlike almost every other creature examined in this book, the vampire and the zombie as currently imagined have no analogue in American folklore and/or urban legend. These voracious living corpses are almost pure creations of American popular culture, their motifs lifted from European and Caribbean legend and transformed into horrific celebrities. Perhaps more than any other monster, they are "made in America" as commodities for sale and distribution. This makes them important representations of what Americans fear, or desire, from the monster at the beginning of a new millennium.[8]

The vampire and zombie are, like all monsters, shaped by their historical context. Historical events of the last third of the twentieth century helped prepare the way for the resurrection of the undead in movies and television. The legacy of the Vietnam War in particular became a silent partner in the birth of modern horror. Many conservatives saw the war as creating what Ronald Reagan later called the "Vietnam syndrome," a profound loss of national confidence. Backlash against feminism would be motivated by the sense, sometimes inarticulate but always present, that American women and other minorities had gained political conscious-ness in the 1960s and 1970s while white men had lost a war. Returning veterans came home to a world where the ground had fundamentally shifted. For Americans who had watched the war from their living rooms and mourned the deaths of their children, parents, and spouses at tens of thousands of funerals, the war itself became a kind of undead monster, one that overcame every attempt to keep it in the ground.[9]

Body Bags

The entrance of the United States into a postcolonial conflict in Southeast Asia became a multi-decade commitment that killed 58,000 Americans and wounded 153,303 more. An incalculable number of Vietnamese died in the conflict as well. At least half a million civilian deaths occurred in South Vietnam alone, America's ally that suffered as much if not more from American occupation forces as victims of American carpet bombing, search and destroy missions, helicopter gunships, and chemical warfare.[10]

This massive loss of life was born of the frustrated efforts of an impe-rial power trying to squelch an armed peasant revolution. General William Westmoreland, commander of American forces in Vietnam between 1964 and 1968, implemented a strategy of "attrition," or the killing of as many Vietnamese as possible in order to break the revolutionary's will to fight. The idea of attrition made the creation of a Vietnamese "body count" central to war-winning strategy. This attitude filtered down through the ranks to exert pressure on every officer that commanded a platoon. Former Marine lieutenant Phillip Caputo remembered that "the pressure on unit commanders to produce enemy corpses was intense." Platoon members took souvenirs of ears, noses, and even scalps to impress their command-ers and substantiate claims of a high body count. Some platoons actually padded their kill ratio ("box scores" some called it) by counting small blood traces, and at least some unit commanders demanded severed body parts as clear testimony that their troops had performed their duty.[11]

Bureaucratic pressure to produce Westmoreland's desired rate of attrition degenerated into careless brutality. The infamous My Lai massa-cre represents the most egregious case of the everyday horrors American forces visited on their hidden enemy, an incident with a particularly high box score. On May 16, 1968, a company of U.S. soldiers entered the small village of My Lai, rounded up the inhabitants (mostly women and children), placed them in a ditch, and turned murderous gunfire on them over the course of an entire day. The company stopped to eat lunch before continuing the slaughter. Soldiers raped many of the women and young girls before shooting them. Army investigators later placed the death toll at between four hundred and fifty and five hundred people, some of them infants in their mother's arms.[12]

Unfortunately, the war crimes of My Lai resulted in the claim that the military contained "a few bad apples" that perpetrated such acts. Journalist Nick Turse, working in the National Archives in the summer of 2001, came across an unused cache of records related to a secret Pentagon task force called the Vietnam War Crimes Work Group. This evidence, combined with interviews with Vietnam veterans and the armed forces' own accounts of their operations, revealed what Turse called "a system of suffering." My Lai represented only one of the inhuman cruelties that involved part of every major military unit operating in Vietnam. These units acted on the wishes of the military hierarchy and the civilian architects of American intervention in successive administrations, from Kennedy to Nixon.[13]

Wanton cruelty became the everyday result of American policy. One marine described the "fun game" of tossing candy out of the back of a transport truck, leading Vietnamese children to run for it and possibly be mangled by the next truck in line. A Vietnamese peasant woman remembered how passing soldiers in a truck grabbed her son's hat and pulled him (it was held to his head with string) under the vehicle's tire, killing him. These random acts by some individual soldiers are dwarfed by the death and destruction wrought on the Vietnamese people by the indiscriminate use of artillery and airpower.[14]

Many American military personnel had the horrors they perpetrated on the Vietnamese partially replicated in the horrors they themselves endured, both in terms of bodily wounds and psychological damage. To the 58,000 American dead would be added 75,000 physically disabled veterans. The trauma of the war left tens of thousands more with nightmares, severe depression, and other psychological maladies. In at least one case analyzed by anthropologist Mai Lan Gustafsson, a veteran came to believe himself haunted by the angry spirit of a Viet Cong fighter whose ID tag he had taken in 1968. The vet found peace only when he returned to Vietnam and gave the tag to the fighter's mother.[15]

American journalism made Vietnam the first truly televised war, and magazines such as *Time* and *Life* created a massive photographic record of wounded, dead, and dying Americans. Vietnam came to be known as "the Living Room War," with images of troops returning in body bags becoming an indelible image of the failure of American policy in Southeast Asia. Dismemberment entered the public record and became part of popular culture.[16]

Romero's zombies shambled onscreen as Americans became increasingly used to real-life images of graphic death, gore, and body parts blown to pieces. In January of 1968 the Tet Offensive inaugurated a new period in the Vietnam conflict and initiated house-to-house and hand-to-hand fighting. American casualties soared throughout the year with one week in February of 1968 bringing news of five hundred thirty-four American deaths. Romero's images of rotting corpses on a violent landscape covered with entrails and viscera, and a band of survivors battling it out with faceless hordes and deeply divided among themselves, perfectly suited the American mood.

In the years ahead, Tom Savini would do an even better job of bringing these rotted corpses to life. Savini had been friends with George Romero during their youth in Pittsburgh and would likely have worked with him on *Night of the Living Dead* had he not been called up to serve in the army the same year. Savini carried a makeup kit with him through basic training and even used collodion, a liquid plastic, to make up a drill sergeant who wanted to frighten his next platoon. Sent to Vietnam as a combat photographer, Savini brought home a blend of trauma and creativity that made him the greatest makeup effects artist since Lon Chaney Sr.[17]

Savini's first film assignment drew directly on his personal horrors. *Deathdream* (1974; also released as *Dead of Night*) told the story of a Vietnam vet who returned home to his horrified family as a rotting zombie-vampire. Working with Romero on *Dawn of the Dead*, Savini brought the war home again with images of a zombie head exploding from a gunshot and arms and legs torn apart. These scenes of gore replicated what he had seen in South Vietnam. In his 1983 book *Bizarro*, which explains special effects techniques (with a preface by George Romero and introduction by Stephen King), Savini remembers a moment in Vietnam when he "nearly stepped on a human arm, one end of it jagged and torn, its fist clenched and grabbing the ground." When not photographing horror, Savini visited friends in the hospital who had been catastrophically wounded by land mines. In *Bizarro* he suggests that he trained his mind to see these things as special effects in an effort to deal with the trauma.[18]

The Vietnam War did not create the zombie genre or make way for the vampire. However, like the Civil War, Vietnam produced a graphic iconography of death and bodily dissolution that has remained a permanent part of American culture. Horror images for the next forty years, in a very literal sense, owed their blood and gore to the disaster of Vietnam. Unlike the Second World War, in which images of veterans seldom included evidence of wounds, the corpses and the physically traumatized human body became a focus of America's memory of Vietnam. The zombie and the vampire (joined by the serial killer) feasted off these images, and Americans turned to these monsters that resonated with the national horror.[19]

Vietnam created a sense of malaise in American society, the feeling that the dynamism of the post–World War II years had fully dissipated. The trauma of the war remained with veterans and the American public after a decade of body bags and the military defeat of the United States in 1974–1975. Events of the 1970s only deepened the growing sense of gloom and prepared the way for an apocalyptic sensibility in American cultural life.

Undead Apocalypse

Night of the Living Dead offered a vision of horror that could not be contained. The beast could not be easily slain or the social order restored to the *status quo ante-monstrum*. At the end of the film, every character that took refuge in the farmhouse has been killed, including Ben, the hero we expected to make it out alive. Perhaps even worse, Ben, one of the first Black action heroes in a film seen by a large number of whites, meets his death at the hands of a redneck posse, local hunters who go after zombies with the glee of a lynch mob. This rifle-toting gang of white men with dogs actually mistake Ben for one of the undead, burning him alongside the zombie that attacked Barbara and Johnny at the beginning of the film.

A few film scholars and critics have read the conclusion of *Night of the Living Dead* as a suggestion that order had been restored through mob violence. In fact, it suggests that the social order has broken down entirely, with gun-toting vigilante killers replacing civil law and images of carnage and destruction everywhere. Romero makes this point more fully in his 1978 sequel *Dawn of the Dead*, in which the zombie apocalypse has led to a general collapse of society, forcing human beings to run for their lives and battle one another over the remaining scraps of American consumer culture in a shopping mall. The 1985 *Day of the Dead* and the 2005 *Land of the Dead* reveal that the zombie plague has so utterly destroyed civilization that only a few human enclaves are left, and those are riven apart by various kinds of social strife.[20]

The zombie managed what no other monster had ever been able to do: it destroyed the world. This new monster perfectly suited American culture that, in the 1970s and 1980s, entered into an apocalyptic mode, a widespread expectation that the clock had run out, not only on American society but the whole human race. A number of social and historical forces generated this feeling. In the early 1970s American defeat in the Vietnam War and the crimes of the Nixon administration led to a collapse of the public trust. By 1980 anxiety ran rampant over the increasingly dangerous global situation brought on by worsening U.S.–Soviet relations and the Arab-Israeli conflict in the Middle East.

Fears of a nuclear or environmental apocalypse, for many Americans, went hand in hand with theological conceptions of "the end of time." A view of the end of history known as "dispensationalism" had long been influential among conservative evangelical Christians. In this interpretation of the book of Revelation and other key biblical passages, human extinction does not come suddenly but in a series of predestined theological events beginning with the "rapture" (or taking up) of all true Christians. This departure of God's faithful inaugurates a seven-year period known as the "Tribulation." During these seven years, plagues, warfare, and various kinds of environmental disasters batter the earth until the second coming of Christ and the battle of Armageddon. The second coming would include a resurrection of the dead and a final judgment.[21]

This elaborate and baroque belief system remained marginal in American society for most of the twentieth century. Hal Lindsey's 1970 *Late Great Planet Earth* changed that, rocketing to the top of the bestseller list and shaping views about the end of the world that proved influential far outside of fundamentalist sects. Lindsey, a recent convert to an informal, West Coast style of evangelicalism, combined a use of au courant 1970s lingo with a tendency to slide between biblical narrative and current events. He created a kind of hip theological techno-thriller that promised its readers secret knowledge of the meaning of world events. Troubles in the Middle East and conflict with the Soviets meant that the rapture would come soon with the Antichrist and the Tribulation period trailing close behind.[22]

America's apocalyptic tendencies grew throughout the 1980s and by the 1990s had become intertwined with technological fears regarding the new millennium. Early computer designers represented the year with two digits rather than four, raising the possibility that January 1, 2000, would become an event horizon that threatened to crash computer systems all over the world. As computer programmers worked to successfully prevent any severe consequences from this design flaw, the possibility of a "Y2K bug" creating a massive societal catastrophe generated hysterical responses. Conservative evangelicals sometimes latched on to fears of Y2K as further proof of theological armageddon. Jerry Falwell, by the 1990s the face of the evangelical right, described Y2K as "God's instrument for humbling this nation."[23]

The very complexity of modern society, the intricate support systems that keep the lights on, the water running, the gas pumping, and the ATMs dispensing cash, gave a special twist to the theme of apocalypse in modern America. Fears of Y2K focused entirely on the results of the breakdown of systems on which modern Americans depend. These fears were transferred after 2001 to the possibility of some kind of high-tech terrorist attack that would render modern conveniences inoperable. Zombie fictions took these anxieties and magnified them. Not only would the hungry undead wreak havoc on the social order, they would turn the human body against itself and transform flesh into food. Zombies represented the end of the world, the complete breakdown of human society, and the cannibalization of humanity.

Vampires have seldom been messengers of apocalypse, although the idea certainly forms a subtext in Stoker's novel. Dracula leaves Transylvania and comes to London to create an army of vampires to overturn the social order, not unlike the scenario imagined in the Guillermo Del Toro–produced television series (adapted from a novel trilogy) *The Strain* (2014–2017). Stoker's sexual cautionary tale never lets things go that far, and the vampire is driven back to his homeland. *Dracula* is, in some sense, the tale of apocalypse averted. Richard Matheson's 1954 novella *I Am Legend*, on the other hand, imagines what might become of the world after a vampire apocalypse. Protagonist Robert Neville has watched the entire world succumb to a plague that has transformed them into vampiric creatures, eager to drink blood and unable to go out in sunlight. Neville, who assumes he is the last human left, lives in a boarded-up suburban home in Los Angeles. During the day, he ventures out to kill vampires, gather supplies, and prepare his domestic fortress for the coming nighttime assault.[24]

Matheson does not portray his character as a heroic monster-hunter keeping the flame of humanity alive. Instead, Neville's hatred of the vampires makes him into more of a monster than they are. He is finally killed when he meets a woman who turns out to be a new breed of plague victim, a representative of a community of supervampires who have learned to integrate their humanity with their new condition. From her, Neville learns that this emerging new society sees him not as a hero but as a maniac killer who spends his days slaughtering and killing. The title of *I Am Legend* refers to Neville's realization that he has become a nightmare story to be told by the people of the new world, the legend of a mythic monster that had to be slain. The zombie genre, especially in Romero's iteration, relied heavily on Matheson's novel, especially its explicit satire of human attitudes toward the monster.[25]

In 1975 Stephen King's modern American retelling of *Dracula* considered what might happen if a vampire created a mini-apocalypse and turned an entire community into its undead servants. *Salem's Lot* tells the story of a small New England town visited by a "Master-Vampire" named Barlow. Riven by small-town conflict, and full of secrets even before the coming of the undead, the townspeople are transformed into monsters by the vampire. Ben Mears, a writer who has returned to "the Lot" that was his childhood home, and Mark Petrie, one of King's prescient child-heroes, kill the vampire-king. In a nod to the "monster kids," Petrie knows how to kill vampires because he lives on a steady diet of late-night monster movies and horror comics.[26]

King, who soon became not only America's best-selling horror novelist but also its best-selling novelist, has said that *Salem's Lot* drew part of its inspiration from his writing the novel just as the full story of Watergate unfolded on television in 1973–1974. King commented that his story of vampires remaking the social order of a small town came directly from the ongoing horrors being revealed about the Nixon administration:

> In my novel *Salem's Lot* the thing that really scared me was not vampires, but the town in the daytime, the town that was empty, knowing that there were things in closets, that there were people tucked under beds ... and all the time I was writing that, the Watergate hearings were pouring out of TV ... Howard Baker kept asking "What I want to know is 'what did you know and when did you know it?'" That line haunts me. It stays in my mind. That might be the classic line of the twentieth century.[27]

The secrets hiding under beds and the thing in America's closet became for King the sum of all fears. King has elsewhere compared *Salem's Lot* to *Invasion of the Body Snatchers* with its conceit that the social order could collapse as one's neighbors, one by one, become victims of a corrupting evil with which they seem willing to collaborate. King would go on to write a number of the most important monster tales of the twentieth century, including perhaps the definitive novel of the apocalypse, *The Stand*, published in 1978.[28]

Vampires have usually offered a much more intimate kind of threat than the reanimated zombie. In an America anxious over the fate of the social order, the zombie offers a talisman, a laughably horrific symbol about a fake apocalypse that keeps at bay real fears about social degeneration and collapse. Max Brooks' best-selling *Zombie Survival Guide: Complete Protection from the Living Dead* presents itself as a civil defense manual for the zombie apocalypse, complete with strategies to kill zombies in every conceivable environment (even underwater) and descriptions of armor (including "tight clothes and short hair"). Meanwhile, zombie walks or zombie pub crawls, in which fans use simple makeup to turn themselves into zombies, are becoming increasingly popular in urban areas. In the early twenty-first century, Philadelphia zombie fans linked the theological notion of resurrection of the dead with their favorite monster by holding an annual Easter zombie walk known as "Crawl of the Dead." Advertised with an image of "zombie Jesus," the zombie walk had grown enough by 2006 to become part of a schedule of annual events, including a zombie beach party in July.[29]

If the zombie articulated fears of apocalypse while containing that fear with dark humor, the undead also encoded the anxiety of Americans over their bodies, and the threats and possibilities of those bodies, at the end of the twentieth century. The vampire's desire for blood and the zombie's hunger for flesh represented brutal articulations of the social and cultural dynamics of America's politics of the body.

Rotting Corpses and Bad Blood

At the close of the twentieth century, Americans became increasingly concerned over the possibility of a personal apocalypse taking place within their own bodies. In 2001, according to the American Society for Aesthetic Plastic Surgery, 8,470,363 Americans had some form of aesthetic surgery. Fear that the effects of aging represented bodily decomposition drove this desire to reconstruct the self, along with the hope that the body could be transformed into a symbol of erotic appeal. Popular procedures used to achieve these goals included chemical peels using a powerful acid to remove a surface layer of skin, injections of the low-grade poison Botox that paralyzes facial muscles to give the appearance of smooth skin, liposuction that liquefies fat before removing it, and reconstructive surgeries, such as breast augmentation, rhinoplasty, and face-lifts.[30]

All of these procedures, invasive and destructive, have grown in popularity over the last thirty years, with notable spikes in the early twenty-first century. The number of chemical peels in 2001, for example, represented a 2,356 percent increase over the number administered in 1997. Breast augmentation surgery grew from 20,000 procedures a year in 1992 to 200,000 in 2002 and climbed to almost 300,000 by 2015.[31]

This mass desire to transform the body did not emerge organically from the availability of new aesthetic surgery techniques. Instead it represents a carefully orchestrated effort to create a new aesthetic by an industry that views divergence from a universal template of attractiveness as an abnormality. Concerned over failing profits, the American Society of Plastic and Reconstructive Surgery began defining small breast size as a medical problem in 1983. An extensive advertising campaign, and the transformation of plastic surgeons into public figures who as authors and talk-show guests spread the gospel of bodily transformation, convinced many American women that face-lifts, tummy tucks, and breast implants could further their career goals, improve their mental health, and even save their marriages.[32]

The promoters of reconstructive surgery found an unlikely ally in evangelical Christian culture's growing obsession with the body in the 1980s. American Christianity's interest in the body as a carrier of meaning and a path to fulfillment fused theological themes and cultural yearnings in the late twentieth century. Millennialist Christianity, with its emphasis on "the glorified body" in the apocalyptic resurrection of the dead, sought to celebrate an eschatological destiny for the Christian body. A new movement toward Christian dieting and exercise, and even increased sexual fulfillment, suggested that the body could begin its glorification even now.[33]

An evangelical dieting and fitness culture focused both on the disciplining and glorification of the physical body as a spiritual act of devotion emerged in the 1960s and exploded in the 1970s. Books with titles like *More of Jesus, Less of Me*; *Slim for Him*; and *Help Lord! The Devil Wants Me Fat!* encouraged evangelical Christian women (specifically women) to see eating and exercise as integral to their spiritual lives. While this principle may not sound radically different from older Christian ascetic disciplines such as fasting, these new dieting and fitness regimes promised the same rewards as secular fitness culture rather than spiritual growth. God wanted evangelical Christian women to diet so they could enjoy a better self-image, increased sexual attractiveness, and a reversal, or at least a slowdown, of the effects of aging. In *Disciplines of the Beautiful Woman*, one of an avalanche of Christian dieting texts directed at women, the author claimed that preventing weight gain is "a key factor in being a beautiful woman for God" and noted God's special interest in "helping you get to and keep the weight that is right for you."[34]

Americans, Christian or otherwise, proved remarkably uncomfortable in their own skins at the dawn of the twenty-first century. An emphasis on the body's aesthetics and the need to save the body from death (or save it *for* the resurrection) betrays a profound anxiety about physical experience. The obsession of physical aesthetics combined with concerns about infectious disease, the politics of the womb, cultural battles fought over alternative sexual identities, controversy over genetics, and the obsession with physical aesthetics have absorbed enormous amounts of media attention.[35]

Zombies and vampires became the ultimate meaning machines in this era of the body wars. The rotting, and yet animated, bodies of the zombie mapped anxieties about the body, both religious and secular. The immortal, and often eerily beautiful, bodies of vampires sucked the blood that Americans imagined as the carrier of infection and death, creating an iconography of fatal, diseased, erotic pleasure.

The zombie, with its awkward movements, single-minded desire, and rapidly decomposing flesh, manages to combine terror, threat, and humor into a single flesh-eating package. In a grotesque reversal of dieting culture, zombies are the ultimate late-night snackers who have no interest in anything but their victims and no interest in their victims except as a source of food. In some respects, this makes the zombie the regnant nightmare of the culture of dieting, exercise, and bodily transcendence. They are unable to transcend their flesh and its desires. They are frightening, or more generally just described as "gross," because their appetites denigrate the human body, turning it into an abject consumable. Meanwhile, their own bodies, or at least what is left of them, represent a parody of both secular and religious hopes for the flesh as a vehicle for transcendence.[36]

The walking undead, whether they are flesh-eaters or bloodsuckers, evoke images of plague, disease, and infection as well as monstrous consumption. Modern America had worried little about the dangers of disease since the deadly influenza epidemics of the early twentieth century. The 1980s saw the beginnings of new fears of older diseases as well as the metaphor of malignancy and ill health applied to a variety of social problems. The AIDS epidemic and its political and cultural uses became central to a societal discourse about threats to the body. Warnings about sexual permissiveness went hand in hand with warnings about poison and illness in a strange new vocabulary. Social critics Arthur and Marilouise

Kroker dubbed this new vocabulary a "Body McCarthyism," which sought to contain threats to the body and the social order.[37]

The vampire and the zombie became the perfect monstrous metonyms for this era since each spread a kind of infection. The AIDS epidemic seemed to especially resonate with the mythology of the vampire, given the immune disorder's blood-borne disease vector. This comported with a homophobic tendency to imagine gays and lesbians as a kind of vampire. The antigay activist Anita Bryant, who more than anyone helped to initiate fundamentalist Christianity's national backlash against gay liberation, made explicit use of the vampire metaphor. Bryant once wrote, "the male homosexual eats another man's sperm. Sperm is the most concentrated form of blood. The homosexual is eating life." Bryant also argued, in imagery redolent with vampire symbolism, that "homosexuals . . . must recruit, must freshen their ranks." While conservative critics often focused on gay men as a source of moral and physical corruption, film imagery of lesbian vampires became an increasingly common trope beginning in the 1970s. Films like *Daughters of Darkness*, *The Hunger*, and *Embrace of the Vampire* offered men voyeuristic pleasures while evoking fears that imagined women as both bloodsucking freaks and dangerously autonomous in their sexuality.[38]

Conservative politicians and the leaders of the New Right eagerly deployed imagery that connected homosexuality with images of infection, transforming AIDS into a metaphor for a diseased and dying social structure. In 1983 Jerry Falwell urged blood banks to reject gay donors and suggested that gay political influence had stood in the way of stopping the spread of disease. A growing moral panic over infection and gay sex led to the passage of a 1986 Senate bill that legalized the creation of donor pools that individual families could contribute to and thus avoid the use of blood from, as the bill read, "the general population." The Reagan administration had, at this late date in the epidemic, not even acknowledged the existence of AIDS, even as the president made use of the imagery of disease, infection, contagion, poison, and degeneracy to describe the general moral state of American society. When finally speaking publicly about the epidemic, Reagan and his speechwriters used imagery from serial killer narratives when they described AIDS as moving "insidiously through the length and breadth of our society."[39]

The homosexual as vampire and AIDS as a "gay plague" delivered by the blood provided a powerful weapon in the culture wars. The pale gauntness of the vampire and the transmission of his condition through an exchange of bloody body fluids became juxtaposed with gothic imaginings regarding gay sexuality in which infection spread in bathhouses where men allegedly had "30 to 40 sexual encounters a night." Phrases like these became a common way for conservatives to talk about the spread and origins of AIDS. It suggested that gay men must have a supernatural sexual appetite combined with an impossible physical prowess. It further envisioned them as voracious creatures of the night, eagerly infecting as many victims as possible.[40]

The monster would not allow itself to mean only one thing. The vampire became, for many in the age of AIDS, a symbol of transcendence rather than of societal decay and decadence. In the 1980s, in part inspired by Rice's novels, a loose network of local networks, nightclubs, and eventually websites and chat rooms created a "vampire subculture," an offshoot of the goth movement.[41]

Becoming a part of the vampire community could mean anything from dressing in black and wearing high-priced fang implants to taking part in exchanges of blood with willing sexual partners. For the most part, vampire communities encouraged safe practices (AIDS awareness and testing became a common element of vampire clubs), as well as tolerant, and rather fuzzy, New Age–style spirituality. "Real Vampires," a term usually used by those who want to differentiate themselves from vampire fandom and role players, come in two basic types. "Sanguinaries," or "Sangs," drink the blood of a partner or have their blood drunk by a partner. This is often, but not always, in a sexual context. "Psychic vampires," or "Psis," believe they siphon mental energy from their willing victims. This may appear diabolical but is understood as a kind of mental communion between the participants rather than an invasive attack.[42]

Those who do not want to take their vampirism this far could take part in the role-playing game *Vampire: The Masquerade*. Reaching the height of its popularity in the mid-1990s, this live-action role-playing (LARP) game allowed participants to become members of various vampire clans and act out various gothic scenarios. Cultural critic Eric Nuzum describes *Masquerade* as a kind of "improvisational theatre" in which players can perform their vampire fantasies with plastic fangs, blood capsules, and the roll of dice.[43]

Cultures frequently employ an iconography of death to deal with moments of historical horror and rapid social change. Fourteenth-century Europe freely employed the "Dance of Death" imagery during the plague. In the late eighteenth century, daughters of the nervous French aristocracy wore red chokers and affected a deathly pale aesthetic during the days of the guillotine. In an era that desires the transformation of the body, and transcendence through the corporeal, the bloodred lips of the vampire prove enticing, while the zombie, falling apart before our eyes, becomes a Black joke about our worst social fears.

"I'm the Slayer . . . and you're history!"

In the late 1990s the critically acclaimed television series *Buffy the Vampire Slayer* fused, parodied, complicated, and nuanced the American fascination with the apocalyptic and the gothic. Running for one hundred and forty-four episodes over seven seasons, *Buffy* told the story of a teenage girl, seemingly a typical petite blonde in Southern California, interested in cheerleading and boys. Buffy's seemingly pedestrian lifestyle hid her identity as "the Chosen One," the one girl in every generation empowered to fight vampires, demons, and a whole host of monsters. Since Buffy's school, Sunnydale High, sat atop a convergence of dark mystical energy known as a "Hellmouth," the young slayer could be supplied with plenty of monsters, week after week.[44]

Joss Whedon, the creator and sometime writer/director for the series, imagined Buffy as a feminist fairy tale. Media descriptions have underscored this claim frequently, seeing the show as an example of what the late 1990s christened "girl power." The *Village Voice* described *Buffy* as "a female empowerment saga," while critic Micol Ostow saw its lead

character as a model of feminine strength. When the show premiered, most discussions of its politics centered on how Buffy combined a traditional femininity with supernatural monster-killing prowess.[45]

Buffy's feminist inclinations and how that message engages its audience has received more attention than the show's subversive cultural and political comments about

Buffy

the nature of society and how forces in society construct, and seek to destroy, the monster. Incorporating both traditional monster imagery and the apocalyptic concerns of late twentieth-century America, Whedon's series inverted the meaning of its own source material and made Buffy into a different kind of monster slayer from anything audiences had ever seen.[46]

At a time when American society seemed consumed with the idea of the apocalypse as the new millennium drew closer, Buffy and her friends (who came to include a witch, a werewolf, two somewhat reformed vampires, and a centuries-old demon) avert numerous apocalyptic events, so much so that it becomes the running joke of the series. Buffy's some-time boyfriend, Riley, comments in season 4 that his time with the Slayer has made him wonder "what the plural of apocalypse is." When Giles, a heavily redacted Van Helsing who serves as Buffy's father figure through most of the series, announces dramatically in season 5 that, "it's the end of the world," Buffy and her crew respond in unison, "Again!!"

Buffy clearly and deftly satirized the imagery of apocalypse prevalent in American culture. Rather than the foreordained apocalypse of evangelical Christianity, the end of the world is averted again and again through human agency. American millenarianism that imagined the coming of God's judgment on the modern world is replaced in *Buffy* by an apocalypse of evil, engineered by monsters. These apocalyptic events are often prophesied but are never predetermined and are prevented through acts of self-sacrifice and unconditional love on the part of Buffy and her "Scooby Gang."[47]

In the final episode of the final season ("Chosen"), Buffy and her friend Willow (who came out as a lesbian and became a powerful Wiccan in the course of the series) deconstruct the patriarchal source material that formed the very basis of the series. Obviously the idea of the "Chosen One" draws from centuries of monotheistic religion's fascination with messianic male prophets and saviors. *Buffy* had already nuanced that imagery by presenting a woman as the Chosen One. The final episode subverted messianic imagery completely by having the power that male elders channeled through generations of slayers explode its parameters and become the property of women all over the world.

Buffy not only deconstructed American notions of apocalypse, it also complicated the American monster tradition. Although *Buffy* centers on the monster slayer and her allies, it also systematically breaks down the narrative of ordered community of respectability that destroys the monstrous other. The show achieves this by frequently exploring the dangers of becoming a monster while trying to fight them. In the classic season 3 episode "Gingerbread," Buffy's mom and the other adults of Sunnydale band together against "occult influences" in their community, a clear reference to America's satanic moral panics. Joyce Summers issues a rallying cry to rid the town of "the witches, the monsters and the slayers." If this crusade to destroy the monsters succeeded it would mean, of course, the destruction of her own daughter and several of her daughter's friends.[48]

Those who fight monsters should also beware lest they fall in love with them. The dark eroticism of the monster has been a theme running through hundreds of years of American cultural history. *Buffy* explores this idea but goes beyond it. In the first and second seasons, Buffy's friend Xander falls for what turns out to be a cannibalistic giant bug and a millennia-old mummy. He eventually has a relationship with a vengeance demon (that looks like a young woman) and almost marries her. Willow has an Internet relationship with someone who we learn is an ancient demon that has escaped into cyberspace. She later has a long-term relationship with Oz the werewolf and, after she comes out, experiences a fulfilling, deeply moving, and doomed romance with Tara, fellow female Wiccan.

Buffy's own romance with two very different vampires became central to the narrative arc of the series. The relationship between Buffy and Angel, a brooding Byronic "vampire with soul," became the centerpiece of the early seasons. Angel, though reformed and tortured by his past deeds, is presented to us as having once been the cruel and lethal vampire Angelus. In season 2, Angel reverts to his monstrous self, though he later finds redemption once again. After season 5, Buffy's romantic interest centers on Spike, another vampire of legendary evil, who seeks and finds redemption in an effort to win Buffy's love and admiration. Along the way, these "monsters" not only form a romantic connection with Buffy, they become a part of her community of misfits whose bonds of love and friendship often prove essential to the salvation of the world. The possibility that the vampire, and the monster more generally, could be loved and cared for as well as darkly desired marks a new departure for the American monster tradition. The monsters of *Buffy* are sometimes creatures that must be destroyed or made into sexual fetishes. But they are also potential "life" partners and members of a community in which difference and the most extreme varieties of otherness prove no barrier to companionship. The Slayer calls into question the need for slayers.

The end of *Buffy* in 2003 coincided with the growth of an even more popular manifestation of the vampire craze, one that borrowed heavily from certain aspects of other undead narratives while rejecting wholesale most of the vampiric tradition. If *Buffy* called into question the notion of slaying monsters, Stephenie Meyer took a very different route. Her monsters are not monsters at all.

Twilight of the Gods

The creature came to Stephenie Meyer in a dream. Meyer, a conservative Mormon, dreamed of a vampire in love with a human girl. The vampire also thirsted to drink the girl's blood. Originally, Meyer wrote the book for her own enjoyment, creating it as something on the order of Internet fan fiction. Having been submitted to fourteen agents before finding someone interested in marketing the book, Meyer's *Twilight* series had, by 2008, sold over one hundred million copies and been translated into thirty-seven languages. In 2008 *Time* magazine included her on its list of the "100 most influential people" of the year.[49]

Twilight tells the story of a romance between teenager Isabella (Bella) and Edward Cullen, a century-old vampire who masquerades as a teenager at a high school in Forks, Washington. Edward and Bella are typical star-crossed lovers, kept apart not by circumstance but by the fact that Edward's attachment to Bella includes a strange mixture of lust and predatory hunger, a desire to literally fuck her to death. Readers are asked to empathize (indeed idealize) Edward for his effort to keep himself from ripping Bella apart and eating her.[50]

Over the course of four books, readers watch Edward become Bella's protector and eventually her husband, introducing her into a secret world of supernatural creatures. Maintaining sexual purity until their marriage, the rather flat characters managed to hold reader interest with the titillation of whether or not they would ever consummate their love. It also gave the opportunity for Meyer to endanger Bella repeatedly, allowing Edward in turn to save her.

Notably, Edward and his fellow vampires are an odd set of monsters, missing almost all the trappings of either traditional folklore or Hollywood legend. Edward comes from a nuclear family, a loving, highly traditional family that seems representative of 1950s dreams of domestic bliss. Unaffected by crosses or holy water, these rather bourgeois vampires can even walk in the sun (sunlight makes them "sparkle" rather than burst into flame). Moreover, many of them are termed "vegetarian vampires," a particularly silly misnomer given that they use their speed and strength to hunt, kill, and feed on various woodland creatures instead of humans.

Perhaps most notably, Meyer's creatures are shorn even of fangs, the most basic accoutrement of vampire mythology.

Meyer's reworking of the vampire mythos, to the point that Edward and friends are best thought of as another fantasy creature entirely different from the vampire, reflects a culture of conservatism from which the book came and to which it appeals. Stephenie Meyer's deeply conservative religious faith worked its way into her dream of vampires. In a time when conservative religious organizations waged "abstinence only" campaigns, Edward fought to control his appetite for Bella's blood while simultaneously refusing to have sex, since the act itself would likely overwhelm his self-control and lead to her brutal death. Meyer contains the imagery of alternative sexuality almost always associated with vampires, first by completely ignoring the homoerotic dimensions of the vampire present since Stoker's novel and, second, by allowing Edward and Bella to consummate only within the confines of a highly traditional, hyper-heterosexual marriage.

Meyer's books, and to a degree the films based on them, attempt to reconstruct the vampire legend as a tale of the struggle for "family values." In fact, Travis Sutton and Harry M. Benshoff called an essay in which they explored the books' religious underpinnings "Forever Family Values," taking note of the Mormon belief that families last quite literally into eternity. The Cullens, Sutton and Benshoff point out, are a kind of "chosen people" in the midst of the less-than-special denizens of Forks. They are not only wealthy and wise but presented as so physically beautiful, at least by white, heteronormative standards, that they seem unreal even before we learn they are actually creatures of fantasy.[51]

Christine Seifert of *Bitch* magazine coined the term "abstinence porn" to describe *Twilight* in a 2009 article. Seifert writes that the first three novels in the series are really about the pair's successful "struggle to keep their pants on" and a celebration of the patriarchal family wrapped up in literally sparkling supernatural elements. The final book, *Breaking Dawn*, sees the pair finally married when Bella becomes a teenage bride of nineteen to the significantly older Edward. Their marriage replicates traditionalist assumptions about marriage with Bella offering her body to Edward and subsuming herself into the power relationships within his family. When not being brutalized in bed (she is covered in welts and wounds after her first sexual encounter with Edward), she makes dinner for his mother or is engaged in other domestic chores.[52]

Twilight also deals with the politics of the womb. Edward immediately impregnates Bella after their marriage in *Breaking Dawn* and, despite the risk to her own life, she brings a monstrous baby to term. Bella must allow her humanity to die in order for the baby to live, in an absurdly allegorical symbolization of traditionalist expectations about motherhood. Bella's willingness to sacrifice herself is matched by Edward's ferocity at saving his spawn as he tears the baby from Bella's womb with his teeth. Bella loses both her humanity and any semblance she had of control over her own body. Bella (Kristen Stewart) makes this plain in the film version of the first book during which, in a voice-over in the film's opening moments, the seventeen-year-old proclaims, "I'd never given much thought to how I would die, but dying in the place of someone I love seems like a good way to go."

The religious themes in *Twilight*, combined with its traditionalist ideology, have made it appealing to the Christian Right, some of whom even see it as an ally in the culture wars. The Facebook site "Jesus Christ Is My Edward Cullen," created by a high school student in 2009, both praised the books for their traditional representation of romance while investing them with theological meaning. "Only Christ is the true gentleman, the one who will sweep us off our feet," the site promises. The immature though reactionary cultural agenda of the page is made clear when the author encourages males who want to join to declare their heterosexuality by writing "No homo" on the page's wall.[53] Conservative evangelical youth minister Kimberly Powers sees in *Twilight* a kind of mythical analogue to her own cultural agenda. In her writings, Powers approvingly quotes the teenage girls who have told her that Edward is the "perfect boyfriend" because he "comes from a good family," and "he continually holds himself back from getting too physically close to Bella." Powers herself praises Edward's "insatiable desire to know everything about Bella" and suggests to her readers that "you would be crazy over this too, if someone cared for your every interest, if he wanted to know each of your thoughts so that he could better protect and honor you."[54]

Notions of male figures who "protect" and "honor" are key to patriarchal discourses about family, marriage, and sexuality. These views comport well with Powers' broader agenda. Powers leads a series of successful weekend conferences she calls "In Search of a Princess: A Weekend Celebration." In sessions entitled "Daddy, I Need You" and "Soul-Tie to the Father," Powers suggests that the failure of the patriarchal household leads to numerous social and psychological problems.[55]

The willingness of conservative evangelicals to either praise or borrow imagery from the *Twilight* series shows that Meyer has not so much created a new American monster as sought to defuse the monster's subversive power. Meyer's vampires are literally defanged, their immemorial associations with sex and excess fully domesticated. *Twilight* seeks to legitimize white, middle-class, heterosexual values by introducing elements that appear to test that normative worldview and then holding those elements at bay. Meyer fully conscripts the vampire into the forces of reaction. Women frightened of the demands of sexual and political liberation can have their vampire and not be eaten by him, too.

The refusal to allow the monster to be the monster, more than its obviously reactionary politics, is the chief reason that *Twilight* will likely make no enduring mark on the American monster tradition. The narrative literally has nowhere to go except to the safe confines of an idealized married life. Robbed of its adolescent romantic tensions by the marriage of Edward and Bella in *Breaking Dawn*, Meyer's cycle of stories has not produced a larger, cohesive mythology.

HBO's *True Blood*, on the other hand, became for a time a major milestone in the development of vampire mythology. Often knowingly schlocky and over-the-top in its portrayal of extreme violence and polysexual eroticism, *True Blood* managed to create a truly American vampire.

True Blood cast

Set primarily in the fictional Louisiana town of Bon Temps, the early seasons of *True Blood* intertwined its living dead in a rich regional mythology, a dirty South world of pickup trucks, juke joints, and evangelical religion as a patina for a seamy and steamy world of sex and violence. The series followed the fortunes of a Sookie Stackhouse and her beau, the century-old vampire and Confederate veteran Bill Compton. Bill and Sookie attempt to find vampire–human love in a modern America in which vampires have "come out of the closet" after the discovery and marketing of a blood substitute known as "Tru Blood."

The modern American setting, and the willingness to explore sexuality with humor and frankness, made the show *True Blood* cast both a controversial and a critically acclaimed hit during its first three seasons, though many viewers and critics felt it declined in value significantly after season 4. Series creator Alan Ball sees himself as not so much revising the vampire myth as returning it to its roots and giving it an American, indeed a Southern, accent. This allowed for all manner of satire and comment, especially in relation to America's struggle to come to terms with sexual identity and the rights of sexual minorities. In this, *True Blood* represented the antithesis of *Twilight*, a point that series creator Alan Ball made when he told *Rolling Stone*, "Vampires are sex. I don't get a vampire story about abstinence."[56]

True Blood enveloped its viewers in a sometimes uncomfortably alternative sensuality that encourages an equally uncomfortable social critique. *Twilight* represents a supernatural escape from the historic demands of feminism and the results of the sexual revolution. In some ways, the popularity of these franchises highlights the American cultural divide, the two Americas of the culture wars. The zombie genre has, meanwhile, taken a strongly political turn as well, becoming, since 2001, a standing (or rather shambling and stumbling) critique of America's foreign and domestic policy since 9/11.

Zombie Crawl Through History

Zombie narratives have proven the perfect vehicle for social satire. This is not because of any inherent quality of the zombie as a character but rather because zombies always bring an apocalypse with them. Any apocalyptic narrative represents a deconstruction of the social contract, either as a complete revolution, a fairly severe redefinition, or, in the case of evangelical eschatology, a reactionary insistence that departing from religious values has triggered God's judgment. Imagining the world as we know it collapsing around us gives us the opportunity to take a long look at what that dead world valued and call it into question.

Moreover, zombies are, more than any other monster, truly human. The vampire is a fully transformed human being, in essence a superior being and the aristocracy of the monster world. Other creatures of the night have little or no human connection, born from beyond the stars or out of satanic darkness. The zombie, on the other hand, is one of us. They are recognizably human even as their bodies are always shown in varying states of decay. Romero's films often emphasized this by making zombies representative of specific occupations and pastimes ranging from cheer-leader zombies to zombie brides and zombie doctors (and, infamously, a zombie Hare Krishna).

Zombie films often force our identification with the walking dead by revealing human beings as the real monsters. In Romero's *Night of the Living Dead*, the besieged humans cannot put aside their own desire for power and control in order to help one another. Frequently, humans murdering zombies with abandon and relish are some of the more fright-ening scenes in the best zombie films. Almost every zombie feature ends in the death of most or all of the major characters because of their own pride, self-absorption, or tyrannical impulses.[57]

Apocalyptic narratives in which everyday people are transformed into monsters allow for significant social critique. Although George Romero has frequently insisted that *Night of the Living Dead* offers no political satire, audiences of the film have read it as a statement about both the Vietnam War and American racism. Romero's later films suggest that he crafted them around efforts to critique American society. The 2005 *Land of the Dead*, for example, alluded both to the war in Iraq and to the American class structure. *Diary of the Dead* (2008) is a sendup of reality TV, celebrity culture, and America's growing reliance on the Internet for news and social interaction.[58]

Horror auteurs in recent years have used the zombie genre not only to launch a broad critique of American society but also to comment on particular political issues. Joe Dante's 2005 "Homecoming," an episode in Showtime's *Masters of Horror* series, features a right-wing commentator named David Murch. On a popular cable television show, Murch tells a mother who lost her son in Iraq that if he could have "one wish" it would be that her son would come back from the dead. Murch adds that if the distraught woman's son could return, he would come back to remind Americans of the importance of the war. In the dark fairy-tale logic of horror, the American war dead from Iraq do begin to return, not to feast on the living or to praise American foreign policy but to "vote for anyone who will end this war." Commenting on the Bush administration's ban on photographs of body bags, dead soldiers, and even soldiers' funerals, Dante has flag-draped coffins that burst open to reveal the walking undead veterans. The left-leaning *Village Voice* described "Homecoming" as "easily the most important political film of the Bush II era."[59]

Zombie films have also proved adept at satirizing a number of issues in American society more generally. Danny Boyle's *28 Days Later* portrayed its "running zombies" as uncontrollable mobs and the infection as both an AIDS-like plague and a kind of terrorist threat. *Zombies of Mass Destruction*, as the title makes clear, references the Iraq War and its domestic effects, portraying the inhabitants of a small island becoming zombified and turning on their neighbors. Director Kevin Hamedani shows us the action partially through the experience of an Iranian-American woman who local residents believe has ignited the zombie apocalypse as part of a terrorist attack. She is tortured, Abu Ghraib-style, by one of her hysterically paranoid neighbors.

The zombies of popular culture are situated in the trajectory of American history. Undead revenants from popular culture rather than monsters of folk belief, zombies symbolize for many Americans the current state of their own society or its eventual direction. The hopelessness of the genre, with its images of civilization's dissolution and human beings cannibalizing one another, captures a sentiment that, in retrospect, has been a theme in American life since the 1960s. The forced optimism of the Reagan years, the glorification of the World War II generation ("the greatest generation"), the generalized nostalgia for an earlier era, and the visceral appeal many found in the 2016 political slogan "Make America Great Again" points to profound unease about current American society and its place in global history. America after 9/11, a place that now must experience history with the rest of the world, is a veritable buffet for the hungry undead. They're not just coming for Barbara. They're coming for us all.

CONCLUSION
Worse Things Waiting

The bats have left the belltower / The victims have been bled / Red velvet lines the black box / Bela Lugosi's dead.

—Bauhaus

There are worse things awaiting man than death.

—Bela Lugosi, *Dracula*

In 1994 Freddy Krueger invaded America's nightmares once again. Ten years after the trash-talking slasher first entered his victims' dreams, *New Nightmare* reimagined the Elm Street mythology in a radical fashion. Director Wes Craven's monster escapes the realm of imagination and stalks Heather Langenkamp and Robert Englund, the actors who portrayed the final girl and Freddy himself in the first film. He even stalks his creator, Craven himself.[1]

New Nightmare was the first of the Elm Street films that Craven, a former literature and philosophy professor, directed since the series debut in 1984. In this revisionist reading of his own work, Craven proposes that Freddy was an actual being, a dream demon, whose power had been contained by the telling of stories about him (the first seven films in the series). Now that the character had dimmed in popularity, he was no longer bound by the narrative and freed himself from the prison of the script. This ingenious story makes the monster into something even more dreadful than the horribly burned child-killer who returns from the grave with a razor-fingered glove. He becomes an archetypal monster with many faces, appearing in different times and epochs and wearing many masks.[2]

New Nightmare's use of metanarrative, narrative that discusses its own premises and implicates the audience in the story being told, proved unsuccessful with that very audience. Two years later, America seemed a bit more prepared for the postmodern monster. Craven's runaway hit *Scream* took the basic premise of *Halloween* and deconstructed it. The film contained numerous references to other horror films, and the killers themselves are two slasher film aficionados whose fascination with the genre structures their mayhem. Audiences fell in love with *Scream*'s aesthetic, mirroring as it did other pop culture styles present in everything from MTV to *The Simpsons* and addressing itself to the increasingly blurred lines between media representation and reality. Audiences may have understood Craven's efforts better than some critics. One film critic laughably described *Scream* as "highly derivative."[3]

This has been a book about stories that a culture tells itself and how the line between "story" and "history" is highly permeable. Our creepy survey has looked at how monster tales have been used as exhibitions of power over the oppressed. Yet we have also seen how they can be used by the oppressed and socially marginalized to unsettle and challenge the powerful. For almost every social group in American society, the monster has embodied the terrors of history and been part of a history of terror.

We have witnessed something even more disturbing. The monster in America has come to life. Metaphors of death, blood, and sex have had living analogues in the history of the United States. These metaphors are something more than reflections of anxiety; they are interstitially connected to events of American history and the structure of American society. Analyze the terrors of the colonial era, and the complexity of nostalgia for that era, and you will meet the shapeshifter and the witch. Ask the victims of the American pharmaceutical and cosmetic industry at Holmesburg Prison if they believe in Frankenstein. Consider the experience of Vietnam through the eyes of Tom Savini and you will better grasp the gory monsters he created. Hear the rhetoric of religious conservatives and how it shaped the politics of the AIDS epidemic and you will know the power of the vampire.

The American monster will not disappear. The Enlightenment bred hideous night things while Jefferson slept, and, as cultural critic Mark Edmunds has argued, America entered a deeply gothic phase in the final years of the twentieth century that shows no sign of abating. The vampire and the zombie are likely to continue their reign in the American consciousness for some time. The themes that make them a current cultural obsession will create, and have already created, new monsters for Americans to see in their nightmares and embody in their history.

We can discern at least one future of the American monster in the related anxieties over medicine, disease, and death that influenced the vampire and zombie craze. Technology has lengthened life, made possible miraculous bodily renovations, increased sexual fulfillment for aging Americans, and linked society together in the new social and cultural arena of cyberspace. Embryonic cloning and medicine grounded in the possibility of cell and tissue regeneration raised the possibility of what author and futurist John Harris called "a new phase in Darwinian evolution" in which "our descendants will cease to be human in the sense in which we now understand this idea." We are wired, both as a society and, increasingly, in our bodies.[4]

These new possibilities are becoming realities at the very roots of human consciousness in the study of our genetic code. The map of the human genome allows us to explore new territory, creating, shaping, and growing life in ways that Mary Shelley never imagined. The Dr. Frankensteins of the present have no need to go digging about in graveyards for body parts to reanimate in the lab. They can grow those parts in the lab, allowing them to develop in something that resembles an organic fashion. The modern geneticist's model is not Prometheus, but rather the gods themselves.[5]

New technologies of the body, as well as science fictions about the augmentation of the body, have created a scholarly and popular discussion about the meaning of the posthuman world. Steve Nichols' 1988 *Posthuman Manifesto* suggested that a new phase in human experience had begun already. Elaine L. Graham argues that a belief in the "technological sublime" has led to a "re-enchantment" of the world in which the mythical representations of science fiction and fantasy (what she calls "the promise of monsters") have become forums for discussion of the nature of posthuman experience. Other thinkers, often labeled "bioconservatives," are less sanguine about the benefits of posthuman technology. Francis Fukuyama in *Our Post-human Future* argues for a stable, unchanging human nature that serves as the basis for "human rights and morality." This stance leads Fukuyama to argue for legislation restricting biotechnological research.[6]

The Religious Right has shaped American conservatism's response to techno-human possibilities. The Presidential Commission for the Study of Bioethical Issues (PCB), appointed by George W. Bush in 2001, published a number of controversial documents that made use of Jewish and Christian theological concepts to discuss cloning, stem cell research, and new reproductive technologies. Author Michael J. Hyde, in his book on the cultural and philosophical history of the idea of perfection, describes how the language of "blessing" and "gift" made its way into PCB documents, as well as assertions of an "unalterable human nature." The work of the commission tended to reflect concerns over religious strictures in relation to biotechnological change rather than thoughtful reflection on the possibilities and limitations of biotech.[7]

Anxieties about, and structured critiques of, posthuman possibilities do not always acknowledge how deeply embedded the desire for liberation from constricted human boundaries has been in literature, art, myth, and theology. These possibilities draw on very old human hopes. Literary theorist Myra Seaman, whose scholarship embraces both medieval and modern culture, has argued that visions of the posthuman have assumed aspects of the Christian hope for the glorified body. She reveals remarkable continuities between vastly different worldviews in her examination of medieval texts that express pious hopes for a transformation into "a new creation in Christ" alongside contemporary pop culture expressions of posthuman possibility, texts ranging from *Frankenstein* to *The Matrix*. At the same time, she shows that older, religious conceptions of the posthuman imagine it as a state of perfection, while modern imaginings tend toward dystopic fears about the loss of something essentially human.[8]

Of course, other thinkers have argued that all the talk about terrors or utopian promises of the posthuman ignores some basic facts of human history. Jamais Cascio, a futurist theoretician selected by *Foreign Policy* magazine as one of the one hundred most important global thinkers of 2009, believes that "post human is a term with more weight than meaning." He suggests that once any innovation leaves "the pages of science fiction" and becomes part of daily experience, it ceases to be "the advance forces of technoapocalypse" and becomes "normal, even banal." Human history, beginning with the use of stone weapons and the discovery of fire, is the history of "augmentation."[9]

Cascio ignores the role played by forces other than rational calculation in accepting new cultural premises. He seems to suggest that we should all stop our whining, shut out a millennia of cultural and religious warnings about human hubris, and get on with the business of being posthuman with the recognition that artificial body parts and the cloning of living beings are really all quite banal. Not incidentally, Cascio's worldview would make moral criticism of new technology impossible, brushing it aside with an exasperated "this is how it's always been." Cascio, though this is not his intention, suggests that the Neolithic spear is not so different from the nuclear missile. They are both simply stages in human augmentation and development.

Cascio's assurances aside, pop culture fantasies of the posthuman reveal how profoundly worried we are about the benefits of modern society and the cybernetic human body. The nightmares of the twenty-first century replicate older Victorian fears of premature burial. The mechanical, computerized, or cybernetically enhanced body threatens to become a tomb in which the human consciousness could become buried, a prisoner to artificial limbs and organs.[10]

The manifestations of this fear in popular culture are too numerous to count. The internment of Anakin Skywalker in the metallic casing of Darth Vader in the 2005 *Star Wars: Revenge of the Sith* is the most well-known representation of this anxiety. *The Matrix* (1999) imagined a world in which humans are encased in mechanoid shells like medical oddities, free only in their false, computer-generated consciousness. These anxieties even appear outside of horror and science fiction. Jean-Dominique Bauby's novel (later a 2007 award-winning film) *The Diving Bell and the Butterfly* tells a story of terrifying salvation by medical technology. Bauby, the editor of the fashion magazine *Elle,* suffered a stroke-induced "locked-in syndrome" in 1994 that left him totally paralyzed, able to move only his left eyelid. Breathing on life support, he became a prisoner of his body and the medical technology that kept him alive.[11] Fears of the posthuman are grounded in a terror of a cultural "locked-in syndrome" in which we become prisoners and victims of monstrous machines. Posthuman realities also raise questions about both what is monstrous and why we declare something monstrous. The meaning of the monster raises the question of the human. What will we define as the monster in a world where the category of the human has become elastic? New technologies may reshape the very morphology of the body, redefining the category of the monstrous out of existence and changing basic conceptions of human beauty.

Aimee Mullins provides an example of how aesthetic choices can upset societal conceptions of disability, beauty, gender, and the role of sexuality while also raising questions about the liminality of human identity. Her condition of being born without fibula bones forced doctors to amputate her legs from the knees down at the age of one. Mullins' life since then has been a record of achievement rather than of tragedy. A graduate of Georgetown University, she competed in NCAA Division I sports using carbon-fiber Cheetah® leg prosthetics. Subsequently, she has become a model, actress, and lecturer. In her latter role she advocates for the convergence of form and function in prosthetics that she hopes will redefine notions of disability.[12]

Mullins' work as a runway model and sometime magazine cover girl has brought the image of a posthuman body to a broad audience. Mullins cultivates certain aspects of a fairly standard heterosexual fantasy aesthetic in these contexts. Her clothing, hair, and photographic presentations of her body to the viewer's gaze replicate the highly sexualized imagery of traditional modeling standards. The addition of artificial limbs, especially the inclusion of the Cheetah limbs, both mocks and complicates those traditional standards.

Mullins challenges the very notion of disability by explicitly comparing her experience to that of traditional celebrities seeking aesthetic enhancement. In a 2009 lecture, Mullins quipped that "Pamela Anderson has more prosthetic in her body than I do; nobody calls her disabled." This leads her to reject the label of "disabled" and the effort to replicate humanness. Artificial limbs no longer represent "a need to replace loss." The formerly disabled can become "architects of their own identity by designing their own bodies."[13]

Mullins seems to offer a vision of the posthuman that would liberate us all from the monster by freeing us from a reductive definition of the human. Aspects of Mullins' inarguably inspiring story become, however, highly problematic when examined in connection with social and economic realities. Her prosthetics have been produced for her at great expense by admirers, obviously not an option available to most of the world's disabled people who have neither the cash or the cachet to "become architects of their identities." Moreover, at least part of the fascination with Mullins in the fashion industry has to do with how her body mostly conforms to standards of beauty universalized by that same industry. Slender and blonde with blemish-free skin, Mullins' self-representation raises questions about whether or not people who do not conform to the standards of beauty promulgated by the film/fashion/cosmetic/plastic surgery industries would be viewed in the same light.

Other technological efforts in the direction of a posthuman future raise similar questions. In 2006 Claudia Mitchell, who lost her left arm in a motorcycle accident, became the first person to receive a bionic arm controlled by her own thought patterns. This "myoelectric arm" receives electrical signals directly from her brain through electrodes that jump these signals to the prosthesis where an onboard computer transforms them into commands. The process is not perfect. Mitchell can sometimes feel her elbow being touched when a muscle on her torso is stimulated.[14]

This extraordinary advance in biomedical technology came at a price tag of three million dollars for the surgery alone and, now more than ten years later, the use of this technology has not become widespread. The cost of such radical therapies, in a society in which there are already limitations on access to traditional types of medical care, suggests a continued growth in the divide between the well-heeled who can afford various types of enhancements and those who cannot. Consider the fact that American states with high poverty rates and limited access to health care have an infant mortality rate similar to developing nations, and you get a sense of the gap between posthuman hopes and American realities.[15]

These complexities suggest that the history of medicine and technology will be the history of the American monster for the foreseeable future, despite the efforts of futurists to praise technology's benefits. The questions raised by life-enhancing technology are moral rather than pragmatic. They are questions that live in the intimate roots of the self, the same roots from which monsters grow. Dracula in his dinner jacket with tails may be so old-fashioned that he has lost his power. But we still believe that technology, computers, and genetic enhancements can suck the life out of us.[16]

The terrors of our possible future grow in part from our fear of losing control of that future. If our most intimate physical self can yield to the power of the machine, certainly our society faces a similar threat. We have seen how the fears of apocalypse in the 1990s drew both from evangelical Christianity and the terror of technological catastrophe. The terror of what a posthuman social order might look like has become a persistent theme in American pop culture, fecund ground for images of complete social breakdown (the zombie genre) and for possible futures in which human beings play no role at all.

James Cameron's *The Terminator* has refracted these fears for more than three decades, providing modern America a forum to discuss the nature of humanity and its relationship to a techno-digital environment. As a film trilogy that began in 1984 and continued into the 1990s, Cameron's posthuman mythology has produced a television series, novels, comic books, and follow-up films in 2009 and 2015. This successful (for the most part) franchise imagines a future in which an artificial intelligence known as "Skynet" has unleashed a nuclear holocaust on humanity and mass-produced an army of predatory cyborgs to mop up the survivors. John Connor represents humanity's one hope, the founder and leader of the resistance. Mastering time travel technology, Skynet sends its agents, human-appearing assassins known as "Terminators," into the past to kill Sarah Connor, John's mother, before he is born. Failing at that in the first film, Skynet and its cyborg killers repeatedly try to kill the young Connor in the sequels.

The *Terminator* series combines the American fascination with religion and its anxiety over technological promise. John Connor is something of a messianic figure, and the day on which the machines will trigger nuclear destruction is known as "Judgment Day." Religious questions about the nature of time and the meaning of the soul are key to the mythology's development.

The *Terminator* series suggests that our fear of posthuman possibilities may not be entirely related to a simple fear of technology. The *Terminator* mythos draws heavily on H. P. Lovecraft's image of a universe full of beings devoid of human feeling and utterly indifferent to the human future. Rather than horrifying Cthulhu arising from his ancient sleep, the machines rise against humanity and seek to destroy them "without emotion, without pity, without remorse."

Destruction of the social order at the hands of uncaring machines taps into very old human fears of powerlessness and meaninglessness in the face of an uncaring universe. Cameron's dark vision can be seen to be oddly hopeful in this light. The most well-wrought iterations of the franchise, *T2: Judgment Day* and television's short-lived *Sarah Connor Chronicles*, focus on the possibility of the cyborg learning human feeling and becoming part of a community through willingness to change and sacrifice. More than the atavistic primitivism of religious conservatism or the uncritical optimism of the futurists, Cameron's *Terminator* offers hope based on integrating the monster into the human community, perhaps even creating that community based on the rejection of notions of monstrosity and ultimate difference.[17]

Such a transformation of the idea of the monster will likely not come anytime soon. The BBC series *Black Mirror* (2011–), widely popular in America after its release on Netflix, has borne out the book's 2011 claim that a digital landscape may give birth to a new world of gods and monsters. Most entries in the series layer and contextualize a simple Frankenstein's monster tale by taking the most worrisome aspects of online life to its logical conclusions. The series themes have included how technology interacts with an embittered subculture that harasses and abuses, the complications of gendered expectations of romance mediated by digital lifestyles, the ability to weaponize every technology in the service of powerful systems of military aggression, and how social media offers new opportunities to make class lines more rigid while seeming more "natural."

Online life has become a matrix of monsters. Creepypasta's ability to create monstrous memes such as "Slenderman" blurred the line between traditional conceptions of folklore and the urban legend. The monsters of our wired world can also quickly become commodified, as can be seen in the extraordinary story of the cult PC game *Five Nights at Freddy's*. Once a peculiar little terror known only to the most dedicated gamers, the disturbing game that seemed to open a dread dimension simply by playing it recently became a multimillion-dollar franchise with t-shirts, action figures, and other swag.[18]

Digital monsters—posthuman, online, and integrated into our lives in shockingly intimate ways—will continue to terrorize us. That posthuman terrors have to be added to our list of possible monsters, along with sea serpents and serial killers, underscores the elasticity of the monster's identity, the tendency of monsters to absorb the characteristics of the historical moment in which they appear. Facebook Live has become most well known as a means for the pathological to stream murder, rape, and all forms of abuse. 4Chan and Reddit have become hives of racism, misogyny, and open, self-identified fascism. Unpopular opinions expressed on Twitter or Facebook, or even in print, have sometimes brought out hordes of aptly named "trolls" who bully, threaten, and stalk their victims. This has become such an integral part of online culture that Victor LaValle's 2017 novel *The Changeling* used the idea brilliantly as the core of his dark modern fairy tale.[19]

This book has refused to give a concise definition of the monster, assuming that no abstract definition exists. The creature we are hunting looks different in each historical era. In essence, every historical period creates the monster it needs. Each historic epoch has a multitude of monsters, many of them representing warring discourses and basic cultural conflicts. The terror tales of the slave trade become symbols of a people's oppression, while stories of frontier monsters become metaphors of conquest for the master class. In the twenty-first century, vampires can serve as traditionalist cautionary tales or embodiments of alternative sexuality. They are malleable but often difficult to control, subject to an array of social and historical forces.

September 11, 2001, made explicit America's tendency to use its monster tales to explain the world to itself. Worryingly, our society seems unable to escape the five-hundred-year-old vision of projecting horror on peoples far away and on our citizens closer to home.

Top: Frankenstein
Bottom: Terminator

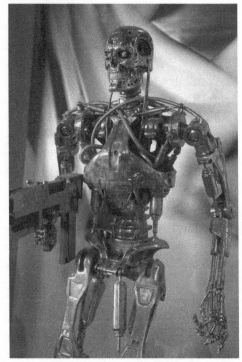

Waging a War on Terror

Many of the best monstrous fictions of the last twenty years, and through-out our history, dwelt on the possibility of sympathetic monsters, inter-rogated us about what we mean by the monster, and asked us to consider ways we project our own monstrous instincts onto the creatures of our imagination . . . and other persons.

Integrating what had formerly been imagined as monstrous into American life reflected one American ideal of the twenty-first century. Indeed, for many so-called millennials (very broadly defined as those born between 1982 and 2004, although those who entered their late teens after the millennium seems a more useful definition), diversity represents a primary social value. The election of Barack Obama in 2008 seemed to many in this generation, and even many like myself who had grown to adulthood in the Reagan years with the freedom struggle still a living memory, to signal a "post-racial America." Younger Americans proved more open, for example, to multiracial friendship groups, romantic rela-tionships, and families, concepts that had remained controversial even in the 1980s.

Horror fans know the monster does not die so easily, especially when it is as deeply intertwined with social, cultural, and even economic life as racism has been in American life. The attack on the World Trade Center and the Pentagon by the relatively small organization of terrorist cells known as al-Qaeda on September 11, 2001, killed 2,750 people (including five hundred visiting foreign nationals and American Muslims who met at a prayer room on the seventeenth floor of the South Tower daily) and has had more effect on our contemporary politics than any event since American defeat in Vietnam.[20]

Al-Qaeda achieved more than it could have ever dreamed with its spectacle of death. September 11 deranged American politics and argu-ably reshaped geopolitics in the Arab, East African, Persian, and Turkish worlds. The event provides an explanation for much of the history of the early twenty-first century. The real-world horror show planned by Osama Bin Laden overdetermined the stance America adopted toward the world. It also created an undercurrent of monstrous thinking among too many Americans that condemned the world's one and a half billion Muslims to the category of the monstrous, the abject, and the irredeemable.

American foreign policy went through a change more decisive than at any time since the beginning of the Cold War. George W. Bush came to power in a controversial presidential election in 2000, the real winner of which will likely never be known given that a split vote in a conservative-leaning Supreme Court ultimately decided the outcome. Embracing many of the same advisers that had been close to his father George H. W. Bush during the Reagan years, George W. Bush surrounded himself with men who held an expansive vision of American power abroad.

An aide to Secretary of Defense Donald Rumsfeld admitted that his boss had been talking about an invasion of Iraq, a country with no links whatsoever to the attack, within hours of the collapse of the Twin Towers. Rumsfield crafted a memo by September 12, 2001, that read in part, "Go massive. Sweep it all up. Things related and not." The same day, Richard Perle informed CIA director George Tenet that "Iraq had to pay a price for what happened yesterday. They bear responsibility."[21]

Encouraged by his powerful vice president Dick Cheney and an enthusiastic White House legal counsel, Bush assumed wartime powers that allowed the executive branch to project American military strength with minimal congressional or judicial oversight. Granted powers that would have stunned even Lyndon Johnson and Richard Nixon in the Vietnam era, the White House centralized war-making to an extraordinary degree. The Obama administration continued to use these enhanced executive powers, in some ways expanding the killing potential of American military power with the use of drone attacks in Yemen and the Philippines as well as the battlefields of Iraq and Afghanistan.[22]

While a massive military intervention into Afghanistan and Iraq began abroad, as well as costly operations in East Africa that frequently caught up civilians in their deadly sweep, American Muslims and recent immigrants from the Islamic world faced a wave of hate crimes and a growing undercurrent of disdain for their communities, religious faith, and culture. Franklin Graham, son of Billy Graham, began a vituperative verbal war against Islam, using ancient language of monstrosity and heroic monster slaying to talk about Muslims everywhere, not just the tiny number influenced by the fundamentalist version of Islam promulgated in Saudi Arabia (a staunch American ally) and embodied in al-Qaeda.

These fantasies of horror reflected on how American tales of dread had come to interact with this terrifying new world. In August of 2007, the New York Police Department released a report called "Radicalization in the West" that referred to "homegrown terrorists" being born out of "extremist incubators." This made them sound like a new race of pod people waiting to be activated, a monster soon to burst forth like the infamous biological horror scene in *Alien*.[23]

Local police departments were not the only ones promulgating such views. An investigation by *Wired* magazine found that the FBI began training many of its agents after 9/11 to view American Muslims as terrorist sympathizers and to view the Prophet Muhammad (570–632 CE) as "a cult leader." The Bureau purged over eight hundred pages from its counter-terrorism training manual after these revelations. It is unclear if they purged the anti-Islamic bias.[24]

Popular prime-time television shows of the two thousand aughts both demonized Muslims of all nationalities and shades of belief and made an implicit argument for the use of torture and extralegal action to deal with the "green peril" of Islam. Mainstream shows like *24*, *The Agency*, *The Unit*, and *Sleeper Cell* all encouraged Americans, as in the fifties, to worry about an insidious invader within as well as without.

The debate about how horror fictions navigate a culture engaged in a "war on terror" remains ongoing. We can point to some fascinating examples of horror films since 9/11 that have offered critically acclaimed entertainment and the opportunity to learn more about parts of the Islamic world, too often imagined as monolithic in the West. The 2014 Iranian film *A Girl Walks Home Alone at Night* both revives the vampire genre and shows a side of Iranian youth culture generally unknown to outsiders. The 2016 *Under the Shadow*, also set in Iran, offers a period piece of the 1980s. Taking place during the Iran/Iraq War, it blended social realism with the supernatural that exposed the undercurrent of horror in the times. Both Kevin Smith's 2011 *Red State* and Jeremy Saulnier's 2015 *The Green Room* ask us to consider the horror of "domestic terrorism," a homegrown horror likely to gain more attention after a white supremacist killed Heather Heyer and badly injured nineteen others at a "Unite the Right" rally in Charlottesville, Virginia, on August 12, 2017.

These films seem lonely islands of reflective horror on a sea of online memes conflating the monster and the image of the Muslim terrorist and all Muslims. Such images have flowed like a bloody tide over the American consciousness, despite the efforts of educators and activists to create thoughtful discussion, to analyze the historical roots of terrorism, to explain that Muslims the world over are the most frequent victims of brutal groups such as ISIS, a boogeyman whose power and internal cohesion have begun to collapse at the time of writing. But many decades and a willingness to open ourselves to different and challenging ideas are required to undo the work of bigotry and fear, not unlike the earthquake of historical change it required for Americans to move beyond monstrous images of the Japanese, and Japanese Americans, after World War II.

American culture shows little current willingness to engage in such a project of discussion, debate, and renewal. The monster tradition, as always, sometimes acts to legitimize the strangely fragile assertions of American exceptionalism. But, just as often, it confronts us with the true terror of the times.

Get Out

In 2017 Jordan Peele released the surprise horror hit *Get Out*. Telling the story of Black photographer Chris going home with his white girlfriend to meet her parents, the production at first suggests we are watching an allegedly post-racial America's version of *Guess Who's Coming to Dinner*. Dad would have voted for Obama a third time, and he is going to tell Chris all about it. We are expecting a comedy of manners with perhaps some slight social commentary.

Something dark from the American past slithers in the film, however, and before the movie's end we learn that the white family represents new incarnations of the Sawyer family, psychotics in a dark wooded American frontier. The tale we are told, intentionally or not, lines up with the macabre realities behind African American folklore about cannibalism we saw even in the slave trade. Those stories reflected the historical experience of an Atlantic economy that ground the bodies of Black men and women into sugar, rice, tobacco, and cotton and a post-Emancipation America where white lynch mobs hunted, tortured, and mutilated the bodies of Black men while raping Black women with impunity.

Get Out also intersected with the horror of contemporary American history. Violence against Black people does not belong to a distant past, and the African American community remains under siege. The metaphor of Black men as Frankenstein's monsters, a trope of white terror reaching back through the era of lynching to the fear of slave revolt, appears in the language of policing and the mass incarceration of Black men that has become part of the very fabric of American life.

On August 9, 2014, Officer Darren Wilson gave his testimony to a grand jury about his shooting and killing of Michael Brown, an African American teen in Ferguson, Missouri. In this testimony, Wilson described Brown as "a demon" who displayed "superhuman" strength. He insisted that he believed that if Brown punched him in the face he "would have died" even though the two are the same height and build. He even suggested that he shot Brown multiple times because the teenager allegedly felt no effect from the bullets, like Michael Myers lurching forward unstoppable in *Halloween*. This language of monstrosity, a demon with supernatural strength who refused to die, helped convince the grand jury not to indict the officer. The people took to the streets to protest.[25]

A significant number of local whites expressed surprise that protestors filled the streets of Ferguson after the killing of Michael Brown. Some claimed that the town had been a "progressive place" where "everyone got along." These claims are belied both by the immediate reaction of local law enforcement and a later Department of Justice investigation into the policing practices. Ferguson, like so many American places large and small, rural and urban, represents a different experience for Black men and women than for white.[26]

The results shocked most observers. The Ferguson Police Department moved against the protests as if mobilizing for war. For weeks, they rolled into neighborhoods in assault vehicles in full-body armor, at times tear gassing families standing in the yards of their own homes.

A national movement emerged out of the protests at Ferguson, Black Lives Matter, that took its defiant name and tone in response to the reality that, in terms of historical fact, Black lives have not mattered in the American experience.

Black Lives Matter has not only critiqued a heavily militarized police. The movement has called into question America's prison-industrial complex, large segments of which are run as a for-profit system in a country that imprisons a larger percentage of its citizens than any other nation on earth. The incarcerated have their citizenship rights, including the right to vote, stripped from them. African American men are disproportionately jailed and serve longer sentences for the same and/or less violent offenses than white offenders. In eleven states, Black men make up one half the prison population.[27]

New American monster tales have emerged around the horror of racist state institutions and police violence. Matt Ruff's novel *Lovecraft Country* (2016) invests the monsters of the *Weird Tales* author with the malefic power of American racial violence. Jordan Peele, at the time of writing, has announced a television series planned around Ruff's work. Victor LaValle's 2016 novella *The Ballad of Black Tom* reimagines one of Lovecraft's most xenophobic tales, "The Horror at Red Hook," from the perspective of an African American named Tommy Tester of Harlem unwillingly caught up in the extra-dimensional horrors at work in Brooklyn. He also must face the horrors of American racism when his father dies in a hail of police bullets. In response, Tester chooses the Great Old Ones over "the devils" that benefit from the white supremacist system.

LaValle, in a 2017 comic series called *Destroyer,* drew on the American tradition of employing the story of Frankenstein to explore the value, or lack thereof, that American society places on human life. The Monster, still alive in 2017, has become understandably nihilistic about the value of human beings after watching our behavior from afar for two centuries. The creature travels from the arctic to contemporary America where an African American woman of the line of Victor Frankenstein has brought her son back to life using modern biotech and her ancestor's famed notebook. Her young son, murdered by a police officer, perhaps will teach the Monster something new about human experience . . . or perhaps the ambiguous title of the series warns us of another outcome.

"All lives matter," or more starkly, "Blue Lives Matter," has been the response of many Americans who don't understand either the history of violence against African Americans in the United States or who have relegated it to a distant past. But, historically, have Black lives mattered? If so, why the frequent inability to convict police officers who murder unarmed Black men? Or who are caught on tape suddenly shooting them repeatedly during a routine traffic stop as in the 2016 case of Philando Castile?

American culture has, time and again, drawn lines around lives that matter and lives that are monstrous. Today in an America decidedly not "post-racial," artists, activists, and scholars seek to wrestle away tales of horror from social and political forces that would use them to legitimize individual and state violence against marginal people. But those forces have been emboldened rather than quieted in recent years. We have learned to live with our monsters, our most vicious, dead-eyed terrors.

We Are the Walking Dead

Zombie fictions grew in popularity, and changed radically, in the shadow of the "war on terror." Using these enormously popular monsters as social commentary seems inescapable, and George Romero, until his death in the summer of 2017, continued to produce films that are, at times, both direct assertions of his moral commitments and, in the current environment, politically unpalatable ideas.

A new kind of zombie fiction emerged after 9/11, however, one that spoke to the inability of many Americans to correlate their personal fears of terrorism and American foreign policy with either their current beliefs about multiculturalism or the myths of American exceptionalism that continue to inundate the cultural atmosphere. The result for zombie fictions has not simply been an apolitical set of zombie tales but rather books, films, and graphic novels that are an ideological morass of competing ideas.

Zack Snyder's kinetic 2004 remake of Romero's 1978 *Dawn of the Dead* reveals these contradictions and results in a very messy adaptation of the Romero original. Romero's opening scene resonated with the concerns of both the 1970s and of the present, as a heavily armed, utterly militarized police urban assault unit slaughters African Americans indiscriminately in a housing project. Much as in *Night of the Living Dead*, the authorities do not discriminate between people of color and zombies.

Snyder's remake opens not in the housing projects but in a peaceful suburb where a young, attractive white couple awaken to find their perfect world shattered by the zombie apocalypse. Snyder follows this incredibly effective set of scenes, in which one catastrophe after another shows the old order having collapsed into chaos overnight, with a now famous montage that uses filmed footage of undead cannibals attacking even the White House press corps with actual news footage of large-scale protests (apparently in contemporary South Korea) and, inexplicably, Muslims peacefully kneeling at prayer.

This directorial decision, invoking social disruption, zombie horror, and Islam made it possible for viewers to read any political message they wished into the sequence, or to simply use it to vent their confusion over world affairs. A series of quick jump cuts of the sort Snyder has become famous for (some of them lasting literally seconds), the sequence washes over the viewer like barely digested cable news, leaving mostly questions and open-ended anxiety (both features of much televised and online media in the twenty-first century).

In a nod to the Romero original, a group of survivors takes refuge in a mall, clearing it of the undead and attempting to remake civilization in the temple of commerce. Romero's original offered a clear critique of American consumerism since the survivors believe they have recreated an Eden for themselves and spend their days exploring all the hedonistic possibilities of being the only survivors left to enjoy the fruits of American capitalism. In the 1978 film, the survivors leave (or die) only after a post-apocalyptic motorcycle gang forces them out of their false paradise and into the world. The brutal intrusion of reality unleashes the dead into their commercial paradise.

Snyder's 2004 version spoke to the economics of the post–9/11 world where, rather than calling on Americans to prepare for ration and sacrifice in response to the new "war on terror," Bush encouraged them to go shopping, take vacations, fuel the American economy, and, in sum, "don't let the terrorists win." This is precisely what the 2004 survivors of *Dawn of the Dead* do, and the film levels no moral critique at their insouciance in the way Romero had done in 1978.[28]

Rather than being forced out of the mall, Snyder's survivors are just bored. They leave their refuge in the last act of the film in hopes of finding "an island" (using the yacht of one of the least admirable characters). The plan seems utterly pointless and designed to end in their deaths, especially since they have absolutely no compelling reason to abandon a very secure fortress where they are well armed and provisioned (the only shortage we hear about is that they've run out of their favorite flavored syrup at the coffee bar). Notably, unlike Romero's ending, there are no survivors in this nihilistic vision. It's not even clear what kind of world they want to survive in.

The enormously successful television series *The Walking Dead*, premiering in 2010 and now in its seventh season, also differs dramatically from Romero's vision. As the thinly veiled metaphor of the title implies, the story explores the struggles of the survivors of the zombie apocalypse who live their lives as "the walking dead." George Romero criticized the series (and faced a fair amount of criticism in return) for being "a soap opera, with a zombie occasionally."[29]

Undoubtedly, the lack of satire in the series troubled Romero. The protagonists of *The Walking Dead* are obviously trying to stay alive, but the enormous arsenal of guns they amass are primarily put to the purpose, at the time of writing, of creating and defending what amounts to a gated community. In Romero's hands this would have become a critique of the idea of the suburb itself. In *The Walking Dead*, the series never really interrogates what the survivors are doing. The values of the group are assumed rather than explored.

We in the audience unwittingly accept the basic good of their effort to return to normalcy without asking if such a regime has value. We are asked to imagine a zombie apocalypse without being urged to imagine a revolutionary new set of social relations such a catastrophe could bring about. *The Walking Dead* provides yet another example of how ideology mystifies us while we aren't looking, or as Slavoj Žižek puts it, films continually succeed in making us believe in the possibility of global apocalypse when many Americans find it impossible to imagine the end of capitalism. This claim certainly holds true for *The Walking Dead*. Just as in Snyder's remake of *Dawn of the Dead*, the monsters are primarily a threat to the

American way of life, not unlike the alien invasion films of the fifties. In these paranoid times, we find in them our fears realized.

These are fears born not out of deprivation but out of prosperity. Never has a society existed in human history in which the middle and upper classes amassed more wealth, mobility, and access to technology. Moreover, like the survivors on *The Walking Dead*, no society in human history has more heavily armed itself and made a fetish of defending its wealth and property either through support for projecting American power overseas or through "stand your ground" laws at home that legalize the murder of fellow citizens during minor altercations.

This suggests the possibly counterintuitive point that many of our zombie fictions since 9/11 have registered our relative contentment rather than our anxiety. Americans in the early twenty-first century found a solution to its problems. We proclaimed ourselves a post-racial society while imprisoning vast numbers of citizens that are seen as problematic, as opposed to truly dangerous. The anxieties of the middle class, and those who aspire to it, find catharsis in superhero films where even the victory of the protagonist results in cities left in ruins and moral ambiguity. America's basic economic systems remain unquestioned and its most irresponsible corporations are subsidized by government bail-out because they are "too big too fail," in a phrase the Obama administration popularized.

Many Americans, particularly the top 30–40 percent who held on to their homes and even prospered after 2008's Great Recession, entered the second Obama term in 2012 with a surprisingly positive view of the direction of the country that seemed both more diverse, more tech savvy, and more economically stable than it had been in decades. This allowed even many liberal white Americans to turn a blind eye to the continuing and growing gap in economic equality, the powerful influence of the billionaire class over politicians and media, and the Obama administration's foreign incursions and aggressive surveillance program at home. Like the threat of "Communist aggression" in the 1950s, the danger of terrorism remained a shadow but one that also seemed distant for relatively prosperous people comfortably watching *The Bachelor* and the other interpersonal dramas served up as entertainment under the misnomer of reality television.

But everything ends.

"American Carnage"

Historians are likely to refer to the text of Donald J. Trump's January 2017 inaugural as the "American Carnage" speech. Inaugurations are known for soaring rhetoric, even if those who give them, from JFK to Ronald Reagan to Bill Clinton to Barack Obama, seldom fulfill the promise of their orations. Trump and Trumpism offered Americans something different: a dark, acrimonious, and bitter vision of the state of the Union. He promised to "eradicate radical Islamic terrorism from the face of the earth," a promise that echoes the conception of the monster hunter since Van Helsing sought to destroy the eastern threat of Dracula in 1897.[30]

The forty-fifth president told "middle class" America that wealth had been "ripped from their homes," an image that perhaps moved those who see themselves as perennially lagging behind the now unreachable 1 percent of Americans who control, by the most conservative estimates, one-fifth of the nation's wealth. The speech alluded to the Rust Belt, single mothers, and a landscape of "tombstones" that have taken the place of the hopes and dreams of many Americans. He was surprisingly perspicacious in describing the reality of many American lives. In some sense, American carnage best describes the last fifty years of the nation's history.

He did not, however, speak for those who have actually suffered from the most lethal effects of what Malcolm X called the American nightmare. Trumpism, a set of free-floating images and slogans rather than a coherent belief system, assumes an oligarchic state in which even the most basic elements of a social safety net are left rotted and frayed. Since his election, the billionaire class has assumed control over many of the major functions of government. In December of 2016, CBS news estimated the combined worth of the forty-fifth president's cabinet at 11 billion dollars, excluding the current president's own wealth. By any standard, it is the wealthiest cabinet in American history.

Trumpism's rallying cry has been "Make America Great Again," a slogan briefly used by Ronald Reagan. Paradoxically, the forty-fifth president always held, and attempted to foment, a brittle sense of ego threatened by marginalized people in American society rather than any belief in American greatness. He has long believed, and encouraged others in the belief, that various kinds of "foreign influences" corrupt American life, even while making tens of millions of dollars in foreign business deals.

Trump's presidency has displayed the characteristics of both reality shows (that made him a public figure) and found footage horror, both of which became popular at the turn of the millennium. As in the past, the horror we consume tells us a great deal about contemporary American history. The popularity of *The Purge* series points us toward our frightening new realities in the twenty-first century, a world in which many current films (superhero flicks, science fiction, actioners, and old school disaster films alongside horror and post-apocalyptic tales) imagine and reimagine the possibility of social chaos, the complete breakdown of civil society, individuals or groups abandoned or even destroyed by powers beyond their control.

The Purge (2013–2016) did something a bit different, imagining horror at the intersection of social breakdown and the creation of a lethal new order. A far right conspiracy of the white and the wealthy known as the "New Founding Fathers" have instituted a yearly "purge" in which all crime, no matter how vicious, becomes legal for twenty-four hours. The regime's official ideology mixes Christian conceptions of shame and guilt with the American passion for violence, telling the populace that the "purge" allows a very literal purgation of their worst instincts, reduces the crime rate to zero for the rest of the year, and revives the American economy.

In reality, the upper middle class remains safe in gated communities during the night of the Purge. The wealthiest Americans hire private security and close themselves off in fortress-like homes, not so different from contemporary America's segregation by privilege in many schools and communities. Black people and Latinos become the direct victims of a night of American carnage when the wealthy supporters of the new Founding Fathers kidnap them so they can "purge" by torturing and killing.

The Purge series sometimes unwittingly extols the explosions of violence it putatively satires. This sits uncomfortably with its sometimes ham-handed attempts at allegory (and the films do veer farther into allegory than any others discussed in this book). The cinematography's use of slow motion photography, elaborate costuming, and heavily stylized bloodshed suggests that many in American culture experience the films as a violent fantasy, a fever dream of infantile regression, in effect a kind of purge. The same could be said for the brilliant 2012 Harmony Korine cult horror film *Spring Breakers*, a film whose message may have been lost in the veteran auteur's unforgettable choreographies of violence.

What do such films tell us about our ongoing state of national emergency? Historians will likely debate whether Trumpism represents an aberration in the American experiment or the result of social forces long at work behind the sleight-of-hand of American exceptionalism. An analysis of the American monster tradition suggests the latter. The utter eruption of the national id that Trumpism encourages and employs has roots in American notions of a manifest destiny to destroy monsters of the frontier, the theft of the vote from African Americans after Reconstruction, the national security state's vampiric feeding off the fear of communism, and post-Vietnam America's reactionary response to both defeat in that war and the social changes wrought in the 1960s.

History shows us that the corpses of our victims have long fouled the waters of democracy. Liberal and moderate hopes that a better America would suddenly emerge if Trump and his cadre exit the stage are as misplaced as the broken, wheezing cries to "Make America Great Again."

We can learn much from our history of monsters. But making monsters of our perceived enemies, a political rhetoric that uses monstrous images of ban, deport, imprison, or kill, leaves us in their talons, unable to imagine a different world.

Monsters in America has looked at stories of the monster, told in different eras and by voices with differing interests, class positions, and racialized, gendered, or sexual identities. In contradiction to Craven's *New Nightmare*, this book has suggested that stories do not so much contain the monster as give it life. Story and event, narrative and social structure are never truly separated. The subtext is always looming like a shadow in the text while the text comes to unnatural life in the social order. The victims of these tales are everywhere in American history, a landscape of corpses.

There is reason for hope. Greil Marcus writes, "cultural awakening comes not when one learns the contours of the master-narrative, but when one realizes . . . that what one has always been told is incomplete, backward, false, a lie." Perhaps we can save the victims from the monster by calling into question the script. History is the work of human agency, and its mistakes can be corrected by human action. Understanding history will break its power, putting it in the grave where it belongs.[31]

Of course, they always come back. One of the conventions of modern horror is to portray the death of the monster and the restoration of the social order only to bring the thing horrifyingly back to life in the final frame. History is a bit like that. There could be worse things waiting.

FILMOGRAPHY

Title	Date	Director
28 Days Later	2002	Danny Boyle
28 Weeks Later	2007	Juan Carlos Fresnadillo
Abbott and Costello Meet Frankenstein	1948	Charles T. Barton
Alien	1979	Ridley Scott
Alien 3	1992	David Fincher
American Psycho	2000	Mary Harron
American Werewolf in London, An	1981	John Landis
Beast from 20,000 Fathoms, The	1953	Eugène Lourié
Birth of a Nation	1915	D. W. Griffith
Black Christmas	1974	Bob Clark
Bram Stoker's Dracula	1992	Francis Ford Coppola
Bride of Frankenstein	1935	James Whale
Brood, The	1979	David Cronenberg
Candyman	1992	Bernard Rose
Carrie	1976	Brian De Palma
Dawn of the Dead	1978	George Romero
Dawn of the Dead	2004	Zach Snyder
Day of the Dead	1985	George Romero
Deathdream	1974	Bob Clarke, David Gregory
Deer Woman	2005	John Landis
Diary of the Dead	2008	George Romero
Diving Bell and the Butterfly, The	2007	Julian Schnabel

Dracula	1931	Tod Browning
Dracula	1992	Francis Ford Coppola
Dr. Jekyll and Mr. Hyde	1931	Rouben Mamoulian
Earth vs. the Spider	1958	Bert I. Gordon
Exorcist, The	1973	William Friedkin
Frankenstein	1931	James Whale
Freaks	1932	Tod Browning
Friday the 13th	1980	Sean Cunningham
Friday the 13th, Part 3	1982	Steve Miner
Get Out	2017	Jordan Peele
Gods and Monsters	1998	James Whale
Godzilla: King of Monsters	1956	Terry O. Morse
Gojira	1954	Ishiro Honda
Green Room, The	2015	Jeremy Saulnier
Halloween	1978	John Carpenter
Hellraiser III: Hell on Earth	1992	Anthony Hickox
Homecoming	2005	Joe Dante
Horror of Dracula	1958	Terence Fisher
Hostel	2005	Eli Roth
House of Dracula	1945	Erle C. Kenton
House of Frankenstein	1945	Erle C. Kenton
Howling, The	1981	Joe Dante
I Walked with a Zombie	1943	Jacques Tourner
I Was a Teenage Werewolf	1957	Gene Fowler Jr.
Invaders from Mars	1953	William Cameron Menzies
Invasion of the Body Snatchers	1956	Don Siegel
Invasion of the Saucer Men	1957	Edward L. Cahn
Island of Lost Souls	1933	Erle C. Kenton
It Came from Beneath the Sea	1955	Robert Gordon
It's Alive	1974	Larry Cohen
Jacob's Ladder	1990	Adrian Lyne
Jaws	1975	Steven Spielberg
King Kong	1933	Merian Cooper
Land of the Dead	2005	George Romero
Last House on the Left, The	1972	Wes Craven
Murders in the Rue Morgue	1932	Robert Florey
Natural Born Killers	1994	Oliver Stone
Nightmare on Elm Street, A	1984	Wes Craven
Night of the Living Dead	1968	George Romero
People Under the Stairs, The	1991	Wes Craven
Psycho	1960	Alfred Hitchcock
Rebel Without a Cause	1955	Nicholas Ray
Red Planet Mars	1952	Harry Horner
Red State	2011	Kevin Smith
Return of the Vampire	1943	Lew Landers

Rosemary's Baby	1968	Roman Polanski
Scream	1996	Wes Craven
Shopping Mall	1986	Jim Wynorski
Silence of the Lambs, The	1991	Jonathan Demme
Spring Breakers	2012	Harmony Korine
T2: Judgment Day	1991	James Cameron
Terminator, The	1984	James Cameron
Texas Chain Saw Massacre, The	1974	Tobe Hooper
Them!	1954	Gordon Douglas
The Purge	2013	James DeMonaco
The Purge: Anarchy	2014	James DeMonaco
The Purge: Election Year	2016	James DeMonaco
They Live!	1988	John Carpenter
Thing from Another World, The	1951	Howard Hawks
Under the Shadow	2016	Babak Anvari
Wes Craven's New Nightmare	1994	Wes Craven
When a Stranger Calls	1979	Fred Walton
White Zombie	1932	Victor Hugo Halperin
Wolf Man, The	1941	George Waggner
Zombies of Mass Destruction	2009	Kevin Hamedani

A NOTE ON SOURCES

Monsters are hiding in the traditional raw materials of American history. Many of the primary sources for this book are evidence of this, revealing how traditional sources contain a substratum of gothic beliefs about the borderlands between the monstrous and the human. This book is an archaeological effort to examine what lies beneath these tectonic layers. One archival resource worth special comment is the Robert H. Brisendine collection at Emory University Library Special Collections. This large collection of materials related to late nineteenth- and early twentieth-century traveling circuses, carnivals, and "monster shows" proved especially useful for filling out my discussion of the American freak show with a large number of regional examples. At the Library of Congress, the American Memory Project offered a vast treasure trove of both primary documents and images. Two secondary works, Teresa Goddu's *Gothic America: Narrative, History and Nation* (New York: Columbia University Press, 1997) and Elizabeth Young's *Black Frankenstein: The Making of an American Metaphor* (New York: New York University Press, 2008), provided both guidance and interpretation of a number of nineteenth-century sources, especially newspapers.

There are several necessary guides for the traveler searching for monsters in the dark forests of American pop culture. David J. Skal, the acknowledged dean of monster culture, provides a wonderful guide to monsters on film and in literature in a number of works, most especially his magnum opus, *The Monster Show: A Cultural History of Horror* (New York: Farrar, Strauss & Giroux, 1992). Skal's work has been a great inspiration for my own in his exploration of the relationship between pop culture of the fantastic and its social and political context. His work almost always avoids the errors of simple, reductive psychological interpretation of monstrous imagery.

A general guide to monsters on film, crucial material for my argument in the latter chapters of this book, is John Stanley's *Creature Features: The Science Fiction, Fantasy and Horror Guide* (New York: Berkley Boulevard Books, 1997). Stanley was the "horror host" for the longtime San Francisco–area TV series *Creature Features*, and his book is the Baedekers of horror movies.

Several works on the relationship between American culture and history helped me to describe the relationship between pop images, folklore, and the historical process. These include Richard Slotkin's *Gunfighter Nation: The Myth of the Frontier in Twentieth Century America* (New York: Macmillan, 1992), Michael Kammen's *American Culture, American Tastes: Social Change and the Twentieth Century* (New York: Alfred A. Knopf, 1999), Lawrence W. Levine's *Black Culture, Black Consciousness: Afro-American Folk Thought from Slavery to Freedom* (Oxford: Oxford University Press, 1977), and Orlando Patterson's *Rituals of Blood: Consequences of Slavery in Two American Centuries* (New York: Basic Civitas Books, 1998).

The work of several historians has been especially influential in shaping how I understand the narrative of American history. Sean Wilentz's work, both in *The Rise of American Democracy: Jefferson to Lincoln* (New York: W. W. Norton, 2006) and the *Age of Reagan: A History, 1974–2008* (New York: Harper, 2008), has informed my reading of nineteenth-century America and the late twentieth century. Two other historians, Lynn Dumenil and Andreas Killen, have written works that provide skeleton keys to crucial moments in twentieth-century American culture. Dumenil's *The Modern Temper: American Culture and Society in the 1920s* (New York: Hill & Wang, 1995) and Killen's *1973 Nervous Breakdown: Watergate, Warhol and the Birth of Post-Sixties America* (New York: Bloomsbury Press, 2007) use a close reading of a specific era to draw larger, brilliant conclusions about the American historical/cultural process.

Exploring and explaining the convoluted history of race and racism is crucial to this book's task. The discussion of the origins of American racial attitudes in the colonial period depended on my late teacher Winthrop

Jordan's classic work *White over Black: American Attitudes Toward the Negro, 1550–1812* (Chapel Hill: University of North Carolina Press, 1967). I was lucky in that Nell Irvin Painter's monumental *The History of White People* (New York: W. W. Norton, 2010), which details the history not only of racism in the Western world but the concept of race itself, appeared while I was in the midst of this project. My discussion in chapter 4 bene-fited greatly from her work. Books that helped me explore how attitudes about interracial sex informed conceptions of the other include Cather-ine Clinton and Michelle Gillespie's collection *The Devil's Lane: Sex and Race in the Early South* (New York: Oxford University Press, 1997) and Martha Hodes, *White Women, Black Men* (New Haven: Yale University Press, 1999).

Scholarship on gender and sexuality has informed this project throughout, especially my analysis of the imagery of the vampire and certain aspects of American folklore and urban legends. Scholars will certainly detect the influence of Judith Butler's paradigm-changing *Gender Trouble* (New York: Routledge, 1999). Her reading, interpretation, and problematizing of the work of Kristeva and Foucault have deeply influ-enced my own understanding of them. Also influential for me has been Anne McClintock's *Imperial Leather: Race, Gender and Sexuality in the Colonial Contest* (New York: Routledge, 1995) and Anne Stoler's *Race and the Education of Desire: Foucault's "History of Sexuality" and the Order of Things* (Durham, N.C.: Duke University Press, 1995). Both works look primarily at structures of power and sexuality in a colonial/postcolonial context. However, their expositions of raced notions of gender and their interpretations of the construction of sexualities within the politics of the body and culture have been very determinative for my own analysis of American society's constructions of deviance and normalcy.

Two works on the relationship between gender and the horror genre are acknowledged throughout the book, but both deserve some mention here: Judith (Jack) Halberstam's *Skin Shows: Gothic Horror and the Tech-nology of Monsters* (Durham, N.C.: Duke University Press, 1995) and Carol J. Clover's *Men, Women and Chainsaws: Gender and the Modern Horror Film* (Princeton: Princeton University Press, 1993). Halberstam's *Skin Shows* illuminates the nature of gender in relation to gothic fictions and includes a compelling reading of both the novel *Frankenstein* and the 1991 film *The Silence of the Lambs*. Her definition of the monster as a meaning machine, productive of a variety of gendered cultural dynamics, can be seen on almost every page of my study. Her more recent work is some of the most articulate and revolutionary expositions of transgender theory, including *In a Queer Time and Place: Transgender Bodies, Subcultural Lives* (New York: New York University Press, 2005).

Clover's *Men, Women and Chainsaws* provided a breakthrough in feminist readings of the horror genre, especially with regard to the gendered politics of the slasher film. Her interpretation of the importance of the final girl is key to my own reading of this genre's significance in late twentieth-century American history. Also worth examining is an excellent essay collection edited by Annette Burfoot and Susan Lord entitled *Killing Women: The Visual Culture of Gender and Violence* (Waterloo, Ontario: Wilfred Laurier University Press, 2006). Especially useful in this collection is the essay by Steven Jay Schneider entitled "The Madwomen in Our Movies: Female Psycho-Killers in American Horror Cinema."

The revised edition contains much-needed material on monsters after 9/11. Readers will note the influence of the collection *Horror After 9/11: World of Fear, Cinema of Terror* (Austin: University of Texas Press, 2012) edited by Aviva Briefal and Sam J. Mille and, most importantly, film scholar Victoria McCollum's *Post 9/11 Heartland Horror: Rural Horror Films in an Era of Urban Terrorism* (New York: Routledge, 2016).

An enormous amount of work has appeared on zombies and vampires even since 2011, and I have become aware of work I simply had been ignorant of when working on the book originally. New insights I tried to include came from excellent books such as Kyle Williams Bishop's *American Zombie Gothic* (Jefferson, N.C.: McFarland, 2010). No one who wants to understand our fascination with vampires should be without M. Jess Peacock's excellent, and at times philosophical, study *Such a Dark Thing: Theology of the Vampire Narrative in Popular Culture* (Eugene, Oreg.: Resource Publications, 2015).

A number of readers, including many classroom teachers, noted that in their use of the book they noted that the American West had simply not received the attention it deserves. I agree, and the revised edition tries to correct this though space prevented me from including the whole horrific story. I made much use of Karl Jacoby's *Shadows at Dawn: An Apache Massacre and the Violence of History* (New York: Penguin, 2009). Dee Brown's *Bury My Heart at Wounded Knee* (New York: Picador, 2007) and Peter Matthiessen's *In the Spirit of Crazy Horse* (New York: Penguin, 1992) talk about the genocide on the plains and, in the latter case, the rise of the American Indian Movement that has had a rebirth in our own times at the Standing Rock Dakota Pipeline and Tar Creek, Oklahoma.

More than in the first edition, I hope readers will note the new emphasis on the idea of American empire and how some of the new primary sources noted, especially in the conclusion, helped me to discuss this idea. I also used Joshua Freeman and Eric Foner's comprehensive *American Empire: The Rise of a Global Power, the Democratic Revolution at Home, 1945–2000* (New York: Penguin, 2013). Another significant work that helped me expand on what I have come to see as a central moment in modern American experience is Nick Turses' *Kill Anything That Moves: The Real American War in Vietnam* (New York: Picador, 2013).

Now and again, I made use of the expanded version of the somewhat controversial *The Untold History of the United States* by Oliver Stone and Peter Kuznick (New York: Gallery Books, 2012). Stone's somewhat unfair reputation as conspiracy theorist and recent controversies concerning his odd interviews with Vladimir Putin should not hide the fact that the highly regarded Cold War historian Peter Kuznick primarily wrote the book as a companion to Stone's film series. In this book, I use only the text (not the documentary films) and sections that Kuznick heavily sources.

The work of scholars of religious studies and especially religion in American history is key to a number of aspects of this book. Douglas E. Cowan's *Sacred Terror: Religion and Horror on the Silver Screen* (Waco, Tex.: Baylor University Press, 2008) provides all of us working in this field with a learned discussion of how cultural fears are represented in our collective dream-life of film and literature. I am a great admirer of George Marsden. His work, especially *Religion and American Culture* (New York: Harcourt, Brace, Jovanovich, 1990) and *Fundamentalism in American Culture: The Shaping of Twentieth Century Evangelicalism, 1870–1925* (Oxford: Oxford University Press, 1980) informed all of my writing about American religious history. Gary Ladderman's studies of the American "way of death" are essential to my interpretation in chapter 2 of the late Victorian period, especially *The Sacred Remains: American Attitudes Toward Death: 1799–1883* (New Haven: Yale University Press, 1999).

Finally, many of my source materials for my discussions of the twentieth century are drawn from my own collection of comics, fan magazines, memorabilia, and films. I hope that it is clear how much I am immersed in the material I write about; all my criticisms of the various tropes and metaphors of pop culture are best seen in this light. *Twilight* may well be the only work discussed that I consider so ideologically and aesthetically repugnant that I see no value in it. If I have a quarrel with *King Kong* or *The Bride of Frankenstein* it is most assuredly a lover's quarrel.

NOTES

Preface to the Original Edition

1 Halberstam writes, "The Monster's body is a machine that, in its Gothic mode, produces meaning and can represent any horrible trait that the reader feeds into the narrative." I am here elaborating on Halberstam's meaning and suggesting that American monsters, in the gothic mode, are productive and representative of meanings granted them by a particular epoch and its historical discourses. I also find useful Halberstam's argument that the meanings of the monster are connected to "a particular history of sexuality" in which the other, the monster, becomes a sexualized foreigner. According to her reading, this begins in nineteenth-century gothic literature and continues through the modern slasher film. See Judith Halberstam, *Skin Shows: Gothic Horror and the Technology of Monsters* (Durham, N.C.: Duke University Press, 1995), 7–9, 21–27.

2 In the discussion that follows, it is important for the reader to remember the distinction between horror narratives and their most common subject, the monster. The monster, while most commonly showing up in the context of a horror aesthetic, is a being that moves in and out of these narratives and can find real-world incarnations. Part of this book's argument is that the monster can become "materialization of ideology" (Slavoj Žižek, "Fantasy as a Political Category: A Lacanian Approach," in *The Žižek Reader*, ed. Elizabeth Wright and Edmond Wright [Oxford: Blackwell, 1999]).

3 Greil Marcus, *The Dustbin of History* (Cambridge, Mass.: Harvard University Press, 1995), 24.

4 See Žižek, "Fantasy as a Political Category," 91.

5 Ironically, Žižek uses the phrase "the truth is out there" to explain Lacan's notion that "the unconscious is outside." This book assumes something similar in its interpretation of cultural images of the monster. They assume a "corporeal form" in the

events of American history and how that history shapes American culture. In this way, their "external materiality renders visible inherent antagonisms." They become for American historical consciousness what Žižek labels "the imp of perversity." See Žižek, "Fantasy as a Political Category," 89.

6 Barbra J. Fields, "Ideology and Race in American History," in *Region, Race, and Reconstruction: Essays in Honor of C. Vann Woodward*, ed. J. Morgan Kousser and James McPherson (New York: Oxford University Press, 1982), 153.

7 Stuart Hall, "Encoding/Decoding," in *Culture, Media, and Language*, ed. Stuart Hall, Andrew Love, and Paul Willie (London: Hutchinson Press, 1980), 170–73.

8 Žižek makes this comment in the introduction to the film *A Pervert's Guide to Ideology*, directed by Sophie Fiennes (Absolut Medien, 2012).

9 The historians among my readers will, I hope, recall the foundational social historian E. P. Thompson's effort to free his subjects from "the enormous condescension of the past." See Thompson, *The Making of the English Working Class* (New York: Vintage Books, 1963), 12. This is the most basic goal of every historian and every work of history.

Introduction

1 Account taken from Dwight Taylor, *Joy Ride* (New York: G. P. Putnam & Sons, 1959), 240–48.

2 Taylor, *Joy Ride*, 240–48.

3 A brief description of the film's reception appears in Melvin E. Matthews Jr., *Fear Itself: Horror on Screen and in Reality During the Depression and World War II* (Jefferson, N.C.: McFarland Press, 2009), 53–58.

4 This argument follows Nancy Bombaci, who suggests that films of this era, especially by Mayer, tried to create the ideal middle-class experience with an emphasis on idealized white female beauty. She notes the irony that the villain/victim in *Freaks* replicates the statuesque blonde heroine of most of Mayer's films. See Nancy Bombaci, *Freaks in Late Modernist American Culture* (New York: Peter Lang, 2006), 81–83, 100–101.

5 A few have come close. Kendall R. Phillips in *Projected Fears: Horror Films and American Culture* (Westport, Conn.: Praeger Publishers, 2005) looks at how the historical context of certain horror films affected and reflected their subject matter. Most of these are, however, post-1960. His excellent analysis does not deal with the larger story of the monster in America. My reading of late twentieth-century horror film is deeply influenced by Linnie Blake's *The Wounds of Nations: Horror Cinema, Historic Trauma and National Identity* (Manchester, UK: Manchester University Press, 2008). It is outside of Blake's purpose to examine the phenomenon of the monster in American history.

6 Jeffrey Jerome Cohen writes that "the monstrous body is pure culture" or, in other words, is born of a very specific cultural moment. He notes, for example, that in the nineteenth century, "Native Americans were presented as unredeemable savages so that the powerful political machine of Manifest Destiny could push westward with disregard." Much of my own view of the monstrous depends on Cohen's "Monster Culture (Seven Theses)" as well as other essays in *Monster Theory: Reading Culture*, ed. Jeffrey Cohen (Minneapolis: University of Minnesota Press, 1993). See esp. Cohen's essay, 3–25.

7   See Richard Kearney, *Strangers, Gods and Monsters* (New York: Routledge, 2003). Kearney argues that monsters are the face of historical and cultural ambiguity, a challenge thrown down in the face of "neat divisions and borders." See esp. 115–21.

8   James Twitchell, *Dreadful Pleasures: An Anatomy of Modern Horror* (New York: Oxford University Press, 1985), 5–7.

9   See Jonathan Kirsch, *God Against the Gods: The History of the War Between Monotheism and Polytheism* (New York: Viking Compass, 2004), 28–32.

10 Timothy Beal, *Religion and Its Monsters* (New York: Routledge, 2001), 30–31.

11 Stephen Asma, *On Monsters* (New York: Oxford University Press, 2009), 64–67; Beal, *Religion and Its Monsters*, 55. Both are drawing on the work of German scholar Rudolph Otto, who, in his 1917 *Idea of the Holy*, described what he called "mysterium tremendum" as the typical human response to true religious experience, the sense of horror that comes with an encounter with the "Wholly Other."

12 Elaine Pagels provides the best guidance through this complex story in *The Origins of Satan* (New York: Vintage Books, 1995). See esp. chaps. 5 and 6.

13 Jeffrey J. Cohen, *Of Giants: Sex, Monsters and the Middle Ages* (Minneapolis: University of Minnesota Press, 1999), 10, 11.

14 Jeffrey Burton Russell, *Lucifer: The Devil in the Middle Ages* (Ithaca: Cornell University Press, 1984), 63, 73–74.

15 Asma, *On Monsters*, 81–82.

16 One of the more interesting discussions of the folklore, and the possible medical roots of the folklore, of the vampire can be found in Paul Barber's *Vampires, Burial and Death: Folklore and Reality* (New Haven: Yale University Press, 1988).

17 Brian P. Levack, *The Witch-Hunt in Early Modern Europe*, 2nd ed. (New York: Longman, 1995).

18 Peter Burke, "Frontiers of the Monstrous: Perceiving National Character in Early Modern Europe," in *Monstrous Bodies/Political Monstrosities in Early Modern Europe*, ed. Laura Lunger Knoppers and Joan B. Landes (Ithaca: Cornell University Press, 2004), 128–29.

19 Behind my interpretation that follows is the awareness that French theorist Michel Foucault's work shows how Enlightenment modernity created a regime of knowledge that defined the human in relation to how discourses of power circulated through the culture of the prison and the asylum, and constructed the deviant and the abnormal. Science is no neutral arbiter or observer that studies the human subject and the physical world. The Enlightenment itself is a construction of a "normal" human ontology that celebrates the "enlightened" subject. See Michel Foucault, *The Origin of Things: An Archaeology of Human Sciences* (New York: Vintage Books, 1994), 328–35; idem, *Discipline and Punish: The Birth of the Prison* (New York: Vintage Books, 1991), 141–49, 195–228.

20 Eric Foner, *Tom Paine and Revolutionary America* (New York: Oxford University Press, 1976), 246–48.

21 Sean Wilentz, *The Rise of American Democracy: Jefferson to Lincoln* (New York: W. W. Norton, 2005), 18–20.

22 A full discussion of Voltaire and the eighteenth-century Enlightenment's view of monstrosity appears in Andrew Curran and Patrick Graille, "The Faces of Eighteenth-Century Monstrosity," *Eighteenth-Century Life* 21, no. 2 (1997): 1–15.

23 Darren Oldridge, *Strange Histories* (London: Routledge, 2007), 9.

24 Julia V. Douthwaite, *The Wild Girl, Natural Man and the Monster: Dangerous Experiments in the Age of Enlightenment* (Chicago: University of Chicago Press, 2002), 12–13, 15–17.

25 Stephen Asma, *Stuffed Animals and Pickled Heads: The Culture and Evolution of the Natural History Museum* (New York: Oxford University Press, 2003), 84.

26 Douthwaite, *Wild Girl*, 12–17.

27 David D. Hall has explored this idea in *Worlds of Wonder, Days of Judgment: Popular Religious Belief in Early New England* (Cambridge, Mass.: Harvard University Press, 1989).

28 Jan Bondeson, *A Cabinet of Medical Curiosities* (New York: W. W. Norton, 1997), 83, 84.

29 Paul Semonin, *American Monster* (New York: New York University Press, 2000), 4, 7–12.

30 Semonin, *American Monster*, 7–12.

31 The work of Robin Wood opened up this scholarly field. His "An Introduction to the American Horror Film" represents a touchstone in cultural studies for reflections on monsters and their meaning. First appearing in 1979, it is reprinted in Barry Keith Grant and Christopher Sharrett's *Planks of Reason: Essays on the Horror Film* (Lanham, Md.: Scarecrow Press, 2004), 107–41.

32 French theorist Pierre Bourdieu, for example, argues, "disgust is the paradoxical experience of enjoyment extorted by violence, an enjoyment which arouses horror." Bourdieu also argues that monstrosity inspires a kind of "value-added disgust" in which those who experience it are often disturbed by their own enjoyment. See Bourdieu, *Distinction: A Social Critique of the Judgment of Taste* (Cambridge, Mass.: Harvard University Press, 1984), 488–89.

33 An excellent exposition of this view appears in Richard Kearny, *Strangers, Gods and Monsters: Interpreting Otherness* (New York: Routledge, 2003). Kearny sees a societal tendency to reject the "experience of strangeness" and to transform the other into the enemy. See 3–8 and 39–41.

34 Sigmund Freud, *The Uncanny* (New York: Penguin Books, 2003), 123–62. For a different reading of the monstrous and castration, see Slavoj Žižek, "Grimaces of the Real, or When the Phallus Appears," *October* 58 (1991): 44–68. Žižek views monsters as screens on which sexualized meanings can be represented. Halberstam contends that Žižek does not leave behind psychoanalysis of the Lacanian variety as his primary analytical tool. See Judith Halberstam, *Skin Shows: Gothic Horror and the Technology of Monsters* (Durham, N.C.: Duke University Press, 1995), 9, 10.

35 Freud, *Uncanny*, 132.

36 See Sue Short's discussion of this idea in *Misfit Sisters: Screen Horror as Female Rites of Initiation* (New York: Palgrave Macmillan, 2006), 10–21.

37 Julia Kristeva, *Powers of Horror: An Essay in Abjection* (New York: Columbia University Press, 1983), 1.

38 Judith Halberstam shows that sexuality, emerging in the nineteenth century as a cultural identity, proved crucial to the creation of the monster. The contemporary monster, she writes, represents "an amalgam of sex and gender." See *Skin Shows*, 6.

39 Kristeva, *Powers of Horror*, 1.

40 On Ramirez, see William Hart, *Evil: A Primer* (New York: St. Martin's, 2004), 76.

41 Jeffrey Cohen sees the monster as embodying both "repulsion and attraction," though not necessarily an erotic attraction. Working off Kristeva, Cohen argues, "the monster is the abjected fragment that enables the formation of all kinds of identities,"

a desire "always at the verge of eruption." See Cohen, "Monster Culture," 19–20. I would argue that the erotic is present in all sorts of attractions to the monster, a desire inspired by the simultaneous experience of wonder and discussion, the thrill of the different and the strange.

42 Dolf Zillman and James B. Weaver III, "Gender Socialization Theory of Reactions to Horror," in *Horror Films: Current Research on Audience Preferences and Reactions*, ed. James B. Weaver III and Ron Tamborini (Mahwah, N.J.: Lawrence Erlbaum, 1996), 81–102.

43 Twitchell, *Dreadful Pleasures*, 127–31.

44 Twitchell's arguments regarding monster tales and their warnings about human sexuality cannot, however, be entirely dismissed. Tales of monsters cannot be divorced from family dynamics, cultural conversations about gender, domestic life, and the politics of reproduction and sexuality. But even these topics, often evoked and addressed by our fascination with the world of the monster, have a clear political dimension and are more than simply the unraveling and rebuilding of the adolescent psyche. The politics of the family and of sexuality are not outworkings of the inward psyche. In the United States, and in human societies more generally, family and sexuality are highly politicized with public meaning that goes far beyond psychological dynamics.

45 Douglas E. Cowan, *Sacred Terror: Religion and Horror on the Silver Screen* (Waco, Tex.: Baylor University Press, 2008), 263.

46 Jonathan Lake Crane, *Terror and Everyday Life: Singular Moments in the History of the Horror Film* (Thousand Oaks, Calif.: Sage, 1994).

47 Slavoj Žižek shows the role played by fantasy in the structuring of ritual acts and ideological systems in "Fantasy as a Political Category: A Lacanian Approach," in *The Žižek Reader*, ed. Elizabeth Wright and Edmond Wright (Oxford: Blackwell, 1999), 86–101. This essay informs my own understanding of how monsters are historicized and how history becomes monstrous.

48 "A Monstrous Sea Serpent, Boston" (printed and sold by Henry Bowen, Devonshire Street, 1817).

49 Neptune, "The Great Sea Serpent, upon the Coast of New England," *Early American Imprints*, Series II, no. 43432, 15–16.

50 Neptune, "Great Sea Serpent," 16, 18

51 Neptune, "Great Sea Serpent," 16, 18.

52 Richard Slotkin, *Gunfighter Nation: The Myth of the Frontier in Twentieth-Century America* (Norman: University of Oklahoma Press, 1998), 13, 14.

53 Cohen has also described the monster as "the harbinger of category crisis." He notes that monsters are always "disturbing hybrids" and thus threaten to "smash distinctions." See Cohen, "Monster Culture," 6.

54 Michael Bimbaum, "Historians Speak Out Against Proposed Texas Textbook Changes," *Washington Post*, March 18, 2010.

55 Lauri Lebo, "Don McLeroy's Texas Textbooks Would Replace Historical Characters with Fictional Ones," *Religion Dispatches*, May 26, 2010 (http://www.religion dispatches.org/dispatches/laurilebo/2687/don_mcleroy's_texas_textbooks_would _replace_historical_characters_with_fictional_ones), and "Conservatives Put Stamp on Texas Textbooks," (http://www.msnbc.msn.com/id/35839979/).

56 A good discussion of the problem of American exceptionalism appears in Robert Jewett and John Shelton Lawrence, *Captain America and the Crusade Against Evil: The Dilemma of Zealous Nationalism* (Grand Rapids: Eerdmans, 2003).

57 Quote from Mary Shelley's *Frankenstein* (New York: Penguin Books, 1963), 52. Perhaps the best discussion of American exceptionalism can be found in Andrew Bacevich, *American Empire: The Reality and Consequences of American Diplomacy* (Cambridge, Mass.: Harvard University Press, 2002). I explore the relationship between American religion, folklore, pop culture, and the notion of exceptionalism in *Satan in America: The Devil We Know* (Lanham, Md.: Rowman & Littlefield, 2009). See esp. xviii–xxiii, 120–21. Paul Starobin calls exceptionalism America's "presiding myth" in *After America: Narratives for the Next Global Age* (New York: Viking, 2009), 35.

58 The term "torture porn" first appeared in David Edelstein, "Now Playing at Your Local Multi-Plex: Torture Porn," *New York Magazine*, February 6, 2006. The term is primarily used by critics of the genre.

59 Alice Walker, *Her Blue Body Everything We Know, 1965–1990* (New York: Houghton Mifflin Harcourt, 2004), 374.

60 Quoted in Howard Zinn, *A People's History of the United States* (New York: Harper Perennial, 2003), 15.

61 Increase Mather, "A Brief History of the War with the Indians of New England," Early American Imprints, Series I, no. 220, 45–46.

Chapter 1

1 In a peculiar way, the uprising of Fool, "the people under the stairs," and the people of the neighborhood replicates the story of the 1676 Bacon's Rebellion in Virginia, a class-based uprising that included a few Native Americans and slaves as well as landless whites.

2 Annalee Newitz, *Pretend We're Dead: Capitalist Monsters in American Pop Culture* (Durham, N.C.: Duke University Press, 2006), 114–15.

3 Michael Palencia-Roth, "Enemies of God: Monsters and the Theology of Conquest," in *Monsters, Tricksters and Sacred Cows: Animal Tales and American Identity*, ed. A. James Arnold (Charlottesville: University of Virginia Press, 1996), 23.

4 See Fernando Cervantes, *The Devil in the New World: The Impact of Diabolism in New Spain* (New Haven: Yale University Press, 1994), 13–15.

5 Peter Burke, "Frontiers of the Monstrous: Perceiving National Character in Early Modern Europe," in *Monstrous Bodies/Political Monstrosities in Early Modern Europe*, ed. Laura Lunger Knoppers and Joan B. Landes (Ithaca: Cornell University Press, 2004), 28–29.

6 Burke, "Frontiers of the Monstrous," 239.

7 Laura Lunger Knoppers and Joan B. Landes, "Introduction," in *Monstrous Bodies/ Political Monstrosities*, 1–3.

8 See David Armitage, "Monstrosity and Myth in Mary Shelley's *Frankenstein*," and Andrew Curran, "Afterword: Anatomical Readings in the Early Modern Era," in Knoppers and Landes, *Monstrous Bodies/Political Monstrosities*, 200, 228–29.

9 Winthrop Jordan, *White over Black: American Attitudes Toward the Negro, 1550–1812* (Chapel Hill: University of North Carolina Press, 1968), 29.

10 Jordan, *White over Black*, 30.

11 Robert Weir, *Colonial South Carolina: A History* (Columbia: University of South Carolina Press, 1997), 8.

12 Fernando Cervantes provides a full discussion of this material in *Devil in the New World*, 13–15, 35.

13 Quoted in Palencia-Roth, "Enemies of God," 38–39.

14 Palencia-Roth, "Enemies of God," 40, 43.
15 See Raymond DeMallie and Elian Jahner, *Lakota Belief and Ritual* (Lincoln: University of Nebraska Press, 1991), 166–70. Many thanks to Professor Lee Irwin, Religious Studies at the College of Charleston, for pointing me to this source. A variant of this folktale is the "Mysterious Deer." This tale, common in the Appalachians, uses the white doe as a symbol of the vengeance of nature in which hunters shoot a mysterious white deer and wound only themselves. See "The Mysterious Deer," in *The Greenwood Library of American Folktales*, ed. Thomas A. Green (Westport, Conn.: Greenwood Press, 2006), 2:197–98.
16 Full descriptions of the earliest colonization efforts by Europeans appear in works such as James Axtell's *Beyond 1492: Encounters in Colonial North America* (New York: Oxford University Press, 1992); and Karen O. Kupperman's *Settling with Indians: The Meeting of English and Indian Cultures in America, 1580–1640* (Ithaca: Cornell University Press, 2000).
17 Michael Leroy Oberg offers the best discussion of Roanoke in *The Head in Edward Nugent's Hand: Roanoke's Forgotten Indians* (Philadelphia: University of Pennsylvania Press, 2008). On the failed French settlement see Walter Edgar, *South Carolina: A History* (Columbia: University of South Carolina Press, 1998), 27.
18 In 1965 Virginia Dare became the lead character in Phillip Jose Farmer's tale of the lost colonists being abducted by aliens. See *Dare* (New York: Ballentine Books, 1965). Author Neil Gaiman also used the character in his Marvel comics series entitled *1602* and borrowed the mythology of Dare as shapeshifter.
19 Roger Manley, *Weird Carolinas* (New York: Sterling Publishing, 2007), 18–19.
20 Sallie Southall Cotten, *The White Doe: The Fate of Virginia Dare* (Philadelphia: J. B. Lippincott, 1902), 12.
21 O. R. Mangum, "The Lost Colony Found," *Wake Forest Student* 25 (1906); A. Denison Heart, "Raleigh's Lost Colony," *Southern Workman*, 1913.
22 James W. Baker, *Thanksgiving: The Biography of an American Holiday* (Lebanon: University of New Hampshire Press, 2009); and Robert S. Tilton, *Pocahontas: The Evolution of an American Narrative* (New York: Cambridge University Press, 1994).
23 Marjorie Hudson, *Searching for Virginia Dare* (Wilmington, N.C.: Coastal Carolina Press, 2003), 87–88.
24 A good introduction to this genre, complete with some examples of these narratives, can be found in Alden T. Vaughan and Edward W. Clark, eds., *Puritans Among the Indians: Accounts of Captivity and Redemption, 1676–1724* (Cambridge, Mass.: Belknap Press), 1981.
25 Edward Ingebretsen, *Maps of Heaven, Maps of Hell: Religious Terror as Memory from the Puritans to Stephen King* (Armonk, N.Y.: M. E. Sharpe, 1996), 39.
26 See Henry Nash Smith's classic discussion of the Western folk hero and his relationship to nature in Smith's *Virgin Land: The American West as Symbol and Myth* (Cambridge, Mass.: Harvard University Press, 1978).
27 The anti-immigrant hate site http://www.VDARE.com provides one example in which Virginia Dare serves as a symbol.
28 The classic argument for the significance of the Puritans for American culture can be found in Sacvan Bercovitch's *Puritanism and the Origins of the American Self* (New Haven: Yale University Press, 1975). A newer emphasis on regionalism and race in the development of American identity has complicated Bercovitch's claims.
29 Owen Davies and Jonathan Barry, "Introduction," in *Witchcraft Historiography*, ed. Owen Davies and Jonathan Barry (New York: Palgrave Macmillan, 2007), 4.

30 David D. Hall, *Witch-Hunting in Seventeenth-Century New England: A Documentary History, 1638–1693* (Boston: Northeastern University Press, 1999), 22.

31 Richard Godbeer, *The Devil's Dominion: Magic and Religion in Early New England* (Cambridge: Cambridge University Press, 1992), 192.

32 Ingebretsen, *Maps of Heaven*, 47.

33 Marion L. Starkey, *The Devil in Massachusetts* (New York: Doubleday/Anchor Books, 1949), 239.

34 An examination of these misogynistic beliefs from a psychological and cultural perspective can be found in Lyndal Roper, *Oedipus and the Devil: Witchcraft, Religion and Sexuality in Early Modern Europe* (New York: Routledge, 1994).

35 Bryan F. Le Beau, *The Story of the Salem Witchcraft Trials*, 2nd ed. (Upper Saddle River, N.J.: Prentice Hall, 2010), 31.

36 Charles Upham, *Salem Witchcraft* (Boston: Wiggin & Lunt, 1867), 451–52.

37 Herbert Leventhal, *In the Shadow of the Enlightenment: Occultism and Renaissance Science in Eighteenth-Century America* (New York: New York University Press, 1976), 77.

38 Yvonne P. Chirau, *Black Magic: Religion and the African American Conjuring Tradition* (Berkeley: University of California Press, 2003), 67, 70–71.

39 Frank J. Klingberg, ed., *The Carolina Chronicle of Dr. Francis Le Jau, 1706–1717* (Berkeley: University of California Press, 1956), 25, 30.

40 Richard Godbeer, *The Devil's Dominion*, and David D. Hall's *Worlds of Wonder, Days of Judgment: Popular Religious Beliefs in Early New England* (Cambridge, Mass.: Harvard University Press, 1989).

41 Cotton Mather quoted in James A. Morone, *Hellfire Nation: The Politics of Sin in American History* (New Haven: Yale University Press, 2004), 86.

42 Richard M. Dorson, *Man and Beast in American Comic Legend* (Bloomington: Indiana University Press, 1983), 64.

43 The best description of this pastime appears in Burkhard Bilger, *Noodling for Flatheads: Moonshine, Monster Catfish and Other Southern Comforts* (New York: Scribner, 2002).

44 Jan Harold Brunvand, *American Folklore: An Encyclopedia* (New York: Routledge, 1998), 270–72.

45 Thomas Jefferson, *Notes on the State of Virginia* (New York: Harper & Row, 1964), 37–57.

46 Paul Semonin, *American Monster* (New York: New York University Press, 2000), 6, 176.

47 See Robert Annan, "Account of a Skeleton of a Large Animal, Found Near Hudson's River," in *Memoirs of the Academy of Arts and Sciences* (Boston: Isaiah Thomas, 1793), 160–68.

48 Jefferson, *Notes on the State of Virginia*, 37–43.

49 Quoted in Semonin, *American Monster*, 178.

50 John Filson, *The Discovery, Settlement, and Present State of Kentucky* (New York: printed and sold by Samuel Campbell, no. 37, 1793), Early American Imprints. Series I, no. 25648, 32.

51 Filson, *Discovery*, 36.

52 Richard Slotkin, *Regeneration through Violence: The Mythology of the American Frontier, 1600–1860* (Middletown, Conn.: Wesleyan University Press, 1973), 278–312.

53 Jefferson, *Notes on the State of Virginia*, 133.

54 Semonin, *American Monster*, 219–20.

55 David Brion Davis, *Inhuman Bondage: The Rise and Fall of Slavery in the New World* (New York: Oxford University Press, 2008), 84–102, 124–40.

56 A layperson's history of the trade can be found in Hugh Thomas, *The Slave Trade: The Story of the Atlantic Slave Trade: 1440–1870* (New York: Simon & Schuster, 1999).

57 Marcus Rediker, *The Slave Ship: A Human History* (New York: Viking, 2007), 299.

58 Paul Edwards, ed., *Equiano's Travels: His Autobiography*, abridged ed. (London: Heineman Press, 1967), 25–26.

59 A full account of these beliefs and a sampling of the mountain of evidence for them appears in William D. Pierson, "White Cannibals, Black Martyrs," *The Journal of Negro History* 62, no. 2 (1977): 147–49.

60 John Thornton, "Cannibals, Witches and Slave Traders in the Atlantic World," *The William and Mary Quarterly*, 3rd ser., 60, no. 2 (2003): 273–94.

61 Josiah C. Nott, "Two Lectures on the Natural History of the Caucasian and Negro Race," in *The Ideology of Slavery: Proslavery Thought in the Antebellum South, 1830–1860*, ed. Drew G. Faust (Baton Rouge: Louisiana State University Press, 1981), 206–38.

62 For a discussion of Hammond and of paternalism more generally, see Drew Gilpin Faust, *James Henry Hammond and the Old South: A Design for Mastery* (Baton Rouge: Louisiana State University Press, 1982), esp. 72–73.

63 "Charlestown," *South Carolina Gazette*, February 25, 1737, special collections, Charleston County Library.

64 A number of scholars have discussed the paradox of the slave as monster and faithful servant. On the varieties of slave resistance, see Peter Kolchin, *American Slavery: 1619–1877* (New York: Hill & Wang, 1993), 155–68. On paternalism and its contradictions, see Eugene Genovese, *Roll Jordan Roll: The World the Slaves Made* (New York: Vintage Books, 1996), esp. 89–93.

65 Elizabeth Young, *Black Frankenstein: The Making of an American Metaphor* (New York: New York University Press, 2008), 19–20.

66 William T. Cox, *Fearsome Creatures of the Lumberwoods* (Whitefish, Mont.: Kessinger Publishing, 2007), 15.

67 The story about a South Carolina planter who disguised himself in a devil costume is described in a religious tract from the early nineteenth century entitled "The Devil Let Loose" (author unknown) (New York: n.p., 1805).

68 See Charles Sellers, *The Market Revolution* (New York: Oxford University Press, 1991), 5–10. For a different view of the same process, see Gordon S. Wood, *The Radicalism of the American Revolution* (New York: Vintage Books, 1993) 254–55, 365–69.

69 A discussion of Douglass' 1860 speech appears in Young, *Black Frankenstein*, 45–46.

Chapter 2

1 A good overview of *Candyman* and its relation to notions of place and space can be found in Avivia Breifel and Sianna Naigal, "How much did you pay for this place? Fear, Entitlement and Urban Space in Bernard Roses' *Candyman*," *Camera Obscura* 37 (1997): 70–91.

2 One of the best studies of the antebellum era, and one that emphasizes the unbelievable tensions in American society, is William H. Freehling's *The Road to Disunion: Secessionists at Bay, 1776–1854* (New York: Oxford University Press, 1990).

3 On the end of Reconstruction and its effects, see some examples in Joel Williamson, *After Slavery* (Hanover, N.H.: University Press of New England, 1990).

4 See Paul Hodkinson, *Goth: Identity, Style and Sub-culture* (Oxford: Berg Publishers, 2002); and Gavin Baddely, *Goth Chic: A Connoisseur's Guide* (Medford, N.J.: Plexus Publishing, 2002).

5 Anne Williams has argued that mythoi of gothic, their basic structure despite differing motifs, all relate in one way or another to the "terrors" of the patriarchal family. See her *Art of Darkness: A Poetics of Gothic* (Chicago: University of Chicago Press, 1995).

6 A voluminous literary scholarship exists on the nature and definition of the gothic, and it is beyond my purpose to explore that scholarship here. I find especially useful Mark Edmundson's formulation in his brilliant meditation *Nightmare on Main Street: Angels, Sadomasochism and the Culture of the Gothic* (Cambridge, Mass.: Harvard University Press, 1997). Edmundson writes that "Gothic is the art of haunting, the art of possession." He argues that, in contemporary America, "not all our gothic modes are fictive" and that the art of haunting has found its way into the very real occurrences of cultural, social, and political history. See pp. xi–xviii.

7 Valdine Clemens, *Return of the Repressed* (Albany: State University of New York Press, 1999), 15–16. See also Clive Bloom's *Gothic Histories: The Taste for Terror, 1764 to the Present* (London: Continuum, 2010), esp. 4, 5.

8 Washington Irving, *The Legend of Sleepy Hollow and Rip Van Winkle* (Mahwah, N.J.: Watermill Press, 1980), 3.

9 Irving, *Legend*, 5.

10 A good discussion of the 1819 Panic and its causes and effects appears in Sean Wilentz, *The Rise of American Democracy: Jefferson to Lincoln* (New York: W. W. Norton, 2005), 206–17.

11 Wilentz, *Rise of American Democracy*, 207–8.

12 Irving, *Legend*, 12–13.

13 See Kent L. Steckmesser, "The Frontier Hero in History and Legend," *The Wisconsin Magazine of History* 46, no. 3 (1963): 168–79. Steckmesser gives numerous examples from the nineteenth-century accounts of the exploits of Daniel Boone, Kit Carson, Davy Crockett, and less well-known figures.

14 Irving, *Legend*, 36.

15 On the origins of vampire folklore, see Paul Barber, *Vampires, Burial, and Death: Folklore and Reality* (New Haven: Yale University Press, 1988).

16 James Twitchell, *Dreadful Pleasures: An Anatomy of Modern Horror* (New York: Oxford University Press, 1985), 112.

17 David J. Skal, *The Monster Show: A Cultural History of Horror* (New York: Farrar, Strauss & Giroux, 1992), 82.

18 Skal, *Monster Show*, 82.

19 Susan Tyler Hitchcock, *Frankenstein: A Cultural History* (New York: W. W. Norton, 2007), 93; Mary Shelley, *Frankenstein* (New York: New American Library, 1978), x–xi.

20 See Michael Sappol, *A Traffic of Dead Bodies: Anatomy and Embodied Social Identity in Nineteenth-Century America* (Princeton: Princeton University Press, 2002), 213–17.

21 On how quickly the creature in Shelley's work became associated with industrial change and mechanical processes, see Hitchcock, *Frankenstein*, 101–6. See also Laurence A. Rickels' discussion of Frankenstein and the birth of the "dark twins" in *The Vampire Lectures* (Minneapolis: University of Minnesota Press, 1999), 277–86.

22 Elizabeth Young, *Black Frankenstein: The Making of an American Metaphor* (New York: New York University Press, 2008), 5.

23 On Poe's vampires, see Twitchell, *Dreadful Pleasures*, 121. The unpublished novel is entitled "The Last of the Vampires: A Tale of Baltimore City," John Hill Hewitt Papers, box 5, Emory University Special Collections.

24 H. P. Lovecraft, *Dagon and Other Macabre Tales* (Sauk City, Wisc.: Arkham House Publishers, 1965), 14–19.

25 Sherrie Lynne Lyons, *Species, Serpents, Spirits and Skulls* (Albany: State University of New York Press, 2009), 34.

26 Lyons, *Species*, 30.

27 Lyons, *Species*, 40.

28 "The Sea Serpent Caught at Last!" *New York Tribune*, February 1852; reprinting of Captain Seabury's account in Antoon Cornelis Oudemans and Loren Coleman, *The Great Sea Serpent* (New York: Cosimo Classics, 2008), 45–51.

29 Lyons, *Species*, 47.

30 Herman Melville, *Moby-Dick or, The Whale* (New York: Penguin Classics, 1992), 498.

31 "Hydrarchos or Great Sea Serpent," September 19, 1845; American Memory Project, Library of Congress.

32 M. Strakosch, "Sea Serpent Polka" (Boston: G. P. Reed), Rare Book, Manuscripts and Special Collections Library, Duke University.

33 Robert H. Brisendine Papers, box 11, file folder 22, Emory University Special Collections.

34 Brisendine Papers, box 24, file folder 82.

35 For an introduction to this vast critical commentary, see *Herman Melville's Moby-Dick*, intro. and ed. Harold Bloom (New York: Chelsea House, 2007). Melville quote taken from *Moby-Dick* (New York: Penguin Classics, 2003), 498.

36 Andrew Delbanco, "Introduction," in *Moby-Dick*, xiii.

37 Melville, *Moby-Dick*, 13, 14.

38 Melville, *Moby-Dick*, 13–15.

39 Melville, *Moby-Dick*, 624.

40 Melville, *Moby-Dick*, 259.

41 See Bruce Levine, *Half-Slave and Half-Free: Roots of the Civil War* (New York: Hill & Wang, 1992). Sean Wilentz describes the context of Moby-Dick, which he sees as a "prophecy of America's destruction," in *Rise of American Democracy*, 653–55.

42 Gross quoted in Teresa A. Goddu, *Gothic America* (New York: Columbia University Press, 1997), 133; Morrison quoted in Bettye J. Parker, "Complexity: Toni Morrison's Women—An Interview Essay," in *Sturdy Black Bridges: Visions of Black Women in Literature* (New York: Anchor Books, 1979).

43 Goddu, *Gothic America*, 133ff.

44 See Eric Foner, *Free Soil, Free Labor, Free Men* (New York: Oxford University Press, 1995), 97–102, 119–20.

45 Quoted in Young, *Black Frankenstein*, 49–50.

46 Goddu, *Gothic America*, 133.

47 Goddu, *Gothic America*, 133–36.

48 W. Scott Poole, *South Carolina's Civil War* (Macon, Ga.: Mercer University Press, 2005), 23.

49 See Annalee Newitz's brilliant examination of Crane in *Pretend We're Dead: Capitalist Monsters in American Pop Culture* (Durham, N.C.: Duke University Press, 2006), 16–19.

50 R. B. Rosenburg, *Living Monuments: Confederate Soldiers' Homes in the New South* (Chapel Hill: University of North Carolina Press, 1993), 14.

51 Anthony Lee and Elizabeth Young, *On Alexander Gardner's Photographic Sketchbook of the Civil War* (Berkeley: University of California Press, 2007).

52 Gary Laderman, *The Sacred Remains: American Attitudes Toward Death, 1799–1883* (New Haven: Yale University Press, 1999), 78.

53 See Michael Griffin, "The Great War Photographs: Constructing Myths of History and Photojournalism," in *Picturing the Past: Media, History and Photography*, ed. Bonnie Brennen and Hanno Hardt (Urbana: University of Illinois Press, 1999), 135–39. See also an excellent survey of the Brady photographs in Jarret Ruminski, "A Terrible Fascination: Civil War Photography and the Advent of Photographic Realism" (M.A. thesis, Youngstown State University, 2007), esp. 4, 6, 63–80.

54 Newitz, *Pretend We're Dead*, 19–20.

55 Described in Laderman, *Sacred Remains*, 100.

56 Laderman, *Sacred Remains*, 168–69.

57 This turn in theology is explored fully in Drew Gilpin Faust's *This Republic of Suffering* (New York: Alfred A. Knopf, 2008), 177–89.

58 Ambrose Bierce, *Ghost and Horror Stories of Ambrose Bierce* (Toronto: Dover Publications, 1964).

59 Quoted in David Schmid, *Natural Born Celebrities: Serial Killers in American Culture* (Chicago: University of Chicago Press, 2006), 44.

60 Schmid, *Natural Born Celebrities*, 46.

61 The best-known account of Holmes is Eric Larson's *The Devil in the White City: Murder, Magic and Madness at the Fair That Changed America* (New York: Vintage Books, 2004). See also Schmid, *Natural Born Celebrities*, 49–65.

62 Mary P. Ryan examines the social and economic origins of "the cult of true womanhood" ideology in *Cradle of the Middle Class* (Cambridge: Cambridge University Press, 1981), 191–229. See also Nancy F. Cott, *The Bonds of Womanhood: "Women's Sphere" in New England, 1780–1835* (New Haven: Yale University Press, 1997), esp. 197–206.

63 Literary criticism of Nathaniel Hawthorne's work in relation to the gothic is truly voluminous. One good place to begin is an excellent essay by Robert K. Martin entitled "Haunted by Jim Crow: Gothic Fictions by Hawthorne and Faulkner," in *American Gothic: New Interventions in the National Narrative*, ed. Robert K. Martin and Eric Savoy (Iowa City: University of Iowa Press, 1998), 129–42. Martin sees in Hawthorne a return of the "national repressed."

64 This reading of "Young Goodman Brown" draws on the work of James C. Keil, "Hawthorne's Young Goodman Brown: Early Nineteenth-Century and Puritan Constructions of Gender," *New England Quarterly* 69, no. 1 (1996): 33–55.

65 See Scott Peeples, *The After-Life of Edgar Allan Poe* (Rochester, N.Y.: Camden House, 2004), 108–15. Peeples argues, "addressing gender in Poe involves acknowledging his benighted thinking on the subject while also recognizing the ways he exposes the dangers of the dominant (sexist) ideology in his work."

66 Goddu, *Gothic America*, 78.

67 In *Hearths of Darkness: The Family in the American Horror Film* (Cranbury, N.J.: Associated University Presses, 1996), Tony Williams makes the argument that what he calls "family horror" has been central to both gothic literature and later film conventions in America. See esp. 26–30.

68 Edgar Allan Poe, "The Fall of the House of Usher," in *Complete Stories and Poems of Edgar Allan Poe* (New York: Doubleday, 1966), 181–82.

69 Poe, "Fall of the House of Usher," 190–91.

70 Sandra M. Gilbert and Susan Gubar in *The Madwoman in the Attic: The Woman Writer and the Nineteenth-Century Literary Imagination* (New Haven: Yale University Press, 1984) describe the common nineteenth-century trope of "the monster-woman threatening to replace her angelic sister [who] embodies intransigent female autonomy and thus represents both the author's ability to allay his anxieties by calling their source bad names (witch, bitch, fiend, monster) and, simultaneously, the mysterious power of the character who refuses to stay in her textually ordained 'place'" (28). This describes most of Poe's female characters and their narratives.

71 The most detailed study of Woodhull's construction in the press is Amanda Frisken's *Victoria Woodhull's Sexual Revolution: Political Theater and the Popular Press in Nineteenth-Century America* (Philadelphia: University of Pennsylvania Press, 2004). Frisken looks into how men's "sporting papers" often feature attacks and cartoons on Woodhull. See esp. 16, 17, 140–45.

72 Anthony Comstock, "Vampire Literature," *North American Review* 417 (1891): 161–62; and Gabriel, *Notorious Victoria: The Life of Victoria Woodhull, Uncensored* (Chapel Hill, N.C.: Algonquin Books, 1998), 185.

73 Frisken, *Victoria's Woodhull's Sexual Revolution*, 46–47.

74 Andrea Tone, *Devices and Desires: A History of Contraceptives in America* (New York: Hill & Wang, 2001), 14, 15.

75 Carole Smith-Rosenberg, *Disorderly Conduct: Visions of Gender in Victorian America* (New York: Alfred A. Knopf, 1985), 226–28.

76 The events surrounding the Sand Creek massacre are well documented as the participants saw little reason to hide their actions. I follow Dee Brown's classic account in *Bury My Heart at Wounded Knee: An Indian History of the American West* (New York: Picador, 2000), 86–92.

77 Brown, *Bury My Heart at Wounded Knee*, 86, 90.

78 Richard Slotkin has detailed the conflation of the frontier and the savage in portrayals of native peoples in *Regeneration Through Violence: The Mythology of the American Frontier, 1600–1860* (Norman: University of Oklahoma Press, 1973).

79 Karl Jacoby, *Shadows at Dawn: An Apache Massacre and the Violence of History* (New York: Penguin Books, 2008), 229–42.

80 See Colin Dickey, "The Suburban Horror of the Indian Burial Ground," *New Republic*, October 19, 2016.

81 The most detailed history of interracial sex, combined with the racial anxieties and obsessions that went with it, can be found in Martha Hodes, *White Women, Black Men: Illicit Sex in the Nineteenth-Century South* (New Haven: Yale University Press, 1999).

Chapter 3

1 A full exploration of Frankenstein as a cultural symbol appears in Susan Tyler Hitchcock, *Frankenstein: A Cultural History* (New York: W. W. Norton, 2007).

2 Christa Knellwolf and Jane Goodall, "Introduction," in *Frankenstein's Science: Experimentation and Discovery in Romantic Culture, 1780–1830* (Burlington, Vt.: Ashgate Publishing, 2008), 2.

3 Melinda Cooper, "Monstrous Progeny: The Teratological Tradition in Science and Literature," in Knellwolf and Goddall, *Frankenstein's Science*, 87–89. Michael J. Hyde in *Perfection: Coming to Terms with Being Human* (Waco, Tex.: Baylor University Press, 2010) shows that Shelley also revolted against her father's fascination with

famed chemist Humphry Davy, who regarded nature as a "she" whose mysteries had to be uncovered. See 98–104.

4   Julia V. Douthwaite, *The Wild Girl, Natural Man and the Monster: Dangerous Experiments in the Age of Enlightenment* (Chicago: University of Chicago Press, 2002), 216.

5   Scott L. Malcomson, *One Drop of Blood: The American Misadventure of Race* (New York: Farrar, Straus & Giroux, 2000), 352–54. Malcomson suggests that emancipation terrified whites, by calling the meaning of whiteness into question. Only in this way can we make sense of the "pathological" fears that created the horrifying spectacles of lynching.

6   Gregory quoted in Elizabeth Young, *Black Frankenstein: The Making of an American Metaphor* (New York: New York University Press, 2008), 212.

7   Clive Bloom, *Gothic Histories: The Taste for Terror, 1764 to the Present* (London: Continuum, 2010), 171.

8   David Robinson, *From Peep Show to Palace: The Birth of American Film* (New York: Columbia University Press, 1996). On the "purpose-built cinema," see 89–98.

9   Amy Louise Wood, *Lynching and Spectacle: Witnessing Racial Violence in America* (Chapel Hill: University of North Carolina Press, 2009), 119, 137.

10   Wood, *Lynching and Spectacle*, 121–22.

11   George M. Fredrickson, *The Black Image in the White Mind: The Debate on AfroAmerican Character and Destiny, 1817–1914* (Middletown, Conn.: Wesleyan University Press, 1971), 278.

12   Quoted in Fredrickson, *Black Image in the White Mind*, 277.

13   Fredrickson, *Black Image in the White Mind*, 279.

14   A general description of post–Civil War violence against African Americans appears in Leon F. Litwack, *Been in the Storm So Long: The Aftermath of Slavery* (New York: Vintage Books, 1980), 276–80. See also Steven Hahn, *A Nation Under Our Feet: Black Political Struggles in the Rural South from Slavery to the Great Migration* (Cambridge, Mass.: Belknap Press, 2003), 426–27.

15   Quoted in Orlando Patterson, "Feast of Blood," in *Rituals of Blood: Consequences of Slavery in Two American Centuries* (New York: Basic Civitas Books, 1998), 194, 195.

16   Patterson, "Feast of Blood," 198.

17   Quoted in Melvin E. Matthews Jr., *Fear Itself: Horror on Screen and in Reality During the Great Depression and World War II* (Jefferson, N.C.: McFarland Press, 2009), 254.

18   A complete discussion of *Birth of a Nation* appears in John Hope Franklin, "Birth of a Nation—Propaganda as History," in *Hollywood's America: United States History through Its Films*, ed. Steven Mintz and Randy Roberts (St. James, N.Y.: Brandywine Press, 2001), 42–52.

19   Jonathan Lake Crane, *Terror and Everyday Life: Singular Moments in the History of the Horror Film* (Thousand Oaks, Calif.: Sage Publications, 1994), 26.

20   Readers should be aware that while the term "freak" carries derogatory connotations, it is the preferred term for both disabled people who work in sideshows and those who theatrically create abnormal differences in themselves for display and profit. See Robert Bogdan, *Freak Show* (Chicago: University of Chicago Press, 1988), xi. I discovered in my research that entering the term "freak" into search engines and library catalogs results in the message that "this library does not use the term 'freak.' Search under monster." (!)

21   See P. T. Barnum, *The Life of P. T. Barnum Written by Himself* (Urbana: University of Illinois Press, 2000), 225. An excellent examination of Barnum and his world can

be found in James W. Cook, *The Arts of Deception: Playing with Fraud in the Age of Barnum* (Cambridge, Mass.: Harvard University Press, 2001). See esp. 1–6 on his career and 80–118 on the Feejee Mermaid.

22 Barnum, *Life of P. T. Barnum*, 234–45. See also Joe Nickell, *Secrets of the Sideshow* (Lexington: University Press of Kentucky, 2000), 10–15; and Stephen Asma, *On Monsters* (New York: Oxford University Press, 2009), 136.

23 Robert H. Brisendine Papers, box 9, file folder 28, Emory University Special Collections.

24 Brisendine Papers, box 9, file folder 28.

25 Brisendine Papers, box 10, file folder 16 and box 11, file folder 22. For ethnographic shows more generally, see Joy S. Kasson, *Buffalo Bill's Wild West* (New York: Hill & Wang, 2000), 212–19.

26 Rachel Adams, *Sideshow U.S.A.: Freaks and the American Cultural Imagination* (Chicago: University of Chicago Press, 2001), 29–31.

27 See Dean Jensen's *The Lives and Loves of Daisy and Violet Hilton* (Berkeley, Calif.: Ten Speed Press, 2006), 151–54, 193, 312–14; Adams, *Sideshow U.S.A.*, 73–74; Nickells, *Secrets of the Sideshow*, 125–26; and Bogdan, *Freak Show*, 166–73.

28 Daniel P. Mannix, *Freaks: We Who Are Not as Others* (New York: Powerhouse Books, 2000), 70–71.

29 Thomas G. Dyer, *Theodore Roosevelt and the Idea of Race* (Baton Rouge: Louisiana University Press, 1980), 141–45. See also Lynn Dumenil, *Modern Temper: American Culture and Society in the 1920s* (New York: Hill & Wang, 1995), 35–45.

30 Adams, *Sideshow U.S.A.*, 31.

31 See *Evolution and Eugenics in American Literature and Culture*, ed. Lois A. Cuddy and Claire M. Roche (Lewisburg, Penn.: Bucknell University Press, 2003).

32 The full story of eugenics is explored in Nell Irvin Painter's *The History of White People* (New York: W. W. Norton, 2010), 256–77.

33 For more on audience reactions to the film *Freaks*, see Matthews, *Fear Itself*, 54–58. Rachel Adams writes that "*Freaks* is less concerned with establishing the normality of its disabled characters than with subverting the notion of normative standards altogether." Adams, *Sideshow U.S.A.*, 72.

34 See George M. Marsden, *Fundamentalism and American Culture: The Shaping of Twentieth-Century Evangelicalism, 1870–1925* (New York: Oxford University Press, 1980).

35 See Marsden, *Fundamentalism and American Culture*, 212–21, for a detailed discussion of the Scopes trial and its antecedents.

36 See Painter on the "American School" and Agassiz in particular in Painter, *History of White People*, 190–200.

37 Painter, *History of White People*, 112–13, 212–13.

38 Edward Spitzka, M.D., "The Development of Man's Great Brain," *Connecticut Magazine* 9 (1909): 327.

39 See Phillips Verner Bradford and Harvey Blume, *Ota Benga* (New York: St. Martin's, 1992).

40 Adams, *Sideshow U.S.A.*, 32. This comports with Linda Frost's contention in *Never One Nation: Freaks, Savages and Whiteness* (Minneapolis: University of Minnesota Press, 2005) that whites came to see blackness as a kind of spectacle. See esp. 57–62.

41 "Negro Ministers Act to Free the Pygmy," *New York Times*, September 11, 1906; "Bushman's Champions Angry," *New York Tribune*, September 12, 1906; and "Still Stirred About Benga," *New York Times*, September 23, 1906.

42 Cook, *Arts of Deception*, 128.
43 Quoted in Adams, *Sideshow U.S.A.*, 40.
44 Edward J. Larson, *The Summer for the Gods: The Scopes Trial and America's Continuing Debate over Science and Religion* (New York: Basic Books, 1997), 239–46.
45 "Reading Race into the Scopes Monkey Trial: African American Elites, Science and Fundamentalism," *Journal of American History* 90, no. 3 (2003): 891–911. See esp. 902–3.
46 Quoted in Adams, *Sideshow U.S.A.*, 39–40.
47 Philip A. Shreffler, *The H. P. Lovecraft Companion* (Westport, Conn.: Greenwood Press), xi.
48 "Call of Cthulhu," in *More Annotated H. P. Lovecraft*, ed. S. T. Joshi (New York: Dell Trade Paperback, 1999), 172–216.
49 T. E. D. Klein, "A Dreamer's Tale," in *Dagon and Other Macabre Tales* (Sauk City, Wisc.: Arkham House Publishers, 1965), xxiv, xxv.
50 Susan Bordo discusses a similar image that appeared in a Guess jeans ad in the midst of the O. J. Simpson trial. A blonde Nicole Brown look-alike is shown being grasped from behind by a large African American man, himself an O. J. look-alike. The caption reads, "If you can't be good, be careful" (*Twilight Zones: The Hidden Life of Cultural Images from Plato to O.J.* [Berkeley: University of California Press, 1997], 102–5).
51 Joshua David Bellin examines the racial imagery of *King Kong* thoroughly in *Framing Monsters: Fantasy Film and Social Alienation* (Carbondale: Southern Illinois University Press, 2005), 1–2, 9–10, 21–47. Elizabeth Young writes that *King Kong's* "distance from realism enables the explicitness of its rape imagery." See Young, *Black Frankenstein*, 182–83.
52 Harvey Roy Greenberg explores this from another angle, pointing out how Denham himself kills the beast by summoning the Air Force, suggesting that the destruction of the monster makes the final line of the film an example of "preadolescent fascism." See Greenberg, "King Kong: The Beast in the Boudoir—or, 'You Can't Marry That Girl, You're a Gorilla,'" in *The Dread of Difference: Gender and the Horror Film*, ed. Barry Keith Grant (Austin: University of Texas Press, 1996), 350.
53 Karen Grigsby Bates, "Race and King Kong," NPR, December 22, 2005, http://www.npr.org/templates/story/story.php?storyId=5066156. Noel Carroll explores the relationship between *King Kong* and the evolution controversy thoroughly in "King Kong: Ape and Essence," in Christopher Sharrett, *Planks of Reason: Essays on the Horror Film* (Lanham, Md.: Scarecrow Press, 2004), 212–39.
54 Aesthetic documents such as *Birth of a Nation* make their intention clear; this is not a matter of "reading too much into" a cultural production.
55 Young, *Black Frankenstein*, 183.
56 Young, *Black Frankenstein*, 184.
57 Brian Donovan, *White Slave Crusades: Race, Gender, and Anti-vice Activism, 1887–1917* (Urbana: University of Illinois Press, 2006), 22–23.
58 Donovan, *White Slave Crusades*, 26, 27.
59 The classic study is John Higham, *Strangers in the Land: Patterns of American Nativism, 1860–1925* (New York: Athenaeum, 1963).
60 Quotes in Donovan, *White Slave Crusades*, 29–30.
61 See David J. Skal, *Hollywood Gothic: The Tangled Web of Dracula from Novel to Stage to Screen* (New York: Faber & Faber, 2004), 172–74, 176–79.

62 Quoted in David J. Skal, *The Monster Show: A Cultural History of Horror* (New York: Farrar, Strauss & Giroux, 1992), 125. For more on reviewer reaction, see Skal, *Hollywood Gothic*, 199–200.

63 Matthews, *Fear Itself*, 25.

64 William Patrick Day, *Vampire Legends in Contemporary American Culture* (Lexington: University Press of Kentucky, 2002), 5, 6.

65 Bloom, *Gothic Histories*, 69.

66 Glen Scott Allen contends that American culture has moved back and forth between seeing the scientist as a "master mechanic" or a "wicked wizard." See his *Master Mechanics and Wicked Wizards: Images of the American Scientist as Hero and Villain from Colonial Times to the Present* (Amherst: University of Massachusetts Press, 2009). See esp. chap. 4 for his discussion of the image of the scientist in the 1930s.

67 See John Cornwell, *Hitler's Scientists: Science, the War and the Devil's Pact* (New York: Penguin, 2004).

68 The complete history of the crimes at Tuskegee can be found in James H. Jones, *Bad Blood: The Tuskegee Syphilis Experiment* (New York: Free Press, 1993).

69 Along with Washington's work, readers should consult Michael Sappol's *A Traffic of Dead Bodies: Anatomy and Embodied Social Identity in Nineteenth-Century America* (Princeton: Princeton University Press, 2002). See esp. his discussion of race and dissection, 253–59, and his description of the "body trade" on 122–35.

70 A complete history of the Brisendine Papers appears in Allen M. Hornblum, *Acres of Skin: Human Experiments at Holmesburg Prison* (New York: Routledge, 1999).

71 Harriet A. Washington, *Medical Apartheid* (New York: Anchor Books, 2006), 250.

72 Washington, *Medical Apartheid*, 250–51. This was part of the CIA MK-ULTRA program, a long-term research project that hoped to use mind-altering drugs as a covert weapon. Washington further shows that experiments on prisoners were not uncommon, with African Americans making up the majority. In 1952, for example, researcher Chester M. Southam from Sloan-Kettering Cancer Center injected almost four hundred inmates in the Ohio correctional system with cancerous cells. See 252–54.

73 See Paul Fussell, "The War in Black and White," in *The Boy Scout Handbook and Other Observations* (New York: Oxford University Press, 1982), 230–24.

74 Matthews, *Fear Itself*, 167–68.

Chapter 4

1 J. Robert Oppenheimer, "Atomic Weapons and American Policy," *Foreign Affairs* (July 1953): 529.

2 A good introduction to the Cold War era appears in the editor's introduction to Peter J. Kuznick and James Gilbert, eds., *Rethinking Cold War Culture* (Washington, D.C.: Smithsonian Institution Press, 2001), 1–15.

3 A detailed description of popular tastes and their cultural meanings during the Cold War appears in William H. Young and Nancy K. Young, *The 1950s* (Westport, Conn.: Greenwood Press, 2004).

4 Andrew Tudor, *Monsters and Mad Scientists: A Cultural History of the Horror Movie* (Oxford: Blackwell, 1989), 220.

5 For a very different view of 1950s notions of the monster, see Mark Jancovich's *Rational Fears: American Horror in the 1950s* (Manchester: Manchester University Press, 1996). Jancovich argues that too much focus on "invasion narratives" and an

unwillingness to look more closely at films that offer dissenting visions has led to a misunderstanding of 1950s horror narratives. See esp. 3, 4, 72–79.

6 Quoted in Rachel Adams, *Sideshow U.S.A.: Freaks and the American Cultural Imagination* (Chicago: University of Chicago Press, 2001), 211.

7 On the medicalization of freaks, see Robert Bogdan, *Freak Show: Presenting Human Oddities for Amusement and Profit* (Chicago: University of Chicago Press, 1988), 62–68, 277–78; and *Invaders from Mars*, directed by William Cameron Menzies, special edition DVD with illustrated collector's booklet by Wade Williams (2000).

8 A number of scholars have used the "containment" concept as a general metaphor for 1950s America. See Martin Haliwell, *American Culture in the 1950s* (Edinburgh: Edinburgh University Press, 2007), 8–10.

9 See Paul M. Boyer, *Fallout: A Historian Reflects on America's Half-Century Encounter with Nuclear Weapons* (Columbus: Ohio State University Press, 1998).

10 *Boxoffice*, February 25, 1956.

11 Boyer, *Fallout*, 73.

12 William Tsutsui in *Godzilla on My Mind: Fifty Years of the King of Monsters* (New York: Palgrave Macmillan, 2004) describes how the original *Godzilla* film dealt with "the most profound, contentious and chilling issues of the day" (19), addressing itself to the scars of Hiroshima as well as to American environmental irresponsibility in atomic testing. The American version, on the other hand, removed "all nuclear anxiety and memories of World War II" (20).

13 Margot A. Henriksen, *Dr. Strangelove's America: Society and Culture in the Atomic Age* (Berkeley: University of California Press, 1997), 45.

14 The United States refused to accept responsibility for this incident, claimed the fishermen had not really been harmed, and came close to blaming them for being in the vicinity. See Robert T. Hartman, "AEC Chief Bares Facts on H-Bomb," *Los Angeles Times*, April 1, 1954.

15 See comments by a top Roosevelt administration official in "Japan Beaten Before Atom Bomb, Byrnes Says, Citing Peace Bids," *New York Times*, August 30, 1945. See also Gar Alperovitz, *The Decision to Use the Atomic Bomb and the Architecture of an American Myth* (New York: Vintage Books, 1996). For a full discussion of Hersey, see Paul Boyer, *By the Bomb's Early Light: American Thought and Culture at the Dawn of the Atomic Age* (New York: Pantheon Books, 1985), esp. 203–9.

16 The director of the exhibit scrapped it under congressional pressure (fomented by the politically powerful American Legion) and a planned congressional hearing. He claimed to cancel the interpretative exhibit because the concept had been ill conceived, and admitted that various personnel who had planned the exhibit might end their tenure with the Institute. Republicans in Congress moved ahead with hearings anyway to ensure that the museum adhered to "interpretative standards." A stripped-down version commemorating the event featured the B-29 *Enola Gay*, a short video about the crew, and no interpretative text. See Eugene L. Meyer and Jacqueline Prescott, "Smithsonian Scuttles Exhibit," *Washington Post*, January 31, 1995.

17 Peter Kuznick and Oliver Stone, *The Untold History of the United States* (New York: Gallery Books, 2012), 330; and Nick Turse, *Kill Anything That Moves: The Real American War in Vietnam* (New York: Picador Press, 2013), 77–79, 93–94.

18 "Shaking Hands with Saddam Hussein: The U.S. Tilts Toward Iraq, 1980–1984," National Security Archive Briefing Book no. 82, ed. Joyce Battle, February 25, 1983. See http://nsarchive.gwu.edu/NSAEBB/NSAEBB82/; accessed May 12, 2017.

19 Scott Allen, "Radiation Tests Used Retarded Children at Wrentham Hospital," *Boston Globe*, February 9, 1994.
20 See James W. Trent, *Inventing the Feeble Mind: A History of Mental Retardation in the United States* (Berkeley: University of California Press, 1994). See esp. 241–46, in which parents of retarded children came to be seen as the true victims because they had to house "low grade defectives."
21 David J. Skal, *The Monster Show: A Cultural History of Horror* (New York: Farrar, Strauss & Giroux, 1992), 289–90.
22 "Mrs. Finkbine Undergoes Abortion in Sweden," *New York Times*, August 19, 1962.
23 A complete history and analysis can be found in Elizabeth D. Blum, *Love Canal Revisited: Race, Class and Gender in Environmental Activism* (Lawrence: University Press of Kansas, 2008).
24 Eckardt C. Beck, "The Love Canal Tragedy," *EPA Journal* (January 1979).
25 A full history of the first generation of Marvel comics appears in Ronin Ro, *Tales to Astonish: Jack Kirby, Stan Lee and the American Comic Book Revolution* (New York: Bloomsbury, 2004).
26 "Synopsis: The Fantastic Four July '61 Schedule," in *Marvel Vault* (Philadelphia: Running Press, 2007).
27 *Marvel Vault*, 76–77.
28 Stan Lee interview, in *Stan Lee's Mutants, Monsters and Marvels* (Sony Pictures, 2002), DVD.
29 Complete script available in *Invasion of the Body Snatchers*, ed. Al Lavelley (New Brunswick, N.J.: Rutgers University Press, 1989).
30 See David M. Oshinsky, *A Conspiracy So Immense: The World of Joseph McCarthy* (New York: Free Press, 1983).
31 J. Edgar Hoover, *Masters of Deceit* (New York: Henry Holt, 1958), 186–87.
32 Sara Hamilton, "Invasion of the Body Snatchers," *Los Angeles Examiner*, March 1, 1956; and Jack Moffit, "Invasion of the Body Snatchers," *The Hollywood Reporter*, February 16, 1956.
33 Henriksen, *Dr. Strangelove's America*, 91.
34 Examples can be found in the film *Atomic Café*, directed by Jane Loader, Kevin Rafferty, and Jane Rafferty (1982). DVD release by New Video Group (2002).
35 Tudor, *Monsters and Mad Scientists*, 114.
36 Stephen J. Whitfield, *The Culture of the Cold War* (Baltimore, Md.: Johns Hopkins University Press, 1996), 59.
37 See Jancovich's discussion in *Rational Fears*, 34–41. Jancovich emphasizes how the film deals with conceptions of both language and gender. He is right to show how it is nuanced, yet, in terms of production and distribution, the majority of American horror films in the 1950s were rather simple invasion narratives.
38 Almost every sensational work by UFO hunters contains a detailed description of the tale. See Jerome Clark, *Unexplained! Strange Sightings, Incredible Occurrences and Puzzling Physical Phenomena* (Detroit: Visible Ink Press, 1993).
39 Obituary of Kenneth Arnold, *Idaho Statesman*, January 22, 1984.
40 Curtis Peebles, *Watch the Skies! A Chronicle of the Flying Saucer Myth* (Washington, D.C.: Smithsonian Books, 1994), 247, 249, 280. Peebles shows that belief in UFO conspiracy comported well with the increasingly "nihilistic mood" of the United States. See 275–80.
41 Peter Knight, ed., *Conspiracy Nation: The Politics of Paranoia in Post-war America* (New York: New York University Press, 2002), 7.

42 Athan G. Theoharis, ed., *Culture of Secrecy: The Government Versus the People's Right to Know* (Lawrence: University Press of Kansas, 1999), 2, 3. See Ted Gup, *A Nation of Secrets: The Threat to Democracy and the American Way of Life* (New York: Doubleday, 2007).

43 Arthur Ruppelt, *The Report on Unidentified Flying Objects* (Garden City, N.Y.: Doubleday, 1956), 201.

44 Peebles, *Watch the Skies!*, 99–101.

45 Nigel Watson, *Fortean Times*, March 23, 1999.

46 See Vern L. Bullough's "Alfred Kinsey and the Kinsey Report," in *The Sexual Revolution*, ed. Mary E. Williams (San Diego: Greenhaven Press, 2002).

47 Nancy K. Young and William H. Young, *The 1950s* (Westport, Conn.: Greenwood Press, 2004), 24–25.

48 Quoted in Beth L. Bailey, *From Front Porch to Back Seat: Courtship in Twentieth-Century America* (Baltimore, Md.: Johns Hopkins University Press, 1989), 86.

49 "Hearing in Student's Case Continued," *Ann Arbor News*, January 25, 1947.

50 Albert Ellis, *Sex and the Single Man* (New York: Lyle Stuart Press, 1963), 83. Beth L. Bailey shows that, elsewhere, Ellis made the case that rape was "neither dangerous nor health destroying." See Bailey, *From Front Porch to Back Seat*, 166n.

51 See a full discussion of body panic and alien abduction in Bridget Brown's "'My body is not my own': Alien Abduction and the Struggle for Self-Control," in Knight, *Conspiracy Nation*, 107–32.

52 A good discussion of the postwar religion boom appears in George R. Marsden's *Religion and American Culture* (New York: Harcourt, Brace, Jovanovich, 1990), 213–18.

53 Whitfield, *Culture of the Cold War*, 89.

54 Whitfield, *Culture of the Cold War*, 81.

55 Peebles, *Watch the Skies!*, 93–99.

56 Fry's account appears in Daniel W. Fry, *The White Sands Incident* (Louisville, Ky.: Best Books, 1966). See also Orfeo Angelucci, *The Secret of the Saucers* (Amherst, Wisc.: Amherst Press, 1955).

57 H. Taylor Burkner, "Flying Saucers Are for People," *Trans-Action* (May/June 1966): 10–13.

58 A detailed discussion of and critical response to this phenomenon appear in Morris Goran, *The Modern Myth: Ancient Astronauts and UFOs* (London: Thomas Yoseloff, 1978).

59 Douglas E. Cowan, *Sacred Space: The Quest for Transcendence in Science Fiction Film and Television* (Waco, Tex.: Baylor University Press, 2010), 180–88.

60 Jason Colovito, *The Cult of Alien Gods: H. P. Lovecraft and Extraterrestrial Pop Culture* (Amherst, N.Y.: Prometheus Books, 2005).

61 Frank De Caro, ed., *An Anthology of American Folktales and Legends* (Armonk, N.Y.: M. E. Sharpe Press, 2009), 281; and Loren Coleman and Jerome Clark, *Cryptozoology A to Z: The Encyclopedia of Loch Monsters, Sasquatch, Chupacabras and Other Authentic Mysteries of Nature* (New York: Simon & Schuster, 1999), 41.

62 Andrew Genzoli, "Giant Footprints Puzzle Residents Along Trinity River," *Humboldt Times*, October 5, 1958.

63 Michael McLeod, *Anatomy of a Beast: Obsession and Myth on the Trail of Bigfoot* (Berkeley: University of California Press, 2009), 25, 30–36.

64 Charles Fort, *The Complete Works of Charles Fort* (New York: Dover Publications), 3.

65 McLeod, *Anatomy of the Beast*, 52–57.

66 Bernard Heuvelmans, *In the Wake of the Sea Serpents* (New York: Hill & Wang, 1968), 44.

67 A good discussion of the scientific creationism movement appears in George E. Webb, *The Evolution Controversy in America* (Lexington: University Press of Kentucky, 1994). See esp. 154–79.

68 McLeod, *Anatomy of the Beast*, 54.

69 George Webb has argued that the growth of support for creation science, in some quarters, is in proportion to a decline in science education in the United States. See Webb, *Evolution Controversy in America*, 221–22.

70 Tudor, *Monsters and Mad Scientists*, 143, 154.

71 Skal, *Monster Show*, 239.

72 Iain Topliss, *The Comic Worlds of Peter Arno, William Steig, Charles Addams and Saul Steinberg* (Baltimore: Johns Hopkins University Press, 2005), 146–50, 178–80.

73 Charles Addams, *Monster Rally* (New York: Pocket Books, 1950), 57, 122–23.

74 Addams, *Monster Rally*, 114–15.

75 Wini Breines, "Postwar White Girl's Dark Others," in *The Other Fifties*, ed. Joel Foreman (Champaign: University of Illinois Press, 1999), 56.

76 Patricia Bosworth, *Diane Arbus: A Biography* (New York: W. W. Norton, 1984), 162, 168. The film *Freaks* also inspired a significant new scholarship on the meaning of sideshow freaks in American cultural history. See Leslie Fiedler, *Freaks: Myths and Images of the Secret Self* (New York: Anchor Books, 1998), 18. Fielder referred to Browning's work as a "masterpiece."

77 Jancovich in *Rational Fears* sees this shift occurring by the mid-1950s, especially in the work of schlock-auteur Roger Corman. See esp. 262–84.

Chapter 5

1 See Slavoj Žižek's discussion of the film *Psycho* in *Everything You Always Wanted to Know about Lacan but Were Afraid to Ask Hitchcock*, ed. Slavoj Žižek (New York: Verso Books, 1992), 226–31.

2 Reviews quoted in Kendall R. Phillips, *Projected Fears: Horror Films and American Culture* (Westport, Conn.: Praeger Publishers, 2005), 62.

3 A full examination of how *Psycho*'s critical reputation grew over time can be found in *Alfred Hitchcock's Psycho: A Casebook*, ed. Robert Kolker (New York: Oxford University Press, 2004), 61–100.

4 William E. Leuchtenburg, *Troubled Feast: American Society Since 1945* (New York: Scott Foresman, 1983), 104.

5 Henriksen, *Dr. Strangelove's America: Society and Culture in the Atomic Age* (Berkeley: University of California Press, 1997), 107.

6 Todd Gitlin, *The Sixties: Years of Hope, Days of Rage* (New York: Bantam, 1987), 22.

7 For a complete history of hysteria over the comic book, see David Nadju, *The Ten Cent Plague: The Great Comic Book Scare and How It Changed America* (New York: Farrar, Strauss & Giroux, 2008).

8 History of EC taken from Grant Geissman, *Foul Play! The Art and Artists of the Notorious 1950s E.C. Comics* (New York: Harper Design, 2005).

9 Descriptions of comics taken primarily from Geissman, *Foul Play!*

10 Bradford W. Wright, *Comic Book Nation* (Baltimore: Johns Hopkins University Press, 2003), 148.

11 Wright, *Comic Book Nation*, 149.

12 Robert Whitaker, *Mad in America: Bad Science, Bad Medicine and the Enduring Mistreatment of the Mentally Ill* (Cambridge, Mass.: Perseus Publishing, 2002). See esp. 169–75, on how social tensions and attitudes about nonconformity informed the treatment of the mentally ill, as well as the racist underpinnings of the treatment of African Americans by the mental health community.

13 This representation of life in American mental institutions as oppressive and inhumane presaged Ken Kesey's 1962 *One Flew over the Cuckoo's Nest* (New York: Viking, 1962).

14 Wright, *Comic Book Nation*, 138–40, 145.

15 Quoted in Wright, *Comic Book Nation*, 167.

16 Description of Gaines and Wertham's testimony taken from Wright, *Comic Book Nation*, 165–72.

17 "The Code for Editorial Matter General Standards Part A and General Standards Part B," reprinted in Robert Michael "Robb" Cotter, *The Great Monster Magazines* (Jefferson, N.C.: McFarlane Press, 2008), 12–13.

18 E. Nelson Bridwell, ed., *Superman from the 30's to the 70's* (New York: Bonanza Books, 1979), 209.

19 See Harold Schechter, *Deviant: The Shocking True Story of Ed Gein, the Original Psycho* (New York: Simon & Schuster, 1998). Schechter's account is not as sensationalist as the title sounds and is mostly grounded in primary source research.

20 Phillips Jenkins in *Decade of Nightmares: The End of the Sixties and the Making of Eighties America* (New York: Oxford University Press, 2006) suggests that the seeds of conservative reaction can be found in the struggles of the sixties. He argues, for example, that just as "feminist politics sounded the alarm about sexual dangers to women," conservatives in the coming decade would coopt that language and use it to describe threats against the family and against children (often used as a metonym for family values). See esp. 20–23.

21 Less has been written on the American Indian Movement than other social movements of the 1960s, but the place to begin is the classic Peter Matthiessen, *In the Spirit of Crazy Horse* (New York: Penguin, 1991), where, along with a personalized history of the movement, Matthiessen convincingly suggests that the U.S. government waged a kind of second series of Indian wars in the 1960s and 1970s by crushing dissent through imprisonment and disinformation. See also Paul Chaat Smith and Robert Allen Warrior, *Like a Hurricane: The Indian Movement from Alcatraz to Wounded Knee* (New York: New Press, 1997).

22 Andreas Killen notes that in the early seventies the "institutional failures of American society routinely evoked expressions of systemic, perhaps irreparable crisis." See Killen, *1973 Nervous Breakdown: Watergate, Warhol, and the Birth of Post-Sixties America* (New York: Bloomsbury, 2006), 261.

23 Ginette Castro, *American Feminism: A Contemporary History* (New York: New York University Press, 1984), 191–93.

24 See Christian G. Appy's detailed discussion of these incidents, some forgotten in popular memory and others barely remembered, in *American Reckoning: The Vietnam War and Our National Identity* (New York: Penguin Books, 2015), 186–92, 202–6.

25 The backlash really began in the 1970s with the 1976 Hyde amendment that forbade the use of Medicaid to pay for abortions. The ERA went down to defeat in several crucial states the same year. See Jenkins, *Decade of Nightmares*, 108–11.

26 Phillips Jenkins, *Using Murder: The Social Construction of Serial Homicide* (New York: Aldine Transaction, 1994), offers the best discussion of these trends. See esp. 21–48.

27 Newitz argues that the serial killer narrative since the 1950s has been structured by a "search for normalcy." This search takes place within America's "enraged confusion" over the relationship between society and economics." See Annalee Newitz, *Pretend We're Dead: Capitalist Monsters in American Pop Culture* (Durham, N.C.: Duke University Press, 2006), 27, 42.

28 David Schmid, *Natural Born Celebrities: Serial Killers in American Culture* (Chicago: University of Chicago Press, 2006), 66–67, 96–106. Douglas has also profiled Lizzie Borden and, perhaps most bizarrely, the literary character Othello.

29 Schmid, *Natural Born Celebrities*, 82.

30 John Starr, "The Random Killers," *Newsweek*, November 26, 1984.

31 Schmid, *Natural Born Celebrities*, 196–200.

32 Schmid, *Natural Born Celebrities*, 96.

33 Stephen G. Michaud and Hugh Aynesworth, *The Only Living Witness: A True Account of Homicidal Insanity* (New York: Signet, 1983), 6.

34 Jane Caputi argues that terms applied to serial killers such as "monster" and "enigma" hide the way that American society has valorized the serial murderer and transformed them into pop heroes. See *Goddesses and Monsters: Women, Myth, Power, and Popular Culture* (Madison, Wisc.: Popular Press, 2004), 119–39. This argument assumes that the popularity of serial murder narratives is the same as valorization of those narratives. Discourses of mental illness and the true crime genre itself that identifies serial murder with social aberrance call this reading into question.

35 Phillip Jenkins shows how popular representations of the serial killer in the 1970s and 1980s conformed to images of social degeneracy. He provides examples of how this imagery could be useful to both the Right and the Left as cautionary tales about alternative sexualities or as examples of societal misogyny. See *Decade of Nightmares*, 140–51.

36 Scott Stossel, "The Sexual Counterrevolution," *American Prospect* (July/August 1997).

37 Stossel, "Sexual Counterrevolution."

38 Robert Lindsey, "Officials Cite a Rise in Killers Who Roam U.S.," *New York Times*, January 1984.

39 Quoted in Jenkins, *Using Murder*, 125.

40 Phillip Jenkins argues, "media rhetoric of 'gay serial killers' confounded homosexuals with both pedophiles and child killers, a powerful political weapon at the time of anti-gay reaction." He notes that both the 1977 film *Looking for Mr. Goodbar* and the 1980 film *Cruising* portray gay subculture as having savage and homicidal tendencies. See *Decade of Nightmares*, 149.

41 Dirk Gibson, *Serial Murder and Media Circuses* (Westport, Conn.: Praeger Publishers, 2006), 95, 96.

42 Schmid, *Natural Born Celebrities*, 224–26.

43 Anne Schwartz, *The Man Who Could Not Kill Enough: The Secret Murders of Milwaukee's Jeffrey Dahmer* (New York: Carol Press, 1992), 115.

44 A number of scholars have critiqued the film *The Silence of the Lambs* from this angle. See Elizabeth Young's "The Silence of the Lambs and the Flaying of Feminist Theory," *Camera Obscura* 27 (1991): 5–36; and Christopher Sharrett, "The Horror Film in Neoconservative Culture," *Journal of Popular Film & Television* 21, no. 3 (1993): 100–110.

45 William Bennett, John DiIulios, and John Walters, *Body Count: Moral Poverty and How to Win America's War Against Crime and Drugs* (New York: Simon & Schuster, 1994); and James Q. Wilson, "What to Do About Crime," *Commentary* 98 (1994): 25–34.

46 Kent Byron Armstrong defines the slasher genre in *Slasher Films: An International Filmography, 1960–2001* (Jefferson, N.C.: McFarland Press, 2003), 1–19. Armstrong does not include *The Silence of the Lambs* in his filmography.

47 Antonio Quike, *Jaws* (London: Palgrave MacMillan, 2014), 7.

48 Caroll Kilpatrick, "Nixon Resigns," *Washington Post*, August 9, 1974, A01. On the transformation of the economy and its effects on the 1970s, see Jefferson Cowie, *Stayin' Alive: The 1970s and the Last Days of the Working Class* (New York: New Press, 2010), esp. 1–19, 311, 361–67. On the effect of defeat in Vietnam for American perceptions of national identity and times, see Appy, *American Reckoning*, 228–31.

49 Carter's reputation as peacemaker perhaps has grown out of his post-presidential work with the Carter Foundation. During his tenure as president, however, he authorized cruise missile deployment in Europe, commissioned the first Trident submarine to threaten the Soviet Union with apocalyptic destruction just off their shores, unilaterally ended treaty talks on nuclear limitations (Salt II), and increased defense spending across the board. Ronald Reagan, for his own political ends, admitted that the ballooning military budget had begun under Carter. See Bernard Weinraub, "Reagan Acknowledges Carter's Military Build-Up," *New York Times*, April 6, 1986.

50 "The Texas Chain Saw Massacre: The Shocking Truth," *Texas Chain Saw Massacre, the Ultimate Edition (Blu-Ray)*, DVD, directed by Tobe Hooper (Dark Sky Films, 2008).

51 John Kenneth Muir, *Eaten Alive at a Chainsaw Massacre* (Jefferson, N.C.: McFarland Press, 2002), 12–22, describes the controversial film's complex box office history and its reception by audiences and American culture.

52 Linnie Blake describes *Chain Saw* as "a degenerate vision of the American family" and connects its "apocalyptic climate of utter despair" to the general feeling that America was edging toward social collapse. See *The Wounds of Nations: Horror Cinema, Historic Trauma and National Identity* (Manchester, UK: Manchester University Press, 2008), 135.

53 Killen, *1973 Nervous Breakdown*, 80–81.

54 Hooper quote taken from "The Texas Chain Saw Massacre: The Shocking Truth." See Judith Halberstam's discussion in *Skin Shows: Gothic Horror and the Technology of Monsters* (Durham, N.C.: Duke University Press, 1995), 146–260. The first two *Chain Saw* films provide Halberstam the opportunity to talk about the resistance of the horror film to psychoanalytic readings since they reject the humanist assumptions of that discipline and favor "abjection, loss, revulsion, dread and violence."

55 Alternatively Christopher Sharrett suggests that Leatherface's gruesome mask of skin "re-creates the lampshades of Buchenwald rather than the knife scabbards and buckskin jackets of Daniel Boone and Davy Crockett." Even Sharrett notes, however, that this is a tale taking place in Texas, "a state brimming with folklore and the key signifiers of the frontier experience." The larger history of twentieth-century genocide is not suggested but rather a domestic American horror on which imagery of the American past is fetishized. For Sharrett's view, see "Apocalypse in the Texas Chain Saw Massacre," in Christopher Sharrett, *Planks of Reason: Essays on the Horror Film* (Lanham, Md.: Scarecrow Press, 2004), 300–320.

56 This discussion of the symbolic reconstruction of American history in *The Texas Chain Saw Massacre* borrows Tony Williams' interpretation in *Hearths of Darkness: The Family in the American Horror Film* (Madison, Wisc.: Associated University Presses, 1996), 185–87. I do disagree with Williams' conclusion that the Sawyers are "Puritanism's worst fears" (187). The Sawyers represent the natural outgrowth of the Puritans' violent "errand into the wilderness."

57 For a close reading and analysis, see David A. Szulkin's *Wes Craven's Last House on the Left: The Making of a Cult Classic* (Guildford, UK: FAB Press, 1997).

58 See Adam Lowenstein's discussion of *Last House* in *Shocking Representations* (New York: Columbia University Press, 2005), 111–43. This is a very insightful interpretation, though I disagree with the amount of emphasis Lowenstein puts on advertising copy of the film, as opposed to audience response within the historical context of the final stages of the Vietnam War.

59 See Carol J. Clover, *Men, Women and Chainsaws: Gender and the Modern Horror Film* (Princeton: Princeton University Press, 1993), 35–41. Sue Short makes a convincing argument for horror films' relationship to fairy tale and, by extension, their role as portraying and replicating female initiation rituals. Horror films, particularly slashers, present "misfit sisters," female heroes who discover resources within themselves and assert their independence from various forms of authority. See Short, *Misfit Sisters: Screen Horror as Female Rite of Passage* (New York: Palgrave, 2006). She notes that many of these films are still politically problematic in that they often raise questions about "sexual assertiveness." See 161ff.

60 Alan Brinkley describes the suburbanization of the middle class as an attempt to "escape the diversity and abrasiveness of urban life." See his discussion of uniformity in middle-class culture in "The Illusion of Unity in Cold War Culture," in *Rethinking Cold War Culture*, ed. Peter J. Kuznick and James Gilbert (Washington, D.C.: Smithsonian Institution Press, 2001), esp. 68–70. See also Bernice M. Murphy, *The Suburban Gothic in American Popular Culture* (New York: Palgrave, 2009), 10–11 and 142–46. Murphy notes that Myers becomes "a blank slate upon which all the worst fears of the suburban parent can be projected." He is both "the escaped mental patient" and "the boy next door gone terribly wrong."

61 A full examination of the "white flight" phenomenon, and its political implications, appears in Kevin M. Cruse, *White Flight: Atlanta and the Making of Modern Conservatism* (Princeton: Princeton University Press, 2007). See also Bruce Schulman's *The Seventies: The Great Shift in American Culture, Society and Politics* (New York: Free Press, 2001), 54–58.

62 An alternative reading of the slasher genre can be found in Jane Caputi, *Goddesses and Monsters*. Caputi sees the slasher genre as a kind of misogynistic fairy tale that has its origins in the sensationalistic tales of Jack the Ripper, whose latterday incarnations are Jason and Freddy. Caputi ignores the complex question of audience identification and does not discuss Carol J. Clover's interpretation of the film in relation to the importance of the final girl. Isabel Christina Pinedo, in *Recreational Terror: Women and the Pleasures of Horror Film Viewing* (Albany: State University of New York Press, 1997), argues for "contradictory dynamics" within the genre. Pinedo argues for the use of Judith Butler's "gender trouble" concept in interpreting the genre. See esp. 71–87.

63 Criticisms of Carol Glover's "final girl" thesis have tended to draw their examples from these inferior and much less influential sequels. For an example, see Tony Williams' essay "Trying to Survive on the Darker Side: 1980s Family Horror," in

The Dread of Difference: Gender and the Horror Film, ed. Barry Keith Grant (Austin: University of Texas Press, 1996), 164–80.

64 Schulman, *The Seventies*, 241–46.

65 Deborah Knight and George McKnight claim that Ellis' novel makes the monster its central character and thus "our primary means of access to the events of the fictional world and in fact our narrator." See Knight and McKnight, "American Psycho: Horror, Satire, Aesthetics and Identification," in *Dark Thoughts: Philosophic Reflections on Cinematic Horror* (Lanham, Md.: Scarecrow Press, 2003). Of course, Mary Shelley had given us a novel at least partially narrated by a monster and, in some sense, a more trustworthy narrator than Patrick Bateman.

66 Blake sees the "fetishization of the mass murderer" during the 1980s and 1990s as a product of the conservative Right's insistence on the individual breaking the mechanisms of state control. See *Wounds of Nations*, 105–16. Mark Selzer makes a similar argument in *Serial Killers: Death and Life in America's Wound Culture* (New York: Routledge, 1998).

67 Jenkins, *Using Murder*, 150.

68 Philip L. Simpson, in *Psycho Paths: Tracking the Serial Killer Through Contemporary American Film and Fiction* (Carbondale: Southern Illinois Press, 2000), argues that Ellis' basic theme is "the self-cannibalizing aspects of 1980s capitalism" (149).

69 See http://www.murderauction.com (accessed April 15, 2010).

70 Philip L. Simpson argues that Stone's points are far more obscure than I argue here, noting that the film becomes dominated by "thematic tangents," including the introduction of religious themes of original sin and millenarianism. I would argue that Stone's aesthetic triumphs over the sometimes uncertain plot and murky dialogue to ask difficult question about our fascination with "natural born killers." See Simpson, *Psycho Paths*, 185.

71 On the popular portrayal of the serial killer, see Tim McGirk, "The Monster Within," *Time*, January 19, 2004; and "Murder: No Apparent Motive," HBO documentary, April 24, 1984.

72 On audience identification with Dexter, see David Schmid, "The Devil You Know: Dexter and the 'Goodness' of American Serial Killing," in *Dexter: Investigating Cutting Edge Television*, ed. Douglas L. Howard (New York: I.B. Tauris Press, 2010).

73 It is noteworthy that, in the early episodes, Dexter and Rita are shown as having a sexually dysfunctional relationship, a conceit quickly dropped by the end of the first season as Dexter's daytime existence became increasingly normalized in relation to his nighttime crimes.

74 The idea of the monster being shaped by historic conditions and economic structures borrows from Annalee Newitz's idea that "humans turned to monsters through capitalism" as "one story that has haunted America." See Newitz, *Pretend We're Dead*, 2, 7.

75 Schmid argues in "Devil You Know" that in post–9/11 America, the terrorist has not replaced the serial killer but the serial killer has become a "sympathetic" figure, perhaps even a counterpoint to the terrorist.

Chapter 6

1 For the best scholarly reading of *The Exorcist*, see Carol J. Clover, *Men, Women and Chainsaws: Gender and the Modern Horror Film* (Princeton: Princeton University Press, 1993), 65–72 and 83–90.

2   Audiences in 1973–1974 tended to read the ending of the film *The Exorcist* as a triumph for Satan since both Merrin and Karras meet their end. Friedkin and Blatty have insisted that this is not the message of the film and that the priests' deaths should be seen as sacrificial efforts to free Regan. In the director's cut of the film released in 1998, the triumph of good over evil is more clearly delineated. See "Director's Commentary," *The Exorcist: The Version You've Never Seen*, directed by William Friedkin (Warner Home Video, 2002), DVD.

3   Stephen King, *Danse Macabre* (New York: Berkley Books, 1981), 169; and Andreas Killen, *1973 Nervous Breakdown: Watergate, Warhol, and the Birth of Post-Sixties America* (New York: Bloomsbury, 2006), 111.

4   Michel Foucault sees the policing of moral and sexual boundaries as part of the general effort to discipline the social order. See a thorough discussion of this in Foucault, *The History of Sexuality* (New York: Vintage Books, 1990); and Ann Laura Stoler, *Race and the Education of Desire: Foucault's History of Sexuality and the Colonial Order of Things* (Durham, N.C.: Duke University Press, 1995), esp. 137–49.

5   Bruce Schulman, *The Seventies: The Great Shift in American Culture, Society and Politics* (New York: Free Press, 2001), 159–89.

6   A lively discussion and debate exists over the nature of the culture wars. A full examination of this debate appears in James Davison Hunter and Alana Wolfe, eds., *Is There a Culture War? A Dialogue on Values and American Public Life* (Washington, D.C.: Pew Research Center, 2006).

7   See Barbara Creed's "Horror and the Monstrous Feminine: An Imaginary Abjection," in *The Dread of Difference: Gender and the Horror Film*, ed. Barry Keith Grant (Austin: University of Texas Press, 1996), 35–63. Creed argues that the feminine is constructed as monstrous within patriarchal discourses and that this sign of the monstrous feminine can be seen in films ranging from *The Exorcist* to *Alien*. She notes that this tells us nothing about women's response to horror, although I think seeing such notions in a political context suggests that both men and women read these films as expositions of social and historical problems. See also Shelley Stamp Lindsey's excellent essay on the film *Carrie*, "Horror Femininity and *Carrie's* Monstrous Puberty," in Grant, *Dread of Difference*, 279–95.

8   See Mary E. Williams, "Sexual Revolution: An Overview," in *The Sexual Revolution*, ed. Mary E. Williams (San Diego, Calif.: Greenhaven Press, 2002), 10–25.

9   Morton Hunt, *Sexual Behavior in the 1970s* (Chicago: Playboy Press, 1973), 183–84; and Phillip Blumstein and Pepper Schwartz, *American Couples: Work, Money, Sex* (New York: William Morrow, 1983), 232, 236.

10 Blumstein and Schwartz, *American Couples*, 232–36.

11 *Saturday Evening Post*, January 15, 1966.

12 Toni Grant, *Being a Woman: Fulfilling Your Femininity and Finding Love* (New York: Random House, 1988), 11, 49.

13 George Gilder, *Men and Marriage* (Gretna, La.: Pelican Publishing, 1986), 111, 149. Consider the 1983 slasher and cult favorite *Sleepaway Camp* in which we meet a monstrous mom who raises a boy as a girl and transforms him into a killer. The final shocking scene manages to combine fears of violence, monsters, and transgender people.

14 Gilder, *Men and Marriage*, 84; and Joshua David Bellin, *Framing Monsters: Fantasy Film and Social Alienation* (Carbondale: Southern Illinois University Press, 2005), 115.

15 A more complex, and certainly more friendly, reading of Cronenberg's oeuvre appears in Lianne McLarty, "'Beyond the Veil of the Flesh': Cronenberg and the Disembodiment of Horror," in *Dread of Difference*, 231–52. McLarty notes that in the film *The Brood*, women "both cause and are the monster." See also Adam Lowenstein, who argues that Cronenberg, especially in his 1975 *Shivers*, introduces the idea of a "non-heteronormative sexual community" that presents a revolutionary challenge to conservative images of marriage and family life." Lowenstein, *Shocking Representations* (New York: Columbia University Press, 2005), 145–75.

16 David J. Skal, *The Monster Show: A Cultural History of Horror* (New York: Farrar, Strauss & Giroux, 1992), 298, 300.

17 There are a number of good discussions of the film *Alien* and feminism. See especially Thomas Doherty's "Genre, Gender and the Aliens Trilogy," in Grant, *Dread of Difference*, 181–99. See also the discussion of Ripley in Patricia Melzer, *Alien Constructions: Science Fiction and Feminist Thought* (Austin: University of Texas Press, 2006), 108–48. Melzer concludes that Ripley represents a boundary figure who plays with the intersection of the female, the monstrous, and the technical in ways that challenge certain aspects of the more conservative tradition of science fiction.

18 Leslie Woodcock Tentler, *Catholics and Contraception: An American History* (Ithaca: Cornell University Press, 2004), 204–64.

19 Mary E. Bendyna, RSM, John C. Green, Mark J. Rozell, and Clyde Wilcox argue that, while Catholics have joined with Christian conservatives on a number of issues, they approach the culture wars with their own set of values that give them nuanced positions on the death penalty and social welfare programs. See their article "Uneasy Alliance: Conservative Catholics and the Christian Right," *Sociology of Religion* 62, no. 1 (2001): 51–64. I would argue that, uneasy or not, a clear alliance exists, especially over what many religious conservatives view as core issues related to gender and sexuality.

20 Quoted in Jessica Winter, "Gone to Seed: The Devil's Playground," *Village Voice*, January 21, 2003.

21 Lucy Fischer, "Birth Traumas: Parturition and Horror in Rosemary's Baby," in Grant, *Dread of Difference*, 412–31.

22 The classic definition of urban legend along with plenty of examples appears in Jan Harold Brunvand's *The Vanishing Hitchhiker: American Urban Legends and Their Meanings* (New York: W. W. Norton, 1981), 1–16, 47–57.

23 Steve Neal offers a reading of *Halloween* in his essay "*Halloween*: Suspense, Aggression and the Look," in Christopher Sharrett, *Planks of Reason: Essays on the Horror Film* (Lanham, Md.: Scarecrow Press, 2004), 356–69. Neal examines the point of view of the film's spectatorship to describe audience interaction and to connect the film to certain ideological premises. He does not examine the larger historical context or the role of urban legend in informing the film's direction and plot.

24 A detailed cultural history of the phenomenon of babysitting can be found in Miriam Forman-Brunell, *Babysitter: An American History* (New York: New York University Press, 2009). See especially her discussion of the cultural images of the babysitter, 139–58.

25 Forman-Brunell, *Babysitter*, 2–5.

26 Jan Harold Brunvand, *Encyclopedia of Urban Legends* (New York: W. W. Norton, 2001), 26.

27 See "The Hook," "The Boy Friend's Death," and "The Killer in the Back Seat," in *An Anthology of American Folktales and Legends*, ed. Frank de Caro (Armonk, N.Y.: E. Sharpe Press, 2009), 328, 332–34, for variants of this story.

28 Bill Ellis, "Why Are Verbatim Transcripts of Legends Necessary?" in *Perspectives on Contemporary Legend*, ed. Gillian Bennett, Paul Smith, and J. D. A. Widdowson (London: Sheffield Academic, 1987); and Bill Ellis, *Aliens, Ghosts and Cults* (Jackson: University of Mississippi Press, 2001), 187.

29 Barbara Arneil, "Gender, Diversity and Organizational Change: The Boy Scouts vs. the Girl Scouts of America," *Perspectives on Politics* 8 (2010): 53–68.

30 Abigail A. Van Slyck, *A Manufactured Wilderness: Summer Camps and the Shaping of American Youth, 1890–1960* (Minneapolis: University of Minnesota Press, 2006), xxxvi–xxxvii, 153–54, 159–67.

31 Bill Ellis, "When Is a Legend Traditional?" in Ellis, *Aliens, Ghosts and Cults*, 33–34.

32 "Adventures at Camp Ranger," http://www.campranger.com (accessed May 1, 2010).

33 Quoted in *American Nightmare*, directed by Adam Simon (Minerva Pictures, 2000).

34 See Harold Schechter's discussion of the relationship between urban legend, folklore, and the horror film, in *Bosom Serpent: Folklore and Popular Art*, 2nd ed. (New York: Peter Lang, 2001), 21–40.

35 Libby Tucker, "Cropsey at Camp," *Voices: The Journal of New York Folklore* 32 (2006).

36 *Cropsey*, directed by Joshua Zeman and Barbara Brancaccio (Antidote Films, 2009), explores the legends surrounding Cropsey and their inflection in the Andre Rand case.

37 The satanic panic is explored fully in W. Scott Poole, *Satan in America: The Devil We Know* (Lanham, Md.: Rowman & Littlefield, 2009), 169–79.

38 Jeffrey S. Victor, *Satanic Panic: The Creation of a Contemporary Legend* (Chicago: Open Court Press, 1993), 47–56.

39 For more on the origins of the Christian Right, see Clyde Wilson and Carin Larson, *Onward Christian Soldiers? The Religious Right in American Politics*, 3rd ed. (Boulder: Westview, 2006), esp. 35–41.

40 Victor, *Satanic Panic*, 219–21. These issues are explored in greater depth in Poole, *Satan in America*.

41 Debbie Nathan and Michael Snedecker, *Satan's Silence: Ritual Abuse and the Making of a Modern American Witchhunt* (New York: Basic Books, 1995), 84–87.

42 Victor, *Satanic Panic*, 29.

43 Robert Hicks, *In Pursuit of Satan: The Police and the Occult* (Buffalo, N.Y.: Prometheus Books, 1990). See also Ben M. Crouch and Kelley Damphousse, "A Survey of Occult Cops," in *The Satanism Scare* (New York: de Gruyter, 1991).

44 Victor, *Satanic Panic*, 19–21.

45 Jeff McLaughlin, "Haunted House Abortion Scene Ignites Protest," *Boston Globe*, October 30, 1991; and "Hell House Ignites Debate," *Denver Post*, October 21, 1995.

46 W. Scott Poole, "Jesus Goes to the Dark Carnival: Hell House Gets a Make-over?" in *Religion Dispatches*, October 31, 2009.

47 Jason Bivins, *Religion of Fear: The Politics of Horror in Conservative Evangelicalism* (New York: Oxford University Press), 159, 166.

48 Nina Auerbach points out how frequently the "monster kid" phenomenon has been gendered male. She describes her own experience with the "shadowy monsters" that became "a revelation" to her and what she calls a "secret talisman" against the dull conformism of teen culture in the late 1950s. See *Our Vampires, Ourselves* (Chicago: University of Chicago Press, 1995), 4–5.

49 *American Scary,* directed by John E. Hudgens (POOB Productions, 2006), fully explores the "horror host" phenomenon with interviews and fan recollections. See also Elena M. Watson, *Television Horror Hosts: 68 Vampires, Mad Scientists and Other Denizens of the Late Night Airwaves Examined and Interviewed* (Jefferson, N.C.: McFarland Press, 2000).

50 See Robert Michael "Robb" Cotter, *The Great Monster Magazines* (Jefferson, N.C.: McFarland Press, 2008), 33–41; and Dante interview with David J. Skal quoted in *Monster Show,* 272–73.

51 Gary Cross, *The Cute and the Cool: Wondrous Innocence and Modern American Children's Culture* (New York: Oxford University Press, 2004), 150–51.

52 Cross, *Cute and the Cool,* 150–51.

53 Cross, *Cute and the Cool,* 151; Skal, *Monster Show,* 263; and "The Return of the Monsters," *Look,* September 8, 1964, 47.

54 Cross, *Cute and the Cool,* 152.

55 Paul R. Amato and Alan Booth, *A Generation at Risk: Growing Up in an Era of Family Upheaval* (Cambridge, Mass.: Harvard University Press, 1997), 10.

56 See Matthew J. Pustz, *Comic Book Culture: Fanboys and True Believers* (Jackson: University of Mississippi Press, 1999), 158–68.

57 Cotter, *Great Monster Magazines,* 212–20.

58 Henry Jenkins, *The WOW Climax: Tracing the Emotional Impact of Popular Culture* (New York: New York University Press, 2007), 41–63.

59 Quoted in Roger Luckhurst, *Alien: BFI Classics* (London: Palgrave Macmillan, 2014), 55.

60 Joseph A. McMartin, "The Strike That Busted Unions," *New York Times,* August 2, 2011.

61 See Luckhurst, *Alien,* 42. During the period under discussion, average weekly wages decreased by 10 percent, while workers who received employer-provided insurance fell by almost the same rate. At the same time, the practice of "corporate raiding" became common with companies bought, broken up, and sold and profits invested in the stock market and other parts of the financial sector where raiders could reap quicker profits than in traditional manufacturing. See Joshua B. Freeman, *American Empire: 1945–2000* (New York: Penguin, 2012), 349–54.

62 Francis Fukuyama, *The End of History and the Last Man* (New York: Free Press, 2006).

63 Mark Edmundson, in *Nightmare on Main Street: Angels, Sadomasochism and the Culture of the Gothic* (Cambridge, Mass.: Harvard University Press, 1997), finds tales of gothic terror everywhere in American public life in the '90s. He suggests that the decline in popularity of gothic slasher films may have been due to the fact that the O. J. Simpson case offered a more compelling gothic narrative than anything even the best filmmakers could produce. See esp. 6–7, 12–17, 63–68.

Chapter 7

1 See Adam Lowenstein's discussion of the film in *Shocking Representations* (New York: Columbia University Press, 2005), 154–55.

2 A full description of the *Night of the Living Dead* and its significance appears in Gregory A. Waller, *The Living and the Undead: From Stoker's Dracula to Romero's Dawn of the Dead* (Urbana: University of Illinois Press, 1986), 272–96.

3 On the continuing popularity of the zombie film, see Gendy Alimurung, "This Zombie Moment: Hunting for What Lies Beneath the Undead Zeitgeist," *LA Weekly,*

May 14, 2009. See also Lev Grossman, "Zombies Are the New Vampires," *Time*, April 19, 2009.

4   Tim Kane explores the changing incarnations of the vampire in *The Changing Vampire of Film and Television: A Critical Study of the Growth of a Genre* (Jefferson, N.C.: McFarland Press, 2006). Kane emphasizes both the eroticism of the Hammer films and their willingness to show blood by the bucketful. See esp. 43–50.

5   See Kane, *Changing Vampire*, 107–11.

6   An interesting alternative explanation for our fascination with these creatures appears in Jorg Waltje's *Blood Obsession: Vampires, Serial Murder and the Popular Imagination* (New York: Peter Lang, 2005). Waltje uses Freudian categories to think about our cultural obsession with vampires and serial murderers. At the end of his study, he suggests the compelling notion that capitalism's fascination with the replication of activity in consumerism and concomitant encouragement society gives to addictive behavior has its perfect embodiment in the serial killer and the vampire. Of course, the zombie would fit this paradigm as well, since their whole existence is driven by a replication of consumption. See esp. 139–41.

7   Both vampires and zombies should be read in connection with the serial killer. Philip L. Simpson points out that the narratives of serial murder "plunder the vampire narratives of the last century and a half" and that the mass murderer is frequently identified with biting and eating. See Simpson, *Psycho Paths: Tracking the Serial Killer Through Contemporary American Film and Fiction* (Carbondale: Southern Illinois University Press, 2000), 4–5.

8   A complete history of the evolution of the zombie figure can be found in Kyle William Bishop, *American Zombie Gothic: The Rise and Fall (and Rise) of the Walking Dead in Popular Culture* (Jefferson, N.C.: McFarland Press, 2010). Their increasing popularity can be seen in a *USA Today* story by Craig Wilson, "Zombies Lurch into Popular Culture via Books, Plays, More," April 8, 2009. For an interesting take on the zombie in relation to current American anxieties over change, see also Elizabeth Kent, "Zombie as Parody: The Misuses of Science and the Nonhuman Condition in Postmodern Society" (M.A. thesis, Auburn University, 2009).

9   A complete introduction to the social and cultural crisis of Vietnam appears in Tom Wells, *The War Within: America's Battle over Vietnam* (Berkeley: University of California Press, 1994); and Bruce Schulman's *The Seventies: The Great Shift in American Culture, Society and Politics* (New York: Free Press, 2001), 221–24.

10 One of the best studies of the war in Vietnam is Christian G. Appy, *Working-Class War: American Combat Soldiers and Vietnam* (Chapel Hill: University of North Carolina Press, 1993). For reading on casualties, see 7–15, 247–48, 274–75.

11 Jonathan Neale, *A People's History of the Vietnam War* (New York: New Press, 2004), 93; and Appy, *Working-Class War*, 156–57.

12 Howard Zinn, *A People's History of the United States* (New York: Harper Perennial, 2003), 469.

13 Turse, *Kill Anything That Moves*, 13–14, 21, 44ff.

14 Neale, *A People's History of the Vietnam War*, 96–97. Arnold R. Isaacs points out that the majority of books and films about Vietnam show low-ranking soldiers engaged in acts of violence without representing the innumerable civilian casualties caused by the "unparalleled in human history" bombings of Vietnam. See Arnold R. Isaacs, *Vietnam Shadows: The War, Its Ghosts, and Its Legacy* (Baltimore: Johns Hopkins University Press, 2000), 22.

15   Keith Beattie, *The Scar That Binds* (Baltimore: Johns Hopkins University Press),
     13. A 2006 Harvard Medical School / Columbia University Study found that the
     effects of severe psychological trauma affected about 20 percent of America's three
     million Vietnam veterans thirty years after the end of the conflict. See William J.
     Cromie, "Mental Casualties of Vietnam War Persist," *Harvard University Gazette*,
     August 17, 2006. Mai Lan Gustafsson's perfectly executed and beautifully written
     study focuses primarily on the experience of the Vietnamese people and how their
     folkloric traditions concerned with angry, vengeful, and unquiet spirits expressed
     grief over the millions of Vietnamese lives lost in their postcolonial conflicts. See
     Gustafsson, *War and Shadows: The Haunting of Vietnam* (Ithaca: Cornell University
     Press, 2009), esp. 47–48, 142.

16   See the discussion of war and photography by John Taylor in *Body Horror: Photojour-
     nalism, Catastrophe, and War* (New York: New York University Press, 1998), 160–88.
     Taylor discusses imagery of the Vietnam War in relation to the 1991 Gulf Conflict.

17   Tom Savini, *Bizarro! The Art and Technique of Special Make-Up Effects* (New York:
     Harmony Books, 1983), 11.

18   Savini, *Bizarro!*, 12.

19   Linnie Blake argues in *The Wounds of Nations: Horror Cinema, Historic Trauma
     and National Identity* (Manchester, UK: Manchester University Press, 2008) that the
     "bewildering array of traumatic happenings" at the end of the twentieth century has
     been conjoined with an "escalating public interest in horror films." Her discussion
     of America in the seventies closely examines Romero's oeuvre, including his 1973
     The Crazies, which she sees as an embodiment of American defeat in Vietnam and
     the calamitous Nixon presidency. See *Wound of Nations*, 3, 4, and 82–88.

20   On the ending of the film, see Kim Paffenroth, *The Gospel of the Living Dead: George
     Romero's Vision of Hell on Earth* (Waco, Tex.: Baylor University Press, 2006), 34, 40;
     and Paul R. Gagne, *The Zombies That Ate Pittsburgh: The Films of George Romero*
     (New York: Dodd Mead, 1987), 38.

21   A good description of the origin of apocalyptic belief appears in George M. Mars-
     den, *Fundamentalism and American Culture: The Shaping of Twentieth Century
     Evangelicalism, 1870–1925* (Oxford: Oxford University Press, 1980); see esp. 51–54.

22   Hal Lindsey, *The Late Great Planet Earth* (Grand Rapids: Zondervan, 1970). See
     also Poole, *Satan in America*, 165–66.

23   Daniel Wojcik, *The End of the World as We Know It: Faith, Fatalism, and Apocalypse
     in America* (New York: New York University Press, 1999), 110–12.

24   See Richard Matheson, *I Am Legend* (New York: Tor Books, 2007).

25   My own reading of the novel *I Am Legend* is heavily influenced by Walters in
     Bernice M. Murphy's *The Suburban Gothic in American Popular Culture* (New
     York: Palgrave, 2009). Walters shows that Neville is presented as living "a horrific
     parody of that experienced by the typical middle class male in the 1950s," even
     driving a station wagon, enjoying a martini, and smoking a pipe. At one point in
     his lonely rumination, Walters notes, he "holds a mock-philosophical debate with
     himself" in which he thinks of the vampire as a "minority element" and asks his
     imaginary debate opponent whether he would "let his sister marry one." See 27–39.

26   An excellent discussion of *Salem's Lot* appears in Nina Auerbach, *Our Vampires,
     Ourselves* (Chicago: University of Chicago Press, 1995), 155–61.

27   *Bare Bones: Conversations in Terror with Stephen King*, ed. Tim Underwood and
     Chuck Miller (New York: Warner, 1985), 5.

28 On King's output and technique, see Edwin F. Casebeer, "Stephen King's Canon: The Art of Balance," in *A Dark Night's Dreaming: Contemporary American Horror Fiction*, ed. Tony Magistrale and Michael A. Morrison (Columbia: University of South Carolina Press, 1996), 42–54.

29 Crawl of the Dead, http://www.crawlofthedead.com/crawls/info/philly_zombie_crawl (no longer available); and Max Brooks, *The Zombie Survival Guide* (New York: Three Rivers Press, 2003).

30 Statistics are cited in Deborah Caslay Covino, *Amending the Abject Body: Aesthetic Makeovers in Medicine and Culture* (Albany: State University of New York Press, 2004).

31 Covino, *Amending*, 37.

32 Covino, *Amending*, 38–54. Susan Bordo challenges the notion that plastic surgery represents an individual empowerment for women. She notes that "cosmetic surgery is more than an individual choice; it is a burgeoning industry" that invents the new norms of aesthetic beauty and proscribes certain looks as deformed and defective. See Susan Bordo, *Twilight Zones: The Hidden Life of Cultural Images from Plato to O.J.* (Berkeley: University of California Press, 1999), 42–65.

33 Tim and Beverly LaHaye, two key figures in the foundations of the Christian Right, wrote *The Act of Marriage: The Beauty of Married Love*, in 1976. This rather explicit guide is a Christian sex manual with detailed descriptions of foreplay and even mutual masturbation (sort of). Its patriarchal bias is also clear as it ignores any discussion of female orgasms and describes foreplay as the female's preparation to "receive him."

34 R. Marie Griffith's *Born Again Bodies: Flesh and Spirit in American Christianity* (Berkeley: University of California Press, 2004) explores the origins of Christian dieting culture and also has excellent material on the role played by race in the literature. She views this culture as an extension of earlier efforts at the reformation of the body. See 217, 225–38, 247.

35 See Dorothy Larson, "Machine as Messiah: Cyborgs, Morphs and the American Body Politic," *Cinema Journal* 36, no. 4 (1997): 57–75, for a reflection on the American obsession with the body and its connections to both constructions of the self and the state.

36 For more on the zombie as a kind of eating machine, locked in its own immanence and desire, see Kim Paffenroth's brilliant reading of religious themes in the Romero oeuvre, *The Gospel of the Living Dead* (Waco, Tex.: Baylor University Press, 2006).

37 Discussed in Kenneth MacKinnon, *The Politics of Popular Representation: Reagan, Thatcher, AIDS and the Movies* (Cranbury, N.J.: Associated University Presses, 1992), 27.

38 *Time*, June 12, 1977, 20; David Pirie, *The Vampire Cinema* (New York: Crescent Books, 1977), 100; MacKinnon, *The Politics of Popular Representation*, 122–23; and Bonnie Zimmerman, "Daughters of Darkness: The Lesbian Vampire on Film," in *The Dread of Difference: Gender and the Horror Film*, ed. Barry Keith Grant (Austin: University of Texas Press, 1996), 378–87.

39 See Lloyd deMause's *Reagan's America* (New York: Creative Roots, 1984) for a full discussion of the various metaphors of toxicity and body fluids that became standard conservative political rhetoric during the era. Quote from Reagan in Joyce Carol Oates, *AIDS and Its Metaphors* (New York: Farrar, Strauss & Giroux, 1989), 86.

40 James R. Kellar, *Anne Rice and Sexual Politics: The Early Novels* (Jefferson, N.C.: McFarland Press, 2000), 34–35. For more on images of AIDS and vampirism, see

"Blood Spirit/Blood Bodies: The Viral in the Vampire Chronicles of Anne Rice and Chelsea Quinn Yarbro" and "'A Girl like That Will Give You AIDS!' Vampirism as AIDS Metaphor in Killing Zoe," in *The Fantastic Vampire: Studies in the Children of the Night*, ed. James Craig Holte (Westport, Conn.: Greenwood Press, 1997), 111–22 and 145–50. Richard Dyer shows that gay men have been able to co-opt images of the vampiric monster and give it positive associations. See Richard Dyer, "Children of the Night: Vampirism as Homosexuality, Homosexuality as Vampirism," in *Sweet Dreams: Sexuality, Gender and Popular Fiction*, ed. Susannah Redstone (London: Lawrence & Wishart, 1999), 27–39.

41 The most detailed and comprehensive study of "real vampires" appears in Joseph Laycock's *Vampires Today: The Truth About Modern Vampirism* (Westport, Conn.: Praeger, 2009). A close study of fandom and vampire clubs can be found in Milly Williamson, *The Lure of the Vampire: Gender, Fiction and Fandom from Bram Stoker to Buffy* (London: Wallflower Press, 2006).

42 See Atlanta Vampire Alliance [AVA]: A Real Vampire House, http://www.atlanta vampirealliance.com/missionfaq.html.

43 Eric Nuzum, *The Dead Travel Fast: Stalking Vampires from Nosferatu to Count Chocula* (New York: St. Martin's, 2007), 162–64.

44 An insightful short introduction to the *Buffy the Vampire Slayer* series and why it works so well appears in William Patrick Day, *Vampire Legends in Contemporary American Culture* (Lexington: University Press of Kentucky, 2002), 160–66.

45 Tom Carson, "So-Called Vampires: Buffy Battles Teendom's Demons," *Village Voice*, June 10, 1997, 51; and Micol Ostow, "Why I Love Buffy," *Sojourners: The Women's Forum* 24, no. 3 (1998): 20.

46 The best discussion of Buffy and feminism, in particular the ideas of third-wave feminism, can be found in Elana Levine's "Buffy and the New Girl Order: Defining Feminism and Feminity," in *Undead TV: Essays on Buffy the Vampire Slayer*, ed. Elana Levine and Lisa Parks (Durham, N.C.: Duke University Press, 2007), 168–90.

47 Wendy Love Anderson discusses the role of apocalypse in the Buffyverse in her excellent essay "Prophecy Girl and the Powers That Be: The Philosophy of Religion in the Buffyverse," in *Buffy the Vampire Slayer and Philosophy: Fear and Trembling in Sunnydale*, ed. James B. South (Chicago: Open Court Press, 2003), 212–26.

48 Contrary to my view of Buffy's originality, Bruce A. McClelland argues strongly that Buffy "does not transcend in any significant way" the Vampire tradition that stretches back to Stoker and beyond. In fact, he compares the "Scooby gang" to Stoker's "gentrified posses." See *Slayers and Their Vampires: A Cultural History of Killing the Dead* (Ann Arbor: University of Michigan Press, 2009), 178–83. Here McClelland does not recognize the yawning cultural gap between a representation of vampire hunters as bourgeois Victorian gentlemen and a community made up of a werewolf, a lesbian witch, and several reformed vampires and demons. Even Giles, the uptight British librarian, has a dark past that includes dabbling in demon worship (and in 1970s British punk culture).

49 Lev Grossman, "It's Twilight in America: The Vampire Saga," *Time*, November 23, 2009.

50 *Twilight* is far from the first young adult vampire fiction to deal with vampire–human romance. Deborah Wilson Overstreet examines these narratives in *Not Your Mother's Vampire: Vampires in Young Adult Fiction* (Lanham, Md.: Scarecrow Press, 2006), 45–59. Significantly, many earlier efforts at the genre let the monster

remain a monster, forcing a doomed romance rather than following the interspecies couple into mundane marriage.

51 Travis Sutton and Harry M. Benshoff, "'Forever Family Values': *Twilight* and the Modern Mormon Vampire," in *Horror After 9/11: World of Fear, Cinema of Terror* (Austin: University of Texas Press, 2011), 208–9.

52 Christine Seifert, "Bite Me! (Or Don't)," *Bitch* 42 (Winter), 2009.

53 "Jesus Christ Is My Edward Cullen," http://www.facebook.com/group . php?gid=59988858896 (accessed May 1, 2010).

54 Kimberly Powers, *Escaping the Vampire: Desperate for the Immortal Hero* (Colorado Springs, Colo.: David C. Cook Publishers, 2009), 23–24, 171.

55 Powers, *Escaping the Vampire* (advertisement in book). See also http://www.wttym .org/Walk_the_Talk_Youth_Ministries/Insear-chofaprincess.html.

56 "The Joy of Vampire Sex," *Rolling Stone*, August 17, 2010.

57 Kim Paffenroth explicates these themes fully in *Gospel of the Living Dead*, 9, 10, and 21–22. He analyzes *Night of the Living Dead* on 27–44.

58 Paffenroth, *Gospel of the Living Dead*, 124–31.

59 Dennis Lem, "Dante's Inferno," *Village Voice*, November 22, 2005.

Conclusion

1 The most striking scene in the film *New Nightmare* follows up what appears to be Heather Langenkamp's encounter with the "real" Freddy with her appearance on a Los Angeles interview show where Robert Englund dressed as Freddy makes a surprise appearance. This shocks Langenkamp, and us, as we are not sure at first whether the celebrity is encountering the monster or just another celebrity. The feeling of unease is increased as the studio audience is full of "Fred Heads," horror fans dressed as their favorite killer and/or wearing Freddy t-shirts.

2 In some respects this revision of the *Nightmare* series marks a return to a more original vision of Freddy as a "dream monster" rather than a more traditional slasher. Craven had sought to create both a mythic monster and a mythic heroine who would slay him. Later sequels expanded on this original idea and turned Freddy into a buffoonish monster, equal parts comedy and horror. See Craven quoted on this in Jane Caputi, *Goddesses and Monsters: Women, Myth, Power, and Popular Culture* (Madison, Wisc.: Popular Press, 2004), 135. In the director's commentary for *New Nightmare*, Craven notes that he wants to get back to Freddy as "primal terror" rather than as "jokester and buffoon."

3 Reynold Humphries, *American Horror Film: An Introduction* (Edinburgh: Edinburgh University Press, 2002), 189. The film *New Nightmare* has been attacked more than it has been watched. The reasons for its box-office failure are probably twofold. By 1994, the slasher genre had gone bust, and many audiences probably expected it to be a retread of a tired formula. Genre devotees likely dismissed it, wanting a nostalgic return to Elm Street rather than Craven's philosophical scalpel applied to the genre. Notably, the film *Scream* also started out with small box-office returns. Ticket sales rocketed after its second weekend, contrary to usual audience behavior.

4 Examples of trends in technology that could be described as "post-human" are too numerous to detail. Miniaturization of parts has made possible the union of technology and the human body, while the interactivity and connectivity of human beings and their computers raises philosophical questions about the nature of mind and consciousness. Biotechnological developments have raised questions about the nature of species and the malleability of human nature. For a full discussion of these

examples, see Elaine L. Graham, *Representations of the Post/Human: Monsters, Aliens and Others in Popular Culture* (New Brunswick, N.J.: Rutgers University Press, 2002), 2–6; and John Harris, *Enhancing Evolution: The Ethical Case for Making Better People* (Princeton: Princeton University Press, 2007), 3–4.

5 An interesting counterpoint to this view of progress as monster can be found in Jon Turney's *Frankenstein's Footsteps: Science, Genetics and Popular Culture* (New Haven: Yale University Press, 1998).

6 Graham, *Representations*, 11–17; and Francis Fukuyama, *Our Post-Human Future: Consequences of the Biotechnology Revolution* (London: Profile Books, 2003), 112, 135, 156. See also John Seltin's discussion of "liberal" and "apocalyptic" posthumanisms in "Production of the Post-Human: Political Economies of Bodies and Technology," *Parrhesia* 8 (2009): 43–59.

7 Michael J. Hyde, *Perfection: Coming to Terms with Being Human* (Waco, Tex.: Baylor University Press, 2010), 222–28.

8 Myra Seaman, "Becoming More (Than) Human: Affective Posthumanisms, Past and Future," *Journal of Narrative Theory* 37, no. 2 (2007): 246–75.

9 James Cascio, Post Humanity, http://io9.com/5533833/your-posthumanism-is-boring-me?skyline=true&s=I (accessed May 1, 2010).

10 Graham suggests that the idea of the encased and mechanized body has long been not only a human fear but also a kind of mythic hope. See Graham, *Representations*, 181–84.

11 Seltin, "Production of the Post-Human."

12 "Portraits in Posthumanity: Aimee Mullins," Post Humanity, http://io9.com/5535730/portraits-in-posthumanity-aimee-mullins (accessed May 1, 2010).

13 TED: Ideas worth spreading, http://www.ted.com/talks/lang/eng/aimee__prosthetic_aesthetics.html (accessed May 1, 2010).

14 Ben McGrath, "Muscle Memory: The New Generation of Bionic Prostheses," *New Yorker*, July 30, 2007.

15 See Eric Eckholm, "In Turnabout, Infant Deaths Climb in the South," *New York Times*, April 22, 2007. Notably, so-called cyberpunk literature has, since the 1980s, critiqued the possibility of limited access to techno-biological enhancement based on class and status. Cyberpunk dystopias feature a technocratic society stratified into a wealthy minority with full access to mechanical and genetic modifications and a proletariat denied these advantages due to their lack of wealth and status. A discussion of this genre is in Graham, *Representations*, 194–96. The narrative of the award-winning video game *Bioshock* (2007) also creates a utopia destroyed, in part, by a struggle for genetic enhancements. Augmentation of the body becomes a kind of chemical addiction desperately desired by addicts known as "splicers."

16 The best discussion of the debate over the fate of humanity in a post-human technological environment can be found in Hyde, *Perfection*, 211–41.

17 My reading of the *Terminator* series is somewhat similar to Elaine Graham's in *Representations*, 208–10, though I disagree with her suggestion that the series necessarily "glorifies" technology. Her reading seems heavily based on the 1984 film with its hyper-masculine, action-driven story that relies heavily on big guns and big explosions. These B-movie conventions are transgressed in interesting ways in essentially every other iteration of the myth.

18 Will Wiles, "'Creepypasta': How the Internet Learns Your Fears," *Aeon Essays*, December 20, 2013, https://aeon.co/essays/creepypasta-is-how-the-internet-learns-our -fears (no longer available).

19 Victor LaValle, *The Changeling* (New York: Spiegel & Grau, 2017); on the novel and online "trolls," see Brian Truitt, "LaValle's Changeling: A Creepily Good Modern Fairy Tale," *USA Today*, June 13, 2017. https://www.usatoday.com/story/ life/books/2017/06/13/the-changeling-a-novel-victor-lavalle-book-review/102515950/, accessed July 6, 2017.

20 Samuel G. Freedman, "Muslims and Islam Were Part of Twin Towers Life," *New York Times*, September 10, 2010.

21 Tom Engelhardt, *The End of Victory Culture: Cold War America and the Disillusioning of a Generation* (Amherst: University of Massachusetts Press, 2007), 309, 370, n. 11.

22 Karen DeYoung, "Secrecy Defines Obama's Drone War," *Washington Post*, December 20, 2011; Akbar Ahmed and Frankie Martin, "Deadly Drones Come to Muslims of the Philippines," *Al-Jazeera*, March 5, 2012; Tom Junrod, "The Lethal Presidency of Barack Obama," *Esquire*, July 9, 2012; and Greg Miller and Julie Tate, "Since September 11, CIA's Focus Has Taken a Lethal Turn," *Washington Post*, September 2, 2011.

23 Sewell Chan, "Police Issue Report on 'Homegrown' Terror Threat," *New York Times*, August 15, 2007. The article includes a link to the entire manual: https:// cityroom.blogs.nytimes.com/2007/08/15/police-issue-report-on-homegrown-terror -threat/?mcubz=0&_r=0, accessed May 17, 2017.

24 Spencer Ackermann, "FBI 'Islam 101 Guide' Depicted Muslims as 7th Century Simpletons," *Wired*, July 27, 2011; and Spencer Ackerman, "FBI Purges Hundreds of Documents in Islamophobia Probe," *Wired*, February 15, 2012.

25 The transcript of Officer Wilson's testimony appears here: https://www.nytimes.com/ interactive/2014/11/25/us/darren-wilson-testimony-ferguson-shooting.html?mcubz=0, accessed June 1, 2017.

26 "Investigation into the Ferguson Police Department, United States Department of Justice Civil Rights Division March 4, 2015," https://www.justice.gov/sites/default/ files/opa/press-releases/attachments/2015/03/04/ferguson_police_department_report .pdf, accessed May 2, 2017.

27 On the movement, its historical context, and its goals, see Keeanga-Yamahtta Taylor, *From #Black Lives Matter to Black Liberation* (Chicago: Haymarket Books, 2016). See also Angela Y. Davis, *Freedom Is a Constant Struggle: Ferguson, Palestine, and the Foundations of a Movement* (Chicago: Haymarket Books, 2016), 23–27.

28 Bush made these remarks at O'Hare airport on September 27, 2001. A transcript can be found here: http://www.washingtonpost.com/wp-srv/nation/specials/attacked/ transcripts/bush_092701.html, accessed May 2, 2017.

29 Tim Robey, "George A. Romero: 'Why I Don't like the Walking Dead,'" *The Telegraph*, November 8, 2013.

30 The complete transcript and a video of the speech appears on the official White House website: https://www.whitehouse.gov/inaugural-address, accessed May 23, 2017.

31 Greil Marcus, *The Dustbin of History* (Cambridge, Mass.: Harvard University Press, 1995), 28.

INDEX

9/11, 173–74; *see also* al-Qaeda, terrorism, Twin Towers, World Trade Center, zombies

abortion, 78, 116–17, 148–49, 152, 174, 183–84; as horror theme, 170, 185–86; *see also* feminism; *Roe v. Wade*; women's bodies
Ackerman, Forrest J., 197
Adams, Rachel, 94, 98
Addams, Charles, 144–45, 150
adolescents, 17, 118, 133, 142–43, 149, 189, 196, 199; popularity of horror films with, 17, 107, 136, 160, 186, 198; *Twilight* popularity, 210–13; as protagonists in horror films, 151, 166, 168–70, 178; *see also* "monster kid" phenomenon
Agassiz, Louis, 62, 97

AIDS, 218–20, 230; Reagan-era rhetoric about, 219; *see also* vampires; zombies
Al-Qaeda, 173, 241–42; *see also* 9/11; terrorism; Twin Towers; World Trade Center
aliens, 13, 118, 125, 127, 142, 145, 97, 123–25; abductions by, 132, 136; sexual encounters with, 132, 134, 137; in film, 81, 115, 117, 125, 129, 142, 249; sightings of, 129–31; as religious emissaries, 136, 137–38; popularity in the atomic era, 116, 125, 131, 138; see also *Alien* franchise; containment; H. P. Lovecraft; "Project Blue Book"
Alien franchise, 183–84, 196, 201–2, 242; themes of body politics in, 183, 184, 201; influence of Lovecraft in, 201–2; *see also* women's bodies; science fiction

Printed in the USA
CPSIA information can be obtained
at www.ICGtesting.com
CBHW071613150224
4375CB00004B/118